HANDBOOK OF MARINE
ELECTRONIC & ELECTRICAL
SYSTEMS

Other TAB Books by Ed Safford

Model Radio Control—No. 74
Advanced Radio Control—No. 122
Radio Control Manual–2nd Edition—No. 135
Guide to Radio–*TV Broadcast Engineering Practices*—No. 523
Modern Radar Theory, Operation & Maintenance—No. 575
Aviation Electronics Handbook—No. 631
Electrical Wiring & Lighting for Home & Office—No. 671
Flying Model Airplanes & Helicopters by Radio Control—No. 825
CBers Manual of SSB—No. 959

TO
My beloved wife THELMA INEZ SAFFORD,
who was with me every step of the way.

HANDBOOK OF MARINE ELECTRONIC & ELECTRICAL SYSTEMS

E.L. SAFFORD, Jr.

TAB BOOKS
Blue Ridge Summit, Pa. 17214

FIRST EDITION

FIRST PRINTING— MARCH 1978

Copyright © 1978 by TAB BOOKS

Printed in the United States
of America

Library of Congress Cataloging in Publication Data

Safford, Edward L.
    Handbook of marine electronic & electrical systems.

    Includes index.
    1. Boats and boating—Electronic equipment—Handbooks,
manuals, etc. 2. Ships—Electronic equipment—Handbooks, manuals, etc. 3. Boats and boating—Electric equipment—Handbooks,
manuals, etc.
4. Electricity on ships—Handbooks, manuals, etc.
I. Title.
VM325.S33   623.85'03   77-27824
ISBN 0-8306-8939-7
ISBN 0-8306-7939-1 pbk.

Preface

The sea can be gentle, beautiful, blue, wonderful and refreshing—or it can espouse from its depths forces that can smash and destroy the tiny chips on its surface, chips that we know as ships, boats, and vessels. Yet it is on this sea—or should we say these Seven Seas—that we must travel and navigate for commercial or pleasurable reasons. And because we must do this, we need all the help we can get from electrical equipment related to sea operations to travel quickly and safely from port to port.

This book is about that equipment and the electrical requirements and power sources which provide safety and comfort on board. Some of it is simple and straightforward, and some is a little more complicated. It operates much like our land based equipment in some cases, but there are differences which, if unobserved, might result in a situation involving life or death. How important is this electrical and electronic equipment on board? It is like a great heart of the Master Mariner. It pulses and from its power all other functions are dependent.

As we originally conceived this book we decided that it would be necessary to know more about the environment in which the vessels operate to better understand what the design and operating requirements of the electrical and electronic systems might be. We found this aspect to be particularly interesting—and even somewhat frightening. The sea is not the best place in the world to have such systems, and it requires true diligence to keep them operating *satisfactorily* and *accurately*. Please note these two words. Equipment which lacks proper attention may operate, but if it fails, or *you* fail in knowing how to operate or interpret its information, a life may be endangered—your own. The chapter on environment will inform you of some aspects of sea dangers which must always be considered, as far as your electrical and electronics equipment is concerned.

Next we found that it was necessary to examine power plants, both for ac and dc systems, to examine the wiring used to convey this power to the proper outlets. How important this is. And what violations of the most basic rules of electrical safety and design have been made by makeshift situations. Perhaps a lack of knowledge of what is required and desired causes these violations. We hope everything in this book will help your understanding in this area.

The book then progresses and considers electrical devices for safety, pleasure, and comfort; then, into the various electronic devices which provide navigation, communications, soundings, and movement of and for the boats in a marina, in the harbor, or at sea.

We have made an extensive effort to include everything possible related to marine electrical-electronic systems that we could learn about, analyze, and evaluate. But you might find some equipment missing and wonder why. This equipment will be the TV sets used for pleasure, the stereo phonograph, tape recorders of various types, and such similar devices. We have omitted these purposely because we found them to be identical with those units used in homes and shore based stations, with the same operating characteristics and problems. There are references available for these kinds of equipment which you will find suitable for your needs in these areas.

It is always with great humility that I acknowledge that such a work as this must contain information which is not the possession of any one person, but is due to the many wonderful folks who have generously contributed to the knowledge contained herein. I thank them for their time, patience and help. They are the countless friends we have made at marinas, ship repair yards, on boats, and in so many other locations who have given of their time and knowledge to assist us in this work. We are most grateful to them, and hope as they do, that this book will help and assist those who love the sea in whatever mood she may display.

U.S. Government Printing Office personnel
U.S. Coast Guard personnel
Raytheon Company, Robert P. Saurez
Konel (Narco), Inc., R. Dean Straw
Penril (Data Communications Division), Wayne Saulea
Bennett Marine, Inc., Blake Bennett
Simrad Co., Gilbert N. Nelson
Skyway Communications, Inc., Charles M. Zwinak
Heath Co., Coy Clements
SGE Communications, Inc., Donald L. Stoner
Onan Corp., Virgil C. Gilbertson
Harris Communications Corp., W.A. Kannapel
Morrow Electronics, Inc., Michael G. Duff
Hermes Electronics Industries, G.W. Vincent
Hoffman Electronics Corp., Frank Hall
Sideband Associates, Inc. (SBA), Edward Prystup
Federal Communications Commission, Charles A. Higgin-
    botham
Bonzer, Inc., Max Mason
Airpax Electronics, Inc., Don Tall
Ratelco, Inc., Dennis E. Terpstra
Ocean Technology, Inc., (OTI), Dwight E. Roof
Brookes and Gatehouse, Inc., Rex Turner
George C. Taylor and Son, Pete Taylor
Marine Development Corp. (MDC), R. Kendall Edwards
Chromalloy Electronics Division, Ernest Pistone
Sperry Marine Systems, Carl H. Konkle
Western Marine Electronics (WESMAR), Kurt Coralline
ITT Decca Marine (Decca), Nicholas P. Edmondson
AMF Hatteras Yachts, Kenneth G. Kranz
Soderberg and Bell, E. J. Thompson
International Marine Instruments, Fred Shotz
U.S. Navy Printing and Publications Services
Encron (Energy Control Corp.) personnel

American Yacht Council personnel
U.S. Army

Finally, as always, we thank *you* for accepting our books and hope that this one will also find a place on your bookshelves. We have found that with a work such as this it is sometimes wise to skim through it and see *what* is covered and *where* it is in the text, and then re-read when you find it necessary, those sections or chapters which apply immediately to your current interest or situation.

E.L. Safford, Jr.

Contents

Chapter 1

The Environment at Sea

To understand the building, testing, and installation requirements for electrical and electronic equipment on board pleasure boats and larger craft, we must look at the environment presented to this equipment. To say it can be hostile states the case a bit lightly. But it is not always so, just most of the time.

WATER, AIR, AND SALT

Remember those lovely days when the sun shines on calm waters shimmering slightly in a cool breeze, when living is easy and troubles seem too far away to imagine. You must also be familiar with the opposite situation, though perhaps only vicariously, when the seas are running high under torrents driven by a three day blow rain and lightning strikes all about, showing man to be a puny thing in the clutches of the wrathful gods.

To ask "What is the most destructive element in this kind of environment?" might well evoke a response of "*Corrosion.*" The very presence of salt laden air causes corrosion of nearly all metal parts no matter where they are and sometimes in spite of the best efforts to protect against it. Imagine the effect of parts submerged in sea water, whether on the hull or in the bilge where sea water does inevitably collect. Thus an aware attitude along with constant checking, burnishing, polishing, and painting are required to guard against this detrimental effect.

Fig. 1-1. A corroded ac powerplant. Replacement is necessary at this stage.

Corrosion increases surface resistance to the flow of electrical currents, especially at higher frequencies. This means that antennas must have special protection because, as you know, radio frequency signals travel only on the surface of conductors; thus, when they corrode and pit resistance develops which causes heating, a loss of power that reduces radiation necessary for communication. Also, mismatching of an antenna system from this resistance causes detuning of the transmitter, radar, or other similar equipment. A mismatch can also affect measuring and monitoring equipment.

Higher currents caused by all this overload the sensitive equipment itself so that they tend toward poor operation or failure. An example of corrosion on an ac power plant appears in Fig. 1-1.

Any system is only as good as its weakest link, and in the electrical-electronic world of marine equipment we are about to investigate, that weakest link might be *any* link in the system. Because of this corrosion effect due to the moisture laden air itself, a result of salt spray and wetness, you must check *every part* of every system constantly. Even in situations where you think the fittings and connections are moisture proof or underwater proof, a check must be made once in a while to verify that this is indeed the case. When you are at sea and adverse conditions develop, it is too late then to find that something sprung a leak in your electrical-electronic systems lines or equipment; that corrosion had been happening and finally gave way to render your navigating and communicating equipment a useless pile of junk. So follow the safe rule to check and recheck constantly to be certain everything is okay.

Corrosion resistance across joints can often be measured with a low range ohmmeter, or a very sensitive voltmeter able to display small voltages developed across lengths of wire, batteries, or the connection junctions. When you find that a significant (readable) indication has developed across any of these items, you can be certain that an undesired resistance exists to cause that voltage or resistance reading. Eliminate the problem by replacing the wire, reconnecting the joint, or cleaning the connections before going any further in your system checking.

It might be a good idea to get everything in apple pie order at one time then develop a series of measurement points for wire resistance and joint checks for cable connection tests and for battery and motor generator connection tests. These, then, can be used as a *standard* so future measurements can be compared to them. In this way you will *know* and not be guessing whether equipment is all right or not. Remember, the salt laden air and water environment is always there, working insidiously to nullify your electrical-electronic systems. In some cases a dry dock is necessary for repairs.

VIBRATION

Any vessel on a body of water will be subjected to constant pounding and vibration, not only from the throbbing motors, but also from wavelets, waves, and wind, which are ever present in varying amounts. Since a vessel is a free body when in the water, it is at the whim of all forces acting upon it, even its own as you well know. Let's consider what this means. In the first place the amplitude of the vibration, the pounding on the hull, will range from very small and very fast motions, to very large and very slow motions. This can be a constant rocking, rolling, turning, or a combination of these.

This reminds me of a fishing excursion I made on a small pleasure craft once. Due to all the motions I became too sick to have operated even the voice communications system much less the direction finder or other navigation equipment. So we might also consider the effect on the people who are involved with these devices. For a Sunday sailor, the disorientation could be a factor in the safety and well being of the boat and its crew. Of course there isn't much we can say about the effect as far as this text is concerned. Another text will have to consider the *human side effects* of boating. We will, however, say that Dramamine does work wonders on sea sickness, or motion sickness, and will assume from here on in the book that all aboard are able to function capably, so it will be the equipment which we analyze in detail.

Rolling, turning, and tossing motions (or to use more appropriate technical terms, rolling, pitching, and yawing motions) mean that some equipment must be specially designed to be kept level (if the information one obtains from it is based on a reference level to the earth). This is, in fact, accomplished by a special mounting called a gimbal system, as shown in Fig. 1-2. With this mounting the platform remains in a given plane even though the base may move through various angular directions. When the stabilized platform (the platform of this figure) is provided with a gyroscope the platform will remain in a given orientation—usually parallel to the earth's surface, regardless of the angular motion of the body that carries it, the boat.

If the gyroscope, or several of them, are mounted on the inner platform, suspended in the gimbal system, then a *stabilized platform* results. The rolling, pitching, and yawing motions of the boat will not affect it. The platform will, however, be subjected to *translatory* motion, which means up-down, left-right, and forward-backward movements. These motions do not upset the *angular* orientation of the platform, so any navigation information, such as bearing, will remain correct. This is a required condition for navigation, and we shall learn more about this in Chapter 6.

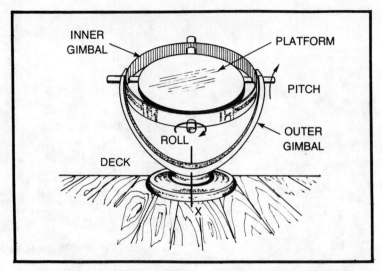

Fig. 1-2. A two-gimbal mounting system. When pivoted at the base, a three-axis system is possible. See Chapter 6.

The gimbal system shown in Fig. 1-2 may be used with a pendulum and a good dampening system (so the pendulum will not oscillate—that is, swing back and forth continuously). In this case a slow roll or relatively slow pitching motion will not cause the platform in the center of the gimbal system to become unlevel. A turning motion of the ship will likewise turn the platform, but if its use allows this, no problem is created. A compass needle which floats in a heavy, dampening liquid has three axes of freedom by the liquid. It responds rather slowly to a change in direction, but doesn't oscillate.

We now turn to the use of gimbal systems in a galley where they support heating and cooking equipment. Here you want to keep the pots and pans level with respect to gravity so the contents won't spill, but a specific *turning* orientation is not required.

An advantage of the open gimbal system shown is that you do not have a ring over the face of whatever may be mounted on the platform. A ring hindering visual or physical access to an instrument is an annoyance. But remember that a gravity stabilized platform may oscillate, but a gyrostabilized platform cannot do so. The pendulous, or gravity stabilized platform, may require a dampening element immersed in a viscous liquid so it takes time to move in it; the effective center of gravity of the pendulum gives the action of a

Fig. 1-3. Modern pleasure boat panel. The floating compass at the top of the panel has all axes of freedom and is reasonably well damped.

very long pendulum, which is not easily put into oscillation. A compound type pendulum also gives the effect of being very long—miles long in fact—while it is physically very small. The compound pendulum consists of several pieces mechanically linked together. Figure 1-3 shows a pleasure boat panel with a compass at the top.

From this discussion it should be obvious that measurements on a ship at sea aren't always easy, or accurate, depending upon conditions and the equipment mounting itself. And certainly a punishing sea is typical of rough conditions. Let us now consider a bit further the effect of the sea as it hammers on the hull. We know that vibrations and shock set up by this can cause great damage to delicate electronic instruments if great care is not used in their construction and mounting. Shock mounts of a special design are generally used and, in fact, should always be used. Solid mounts to the hull should be avoided.

Electrical connections are best secured by strong mechanical fasteners and the joints secured by strong physical connectors, or, in some cases, by *rosin* core solder joints. Use *only* rosin core solder. Soldered connections can help prevent the gradual working apart of these joints to eliminate the resultant high resistance and corrosion which may otherwise take place. One example of defective wiring is shown in Fig. 1-4.

We must be very careful with all electrical cables and wires to insure they cannot whip back and forth or be subject to constant motion at sea or in the harbor. This motion can cause wire fatigue and insulation deterioration—perhaps as loose wiring chafes at a

Fig. 1-4. A makeshift panel. An example of dangerous and bad wiring.

hanger—then sparking, and electrical failure. The electrical cables and wires should be installed in conduit of a proper size and sealed. (See our book *Electrical Wiring for Home and Office*, TAB No. 671, for information on conduit sizes versus cables contained.) Wire must not be permitted to move around in conduits either. In those cases where conduit, be it plastic or metal, cannot be used, fasten the wires securely to the hull at intervals of not over *six inches* between hangers. Allow some slack lengthwise in the wires and cables so that hull strain, tension, and relaxation will not cause an overly tight wire or cable to break. These kinds of forces can be produced by heat and cold as well as by the sea on the hull.

When thinking of conduit for electrical cables, we must remember that metals can corrode and develop rust spots that produce holes to allow the salt air environment inside unless the metal is rust and corrosion resistant. Plastics also resist corrosion, but some types can be cracked by extremes of cold, and some types will shatter into small pieces when subjected to very low temperatures and slight direct physical shock. Plastics also may expand and become soft under extreme heat. The combination of direct sunlight and reflected sun from the sea does produce very high temperatures. Care must be used in the selection of plastics for shipboard use to be sure they are of an approved type and also in the installation procedure.

Electrical wires and cables that have to be exposed to the elements, such as the connections to the battery on small craft, will require constant inspection to insure good and light connections. Battery terminals will corrode naturally and cause a high resistance connection, so they must be kept tight and clean at all times. We will have more on battery care in the next chapter. Electronic equipment poses a real problem if it is not designed for shipboard use. Inside the equipment there may be many tiny wires of some length but with no support. These may break under constant vibration, probably at a time when equipment use is crucial and conditions are at their worst. Any movement of wires inside the equipment, or of components which are not securely fastened to the chassis, may cause complete or intermittent failure at some critical time.

Of course when everything is ideal, on calm seas with a gentle breeze, equipment will perform beautifully. You'll have your navigation and communications gear, and the depth sounding equipment all working fine. But let conditions change, as they can do so quickly, and the differences between equipment designed for marine use and equipment that is simply adapted for marine use quite often becomes obvious. All those delicate parts and wires and adjustments in the adapted gear may come "unglued," which will of course render the equipment inoperative, or perhaps even worse, send it out of adjustment or tuning so you get readings which are wrong. We must have equipment that can be trusted, which means equipment *designed* for the environment in which it will be operated.

Even though equipment may be properly designed and mounted in shock proof and sealed cabinets, such as are provided for military equipment, aircraft and naval use, a boat owner can negate this and become a menace to himself. Sometimes when at sea or when going out for a "Sunday sail" or short boating trip, the owner will decide to move some equipment from its installed location to another, so he jury rigs connections to do so. Yes, it operates all right in the new location as long as everything is well, but only for a short time. Then, even if no storms are encountered, the insidious salt air works into the equipment to corrode connections, or whipping wires soon short or break and real troubles begin. We must realize that equipment designed to work well and have a long life in the hostile environment of the sea may fail and cause trouble if it is moved from a planned professional installation into an inadequate location.

We previously mentioned the vibration caused by engines on board boats. This vibration may be of such slight amplitude that you can't feel it, *but it is there*. High frequency vibrations can cause all sorts of problems if equipment is not installed to counteract it. *Throbbing* vibration we can sense and account for; high frequency vibrations in all likelihood exceed our ability to sense them. Be aware that they exist.

INTERFERENCE

Many potential sources of electrical interference exist on board a boat. These combine with other phenomena to prevent equipment from functioning properly. There are static electricity discharges from any projections on board. In the extreme, St. Elmo's fire can disrupt electronic gear. Then there is ball lightning, which is exactly that, a luminous ball from 2 inches to 2 feet in diameter which may float through the atmosphere around the ship until it finally extinguishes. What causes it is unknown, as are the causes of so many of the other "unearthly" effects one finds in this world of ours. But it is said to be a lightning type of electricity which may be caused by air masses moving with respect to the earth's surface. There is normal lightning which accompanies thunderheads, of course, probably the greatest natural source of electrical interference to our equipment.

When at sea and desiring to fix a position, or when piloting during heavy weather, you often must try to get readings buried in the interference noise level. Only a vast amount of experience will help in this kind of situation, but knowing that your equipment is probably operating correctly goes a long way towards helping you to make vital decisions.

With direction finding equipment requiring an external sense antenna or loop, the antenna system should be located amidship, especially if the hull of the ship is metal. The antenna should be separated from the rigging wires by a distance of at least one fifth the air length; these wires should, when possible, be insulated from the metal hull plates. This not only increases the sensitivity but also provides isolation from possible electrical discharge sources.

Of course, when using a magnetic compass on boats having masses of metal, keep it as far away as possible from them, be they hull, machinery, or motors. This will help to avoid compromising the compass readings. In inclement weather, moving direction finding equipment around the boat may cause such a magnetic field. This would give errors in compass readings, always a dangerous situation. The rule is to know where your equipment is on board ship with respect to every possible magnetic field and to have carefully checked the readings of your equipment when at these locations. Learn the direction and magnitude of these magnetic errors.

Electrical interference from the atmosphere is out of our control so we must live with it or wait it out, then try to find out where you are or establish whatever communications needed at the moment. But the on-board interference can be checked out ahead of time, tracked down, and compensated for so it won't upset your communications or navigation readings later. Of course, you might say, "Well, sometimes the local or on-board interference doesn't exist until we're under way and subject to the movements and buffeting of the high seas." True. That means you must work doubly hard while under way to find these trouble spots or at least obtain sufficient information to later duplicate conditions causing the interference. Isolating and removing them can then be performed at the dock.

We are reminded of a situation when a fine, expensive loran navigation system installed in a large pleasure boat failed during a trial run some 100 miles out at sea. During the run, noise obscured pulse reception to such an extent that navigation with this equipment was impossible. With fine weather during the run, interference had to be an on-board problem. It never appeared at the dock, but only during a run.

Run after run was made, every inch of every electrical system on board was checked and rechecked, yet still the source of the interference eluded everyone. Finally, as a last desperate measure, troubleshooters decided to check the engines more thoroughly, even to remove spark plugs and check their gaps. Lo and behold, the gaps were too wide. The ignition was using a Thunderbolt Booster and spark plugs gaps had been increased to help satisfy the ignition requirements. Reducing the gap caused the noise to vanish. The loran system then worked perfectly.

An example of a lot of electrical wiring associated with a modern boat with twin engines appears in Fig. 1-5. Most wiring like this probably requires some form of suppression.

You cannot assume anything when seeking out sources of electrical interference. Switches, outlets, heating elements, battery connections, recorders, TV antennas, or any other electrical device may cause interference. An electrical connection, plug, or socket becoming loose or corroded can vibrate, thus causing sparking which produces electrical interference. This, of course, must be corrected.

On some metal hulled ships, even the cathodic currents might be a source of noise when your equipment is required to operate at its most sensitive level to pull in weak signals. Of course all electric motors must be properly suppressed, especially those used in air conditioning, heating units, pumps, winches, and other heavy duty

Fig. 1-5. Modern pleasure boat engine compartment with twin engines. Crowding is essential to save space. All types of suppression may have to be used to prevent interference with electronic gear.

equipment. You can probably think of many possible sources of trouble. These must be checked often because the suppression may deteriorate after long operation or with changing environmental conditions. Assuming that "Once suppressed is always suppressed" might bring serious trouble in time of emergency.

Electrical equipment such as battery chargers, generators and alternators, steering motors, ignition systems, circuit breakers, and even lights, which may work loose in their sockets, must all be operated periodically and checked for causing interference. This way conditions are much easier and safer. If trouble does exist, it can be pinpointed and corrected in the safety of the harbor.

HULL CURRENTS

It is extremely interesting, and a problem, that when metals are immersed in an electrolyte, such as seawater, electrical currents will generate due to chemical action. This also happens in long pipelines crossing the country, as they are in moist earth or earth and water. The primary problem with these currents is that they eat away the metals. So from the standpoint of a ship, this continual current may weaken the hull or cause holes, setting up an ultimate disaster.

This deterioration is set up by several possible conditions: dissimiliar metals in the hull, positive and negative areas occurring on the same metal sheet, an oxygen concentration in or on the metal, an ion concentration on the metal due to impurities, or even by cavitation.

Both with pipelines and ships, the designers tend to "fight fire with fire." They generate countercurrents over those areas most subject to this action. Cavitation is the "air space" in the water caused by a rotating propeller, for example, which throws water away so fast that flow can't keep up with the discharge; thus, an air space occurs around parts, or all, of the propeller. The friction of the propeller with these two mediums, liquid and air, causes charges to be built up and, when transferred to the hull, may cause propeller or hull damage.

Of interest is an examination of the relative voltages generated between various metallic electrodes placed in a saltwater solution in Table 1-1. Voltages between the electrodes will be slightly less if the saltwater solution is not saturated. It is possible to determine from

Table 1-1. Voltage Generated in a Saturated Salt Solution.

Voltages Generated Between Metals In A Saturated Salt Solution.		
Electrode 1	**Electrode 2**	**Potential Developed**
Coin Silver	Zinc	0.9V
Silver	Aluminum	0.7V
Silver	Iron	0.32V
Silver	Stainless Steel	0.17V
Brass	Silver	0.10V
Silver	Copper	0.06V

the table what the voltage generated would be between various other combinations; for example, a copper wire and an aluminum hull. These would be 0.7 volts minus 0.06 volts, or a difference of 0.64 volts between these two metals. Thus there is a current flow between them. It is also interesting that the metals listed higher in the table, for example zinc, will be positive with respect to a lower metal on the chart, such as iron. Also, considering that two electrodes make a cell, so the voltage will increase only if the number of cells increase, not necessarily because the cell size or individual electrode size increases.

As has been indicated, local action can occur in metal hulls where steel plates overlap since no two will have an identical composition. While underway an increase in these hull currents is likely as the water passing by the hull creates friction and also removes a film produced by the generation of currents between different metals. If allowed to build up, the film gradually reduces these currents. Thus we see that the effect of localized currents can cause deterioration of metal parts, especially when they are immersed in a saltwater solution.

Now we must delve into spray situations and high humidity salt air conditions, which can cause moisture to gather around parts not really exposed to water. A localized action taking place over a period of time causes deterioration of wiring, connections, cables, and even fittings themselves. Be on constant guard against this insidious destroyer of seemingly protected gear. One method of protection uses small or medium size electrodes precisely located on the hull and furnished with currents from the primary energy supply of the boat. This countercurrent nullifies the destructive currents as they oppose each other. In systems such as this, electrodes are deliberately eaten away by circuit action and must be replaced on a periodic basis.

LIGHTNING

We had previously mentioned thunderstorm activity briefly but now must cover the possibility of damage to electrical and electronic equipment on board should lightning happen to strike, whether an antenna or a wire leading to equipment. Many times, even though no actual lightning flashes or thunder rumbles, the atmosphere becomes so highly charged that sparks from 1/4 to 3/4 inch in length will jump across gaps in switch contacts or between wires. Protective steps against such sparking and the resulting effects on sensitive equipment must be taken. Commercial spark gaps and antenna grounds are a must during storms or high static conditions.

Fiberglass antennas (nonmetallic) do not furnish any protection against lightning even though they may be grounded. Other types of antennas may possibly be grounded below the loading coil, and this, of course, can prevent entry of spurious currents into the equipment. One means of lightning protection is a metallic spike (a lightning rod) rising above the highest point of the rigging. Have this connected to either a grounded hull or to the hull grounding system with nonmetallic boats. These types should have a metal plate underneath for grounding. To combat electrical interference, have all metal objects on board bonded together with good electrical conductors so electrical potentials cannot develop between them. This conductor also will be bonded to the ground plate, or metal hull.

HUMIDITY

During World War II great efforts were made to fungus proof electronic equipment by cleaning thoroughly, coating with a special plastic-like spray, then baking in an oven so the spray hardened. The result was a moisture proof, fungus proof, and mildew proof shield. We need this in shipboard electrical and electronic equipment today too. Humidity is an insidious danger. It is always present, yet, aside from physical discomfort for people, it doesn't give any clues to the real danger presented to the equipment. It can work its way into most every kind of equipment. Then, when exposed to temperature change, becomes liquid. With impurities, this will cause failure or degradation of performance of electrical and electronics equipment.

It is wise here, again, to point out that electronic equipment not designed with proper seals, coatings, or other protection for boat use will be a source of trouble sooner or later, if used on board. The tendency to store this equipment on board in some random manner and not operate it very frequently often leads to inoperative equipment when out for a cruise and in need of it.

Purchasing electrical and electronic equipment for boats is a demanding and exacting duty, and great care must be taken to insure that the equipment is indeed designed for marine use. Only then will it have a chance to operate in the rough environment it will be subjected to. Many old timers say it is not enough just to have well designed equipment. Boat owners must also set up and maintain a periodic schedule of tests and adjustments to maintain such equipment. "It needs to be run, and run often," one craggy seaman emphasized. "You gotta be sure. Most people don't use their stuff enough. They just don't give it the workout it needs," he added. I listened and knew he spoke from years of experience; it is proper to give credence to his words.

FUEL, FUMES, FOREWARNED

A boat, no matter how large or how small may use gasoline, or diesel fuel, or similar combustible liquids for its source of propellant power. Because fumes are generated—indeed, fumes are what make these engines run—and because fumes may get into areas where they should not be, and because a fire can mean total disaster on a boat or ship or vessel, this is an environment which must be rigorously controlled.

One pint of gasoline has the potential for more explosive power than thirty sticks of dynamite. If you consider how many gallons of gasoline might be on board, you must realize that a tremendous explosive danger exists, and it must be treated with extreme respect. The U.S. Coast Guard Auxiliary has some guidelines which are important in this respect:

1. Always try to fuel the boat in good light. It is too easy to spill gasoline when it is dark.
2. Don't smoke or allow anyone near the fueling area to smoke when filling the tank with gasoline or other fuels. It's not a good way to stop smoking.
3. Make certain that all electrical equipment on the boat is shut off, don't operate any switches when you are fueling, and don't allow anyone else to do it either.
4. If you use portable tanks, fill them away from the boat and, when full, put the caps on tightly and wipe them off.
5. Keep the metal nozzle of the gas hose in contact with the tank at all times to prevent a static spark. Some fueling systems have a grounding connection; if they have one use it.
6. Don't spill gasoline. This may be easy to say but it is hard to accomplish on a rocking boat. If gas does spill, don't let it turn to a vapor, which can be set off by even the smallest spark. Wipe it up immediately and get rid of the rag you used to wipe it up with.
7. When you have finished fueling, put the gas tank cap on tightly and check it. A loose cap or one that can become loose will allow gasoline to slosh out, turn to vapor, and present an explosive environment, even if it is mixed with water.
8. Finally, always open up the boat to air it out after fueling. Walk around the inside of the boat and give it the sniff test, especially in low places. Gasoline vapor is heavier than air and sneakier than nitroglycerin. Give the boat a chance to air out before you start the engine or any electrical equipment.
9. Remember that gaoline vapors are extremely explosive. All doors, hatches, and ports should be *closed* while fueling, galley fires and pilot lights extinguished, and smoking strictly prohibited—*always*.
10. Do not operate any electronic equipment on board when fueling, not even a radio. And remember, the electrical system in the motor compartment, including the ignition system, must be off as it might produce a spark to ignite the

accumulation of vapors there during fueling. Always keep the fuel lines tight and the bilges clean—and inspect them often.

There are regulations concerning equipment that must be carried on board to fight a fire. And there are some regulations concerning ventilation and fire prevention equipment too. For example, each boat must have a *backfire* flame arrester; one approved device on each carburetor of all gasoline engines except outboard motors. When there is no fixed fire extinguishing system installed in the machinery space, at least one B1 type must be present. This can be a hand portable unit. On outboard boats less than 26 feet in length this is not required if there is no place where vapor fumes might be trapped and become a hazard. The letter B on the fire extinguisher designates it is for gasoline, oil, and grease fires. A letter A designates fires of ordinary combustible material, and a letter C designates electric type fires.

All too often a careless mistake or lack of planning has been traced as the cause of a serious accident. Once on the water, even if it is only a few miles off shore, your boat is your home, and anything causing it to malfunction or sink places you at the mercy of the water.

The requirements for naval electronic equipment may help you to obtain gear meeting standards found to be acceptable. You can order the following pamphlets from the U.S. Government Printing Office, Washington, DC.

- Vibration Requirements: MIL-STD 167, Type 1
- Shock: MIL-S-901C Grade A, Class 1, Type A
- Temperature: MIL-E-16400F, Class IV (0° to 50° C)
- Humidity: MIL-E-16400F
- Degree of Inclosure: MIL-STD-108, Drip Proof 15°
- Basic Design: MIL-E-16400F
- EMI-RFI (Interference): MIL-STD 461, Class 1C

PEOPLE ENVIRONMENT

Part of the sea environment which affects people but not equipment is the vast loneliness of the oceans, where one may cruise for days, weeks, and months without crossing the wake of another vessel. Another problem can be the confinement in a small craft that makes the living together of just a few persons a task at times. Because of these situations it is necessary to look at some items helping to relieve these problems.

Man needs luxuries and relieving refinements if he is to survive happily. Therefore we find on board pleasure boats, fishing, and on work boats, items such as mechanical refrigerators to keep foods preserved and supply ice cubes. These systems sometimes operate from small fuel powered engines which must be run occasionally to cool the box.

Other items must not be underrated either. The advantages of having music, the spoken word, plays, or comedy tapes to be played on a cassette player or similar machines cannot be overemphasized. The sound of other voices, no matter whose or the subject, can relieve nervous tensions that build up, a desirable situation on a cruise or during travel to and from fishing areas or other destinations. Of course marine voice communications gear may be supplemented by CB equipment which can be used if not too far out from the shore or other boats.

Also keep in mind portable TV sets, many of which can operate from either battery power (12 to 36 volts dc), 110 volts ac, or both. Some multiband receivers will operate on 12 volts dc or 110 volts ac. If you happen to have an amateur radio license and a station license for your boat, you might communicate with other radio amateurs on their assigned bands using either code or voice.

When in the harbor, and most pleasure boats spend a great deal of time there, it is useful to have electric hot plates and other high current gear operable from the shore power 110 volt 60 Hz line. Figure 1-6 shows one type of receptacle for making this connection. Telephone connections are also important if your boat is your home or second home. Electric heaters for 110 volt lines are also useful. If you plan to use these items in foreign ports, have voltage step-up and step-down transformers on board, as well as inverters to convert ac to dc and vice versa. Some power tools may also be useful if you expect to perform repair work along the way, perhaps battery operated drills, screwdrivers, saws, and the like. Of course you would want to have some kind of charging system, either your engine, or an auxiliary generator on board. Boat electrical systems appear in our next chapter. Keep in mind portable lights and

Fig. 1-6. One type of shore electrical connection. Notice the screw type sealing cap for when the socket is not in use.

flashlights for emergency use. Have these on board and regularly checked for corrosion and good battery condition.

With the availability of a full range of entertainment equipment on board, preventing one system from interfering with another becomes a problem. In fact, some may not want any sound at all while at the same time others may want a rock-and-roll blast. To this end, earphones will provide individual listening without disturbing others. They are used in airliners for the movie sound track, and for radio programs to permit some listeners to hear news and weather while others hear progressive rock or opera. Definitely, then, earphones are a necessary item on boats.

At sea or in a marina it is not always cool, below decks, and you may not want to operate air conditioning equipment, or you may not have any. Therefore another electrical item which becomes desirable is the electric fan, or several of them, which can be either line or battery operated to circulate air in below-deck spaces. This will provide some relief, especially in harbors or marinas. However, air conditioning may be very desirable under the hot sun of some cruising areas.

We wrap up this part of the chapter with a hint. Marine light fixtures often corrode, making light bulb replacement difficult. Smear some petroleum jelly on the bases of bulbs (all sizes and kinds) and they will be easier to replace when they burn out. Be careful not to overtighten them in their sockets though.

TEST EQUIPMENT AND TOOLS

Because of the multitude of electrical and electronic devices and supporting electrical systems aboard, you may want to have some basic test equipment on board. Consider for example, a small volt-ohm meter which can read from one volt to at least 600 volts. This is an item which is easy to use and usually furnished with complete instructions when purchased. It is a simple matter to test the various outlets for voltage with one of these meters. In this way isolating a bad socket, an open line, or even a defective generator becomes easy. The bad socket is evident if one receptacle shows a reading while the other does not. An open line is evident if several receptacles on one circuit do not show a voltage reading, while another circuit from the same source does show a voltage. An open circuit breaker or a defective generator would be evident if no voltage readings appeared anywhere.

Since the ohmmeter part of the unit can be used to check continuity (continuity means a continuous circuit) you can determine if individual items such as fans, lights, electric hot plates, and motors are burned out. To make this check you *unplug* the suspected item, connect the meter leads across the plug, turn its switch on, and look for a reading on the meter—full scale, as shown in Fig. 1-7, if the circuit is OK.

Of course the meter must also show a full scale reading when its own leads are connected together *before* you make the test. Nor-

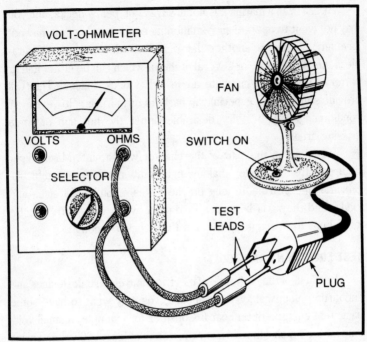

Fig. 1-7. Continuity testing with a volt-ohm meter.

mally on a very low ohms scale there should be some resistance indicated, not a complete full scale reading. But with motors and similar equipment a full scale reading is usual. *Always be sure the test item is disconnected when making any kind of continuity checks, and do not attempt to check continuity of electric lines unless the circuit breaker is opened and the primary power plant fully disconnected.*

If you do not have, nor desire to have, a volt-ohm meter you can still check for voltages by using a small test lamp available from most equipment stores. This consists of a socket with two leads connected to it. You install a small lamp of the proper voltage for the circuit to be tested and put the leads to the wall receptacle to be tested. The lamp will light if a voltage is present. Sometimes you must wiggle the leads around to make contact, but this may indicate a bad connection in the socket. You may then want to replace it.

You should have some tools for electrical repairs, at least long-nosed pliers with insulated handles, a pair of side-cutting pliers, and various sizes of screwdrivers, both chisel tip and Phillips. You should have electrical tape and spare plugs and wall receptacles and wire.

Fig. 1-8. A circuit breaker panel for a boat. The meters read voltages on primary mains.

Because of the hostile environment it is wise to regularly check the cables to fans, lights, radios, and other electrical gear. These can become cracked and frayed due to heat, cold and normal use. They should be replaced as often as they become brittle or when any kind of break or crack appears in the insulation. Remember that plastic will sometimes split under severe cold and may then part under strain in hot weather. Switches and circuit breakers, either in panels as shown in Fig. 1-8 or at individual stations, require attention. We need to be careful working around these circuit breakers. Fuses are not recommended on board water craft. In each case it is again necessary to consider the problems caused by dampness and the salt air environment. We must also consider the accumulation of water on the deck or floor when working around these panels. Everyone knows the extreme dangers of electrocution if a bare electric wire is contacted while a good ground path is offered by water. If you are on a wet deck or standing in water while manipulating electric switches, circuit breakers, or wires, you increase your chances of being electrocuted. Always be certain that all these items are plainly marked as to what they control, where they go, or which circuits they are so you will be better able to operate them safely and surely if the need arises.

ROUTING OF ELECTRICAL CIRCUITS

We normally do not worry about where electrical wires are routed on shore installations except for economy of length, cost, and effort. But on board boats and airplanes, the routing of wires is important—very important. This is because these craft rely on instruments depending upon the earth's magnetic field for their application and if a manmade magnetic field interferes with the earth's field the readings will be wrong. Thus the electrical wiring must be installed so that no stray magnetic fields will be created in the vicinity of compasses, or autopilots, or other such instruments. Normally, wires run close to but not nearer than three feet from areas containing these instruments and must be carefully and somewhat tightly twisted to minimize magnetic fields around them. This is done for both dc and ac wires. Incidentally, on boats and planes the current carrying conductors must be stranded and of an approved size. You *should never* rely on the metallic hull or structure of a boat

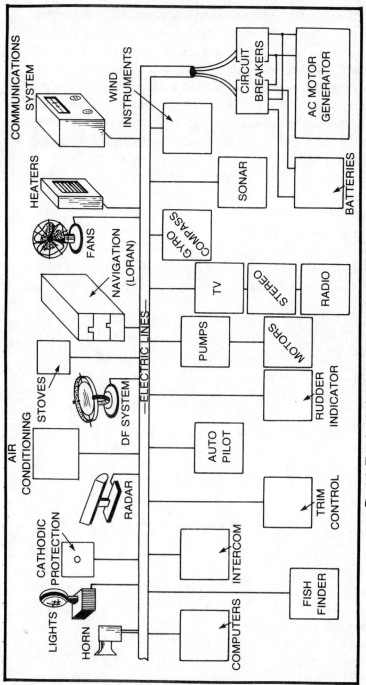

Fig. 1-9. The electrical and electronic environment of a modern boat.

or plane to carry electrical currents even though the electrical system is bonded to these structures. Separate ground wires are always used for the common lead in the electrical systems as we will see in the next chapter.

Figure 1-9 gives you a general idea of the magnitude of electrical and electronic loads on the electrical system of a ship. The next Chapter begins an examination of each of these in more detail as well as a look at the general requirements for the electrical systems for all systems shown.

Chapter 2
Primary Electric
Power and Wiring

Before considering electrical and electronic systems for boats, a closer look at the electrical requirements on board is in order. We have some background from Chapter 1 in which we learned of some environmental conditions and also of some safety precautions. But now it is time to press forward and dig into some primary power systems and electrical wiring requirements.

DIRECT CURRENT SYSTEMS

Relatively small craft will usually have a direct current primary power source. These are usually lead-antimony batteries with a liquid electrolyte. We note that lead-calcium batteries also using the liquid electrolyte have been developed, which are sealed and never need attention as far as replacement of water is concerned. These so called "maintenance free" batteries are ideal, of course, for all you have to do is to keep them properly charged to have electrical power throughout the long lifetime of the cells. Interestingly, the older lead-antimony batteries are now available as "maintenance free" too. Figure 2-1 shows some batteries in an engine compartment. The majority of batteries are the heavy duty, rechargeable lead-antimony cells, so combined to produce from 6 to 48 volts. This serves as the primary dc supply voltage for the boat.

When you consider that voltage times current equals power, a 12 volt battery has to supply only half the current that a 6 volt battery

Fig. 2-1. Marine batteries installed near the engines. Note alternators to the left of engine blocks near batteries.

does for the same power output. Usually the less current drawn from a battery the longer it lasts—or its charge life is increased, so it is more economical to use a higher voltage and lower current than the other way around. Also the higher the current drawn from the battery the more likely the plates are to buckle and flake, causing battery failure. So, low currents are a safety factor also. It takes about the same current-time factor on both kinds of batteries to charge them. That is, a 6 volt battery may take a current of 20 amperes for one hour while a 12 volt battery may require only 10 amperes for 1 hour. The total wattage in both cases, voltage time current, is the same.

Now, to get more current or voltage, it is common to parallel or series connect batteries. Thus two 6 volt batteries in parallel—plus to plus and minus to minus—can deliver twice the current at 6 volts that one battery can deliver. Note that there is no increase in *voltage*. If you series connect the two batteries—plus to minus—and use the two free plus and minus terminals for the cables, you maintain the amperes capability of a single battery but at twice the voltage, or 12 volts. Each boat system is designed for a given voltage. Be careful not to connect multiple batteries to exceed this. You can safely increase the current availability, though, by paralleling batteries at the boat's stated voltage.

BATTERY CHARGING

Most boat batteries will be charged from a generator or alternator, shown in Fig. 2-1. This is usually driven from the same engine that drives the propeller. On very small boats, an outboard engine may not have such a charging system, so the batteries must be charged in the harbor or at a marina. On large craft there will probably be an electrical generating power plant consisting of a gasoline motor and generator combined with regulators and governors for precise control of the power output. Usually these plants supply 110 volts at 60 Hz for the boat's mains. Figure 2-2 shows a typical primary supply system for a large boat.

The location of the batteries is important from the standpoint of ballast and safety. The compartment will generally be arranged with the batteries fastened in place so they cannot move, and they will have covers over them consisting of leadlined trays. Enough area must be available above the battery for a hydrometer to determine the charge of the individual cells. The electrolyte for a well charged lead-acid cell is near 1280 specific gravity. If it is much lower than this check the comparison chart for the amount of charge in the cell. Such charts are provided with hydrometers.

The battery compartment must be ventilated by some forced air means to prevent the buildup of gas from charging or discharging. Nickel-cadmium cells must be ventilated also. Of course all precautions must be taken to prevent spillage of electrolyte. You know what it means to have that problem. If not, just glance at a battery area where spillage has occurred and you will usually get a good idea. Corrosion is terrible. The electrolyte can eat through metals and wood and even some plastics. So the battery compartment must be designed for batteries and must be kept clean at all times. Keep batteries filled with electrolyte as required but do not overfill.

Here is something which we've found important. The use of distilled water will prevent premature failure of the battery—lead-

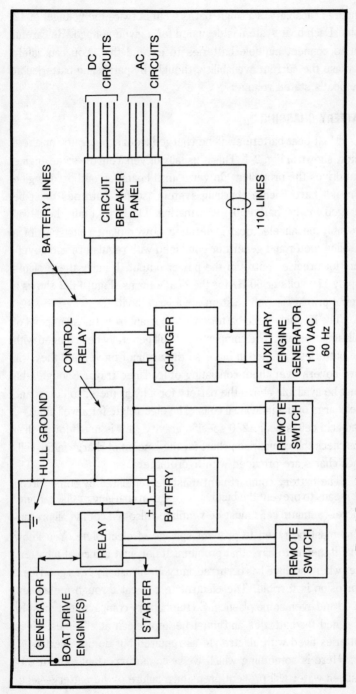

Fig. 2-2. Boat primary electrical power system with batteries and an ac plant both in use.

acid battery of course. Too many times we have found that boat owners fill batteries with tap water. The impurities in the water will actually shorten cell life and capacity. If you make it a firm habit to use only distilled water in your lead-acid cells from the moment you buy them, you'll find the extra life pleasing to you. Other type cells use a different electrolyte, so you must fill them, when required, with the type of electrolyte they use.

BATTERY CONNECTIONS

Usually batteries will be located close to the point of greatest drain. This is because the cables must be large (thus expensive), and long cables reduce the available power due to cable resistance loss. Probably the greatest source of drain will be the starting motor on the engine, so the battery will be located in that area. Never take for granted that a battery connector is making good contact to a battery terminal. We have found that in many cases the appearance of a good connection is given, but the actual contact area is bad due to corrosion which cannot be seen until you take the terminal off. There may also be corrosion in the battery cables, inside the insulating sleeve so that perhaps only a few of the many strands of wire are carrying the current. We suggest a periodic thorough maintenance schedule wherein you take off the battery cables, clean the inside of the connectors and the posts of the battery, and tighten them down to fit securely and snugly again. Check all cables at this time, and be sure that all conductors are solid and full and not corroded. You can sometimes determine this by flexing the cable and thus finding out if it is stiff and strong, or weak and supple. Bending may also cause a fragile point to break, and that is good, for it is better to find it while ashore than while at sea. Never take batteries for granted. They are delicate, in a sense, and need care and attention often.

SOME WIRING REQUIREMENTS

All dc circuits must be a two wire type, and the negative terminal of the battery must be connected to the common ground system of the boat. The negative terminal of the battery on pleasure boats is connected to the negative (ground) terminal on the engine and a circuit breaker installed between the positive terminal of the battery and the electrical circuits of the boat. With a two wire system

Fig. 2-3. Pleasure boat circuit breaker panel. Each circuit has a circuit breaker for protection.

you will have a pair of lines from the battery to the circuit breaker panel. The individual circuits will be protected at this panel, with two wires progressing on to whatever type receptacles or equipment they are to be connected to. The number of two wire circuits from the panel will depend on the boat demand, but each pair will be protected by a circuit breaker. A typical panel is shown in Fig. 2-3.

Receptacles should be polarized, having one large and one small hole for matching plugs so they can be put in but one way. The plugs should also be the self-locking types (screw turn fit) so they cannot loosen with vibration or during heavy weather. The size of the conductors from the battery to the panel must be large enough to prevent more than a 3 percent voltage loss from the battery to the device being used under full load with the battery fully charged. Remember also that voltage at a terminal may mean a defective battery or a low charge condition. Also note that a 10 percent voltage loss may be tolerated on some devices—such as lighting, or heating, or possibly pumps and motors—but for electrical instruments and electronic devices loss must not exceed 3 percent to ensure reliable operation.

CALCULATING WIRE SIZES FOR DC CIRCUITS

A relatively simple formula, requiring only multiplication and division, can be used to determine proper size copper wire for a given load over specific distances.

The formula is:

$$A = \frac{10.7 \times I_L \times D}{V_L}$$

where:

A = Required circular mil area of wire
I_L = Load current
D = Distance of cable run
V_L = Voltage loss permitted (3%)

Let us consider an example calculation. Assume that you plan a circuit to have a maximum load of 20 amperes, and that the distance of this line is 25 feet. Note that when we calculate wire size for maximum load, any load of less demand will result in the voltage loss being less too.

1. Calculate the 3% voltage value: $0.03 \times 12 = 0.36$ volt (Assuming a 12 volt battery supply)

2. Now use the values obtained in the formula:

$$A = \frac{10.70 \times 20 \times 25}{0.36} = 14861 \text{ circular mils}$$

3. Look on Table 2-1 to find the size wire to use. It should be size 8. Two 8 gauge wires would then be used for the circuit.

This is a larger wire in circular mil area than calculated but a standard value, so our voltage loss will be even less than calculated. This is on the safe side. If using stranded copper wire, the total circular mil area will be the sum of the area of each of the individual strands. With this formula, any of the typical voltage source values from 6 to 48 volts can be used (or even 110 or 220 volts dc), and any permitted loss value can be used. Normally, however, circuits aren't designed to have over 20 amperes full load. Use additional circuits to keep the load current from exceeding this value. Table 2-2 shows wire gauge requirements for ac circuit load currents.

OVERLOAD, WIRE COMPOSITION, AND INSTALLATION

There is one precaution. If we have a boat with wiring for a normal complement of equipment, adding electronic or electrical equipment can pull more amperes than the original wiring was intended for. Then, insufficient voltage may be supplied to critical

Table 2-1. Direct Current Circuits, Circular Mils to AWG Gauge for Copper Wire

Direct Current Circuits: AWG Gauge Wire (Copper) To Circular Circular Mils.	
Conductor Size AWG	Circular Mil Area
18	1,620
16	2,580
14	4,110
12	6,530
10	10,530
8	16,530
6	26,240
4	41,740
2	66,360
1	83,690
1/0	105,600
2/0	133,100

Table 2-2. AWG Sizes for Alternating Current Circuits.

AWG Gauge Table For Alternating Current Circuits.	
Wire Size	Amperes
14	20
12	30
10	40
8	55
6	80
4	105
2	140
0	195
00	225
000	300

equipment causing erroneous readings or other failures. Be sure that instrument primary lines are never overloaded—that radar, direction finders, communications equipment, and navigation equipment do in fact have the voltage they are supposed to have. Then your devices will operate as they should and you'll avoid trouble.

When considering the kinds of wires to use and thinking of aluminum, copper, and possibly other types, remember that you do not want to have metals which will corrode or deteriorate when subjected to the galvanic (internal current) action caused by salt moisture upon dissimilar metals. This may happen on switches, panels, or terminals, where screws of a different metal are used. It can occur if you connect aluminum wire to copper wire.

When dissimilar metals are used interchangeably in a power-distritubution system, problems will be created. Connecting dissimilar metals may allow galvanic corrosion at the joints which eventually destroys the usefulness of the equipment. This is of particular concern when aluminum and copper are joined. New materials are especially made for connection to copper or aluminum with no adverse effects. This equipment will be so marked. Except in emergencies, as an expedient installation, dissimilar metals must never be used together. If aluminum is exclusively used in a system, a special joint compound must be applied to all connections or joints to protect them from excess surface oxidation. This is necessary because the oxide of an aluminum conductor differs from copper oxide in that it adds a high resistance in contact with the wire. It is best to use copper wire throughout a boat. Also we don't want any more than four wires connected to a terminal stud, but we surely do want these metals to be compatible to avoid deterioration. Brass or copper terminal used with copper wire are recommended.

Once again we mention that all wiring must be carefully supported. Since boats are subject to choppy or even violent seas, any wire that can move to cause physical fatigue or chafing away of insulation may ultimately break or short. Nonconducting clamps should be used at least every 12 inches or so along any runs. Battery cables should be well fastened both to the batteries and to the bulkloads so they won't vibrate loose. There should always be some looping permitted at terminals and along runs, not enough to permit swing or large movement but enough to allow for stress and strain. Boat twisting then will not pull electrical joints loose or weaken them. Wires in conduits usually have this freedom.

We have mentioned a common physical ground on boats. This may be the hull if it's metal, but remember not to carry load currents through the hull; it is simply for bonding to the common wire return. This common ground does furnish an earth return system for radio or radar waves when immersed in salt water, increasing range and removing, in some cases, high frequency interference as it makes a path for these interfering signals to shunt from the equipment *cases* to "ground" in the sea water. This helps to prevent interfering signals from entering electronic gear to cause incorrect or unreadable signals. You do want everything metallic connected to the common grounding conductor.

The engine itself, being metal, might be a starting point for this large conductor wire which then runs to a metal plate on the underside of a fiberglass or wooden hull. This plate is in constant contact in the water. A common return is also required for ac systems but this is *not* connected to the ground system. These ac lines operate "above" the ground potential, but a common ground wire is still used in the ac system.

The Institute of Electrical and Electronic Engineers (IEEE) recommends that the maximum voltage drop permitted on lines feeding communications equipment be not more than 5 percent. We had recommended a 3 percent level, so staying within this tighter tolerance ensures meeting their recommended tolerance of 5 percent. All connections to communications equipment, except call-bell signalling circuits, should be made in flame retardent connecting boxes using approved fixtures. Again we want to point out that a rigid, mechanically strong and tight electrical connector must be used always to avoid loosening due to vibration, stress, and strain.

Consider for a moment the requirements for bells, buzzers, and other such contact making devices. Each type must be designed for marine service so it will not be affected by vibration, and each should be waterproof. The housings must have a terminal for each wire connection, and, when of waterproof construction, must be of corrosion resistant material and accept a tube conduit able to contain the wires. If a moded composition is used, it must be flame resistant. a 1/4 inch clearance must be maintained between opposite polarity parts which carry 110 volts and at least 1/8 inch air clearance for those parts which handle 24 volts or less. All coils must be able to withstand without damage, for a period of at least 5 seconds, a voltage equal to at least 10 times that of the operating value. Each unit must also be capable of operating on as much as a 20 percent reduced voltage from its source.

COLOR CODED WIRING

Figure 2-4 shows panels for some of the standard electrical circuits that we had previously mentioned, now we must cover the color coding recommended for these circuits. Every insulated conductor must have a color code to permit identification. Insulated bonding conductors, which actually *do not* carry circuit currents, are identified by green. White is reserved for the grounded *current carrying* conductor in any ac circuit.

For three-wire ac systems, black is the hot lead and red is for switch returns. In a four wire ac system, blue will be added. If there are branch circuits, striped colors may be used.

With a dc system under 50 volts, green is the bonding (hull ground) color, white or black is the negative return primary wire color and the source of the negative voltage. Red is the color of the positive voltage wire. There are some additional colors which have been suggested as standard for other type circuits. These are: yellow with a red stripe for the starting circuits of engine , yellow for bilge blower circuits, dark gray for navigation lights and tachometer

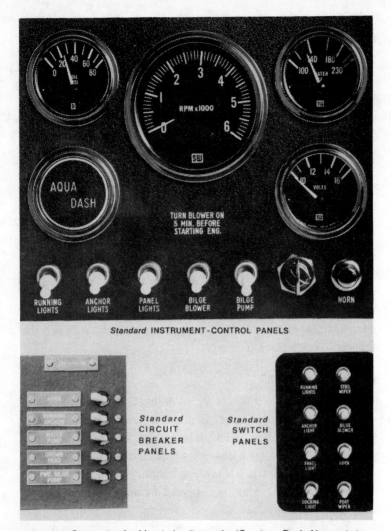

Fig. 2-4. Some standard boat circuit panels. (Courtesy Buck Algonquin.)

circuits, brown for the generator armature to regulator circuit, alternator charging light, and pump circuits. Orange is the color for any accessory feed, such as ammeter to alternator, or to other switches or fuses from the generator. Also, orange is recommended for distribution panel circuits to accessory switches. Purple is the color for ignition and electrical instrument circuits. Blue is used as the primary circuit to electronics instruments. Dark blue is reserved for cabin and instrument light circuits. Light blue is for oil pressure gauge circuits and tan for circuits to temperature sensors. Remember that white or black is used throughout as a common return associated with each of these colors for a particular wiring area. It must be mentioned here also that just in case ac and dc wires are together in a common raceway, you must jacket all ac conductors *separately* so they are isolated from the dc conductors. Separate tubing or conduit does the job nicely. With ac circuits, white is the common wire, green is the ground, and black is the hot. Red is usually the hot switched wire.

CIRCUIT PROTECTION DEVICES

We had briefly mentioned circuit protection devices. Consider now some of their basic requirements for ac distribution circuits. Not more than four receptacles may be fed from a single overcurrent protection breaker. The circuit breaker must not be rated over 20 amperes, and the individual receptacles that are fed must have ratings of at least 15 amperes each. Of course, all motor circuits must have overcurrent circuit breakers that will kick out when the current reaches no more than 125 percent of the full load motor current rating. All conductors carrying ac must, like shore based installations, have insulation with a minimum rating of 600 volts and be specially designed to resist flame, humidity, cold, heat, gas, oil, vibration and other conditions. Conductors must be at least 14 gauge in wiring ac circuits. Receptacles in locations subject to rain, spray, or splashing water will have weathertight spring-loaded covers and the wiring for the receptacles will be such that the grounded conductor (white) attaches to a terminal marked **S** or is a light silver color. The hot conductor shall be connected to the terminals marked **S** which are of a gold, brass, or copper color.

SHIP TO SHORE ELECTRICAL CONNECTIONS

When in marinas or at docks, boats tie into shore electrical systems, as shown in Fig. 2-5. An isolation transformer is advisable for ac electrical systems to minimize chances of getting shorts or other malfunctions. It is advisable, however, to carry the shore ground neutral throughout the boat system. There should be a master switch, easily located, so as to disconnect the power being applied and to prevent application of boat power during the time you

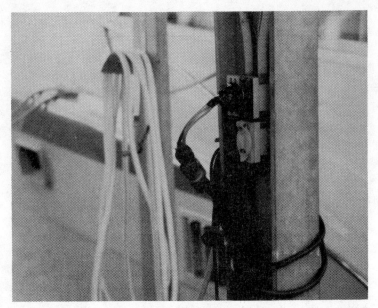

Fig. 2-5. Marina electrical connections.

receive power from the shore. Unless careful interlocking is accomplished, a disaster may result. But there are two-way master switches which in the up position apply shore power and in the down position apply boat power to the distribution circuits on the boat. Since the switch can be in only one position at a time, it is impossible to interconnect sources.

The dc power requirements may be the same except that you probably will be charging batteries from shore chargers. It must be *impossible* to get a polarity reversal from the charger to the battery, either by using polarized plugs, by clearly marked connectors, or by other means. As with a car charging system, if the battery and charger are connected in reverse a danger of fire exists from overheated cables. All cables should be kept out of the water and should be sufficiently supported so they will not move about in winds or bad weather, especially if power is being drawn under these conditions.

SAFETY IN ELECTRICAL CIRCUIT REPAIR

The following safety rules should be used when repairing electrical or electronic circuits or equipment, or when making additions or adjustments to such systems. We strongly recommend that you read them carefully and think about them. It could be the difference between life and death or with being lost at sea.

Take the last thought. If making a temporary repair of some electrical wiring with a knife to strip back the insulation, the conductor may be nicked. When at sea, with the boat vibrating and pounding, that weakened point may give way, taking out the circuit for vital instruments. So if using a knife for stripping insulation from cables, be sure to not nick the cable conductors.

Tools should be designed for electrical repair work and have insulated handles. If a pair of pliers is not insulated, for example, wrap the handles several layers deep with electrical insulating tape, being sure to cover the ends of the handles. This could be used as a temporary solution and may be used with tools too.

Whenever possible completely de-energize all electrical circuits you will come in contact with. Open circuit breaker panels and set the breaker switch to off, or remove one terminal from the battery or primary power source and securely tie it away from any possible contact with anything metallic. Be careful that everybody knows you will be working on circuits so they won't throw the breaker on while you are in contact with the circuits. Sometimes only a switch need be turned off to isolate a circuit. Figure 2-6 illustrates a clearly labeled switch panel. That makes identification of circuits easy. Be sure someone doesn't reset a circuit breaker or turn a switch on, to later find you dangling from some far off hidden terminal. After you turn a switch off it is a good idea to tag it, stating not to close it. As an extra precaution, place tape over the switch.

If a person has to work on hot circuits in an emergency, and remember that only a person with experience should do this, extreme care must be taken. With ac circuits as low as 67 volts and with dc circuits as low as 110 volts, death and serious injury have resulted. The person who knows what to do works on hot circuits only as a last resort and:

- will take extreme care to prevent the body from becoming a conductor path for current flow.
- will only work on one side (wire) of the circuit at a time.
- will always use insulated gloves, stand on insulated material, and use insulated tools.

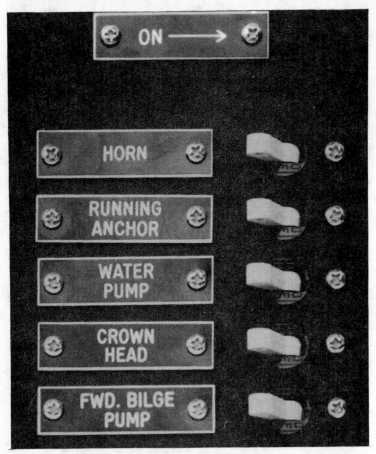

Fig. 2-6. A clearly labeled switch panel. (Courtesy Buck Algonquin.)

• will try to keep all equipment, tools, and clothing dry. This can be difficult at sea, but the attempt must be made. A temporary shelter completely around the person and the work area might have to be constructed to accomplish this.

Again, this would be a "last resort" operation and should not be attempted by inexperienced persons.

Now the electrician may have disconnected the circuit to be worked on by pulling a main switch or turning off a circuit breaker but always recheck the circuit to be sure that it isn't energized through some other path. Do this with a voltmeter or a test lamp known to be good and that will light up on the expected voltage. Sometimes a voltage will exist between a hot lead and ground even though it isn't supposed to exist there. Always test the circuit. Also test nearby circuits that you might accidentally come in contact with. Check the common ground bus or lead and if a metal conduit is used, also check between hot wires and the tubing.

Sometimes errors will exist in color codes, so never take for granted that a designated wire will be the one to check or to assume is turned OFF. If an error was made, you will be in a dangerous situation because a circuit supposedly dead is actually energized. So always check with your meter or test light.

OVERLOADING CIRCUITS

This is a recurring problem. We all have a tendency to add equipment to existing circuits until they are called upon to supply more current than originally intended. Adding air conditioners, pumps, miscellaneous electronics gear, fans, and heaters can pose a real problem if the circuits aren't designed to handle the load. Of course the safety protection is the circuit breaker, which should have been properly specified for the circuit it was installed to protect. But if you change the size of this protective device to be able to add just a bit more load, an overload in the wiring may result in a fire.

On board larger yachts various size motors are used requiring many different load currents. Tables 2-3 and 2-4 show some of the current requirements for the various size single and three phase

Table 2-3. Full Load Current for Single Phase AC Motors.

HP	115V	230V	440V
1/6	4.4	2.2	--
1/4	5.8	2.9	--
1/3	7.2	3.6	--
1/2	9.8	4.9	--
3/4	13.8	6.9	--
1	16	8	--
1 1/2	20	10	--
2	24	12	--
3	34	17	--
5	56	28	--
7 1/2	80	40	21
10	100	50	26

Table 2-4. Full Load Current for Three Phase AC Motors.

	Full Load Current Three Phase AC Motors.								
	Induction Type Motor Squirrel-Cage and Wound Rotor Amperes					Synchronous Type Motor Unity Power Factor Amperes			
HP	110V	220V	440V	550V	2300V	220V	440V	550V	2300V
1/2	4	2	1	.8					
3/4	5.6	2.8	1.4	1.1					
1	7	3.5	1.8	1.4					
1 1/2	10	5	2.5	2.0					
2	13	6.5	3.3	2.6					
3		9	4.5	4					
5		15	7.5	6					
7 1/2		22	11	9					
10		27	14	11					
15		40	20	16					
20		52	26	21					
25		64	32	26	7	54	27	22	5.4
30		78	39	31	8.5	65	33	26	6.5
40		104	52	41	10.5	86	43	35	8
50		125	63	50	13	108	54	44	10
60		150	75	60	16	128	64	51	12
75		185	93	74	19	161	81	65	15
100		246	123	98	25	211	106	85	20
125		310	155	124	31	264	132	106	25
150		360	180	144	37		158	127	30
200		480	240	192	48		210	168	40

electric motors. As you can see the addition of even one small motor represents a considerable increase in current drain for your electrical system.

Aside from overload due to additional electrical devices, the presence of a tripped circuit breaker may indicate troubles of a very serious nature; a shorted cable, a terminal perhaps grounded through buildup of corrosion or salt deposits, or even a defective piece of equipment. Disconnecting all equipment from a given circuit may be required to isolate the problem. If the circuit breaker still trips, the trouble is in the electrical wiring. If it doesn't trip, energize equipment to the line one at a time, until the breaker again trips. You can then repair that unit.

Perhaps one of the greatest dangers with electricity is using bad cables. These may be the plug-in cords from lamps, fans, or the extension wires hanging around the boat. When they are frayed, broken, or cracked, someone could really pay for this negligence. Also, a sloppily routed extension cord dipping into a pool of water is a dandy way to get electrocuted.

We should also mention that ac motors for the 60 Hz frequency of U.S. power may not be able to operate on 50 Hz foreign power.

Voltages may be different too. Many ac motors are synchronous types; thus, speed depends on the applied frequency. For example, a synchronous motor at 60 Hz turns at 1800 rpm. At 50 Hz, its speed reduces to about 1500 rpm. So be careful about attaching to commercial power in a foreign port. Be sure it is the correct voltage and frequency before you connect to it.

GENERAL MAINTENANCE OF ELECTRICAL CIRCUITS

Some routine inspection procedures should be considered when checking electrical systems. While it is impossible to check a run of cable because it is concealed in conduit, at least check for sealing at each of the ends. If a wire is permanently exposed to water, such as in the bilge, some means must be found to check its overall condition periodically even though it may be an approved cable for underwater installations. All conductor enclosure supports must be periodically inspected and maintained. When loose or damaged they should be replaced immediately.

Loose fittings may be a source of trouble. A new boat is tight, but time takes its toll and things begin to work apart. Regularly check electrical fittings of every type for looseness. These include conduit couplings, connectors, box entry fasteners, box covers, cover seals and hinge springs, and all other such items. The conduit or flexible cable connections to engines, generators, and other equipment must also be checked.

INTERFERENCE

Inspection of electrical connections must include all splices and taps if there are any. There aren't supposed to be any in boat wiring, but it is just possible that someone made a jury-rigged connection at one time and didn't bother to make a permanent installation afterwards. These temporary jobs and loose or broken connections can cause short circuits and arcing with resulting radio and instrument interference. High resistance shorts cause heat which in turn can cause fire. So always be sure connections stay bright, tight, and solid.

ELECTRICAL TROUBLESHOOTING PRINCIPLES

An open circuit can occur when one or more conductors are broken, burned into, or otherwise separated. If a piece of equipment doesn't work even though the circuit breaker holds, and the battery or generator connections seem all right, suspect an open circuit. To test for the problem use your test light or voltmeter at the receptacle. Be sure to pick up a ground from the common pin of the socket, not a case ground. Then if no voltage is present trace the circuit wiring physically, looking for bent conduit or any other sign of trouble along the wiring. Test at various points along the wiring, working towards the source of power. The circuit breaker panel may be the next accessible point. From there work towards the battery or ac generator, as the case may be. This way you may find a broken wire or damage indication where it is broken. You may not be able to tell anything, however, except that power is not getting through the line. The line may be concealed in the hull. In this case run a new line, disconnecting the damaged one, but leaving it in place. This new cable doesn't have to follow the old cable run. Just make sure it doesn't go near any navigation instruments. Also be sure to cut off all power before working on cables.

To determine which wire of a two wire ac system is open, if metal conduit or a ground wire (green) is available, connect between the hot line and the ground or the conduit with your test light leads. If the light doesn't come on with the switch on, the hot line may be at fault. If, however, the light just glows then a possibility exists that the neutral grounding wire of the two wire system (single phase) is open. This must be located at the power plant or leading away from it. Establish a temporary wire to complete the circuit and retest. If this was the problem, run a permanent neutral wire. Large boats have electrical generating systems almost exactly like shore based systems and the same philosophy of troubleshooting applies to both. However some requirements of boat wiring are more stringent then shore wiring.

Three types of grounds may short electrical circuits. The direct ground is a complete short circuit and will always cause tripped circuit breakers, possibly burning them out and causing arcing, smoke, and even fire. This could be caused by two wires touching each other because the insulation has failed.

The second type of ground is the partial ground, a resistance connection which permits the flow of current to the ground (or common) wire but not enough to cause the circuit breaker to trip.

This type of malfunction is difficult to locate. It may possibly take place at switches or in cable runs where water has somehow accumulated. It is detectible by a low voltage at receptacles; lights not operating at full intensity, or, if near a socket, one light may be dim and others remain bright.

You may also find that all equipment appears to operate normally but there seems to be an increased loading of the generator. Batteries may discharge quicker, or an ammeter in the line between the battery and the circuits may show a greater than normal discharge.

If accustomed to the sound of your ac generator supplying power, you can tell by ear when the unit is loading down more than normal. Better than this, have current meters or sensitive circuit breakers at the source of electrical power to tell if an increased power drain develops. Current meters may show drain even when all switches are off. Standard circuit breakers won't trip on small currents but specially designed low voltage sensing types will. Figure 2-7 shows a circuit of one such unit.

The third type of ground, and the worst, is the floating ground. This is one in which the resistance between hot lines and ground wires varies from time to time and from one environmental condition to another. It's a bad one. You may not know you have such a condition for a long time, then suddenly a circuit breakers trips.

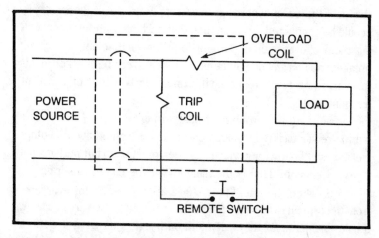

Fig. 2-7. Low voltage and high current circuit breaker schematic. (Courtesy Airpax.)

When reset, the breaker may hold for a while then abruptly trip again for no apparent cause. Of course radio and instrument interference may be higher than normal when this type of partial ground occurs.

One way of checking for these kinds of troubles is to open the ac main power switch and attach a 25 watt light bulb in series with the hot line of the circuit. Remember, in a marina you can check for the hot line with a test lamp by connecting the leads between the receptacle and the metal conduit. The light will glow when connected between the hot line and the conduit. Then disconnect the circuit and insert the lamp in series with this line. Next, disconnect everything from the circuit on the boat side, then close the main switch on the panel. If the light burns, you have a short somewhere in the main boat circuits. If the light doesn't burn, close the switches and circuit breakers one by one. If the light comes on after any such closure, that circuit is suspect.

The most probable cause of short circuit troubles is portable equipment connections or the equipment itself. It has been found that 90 percent of short circuits in electrical systems occur in the exposed flexible cables which feed electrical devices. In many cases just a good eye-ball inspection and feeling of the wires—when equipment and circuits are off—will tell what you want to know about the condition of these wires.

Once you have checked all of the primary circuits through use of the test light, reconnect the primary supply circuits as they normally should be connected. You can then test portable gear by reconnecting them one at a time, turning them on, and seeing if a circuit breaker trips on any one of them. Motors also can be checked in this manner. Operate and test each item individually with all others off or disconnected.

Discussing the problem of boat wiring with one Old Salt at a marine repair facility in Galveston, Texas, I learned about another weakness of boat wiring which has been mentioned but perhaps not stressed enough. That is the hangers for the electrical wiring.

'Too often, he said, "they (and I assume he meant everyone, from the captain to the shipyard repair men) put those wires on light, fragile hangers. Or they put them on hangers which aren't set in strong enough so they won't pull out. You know," he added, "I just finished putting in a complete set of new wiring for a boat. What happened was that they used those little hangers and some pulled out and let those wires come down on a pulley. That pulley wore out them wires and shorted them and almost burned up that darn boat. I sure wish folks would use proper wires and proper hangers—might save their lives—tell them that—yes, tell them that."

ELECTRICAL MOTOR PREVENTIVE MAINTENANCE

All electric motors and similar devices are manufactured to operate below a particular temperature stated in degrees above the ambient temperature. This specification limits the maximum operating temperature of the equipment. It is obtained by adding this rating in degrees to the temperature of the operating location, but be careful to use the specified temperature system: that is, use Fahrenheit or Centigrade, and be sure to use the same scale for both temperatures. For example, if a motor is rated at 30° above ambient, the surrounding temperature is 80°, with both specified in Fahrenheit, then the maximum operating temperature would be 110° F.

It is necessary to keep rotating equipment clean and dry to keep it operating within the temperature tolerance. An excessive amount of dust, grease, oil, or moisture on the equipment surface acts as an insulator, preventing the heat from dissipating through the housing of the equipment. When operating in areas of high humidity and temperature it is vital that the rotating equipment be specified for that environment. In some cases a motor is used to propel small craft. These motors must not be run out of the water. They will become too hot without the water coolant. It is necessary to properly lubricate motors unless they are specified to be permanently lubricated. This type motor has bearings that are oil impregnated. As the motor shaft turns they release tiny globules of oil so that wear is minimized. Eventually, of course, the motor will have to be replaced, but a service life from two to five years is typical.

It is also important that you do not overlubricate electrical rotating machinery. This can cause malfunctioning just as no lubrication can cause malfunctioning. Oil or grease in contact with insulated conductors causes deterioration much quicker than when they are not subject to this contamination. Overlubrication also results in heat buildup and grease leakage, in some cases fire hazard. Of course, dust and dirt, common at harbors and marinas will collect on oily and greasy surfaces producing high wear from surface abrasion on rotating shafts if they are not completely sealed.

EFFICIENT LIGHTING

The efficiency of lighting on board can be vastly reduced when dirt collects on the reflectors, lamps, walls, or ceilings of lighted areas. Of course double covers are often used when these areas are subjected to wetting from spray, rain, or direct immersion. The sea water tends to build up crusts on these outer protective covers, and a reduced amount of light will result from the fixtures if they are not cleaned regularly. Of course high efficiency of all electronic and electrical equipment is necessary on boats, for you have only a limited amount of primary power and every available watt should be converted into useful energy. Keep all lights clean and you may find a 50 percent increase in lighting over that which occurs with dusty, dirty, greasy, or sea water encrusted fixtures.

ELECTRICAL DISTRIBUTION SYSTEMS

The American Boat and Yacht Council recommends that the neutral wire (white) of an ac system be grounded only at the power source, that is, at the on-board ship generator or through the individual shore power connection. They also recommend that individual circuits not be energized by more than one source of electrical power at a time, and that each shore power input be from a separate source of electrical power. Furthermore, the systems should be designed so that the on-board generators and shore based power cannot be used simultaneously. And circuit breakers shall be used to simultaneously open all ungrounded main supply current carrying conductors of the systems. Fuses should not be used on boat wiring.

Each *ungrounded* conductor of a branch circuit shall be provided with overcurrent protection devices at the point of connection to the main switchboard or distribution panel bus. Each trip-free circuit breaker used shall be rated according to (1) the smallest conductor between the circuit breaker and the load or (2) the maximum current rating of the device on this circuit, except by ac motors, whichever is less. In branch circuits the boat shall be equipped with multipole circuit breakers and switches which will simultaneously open all

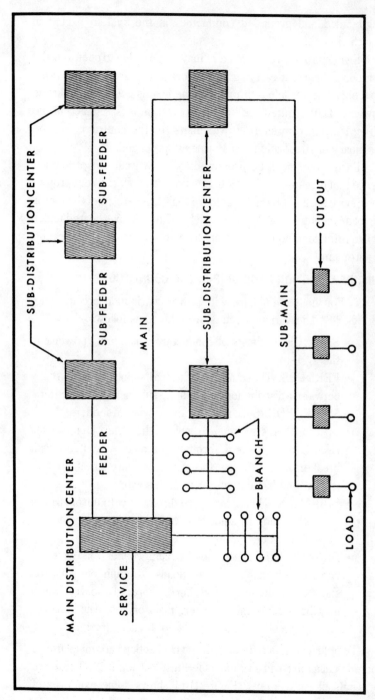

Fig. 2-8. An electrical distribution system.

63

ungrounded and grounded conductors in the system except in branch circuits.

Switches and circuit breakers may be provided to open *only* the ungrounded current carrying conductors in the circuit *if* the wiring from shore power inlets throughout the boat is polarized, including power to light fixtures, *and* a polarity indicator is installed in the wiring leading from shore power inlets, or the neutral leg of the secondary of an isolation transformer is grounded.

Each motor shall be protected by an overcurrent protection device that is responsive to motor current. The overcurrent protection device shall not be rated at more than 125 percent of the motor full load current rating. Motors which will not be overheated under locked rotor conditions are exempt from this overcurrent protection requirement.

CIRCUIT DEFINITIONS AND SHIP-SHORE CONNECTIONS

For those not familiar with power distribution circuits, refer to Fig. 2-8. The various circuits are defined as follows.

- SERVICE. Consists of conductors which bring power into the system.
- FEEDERS. These are circuits that supply power directly between a distribution center and a sub-distribution center.
- SUB-FEEDERS. These are extensions of feeders.
- MAIN. This is a circuit to which other energy consuming circuits are attached through automatic cutouts (circuit breakers). A main has the same size wire throughout its length, and has no cutouts in series with it.
- SUB-MAIN. This circuit is fed through a cutout from a main or another sub-main, and has branch circuits connected to it through cut-outs.
- BRANCH CIRCUIT. These circuits connect one or more energy consuming devices (loads) through one fuse on shore or circuit breaker on ship or shore, to a source, which may be a distribution center, main or sub-main. Interior lighting circuits are an example of branch circuits.

To obtain an idea as to how the ac connections are made from a shore installation to a boat, examine Figs. 2-9 and 2-10. These are for single phase systems. Figure 2-11 shows some examples of

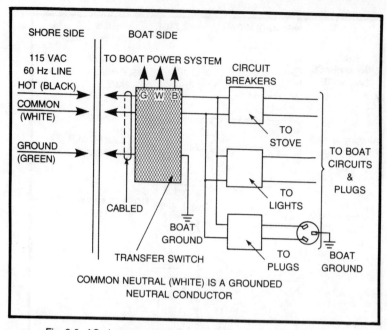

Fig. 2-9. AC shore connections with a grounded neutral conductor.

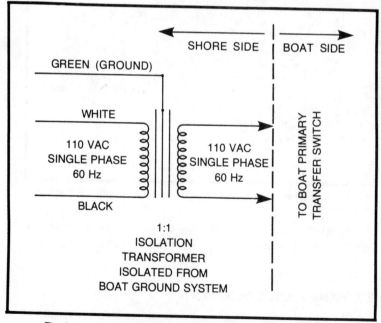

Fig. 2-10. AC shore connections through an isolation transformer.

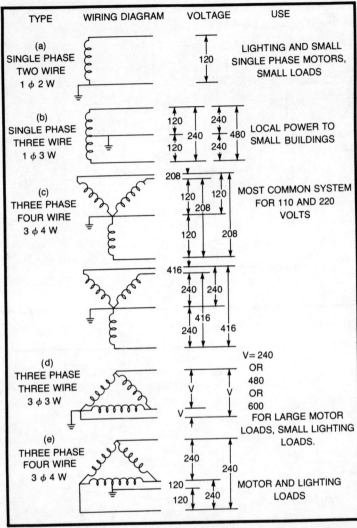

TYPE	WIRING DIAGRAM	VOLTAGE	USE
(a) SINGLE PHASE TWO WIRE 1 ϕ 2 W		120	LIGHTING AND SMALL SINGLE PHASE MOTORS, SMALL LOADS
(b) SINGLE PHASE THREE WIRE 1 ϕ 3 W		120 / 120 240 240 / 240 480	LOCAL POWER TO SMALL BUILDINGS
(c) THREE PHASE FOUR WIRE 3 ϕ 4 W		208 / 120 / 120 / 208 / 120 / 208 416 / 240 / 240 / 416 / 240 / 416	MOST COMMON SYSTEM FOR 110 AND 220 VOLTS
(d) THREE PHASE THREE WIRE 3 ϕ 3 W		V V V	V= 240 OR 480 OR 600 FOR LARGE MOTOR LOADS, SMALL LIGHTING LOADS.
(e) THREE PHASE FOUR WIRE 3 ϕ 4 W		240 / 240 / 120 / 120 / 240	MOTOR AND LIGHTING LOADS

Fig. 2-11. AC connections for single phase and three phase circuits at shore transformers.

connections and the voltages for single and three phase systems. This diagram will also indicate the usage of the various circuits and phases.

ELECTRICIAN'S DUTIES ON SHIPS

Electrician's duties on shipboard are similar to those on shore but with the added precautions necessary for the safety and operational requirements of a boat. The requirements of the National Electrical Code are used as well as specific regulations and recommendations promulgated by other groups such as the American Boat and Yacht Council, the Coast Guard, and the Maritime Commission. The primary requirement is that the electrician must know the field technically as well as understanding all regulations and requirements pertaining to it. On shipboard, one has no room for guessing or unskilled experimentation.

One more item of importance to installation of motors on board should be kept in mind. Normally motors are to be installed with their shafts in the fore and aft direction of the vessel. If the motor is to be mounted athwartship (crosswise) to the longitudinal axis of the vessel, the manufacturer should be notified. There is a reason. When a motor is turning on a boat it acts like a gyroscope. If large enough it can actually be used as a stabilizer, and in some cases this has been done by mounting the motor with the shaft vertical. This tends to resist any roll or pitch of the craft. We will go into the gyroscopic principles more in a later chapter. Right now we just want to note that in the case of smaller motors, the ship's rolling, turning, and pitching can cause the armature to exert undue pressure on the motor bearings, and if this is not allowed for, may well cause bearings to wear prematurely. To avoid trouble, manufacturers will design a motor for boating use a little differently than for shore use, and the installation of the motor is of major importance to this. Any rotating machinery with great mass of the rotating part will have this gyroscopic effect, so it is well to consider its effect and account for it in accord with good installation practices.

Thus concludes this important chapter on wiring and electrical installations. Many persons know the principles expressed here, but many do not put them into practice. We hope you are not one of these persons.

Chapter 3

Batteries,
Charging Equipment,
and Electric Generators

The primary source of electrical power for most small boats will be marine batteries. Large craft probably will have chargers operating from an ac supply, but some may charge from the propulsion engines. But most every large boat will have both ac and dc electrical power systems on board. Small boats usually have only dc as a primary electrical power and it may be from 6 to 48 volts in value. The ac systems are related to the 115 volts, 60 Hz standard used in the United States.

BATTERIES

There are various means of charging batteries, from engine-attached generators (alternators) similar to those used on your car, Fig. 3-1, to completely separate units such as will be described in this chapter. There are many requirements which should be taken into account from a safety as well as an operating standpoint. In most cases, small craft should have a second battery system on board to give a margin of safety should the original battery run down accidentally or through mishap.

Currently there are some types of sealed batteries available which are advertised as "maintenance free." These are said never to need replacement of water or electrolyte. In theory these would be ideal, of course, but marine use may prove to be too severe for these batteries. The kind you do have to top off occasionally have proven themself so we will restrict our discussion to this type.

The ONAN company has stated the dangers of batteries very precisely:

"Few people realize how dangerous a battery can be. The electrolyte in a lead-acid battery is dilute sulfuric acid (H_2SO_4) and in an alkaline battery it is potassium hydroxide (KOH). As dissimiliar as these two liquids are, they have one thing in common: they give off hydrogen gas.

Any battery which has a charge-discharge cycle is known as a secondary cell. In it a chemical change takes place which causes the bubbling you see through the vent hole during charging or rapid discharging. This bubbling is caused by hydrogen gas which is explosive.

When charging or discharging a battery, if this gas is present and a spark or other means of ignition appears, an explosion can occur. Then, not only would immediate physical damage result but also the secondary effect of having sulfuric acid or potassium hyd-

Fig. 3-1. These alternators, driven by the propulsion engines, charge the batteries as they do in automobile systems.

roxide sprayed over everything. You know how sulfuric acid will eat away even the strongest of metals. Be aware that both these are corrosive and dangerous.

When you have to service your battery, do as Fig. 3-2 suggests. If electrolyte splashes on your skin it can cause great irritation and if

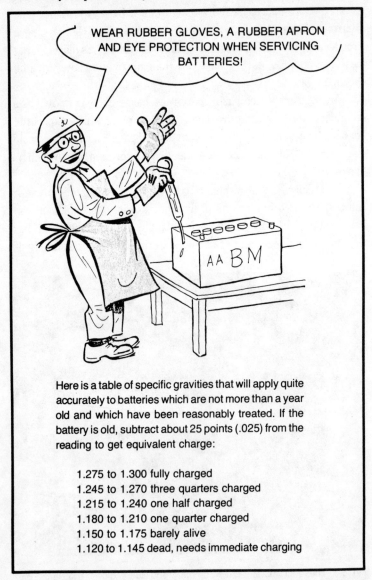

Here is a table of specific gravities that will apply quite accurately to batteries which are not more than a year old and which have been reasonably treated. If the battery is old, subtract about 25 points (.025) from the reading to get equivalent charge:

> 1.275 to 1.300 fully charged
> 1.245 to 1.270 three quarters charged
> 1.215 to 1.240 one half charged
> 1.180 to 1.210 one quarter charged
> 1.150 to 1.175 barely alive
> 1.120 to 1.145 dead, needs immediate charging

Fig. 3-2. Battery servicing precautions and specific gravity. (Courtesy Onan.)

into your eyes very likely serious injury. If unable to have the protective equipment shown and you do get splashed with electrolyte, flush immediately with cold running water—but not sea water. *Salt water combining with electrolyte forms highly poisonous chlorine gas.* So beware if there is sea water in the bilge and the battery spills any electrolyte into it.

When charging batteries with removable caps, lift them free to allow gasses to escape freely. On alkaline (or nicad) batteries, the vents are usually spring loaded in a closed position. Do not wedge these vents open because the potassium hydroxide will become weak (its specific gravity will be lowered) if exposed to air. But do

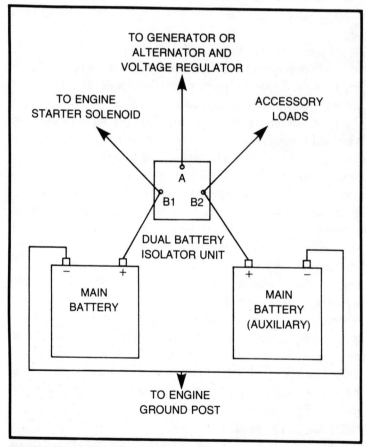

Fig. 3-3. Dual battery isolator block diagram. The isolator may consist of an arrangement of diodes or relays.

check to see that the vents are free to open when internal pressure builds up.

After the batteries are charged, replace the vent covers on lead-acid batteries and wash down the tops with baking soda (sodium bicarbonate) and water but not salt water. Use distilled or drinking water for this purpose. You can also sprinkle some of the baking soda into the lead-acid battery tray to neutralize any spilled electrolyte which may have gotten beneath the battery which may somehow spill out after the boat is at sea.

If it becomes necessary to mix an electrolyte for a lead-acid battery for any reason (specific gravity too low after what would be a good healthy charge), add *acid to water*, never the reverse action. If water is added to acid, the mixture may violently erupt to burn you severely.

If you must mix electrolyte for a nicad (alkaline) battery, add powder to distilled water and stir with a glass rod. Do not handle any component of the electrolyte with your bare hands. The dry powder will burn you as badly as the liquid mixture.

Now, consider again the idea of having a second battery on board with at least enough capacity to start your engine—except for outboards which may be hand started. This battery will not only take up space but will also add weight to your boat. It must be firmly mounted, preferably strapped into position as the original battery should be. Then you must have the proper circuit to charge both batteries to full capacity whenever docked. One such device is the dual battery isolator. These isolators are designed so that batteries will deliver their loads independent of each other, not discharge each other, yet will charge in parallel when required. When charging two batteries from the same source, be certain the circuit can supply the required current. Generators or alternators may overheat if required to supply high current for long charging times. A larger than usual generator or alternator may be required, or an arrangement made to charge each battery separately. Some methods of connecting multiple batteries for charging from generators or alternators are shown in Fig. 3-4.

SHORE BASED CHARGERS

When in a marina you will probably connect to a shore based battery charger. One such unit is the Ratelco Type-VM which is

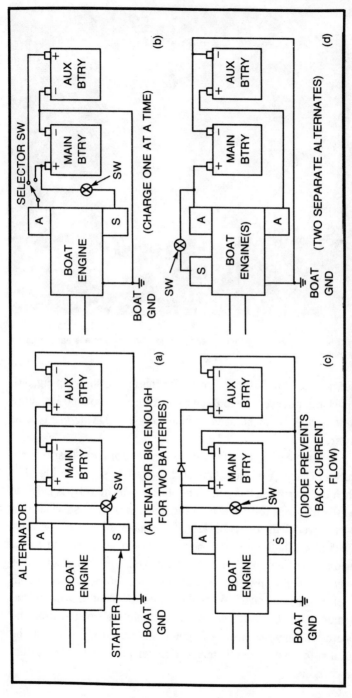

Fig. 3-4. Methods of charging multiple batteries. An auxiliary battery is always a precaution.

73

Fig. 3-5. The Ratelco constant voltage charger. Charging rate is easily read on the meter.

shown in Fig. 3-5. Batteries connect to this unit as shown in Fig. 3-6. This charger delivers up to 20 amps dc from a 110 volt, 60 Hz, single phase ac line. It can be used on board any boat having this type ac power.

In some cases, a boat will have a generator and a charger with which to charge batteries. One such system is shown in Fig. 3-7. When the start switch is energized, the paralleling relay is pulled in and the batteries are connected together, with very small current flowing through the relay contacts. This causes the starter contactor to pull in and both batteries then supply a starting current to the generator engine. When the engine starts, a charging current is generated and it flows through the diode isolators to charge both batteries simultaneously. When the generator is not running and the charger is on, the batteries will be completely isolated from the generator. Only when the charger is energized will the relay be pulled in to connect the batteries together to receive current from the charger.

Installation of a Charger

The charger should be mounted in a cool, dry location with at least four inches of clearance on all sides, top, and bottom. Do not install in a locker or in any other location lacking free air flow.

The case of the charger should be grounded to the nearest good electrical ground (water pipe or electrical grounding system on shore installations and the electrical ground system on shipboard installation). Grounding is very important, not only to conform to the electrical codes and good wiring practices but to protect the charger from transient voltages which could cause erratic operation. The charger case is isolated from both the input and output connections. Never connect any input or output connection to case or ground. With no grounding connection from input or output to the case, the grounding of the case will have no effect on electrolysis or the polarity of the ac connection. Recall that the negative battery terminal is always the one grounded.

Charger Connections

When connecting the charger to the batteries you must be certain that the dc leads are connected with the correct polarity, that the ac and dc leads are the correct wire sizes, and that the charger case is properly grounded as stated previously. Failure to properly connect the charger may result in damage to the equipment. Remember that to charge, connect the positive lead of the charger to the positive battery terminal and the negative charger lead to the negative battery terminal.

Voltage regulation of the charger and battery life are improved when the charger is connected directly to the battery terminals, with a wire size not less than that recommended in the installation instructions. If you are replacing a charger be sure that your wire leads are correct for the new charger. If radio noise from the charger is a problem, the battery leads to and from the charger may be cabled with leads going to the radio equipment. Separate them. Also, it may be necessary to use a 50 to 100 mmF electrolytic capacitor across the dc power leads going to your radio system. Be sure to observe the polarity of the electrolytic capacitor when you install it.

We mentioned the use of proper wire size. It is generally true that at least a 14 gauge wire must be used to connect the charger to

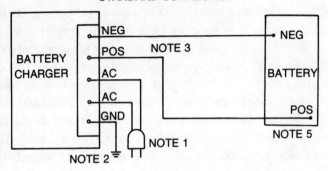

STANDARD CONNECTION

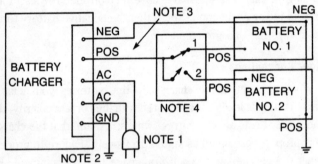

NEGATIVE GROUNDED SYSTEM—MULTIPLE BATTERIES

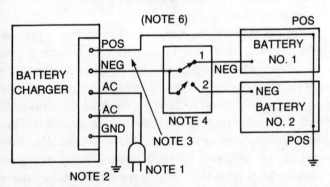

POSITIVE GROUNDED SYSTEM—MULTIPLE BATTERIES

Fig. 3-6. The Ratelco charger installation. This may be a typical ship to shore connection to charge batteries. The charger may be shore based.

NOTES:

1) WIRE SIZE MUST BE CAPABLE OF HANDLING INPUT CURRENT.

2) TO SHIPS GROUND (MAY CAUSE ERRATIC OPERATION IF NOT CONNECTED).

3) CONSULT "WIRE SIZE TABLE" FOR PROPER WIRE SIZE.

4) SELECTOR SWITCHES CAN HAVE AS MANY POSITIONS AS MAY BE NEEDED.

5) EITHER THE NEGATIVE OR POSITIVE TERMINAL MAY BE GROUNDED.

6) POSITIVE GROUND IS NOT RECOMMENDED OR NORMALLY USED IN MARINE INSTALLATIONS.

the ac source. Remember, as the number *decreases* the wire diameter increases, so a 10 gauge wire is larger physically than a 14 gauge wire.

Operation of a Charger

After the charger is connected to the batteries—being careful to have correct polarity—and to the ac source, switch the unit on. If the battery connected to it is not fully charged the ammeter on the charger will show a charging current. If the battery happens to be fully charged the ammeter will indicate little or no current to the battery. To be sure the charger is working properly in this latter case, connect a light of suitable voltage across the dc output of the charger. When this load is placed in parallel with the battery, the charger will supply an additional current equal to that required by the new load. This will show the unit is operating correctly. Be aware that some chargers cannot supply the high currents required to run electric motors; so be careful about using such high current equipment to test the charger or when the charger is connected to the battery. To operate electric motors it is best to turn the charger off,

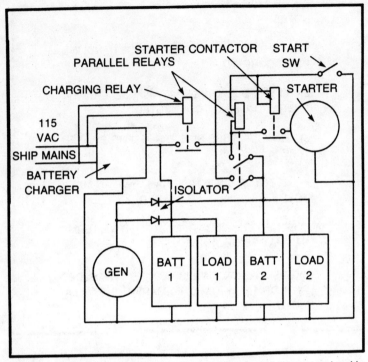

Fig. 3-7. A reliable charging system. Both a shore based charger and a ship generator are used. Batteries may be charged in parallel.

disconnect it and let the battery supply the full load. Only after the electric motor is turned off should you reconnect your charger. Some chargers are built to supply the current needed to run electric motors. Their specifications should tell you if this is possible.

Safety

You should note that most chargers will expose live circuits when their door is open. Charger doors should have interlock switches that turn off the electric power when the door is opened. This prevents accidents. Never disable the interlocking switch unless you are a qualified repairman and know exactly what you are doing. Even then keep all safety precautions in mind. Remember that even if the battery charger is de-energized and isolated from the ac mains or the ac generator, current may possibly be stored in the large capacitors. Always check for discharge of such capacitors before working on any circuit.

Voltage Outputs From Chargers

On a battery charger such as we have been referring to, the usual float voltages are indicated as *normal* on the voltage control. For a 12 volt system this is about 13.3 volts; for a 24 volt system, 26.6 volts; for a 32 volt system, 35 volts; and for a 48 volt system the float voltage is 52 volts. At 120 volts dc, the float voltage at normal charge becomes 130 volts.

Any changes in the NORMAL voltage settings of the charger control should only be done after the battery has completed one charging cycle. If the battery should gas or require the addition of more water (lead-acid cells), the charging rate may be too high and should be reduced until this gassing or consumption of water stops. Conversely, if the battery does not reach full charge (as indicated by a hydrometer reading of 1.250 or greater for lead-acid cells), the voltage must be increased slightly in small steps until the battery does reach a full charge. It is to be noted that new batteries, and old batteries that are still serviceable, will gradually change their characteristics so it is important to keep adjusting the voltage as necessary to meet the full charging condition without causing undue gassing or water evaporation. Always use distilled water in the battery. Tap water can be contaminated with minerals and in some cases will greatly reduce your battery life. Sea water is prohibited.

Charger Protective Features

Some battery charging units are equipped with very effective current limiters which will protect the charger from any secondary short circuit that may exist, such as would be experienced when starting a boat engine. The limiter is usually located on the charger circuit board and is factory set for the output rating of the charger. The adjustment should never be set at a higher value than the charger can handle or was designed for. This is usually stated in the unit's specification. Even connecting more than one battery in parallel to be charged may overload the charger so be sure to check the specifications.

Some chargers will maintain their adjusted output voltage as long as the total current required is less than the maximum rating of the charger. There are others which will taper the current off as the battery charge approaches its full charge state. When this type

Fig. 3-8. A charger suitable for shipboard installation. Note cable clamps for permanent installation.

charger is connected to a discharged battery the meter will show full output current for some time, then gradually taper back to near zero amperes as the battery becomes fully charged. This assumes, of course, there is no load connected to the battery. If lights, a radio, or other gear are pulling current, the meter may indicate those currents even though the battery is fully charged. The charger shown in Fig. 3-8 uses permanently installed cables and has a circuit to protect it in case of an accidental reverse connection to a battery. This means the charger must sense if a small voltage of the correct polarity is being applied accross its charging terminals before starting to charge a battery. Chargers of this type will not start to operate if connected to a completely dead battery or a battery with a heavy load across it. Normally, if a battery has been completely run down but all loads are removed, it will recover sufficiently to produce at least a small residual voltage which can be sensed by the charger. It will then start to charge the battery. If no residual voltage is obtainable from the battery, use another battery and small connecting wires to produce the slight voltage necessary to trigger the sensing unit. Remove the starting wires after a charge is established.

When charging from marina equipment, some of these same precautions are necessary, such as removing all loads from your batteries and checking the charging rates to see if you are getting enough, but not too much, charging current from the dockside charger. Be aware that fast charging, in which a high temperature buildup takes place in your battery, may cause some plates to buckle and distort to later short out under boat vibration or pounding, causing real troubles. Be sure you know what your safe charging current is and do not exceed it, whether your batteries are lead-acid or nicad types.

As has been mentioned, the charger may be a shore based unit, or it may be located on board and driven from the 115 volt, 60 Hz system of the boat. Your battery may be charged from an alternator or generator driven by the same engine as drives the prop, or you may have a small portable gasoline powered dc generator on board to charge the batteries. All methods work satisfactorily if you follow the rules and precautions mentioned previously. A small gasoline powered dc generating plant may cause noise and interference for your radio and navigation equipment, so charging batteries when these devices are not needed may be the rule.

DC TO AC INVERTERS

Among the primary power devices which are used on boats is the dc to ac inverter. This may be one of two types. It may be a dc motor driving an ac generator, or it may be what is a true inverter—a device which uses solid state components to convert the direct current of the battery to an alternating current, usually at 115 volts, 60 Hz, to operate such things as radios, stereo, and fans.

These dc and ac inverters may be obtained with inputs from 12 to 120 volts dc and the output voltages of 120 or 240 volts ac, at 60 Hz. They may be obtained with capacities from 250 volt-amperes to as high as 2500 volt-amperes. This rating means that if you are using 120 volts, then from the 250 watt type you may draw only 2 amperes, while for the larger size you may draw as high as 20 amperes. The battery, of course, must be able to supply the total volt-amperes rating plus an additional large current to make up for in inefficiency of these inverters. For example, at 2500 watts a 12 volt battery must be able to produce about 210 amperes to match the volt-ampere factor and an additional current of perhaps 70 amperes because of inefficiency. You can consider using a 220 volt output to cut the secondary current in half, but the primary volt-ampere requirement must remain the same.

Some requirements which should be met by a good inverter are:

1. That it is designed to inherently protect itself against overload or short circuit without blowing a fuse or tripping a circuit breaker. Some types do have fuses or circuit breaker protection built in.
2. It should have a harmonic distortion in its output voltage of less than 15 percent for all size loads. The specifications will tell you this.
3. It should be designed so that it will not introduce over 30 mV, rms of noise on the dc line.
4. It should have some kind of primary dc protection.
5. It should be supplied in an appropriate package for sea duty, be safe to have on board, and easy to install.

The dc to ac inverter is usually a device without moving parts but with meters to show input and output voltages. They usually have an off-on switch and a light or bell alarm device which will flash or ring if anything goes wrong with the unit. They are an economical means of obtaining ac voltage from your battery supply without the bother of an engine driven ac generator.

Operation of an Inverter

Most inverters have a silicon controlled rectifier (SCR) which is able, through a switching operation, to produce an oscillation similar to that produced by a multivibrator. This alternating voltage is held to a frequency of about 60Hz by a ferro-resonant magnetic circuit. Its tolerance is plus or minus 0.5 percent. The output voltage may be regulated to within plus or minus 5 percent from full load to no load over a nominal range of input voltages.

The inverter is about 65 percent efficient and some units are equipped with transfer switches such that they will go into operations automatically if a line is disconnected from shore ac power, or if that power is suddenly interrupted. They will instantly disconnect themselves and transfer the boat lines to shore power again when that power is reapplied or reconnected.

A good inverter will have instruments to indicate when it is working properly. It will have a frequency meter of some type, possibly a reed unit or a pointer dial meter, and it will have a dc ammeter and voltmeter on the input and an ac ammeter and voltmeter on the output. It will have an output voltage failure alarm, a low battery alarm and a low battery disconnect switch which is automatic and will insure that the unit does not try to supply voltages which are too low or voltage at an incorrect frequency. Too low a frequency or voltage on your ac lines may seriously damage radios, navigation instruments, radar, and other such gear.

Estimating the Electrical Load

The load presented by an electrical device is usually stated in watts, and a watt is simply the current times the voltage. For example, if you have a load of one ampere at a voltage of 120 volts ac, the wattage is $(1) \times (120)$ or 120 watts. You will find inverters and ac generators rated in watts or in VA (volt-amperes). Notice that by our definition the VA is the wattage.

To obtain some idea of what size inverter or ac generating system you might want on board, you must consider the total wattage of all the electrical and electronic equipment you may have or will have on board. When purchasing gear, be it radar or record player, you will find the wattage stamped on it or in its specifications. If you total the wattage of all the equipment then allow about 10 percent more, you should have an idea of the amount of electrical power your inverter or your generating system must produce.

To help with this task we offer the following list of items and the wattage values commonly found for them. Be sure, however, to check your own purchased units as they may differ somewhat. This will simply give you an estimate of what power you might need on board when considering the gear on a cruise.

First look at some motors (capacitor starting types):

Horsepower	Starting Watts	Running Watts
1/6	900	200
1/4	1300	300
1/3	1500	360
1/2	2200	520
3/4	3400	775
1	4000	1000

Repulsion-induction motors require less starting wattage than the capacitor types. Split phase type motors require more starting wattage. There are universal type motors which run equally well on ac or dc. These are brush types, but you must be sure to have the right voltage applied whether it be ac or dc. With this information you can estimate the wattage of any motor driven appliance such as an air conditioner, fan, or bilge pump if you know the horsepower.

Now let us consider some other equipment, courtesy of Onan:

Electrical Device	Wattage Used
Battery chargers (rectifier)	up to 800 watts
Electric blankets	50 to 200 watts
Coffeemakers	550 to 700 watts
Electric drill	see motor size
Electric range (per element)	550 to 1500 watts
Fans	25 to 75 watts
Fry pan	1000 to 1350 watts
Space heater	1000 to 1500 watts
Hot plate (per element)	350 to 1000 watts
Electric iron	500 to 1200 watts

Electrical Device	Wattage Used
Lights (ac)	watts marked on them
Refrigerator	see motor size
Television	200 to 300 watts
Toaster	800 to 1150 watts
Vacuum cleaner	see motor size
Waffle iron	650 to 1200 watts
Water heater	1000 to 1500 watts

Of course this does not include your radio, pleasure items, radar and other such equipment, but it does indicate some items which you might have on board and gives you an idea of how quickly the watts can add up. When calculating wattage, always use the maximum value on the appliance. With an electric iron, for example, use the 1200 watt value even though you may not use it at that rating all the time.

AC GENERATING SYSTEMS

We now consider ac generators and the systems associated with them. They may be small and portable or they may be very large power plants. You may not have one on your boat, using battery power entirely. If this be so you might want to give consideration to at least a small gasoline or diesel driven electric plant as an auxiliary source of electrical power. As dependent as we are on electricity, especially with electronics for navigation, a redundancy of electrical power systems is considered a necessity. We are going to consider small and middle size craft, remembering that large craft have regular power stations or power plants as an integral part of their makeup.

Marine generator sets are usually located in very cramped quarters (Fig. 3-9) and it is because of this that installations should be very carefully engineered. The equipment compartment must be large enough to provide adequate access space for servicing and maintaining the generator, its batteries, and ancillary equipment. The engine driving the generator needs combustion air, and the generator itself needs cooling air. As an example, the Onan MCCK 4.0 kW generator needs 142 cubic feet (4.1 cubic meters) of air for generator cooling and combustion air. Provision must be made to

Fig. 3-9. An ac power plant. The motor generator is tucked under lip of engine compartment deck top. One main propulsion engine is at center, and batteries are to the right.

supply this amount of air on a continuing basis while the generator is in operation. Of course all flammable fumes must be purged from the compartment before the set is turned on. Even with the most perfect commutator or slip ring, the brushes arc. This arcing is sufficient to ignite unpurged fuel fumes and cause an explosion. Just a note here. In the event of fire, use an approved extinguisher. Remember salt water and battery electrolyte cause chlorine gas, and it is deadly poision.

Adequate space around the equipment is important when it becomes necessary to investigate a malfunction on a hot engine. You can get severely burned trying to work in crowded quarters. Of course you must always be sure that exhaust fumes are expelled and not leaking.

Safety Considerations

When dealing with batteries up to about 48 volts dc the probability of shock from electrical current is not as great as it is with the generating equipment where 115 volts or 220 volts may be present. The utmost caution is always of prime importance to avoid shock which, depending upon its magnitude and duration, can produce a range of effects from a simple numbing and paralysis of the hand or arm to death. Here are some words of caution which should be considered by everyone who performs any kind of task on electrical systems, whether on shore or at sea.

DO

- Perform your tasks carefully, without undue haste.
- Provide fire extinguishers (rated A, B, C).
- Provide a first aid kit (for burns and abrasions). Obtain medical attention if necessary.
- Keep your installation clean and dry.
- Use the correct tools for the job you are doing.
- Make sure that all fasteners are secure.
- Use extreme care while making adjustments on equipment while it is running.
- Keep your hands away from moving parts.
- Remember, *horse play is for horses*. It has no place around machinery.
- Tag open switches when working on their circuits.
- Disconnect batteries before starting work on generator set.
- Use screwdrivers, pliers, diagonal pliers, etc., having insulated handles.
- Remember to keep one hand (preferably the left) in your pocket if it is necessary to work on live circuitry. To do so will possibly prevent passage of electricity across the heart in the event of a shock.
- Avoid excessive use of cold weather starting fluids. These can result in serious backfiring, or explosion.

DON'T

- Leave heating devices (e.g., soldering irons) plugged into receptacles after you have finished with them. Should power fail, these devices could be forgotten; when power is restored, which may be after the normal workday, unattended heating equipment may overheat and start a fire.
- Allow inexperienced personnel to work on the generator or electrical equipment.
- Interfere with or bypass interlocks.
- Remove guards or protective devices.

Table 3-1. Gasoline Engine General Troubleshooting.

GASOLINE ENGINE TROUBLESHOOTING GUIDE

CAUSE \ TROUBLE	Sticking Valves	Ring Wear	Poor Compression	Piston Wear (Air Cooled)	Overheating (Water Cooled)	Misfiring	Mechanical Knocks	Loss of Coolant (Water Cooled)	Low Oil Pressure	High Oil Pressure	Governor Hunting	Failure to Start	Engine Stops	Cylinder Wear	Cranks Slowly	Connecting Rod Wear	Burned Valves	Blue Exhaust	Black Exhaust	Bearing Wear	Backfire at Carburetor
STARTING SYSTEM																					
Loose or Corroded Battery Connection												●			●						
Low or Discharged Battery												●			●						
Faulty Starter												●			●						
Faulty Start Solenoid												●									
IGNITION SYSTEM																					
Ignition Timing Wrong					●	●						●									●
Wrong Spark Plug Gap					●	●						●									
Worn Points or Improper Gap Setting						●						●	●								
Bad Ignition Coil or Condenser						●						●	●								
Faulty Spark Plug Wires						●						●	●								
FUEL SYSTEM																					
Out of Fuel - Check												●	●								
Lean Fuel Mixture - Readjust					●	●						●	●				●				●
Rich Fuel Mixture or Choke Stuck												●	●						●		
Engine Flooded												●	●						●		
Poor Quality Fuel							●					●	●						●		
Dirty Carburetor	●											●	●						●		
Dirty Air Cleaner		●		●										●					●	●	
Dirty Fuel Filter												●	●			●			●		
Defective Fuel Pump												●	●								

This troubleshooting chart uses a dot-matrix format. The row labels (listed as column headers in the original rotated layout) are grouped under four system headings. The columns (1–N) represent symptom/condition columns reading left to right across the chart.

INTERNAL ENGINE

Cause	1	2	3	4	5	6	7	8	9	10	11	12	13	14	15	16	17	18	19	20
Wrong Valve Clearance					•		•					•					•			
Broken Valve Spring	•				•		•					•					•			
Valve or Valve Seal Leaking					•		•					•								
Piston Rings Worn or Broken						•					•						•			
Wrong Bearing Clearance									•				•				•			

COOLING SYSTEM (AIR COOLED)

Cause	1	2	3	4	5	6	7	8	9	10	11	12	13	14	15	16	17	18	19	20
Poor Air Circulation				•		•														
Dirty or Oily Cooling Fins				•		•														
Blown Head Gasket		•								•										

COOLING SYSTEM (WATER COOLED)

Cause	1	2	3	4	5	6	7	8	9	10	11	12	13	14	15	16	17	18	19	20
Insufficient Coolant					•															
Faulty Thermostat					•															
Worn Water Pump or Pump Seal					•			•												
Water Passages Restricted					•			•												
Defective Gaskets								•		•										
Blown Head Gasket		•						•		•										

LUBRICATION SYSTEM

Cause	1	2	3	4	5	6	7	8	9	10	11	12	13	14	15	16	17	18	19	20
Defective Oil Gauge						•					•		•	•					•	
Relief Valve Stuck						•					•		•	•					•	
Faulty Oil Pump	•	•	•			•		•			•		•	•					•	
Dirty Oil or Filter	•	•	•			•					•	•	•	•					•	
Oil Too Light or Diluted	•	•	•			•		•			•	•	•		•					
Oil Level Low						•		•												
Oil Too Heavy							•	•							•				•	
Dirty Crankcase Breather Valve							•	•											•	

THROTTLE AND GOVERNOR

Cause	1	2	3	4	5	6	7	8	9	10	11	12	13	14	15	16	17	18	19	20
Linkage Out of Adjustment	•																			
Linkage Worn or Disconnected	•																			
Governor Spring Sensitivity Too Great		•																		
Linkage Binding		•																		

- Wear loose clothing or jewelry in the vicinity of moving parts. These can get in machinery, with disastrous results. Don't wear jewelry while working on electrical equipment. If your hair is long, wear a head covering. Hair caught in a drill press, fan belt or other moving parts can cause serious injury.

- Stand on a wet floor while working on electrical equipment. Use rubber insulative mats placed on dry wood platforms.

- Fill fuel tanks while engine is running.

- Smoke or use an open flame in the vicinity of the generator set or fuel tanks.

- Lunge after a dropped tool. To do so may place you in a position of extreme danger.

- Work in the overhead while machinery or equipment is operating below you.

- Commence any operation until you have taken all the necessary steps to ensure that you are in complete safety.

GASOLINE AND DIESEL ENGINES

While it is not really in the scope of this book to go into the care, servicing, and operation of gasoline and diesel engines, we believe that because they are an integral part of the ac system, and some dc systems, we must give consideration to them. Most of the vital information is listed on the following charts, courtesy of Onan. They are self-explanatory and will serve as a guide and supplement to manuals that may be obtained from libraries or manufacturers. Some troubleshooting guides appear with Tables 3-1 and 3-2 for water cooled and air cooled gasoline engines, and with Table 3-3 for a water cooled diesel engine. We also suggest you obtain from your Coast Guard, a copy of their pamphlet CG-151 titled *Emergency Repairs Afloat*. This contains a section on engine repair and troubleshooting which is valuable.

Next we show, with Table 3-4, the sequence of operations which takes place when you operate a typical ac power plant. This chart will help you to understand better how your system functions, and will also help you understand the text material which follows.

The Starting System

In many generating systems the generator is also used as a starter for the gasoline or diesel engine. There are circuits which transfer the output of a battery from the starting process to the generating process once the motor is operating. Figure 3-10 shows a starting sequence for a diesel engine. Using a generator to start the engine is not unusual because most any generator will act as a motor if it has brushes or is so designed that the application of an electric current causes the armature to rotate. Some which have this capability of acting as either a motor or a generator are called universal type generating devices.

Installation

Since the electric generating units, even the very small portables, are engine-generator combinations, the best location is in the propulsion engine compartment. In any event it needs to be firmly and securely mounted on shock proof mounts, with a drip pan underneath with sufficient lip to prevent spillage. Two types of mounting are shown in Fig. 3-11. It is important that your ac plant not exceed

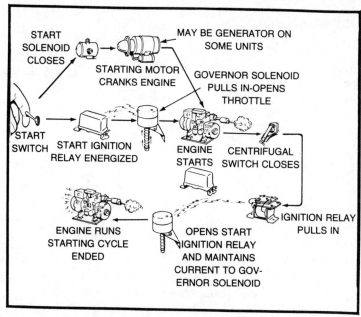

Fig. 3-10. Diesel starting sequence. (Courtesy Onan.)

Table 3-2. Troubleshooting Water Cooled Engines.

TROUBLESHOOTING GUIDE for GASOLINE ENGINES (Water Cooled)

TROUBLE \ CAUSE (SYSTEM: COOLING)	Insufficient Coolant	Faulty Thermostat	Worn Water Pump	Engine Water Passages Restricted	Damaged or Defective Water Pump Seals	Blown Head Gasket	Overheating	Water Lines Restricted or Too Long	Out of Fuel, or Shut-off Valve Closed	Poor Quality Fuel	Dirty Fuel Filter	Fuel Line Leaks
Blue Smoky Exhaust												
Black Smoky Exhaust												
Loss of Coolant												
Coolant Temperature Too High							●					
Mechanical Knocks			●		●	●						
Engine Overheats	●	●	●	●	●	●		●		●		
Engine Backfires at Carburetor	●	●	●	●	●	●		●				
High Oil Pressure												
Low Oil Pressure							●					
Excessive Fuel Consumption										●		
Excessive Oil Consumption							●					
Poor Sensitivity												
No Governor Control												
Hunting Condition												
Engine Speed Too Low												
Engine Speed Too High												●
Engine Misfires												
Starter Motor Doesn't Turn							●		●	●	●	●
Hard Starting or Failure to Start							●		●	●	●	●

FUEL

- Mixture Too Rich or Choke Stuck
- Mixture Too Lean
- Engine Flooded
- Run for Long Periods of Time at No Load
- Restricted Air Intake, Dirty Air Cleaner

GOVERNOR

- Linkage Loose or Disconnected
- Linkage Binding
- Excessive Wear in Linkage
- Incorrect Governor Adjustment
- Spring Sensitivity Too Great

LUBRICATION

- Low Oil Supply
- Defective Gauge
- Excess Oil in Crankcase
- Oil Leaks From Engine Base or Connections
- Crankcase Oil Too Light or Diluted
- Crankcase Oil Too Heavy

STARTING AND IGNITION

- Battery Discharged or Defective
- Loose Battery Connections
- Load Connected When Starting
- Open Solenoid
- Defective Starter
- Wrong Plug or Point Setting
- Incorrect Timing
- Spark Too Far Advanced

TROUBLESHOOTING GUIDE
for
DIESEL ENGINES
(Water Cooled)

Table 3-3. Troubleshooting Diesel Engines.

TROUBLE \ CAUSE	Insufficient Coolant	Faulty Thermostat	Worn Water Pump	Water Passages Restricted	Damaged or Defective Water Pump Seals	Blown Head Gasket	Overheating	Water Lines Restricted or Too Long	Out of Fuel or Shut-off Valve Closed	Poor Quality Fuel	Dirty Fuel Filters	Fuel Line Leaks
SYSTEM	COOLING											
Loss of Coolant												
Coolant Temperature Too High	•	•	•	•	•	•		•				
Mechanical Knocks			•		•	•						
Engine Overheats	•	•	•	•	•	•		•		•		
Diluted Oil												
High Oil Pressure												
Low Oil Pressure							•					
Excessive Fuel Consumption										•	•	•
Excessive Oil Consumption							•					
Poor Sensitivity												
No Governor Control							•					
Hunting Condition												
Engine Speed Too Low												
Engine Speed Too High												•
Engine Misfires												
Starter Motor Doesn't Turn		•				•						
Hard Starting or Failure to Start									•	•	•	•

FUEL

- Air in Fuel System
- Fuel Transfer Pump Diaphragm Leaks
- Incorrect Timing
- Run for Long Periods of Time at No Load
- Restricted Air Intake, Dirty Air Cleaner

GOVERNOR

- Linkage Loose or Disconnected
- Linkage Binding
- Excessive Wear in Linkage
- Incorrect Governor Adjustment
- Spring Sensitivity Too Great

LUBRICATION

- Low Oil Supply
- Defective Gauge
- Excess Oil in Crankcase
- Oil Leaks From Engine Base or Connections
- Crankcase Oil Too Light or Diluted
- Crankcase Oil Too Heavy

STARTING

- Battery Discharged or Defective
- Defective Glow Plug or Lead
- Load Connected When Starting
- Open Solenoid
- Defective Starter

95

Table 3-4. Sequence Of Gasoline Operation Exciter Cranking. This Is Used With Onan MCCK Units Only.

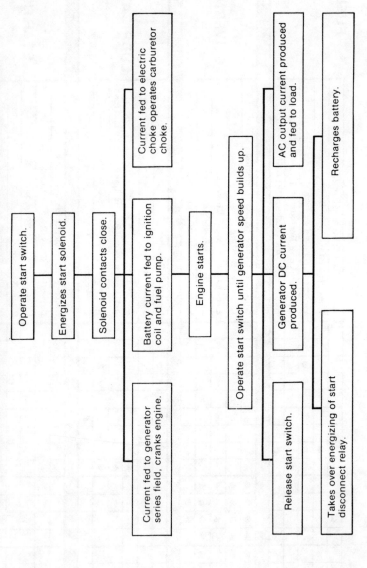

96

the maximum tilt angle specified by the manufacturer. For ONAN units, for example, the maximum tilt angle is 20 to 30 degrees, depending on the type unit installed. Don't tip your ac plant more than this angle with respect to the flooring.

Reducing Power Plant Noises

Because noise from the machine can become a people problem we checked on some methods of reducing this kind of irritation. We found that there are two kinds of noise to be considered. The airborne noise which comes from the pressure waves through the air, and the hull noise which is from the conduction of vibrations through the hull of the boat itself.

Airborne noise is caused by the exhaust. Thus, to reduce this problem area, a good muffler is required. The installation of an exhaust deflector on the exhaust outlet to direct the exhaust toward the water will help too.

Sometimes you will get a lot of noise through the air due to the bouncing off of sound from large surfaces in the installation compartment. In this case, lining the compartment with at least a good two inch thick layer of fiberglass insulation will help reduce the sound penetration. One method of insulating the power plant is shown in Fig. 3-12. This kind of insulation will also be especially effective in

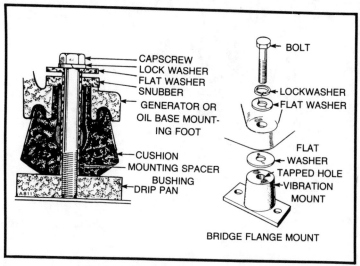

Fig. 3-11. Vibration isolators. (Courtesy Onan.)

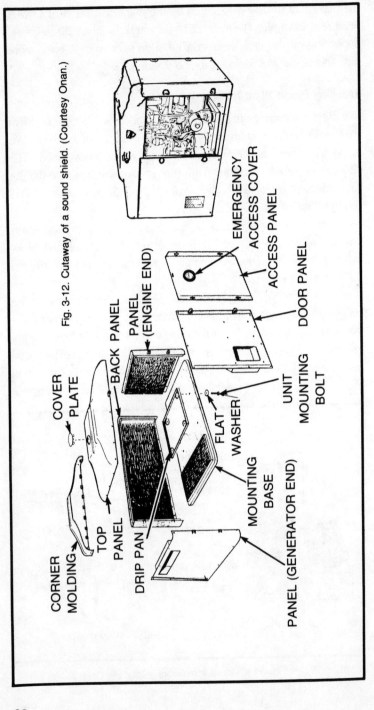

Fig. 3-12. Cutaway of a sound shield. (Courtesy Onan.)

CORNER MOLDING

COVER PLATE

TOP PANEL

BACK PANEL

PANEL (ENGINE END)

DRIP PAN

EMERGENCY ACCESS COVER

ACCESS PANEL

DOOR PANEL

FLAT WASHER

UNIT MOUNTING BOLT

MOUNTING BASE

PANEL (GENERATOR END)

compartment ceilings and in bulkheads which adjoin the living quarters. Of course all cracks and openings into the power plant compartment must be sealed tightly, and all wiring and pipes which pass into the compartment must be securely mounted so they will not vibrate against the boat structure and cause noise. The engine intake air noise can be reduced by installing an air intake resonator kit. But the overall best way to reduce noise is to have the sealed sound shield type compartment shown in Fig. 3-12.

To prevent transmission of sound through the hull, equipment must be mounted on the shock mountings, the rubber isolators shown previously. Be certain there is nothing in the equipment compartment which can rattle, shake, or vibrate in any way against the hull. Anything which does this will set up vibrations to be transmitted throughout the ship and they are almost impossible to cancel out unless done at the source. When your power plant is off you should be able to rock it a little with your hand. It should not hit anything in this motion. You can then see if you have provided sufficient rubber lines, cables, and mountings so that it can vibrate and not transmit this vibration to the hull in any manner whatsoever. A typical major electric generating set installation is shown in Fig. 3-13.

Other Installation Considerations

The engine compartment of the boat must be ventilated. It is usually insulated and is close to the fuel supply. Of course if your propulsion engines are gasoline and the generating equipment is diesel, two fuel systems will be required. Or you may have diesel propulsion engines and gasoline power plant engines. In any event keep the generating equipment well away from the living quarters and away from the bilge area where water and vapors are present. Be sure, when making your installation, to allow yourself plenty of space to work on or adjust the equipment if that becomes necessary—or install it so that it could be removed from its installed position for this purpose.

There is much equipment necessary in the installation of a major electric generating set, as shown by Fig. 3-14. You must always be careful to have a good slope downward from the engine exhaust to the outside of the boat so that water cannot run back up

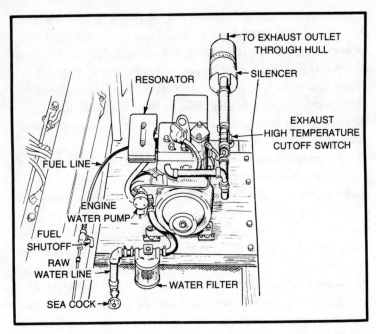

Fig. 3-13. Typical major electric generating set installation. (Courtesy Onan.)

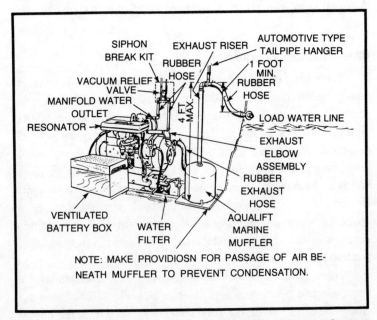

NOTE: MAKE PROVIDIOSN FOR PASSAGE OF AIR BE-
NEATH MUFFLER TO PREVENT CONDENSATION.

Fig. 3-14. Below waterline installation of major electric generating set. (Courtesy Onan.)

into the engine. When installing the exhaust system make certain that back pressure does not exceed the manufacturer's recommendation. In some cases it is advisable to have a manometer (pressure reading gauge) mounted so that it can be read. For some typical units the back pressure should not exceed 3 inches of mercury, or 23.0 ounces per square inch at full loading. Remember also that you will need vibration proof connectors on fuel lines which come from the fuel tank to the vibrating engine, and always ground copper tubing lines to the generating unit with an approved type electrical grounding strap.

Engine Cooling

As with an automobile engine some means is necessary to cool the engine when it is in operation. There are various systems used. One is a closed system that uses a heat exchanger, like your car radiator, mounted under the keel to cool off fresh water which is circulated through it and the engine by a pump. Figure 3-15 shows one such system.

Another system takes water directly from beneath the waterline, circulates it through the engine and exhausts it overboard. Freely circulating water normally is not used for cooling. Thermostats must keep the proper engine temperature. A third system

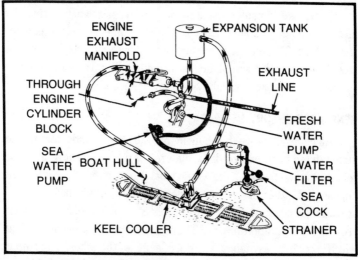

Fig. 3-15. A keel cooling system. (Courtesy Onan.)

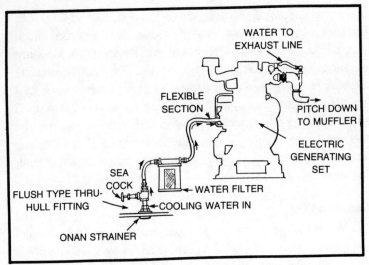

Fig. 3-16. A direct cooling system.

exchanges engine heat to outside water through an internally mounted heat exchanger. This system, however, requires a fresh water working fluid to be run through the exchanger and the engine. We also need to note that in boats the exhaust systems inside the boat must generally be cooled also, so you will find rather bulky equipment attached to this part of the engine. An example of a direct cooling system is shown in Fig. 3-16.

When we consider maintenance and repair we find that the largest number of adjustments for power units are on the engines themselves. The electrical portion of the system usually gives little trouble if normal maintenance is provided. Figure 3-17 shows a neglected power unit which has to be replaced.

GENERATOR THEORY OF OPERATION

All generators are the same in that they have conductors on the stator (fixed part) and rotor (armature) of the unit. There must be relative motion between these two units—notice that this statement implies that either may rotate to get this motion. Normally it is the armature which turns, and the gasoline or diesel engine is what provides this rotation power. There must also be a magnetic field which is cut by the rotating wires of one unit or the other. The output voltage is proportional to the strength of the magnetic field, the speed of rotation of the cutting wires, and the number and size of these wires. It is actually the size of the magnetic field and the size of the conductors which limit the amount of current that can be drawn from the unit.

There is a loading effect which occurs on the prime power source driving the generator, and this is directly proportional to amperes drawn from the generator, and not to the voltage which may be present across the output terminals. If your unit is working properly there is a normal loading of the engine. If a short circuit develops, and the circuit breakers do not open, there will be an immediate loading down of the engine due to the increased demand which is taking place. As we have pointed out previously, always be certain you have circuit breakers in the primary lines leading away from the generator to prevent equipment damage. Most generators of the size we are considering are of either the two pole or the four pole variety; see Figs. 3-18 and 3-19. This simply means that in the case of the two pole generators there will be one magnetic field with a north and south pole presented to the armature. The magnetic field will pass from the north pole to the south pole through the iron in the armature and thus will cut across any windings which are wound on the armature. The four pole type has two such magnetic fields and

Fig. 3-17. A neglected ac engine-generator.

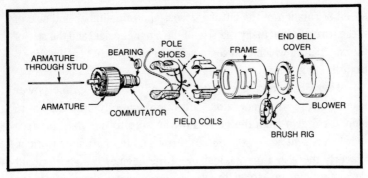

Fig. 3-18. The two pole generator assembly.

the windings on the armature will be increased and so divided that when one winding is under the south poles the other winding will be under the north poles at the same time.

The magnetic field of the generator results from the application of a dc current through the field windings. Notice also that the slip rings are continuous for ac type generators. On dc generators these slip rings are slotted segments instead of complete rings, and it is this *slotted commutator* which makes the difference between a dc and an ac generator. All else about them is just about identical.

ALTERNATORS

An alternator is an ac generator in which the armature is stationary and the magnetic field rotates inside it. This is the reverse of the dc and ac generators previously discussed in which the armature rotates inside the magnetic field. With alternators, the armature coils are held in place in slots in the frame and the field coils are wound on poles or slots in the rotating part of the machine. A salient-pole alternator is merely an alternator with salient (projecting) field poles as contrasted with the turbo-type (slotted) field poles. Just as the usual dc generator can be energized to operate as a motor, so the ac generator can be operated as an ac motor. Similarly, an alternator will operate as a motor without any changes in construction. When so used it is called a synchronous motor. The so called induction generator is simply an alternator of salient pole contruction. It is used in traction work, as an induction motor on level and up grades with streetcars. As a traction unit goes down a steep grade, the motor may speed up beyond synchronization and

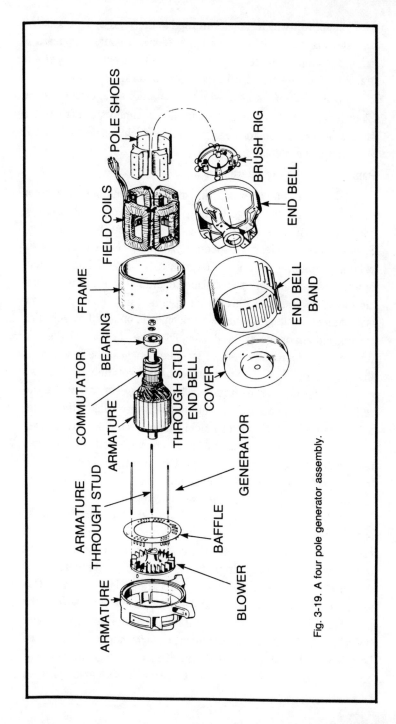

ARMATURE THROUGH STUD

ARMATURE

COMMUTATOR

BEARING

FRAME

FIELD COILS

POLE SHOES

ARMATURE

ARMATURE

THROUGH STUD
END BELL
COVER

GENERATOR

BAFFLE

BLOWER

END BELL
BAND

END BELL

BRUSH RIG

Fig. 3-19. A four pole generator assembly.

105

generate power which is then returned to the source. This is known as regenerative braking. This application, of course, appears in automatic control of the down-grade speed of electrically operated trains that are equipped with induction motors.

Figure 3-20 shows the wiring diagram of an alternator panel. Since it is unsafe to connect measuring instruments directly to the alternator leads, transformers are used, which isolate these leads and reduce the voltages.

Parallel Operation of Alternators

To connect one alternator in parallel with another machine or system, the output voltage of the two must be equal and the two machines must be synchronized as to speed and phase rotation. Speed means the electrical speed or *frequency*. For example, a six pole alternator operating at 1,200 rpm has the same electrical speed, or frequency, as an eight pole machine operating at 900 rpm. Assuming that two alternators are to be operated in parallel, the same instantaneous voltage of the two machines is obtained by adjusting the excitation voltage of the dc supply to the alternator fields. To regulate the electrical speed, or frequency, adjust the governor of the drive engine. To synchronize phase rotation of the two machines, perform an operation called *phasing out*, as will be described later in the book. When all conditions are fulfilled the potential difference between corresponding terminals of the two machines is zero. If the speeds of the machines are not equal, the voltages between corresponding terminals vary from zero to about twice the terminal value voltage at a frequency equal to the difference in speeds (electrical) between the two machines.

In polyphase machines, the coils for each phase are equally spaced about the armature, and the maximum voltage in the coils occurs at different times. When the ends of the coils are brought out to terminals without markings, phase rotation may be determined with a phase-sequence indicator as illustrated in Fig. 3-21. This indicator consists of two lamps and a highly reactive coil such as the potential coil of a watthour meter. If the generator voltage is higher than allowable for the indicator circuit, transformers can be inserted between the line and the indicator to reduce voltage. If lamp 1 is bright, the phase sequence is A, B, C; if lamp 2 is bright the phase is C, B, A.

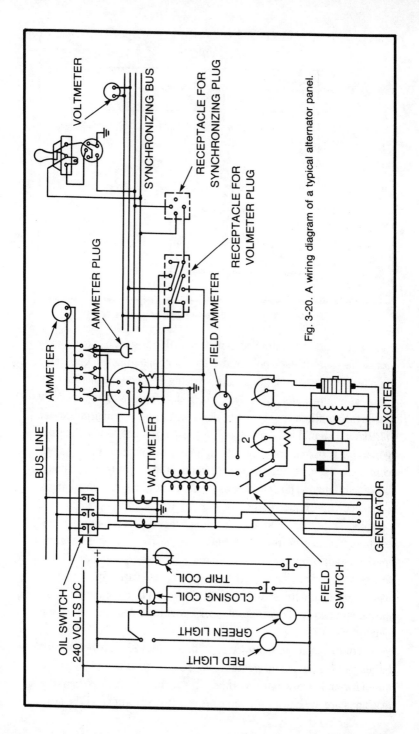

Fig. 3-20. A wiring diagram of a typical alternator panel.

107

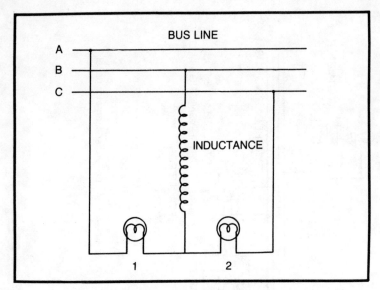

Fig. 3-21. Diagram of a phase-sequence indicator.

The simplest system of synchronization uses a bank of lamps connected across each pole of the switch connecting the generator or alternator to the bus, this bus also being connected to another hot generator, alternator, or ac system. Referring now to Fig. 3-22 you see in (a) a method known as the all-dark method of synchronization. The lamps should have a voltage rating 15 percent higher than the generator terminal voltage, although lamps of standard ratings are commonly used. If these lamps are connected properly, they should become bright and dim *together* as a pair. If they brighten and dim in a sequence, the phase rotation of the two machines is opposite, and one phase must be reversed. The lamps flicker at a frequency equal to the difference in frequency between the two machines. As the machines approach the same frequency the flicker becomes slower and slower so that, finally, when the lamps are dark, the system is synchronized and the switch may be closed to place both generators on the line buses. This system works well for small and low speed generators.

A more sensitive arrangement, (b) of Fig. 3-22, may be used for larger and higher speed generators. This method is known as the one-dark-and-two-bright method of synchronization. When the machines are synchronized, lamps A and B are bright and C is dark.

As one of the two bright lamps is increasing in brilliance the other is decreasing in brilliance, and the instant of synchronization can be determined quite accurately. By noticing the sequence of brightness of the two lamps, it can be determined whether the machine already on the line is fast or slow. Standard practice requires closing the switch when the incoming, or new, machine is gaining speed slowly and is just below synchronous speed.

Voltage and Frequency Regulation

In addition to the governor on the drive engine, the generator equipment is usually equipped with voltage regulators which may be

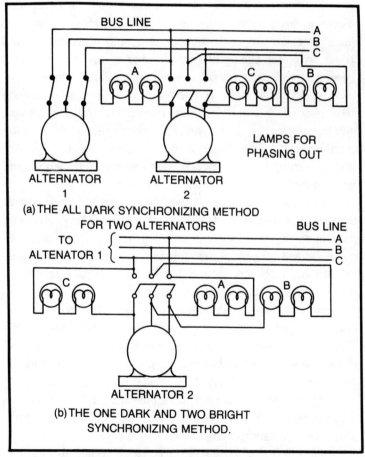

Fig. 3-22. Lamp synchronizing methods for two alternators.

of various types. One kind, which prevents a too-high voltage, uses a saturable reactor to control the current and voltage output. This type has no moving parts and can sense when an overvoltage or undervoltage may be produced at the equipment output due to loading circumstances. This regulator then electrically removes or adds reactor resistance into the generator field line. This, in turn, provides larger or smaller current in the generator field to control output voltage. Notice, however, that to control frequency, the speed of the drive engine must be controlled, as frequency is related to physical speed, always.

Care and Adjustment

As with any machinery, bearings should be periodically oiled or greased, if this is called for. When the unit begins to rust and deteriorate, remove it from the boat, clean and paint metal work and repair or replace bad parts. One of the prime areas of wear on a generator or alternator is the commutator or the slip rings. These become dirty and pitted, and when they do, excessive sparking takes place which not only can cause radio and navigation instrument interference but also can hasten the deterioration process of the armature itself. Since these often are located in out of the way places, checking them regularly is often neglected. Interference and future troubles will result.

Slip rings and commutators must be kept in good condition with the brushes in firm contact and aligned. The mica between the dc commutator segments will wear less than the copper, causing a very rough and uneven surface, which in turn causes faster brush wear and heating, sparking, and electrical noise. The mica separators should always be undercut when required.

Always replace brushes when worn down to 5/8 inch or so. Check the springs for proper tension and for rust deterioration. They probably should be replaced when replacing the brushes. When reassembling the brush and generator parts, be sure to reposition all brushes correctly because, if you don't, excessive sparking will result from brush misalignment. Make certain all electrical connections are tight and positioned so that vibration will not cause short circuiting of any leads.

Tables 3-5 and 3-6 supply a quick reference to possible generator troubles and some remedies for them.

AUTOMATIC DEMAND CONTROLS

These controls automatically start the electric generating system if a load is switched on anywhere in the boat. They will stop the power plant when all loads are switched off. This is an advantage because you don't have to worry about starting the power plant with a separate switch and then having to remember to turn it off when the last light is turned off. Automatic demand control units are available so the owner can utilize a remote control switch and override the system if desired. In this case you can use a switch for dockside power or for the marine load transfer, which can be wired into the demand control output. A typical demand control system is shown in Fig. 3-23.

REPAIR OF WATER DAMAGED GENERATING EQUIPMENT

Equipment that has been subjected to lots of water through any means must of course be cleaned up and dried out thoroughly. Then all insulation must be tested to insure that no damage has been done to it. It is recommended that the units be taken apart completely, cleaned and inspected, and all corroded or damaged parts be re-

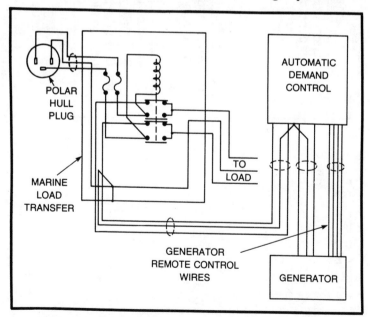

Fig. 3-23. Typical automatic demand and load transfer diagram.

Table 3-5. Troubleshooting AC Revolving Armature Generators.

NATURE OF TROUBLE	CAUSE	REMEDY
Incomplete circuit from DC armature to shunt field.	(b) DC commutator brushes not contacting the commutator.	(b) Replace brush spring which may have broken or come off; replace brushes which may have become worn down too far to make contact. Make brushes free to move in holder.
	(c) Brush leads broken due to vibration.	(c) Check brush shunts with an ohmmeter and replace defective brushes and leads.
	(d) Loose connections at the brush terminals.	(d) Check and tighten all brush terminal connections.
	(e) Open circuit in shunt field coil leads.	(e) Check leads with an ohmmeter and repair as needed.
	(f) Open circuit in rheostat or voltage regulator resistance is high.	(f) Check rheostat or regulator with an ohmmeter and repair as needed.
Short circuit in field	Dampness or deteriorated insulation.	Bake if damp, repair or replace if insulation is deteriorated.

Open circuit in field	Rough usage or original short circuit which may have burned a coil or connection.	Examine field connections and test with an ohmmeter. If a coil is open, replace it.
AC slip rings shorting.	Conducting dirt, dust, grease, or oil shorting out the slip rings.	Clean slip rings with approved solvent.
AC armature short circuit	Insulation or coils broken down.	Rewind or replace.
AC armature open circuit	Rough usage or original short circuit which may have burned a coil or connection.	Test with an ohmmeter and if open replace or rewind the armature.
Incomplete circuit from AC armature to load	Insulating film on slip rings.	Clean slip rings with stone or fine sandpaper and blow out dust. DO NOT USE EMERY CLOTH.
	Slip ring brushes not contacting the slip rings.	Replace brush spring which may have broken or come off or replace brushes which may have become worn down too far to contact the slip rings. Make brushes free to move in holders.

Continued on page 114.

Continued from page 113.

Table 3-5 Continued.

NATURE OF TROUBLE	CAUSE	REMEDY
	Brush shunt broken.	Check brush shunts with an ohmmeter and replace open brushes and shunts.
	Loose connections at the slip ring brush terminals.	Check and tighten all slip ring brush terminal connections.
Armature short circuit	(a) Carbon dust or other conducting dust between adjacent bars.	(a) Clean the commutator. The presence of this trouble will be shown by flashing of brushes or heating of one or more coils.
	(b) Insulation or coils broken down.	(b) Replace or rewind if insulation is beyond repair.
Armature open circuit.	Rough usage or original short circuit which may have burned a coil or connection.	Test adjacent commutator bars; replace or rewind the armature.
Incomplete circuit from DC armature to shunt field	(a) Insulating film on commutator.	(a) Clean commutator with fine sandpaper or a commutator stone and blow out dust. DO NOT USE EMERY CLOTH.

placed. Then reassemble with appropriate lubrication. Use new gaskets and seals, of course, in the reassembly.

To clean the generator, wash all parts with hot water *as soon as possible* after exposure to the bad water environment. Oil and grease can be removed with a good unheated cleaning solvent such as Stoddard, Stainsol, etc. It is wise to have fire extinguishers handy when the electrical components are being cleaned and dried because fumes from solvents may be flammable. You should also follow recognized safety practices: keep in the open, have air flow, etc., because some solvents generate gases that are bad for eyes, nose, throat, or skin.

It is recommended that you do not use water temperatures above 194°F, or a pressure system of more than 40 pounds per square inch to clean the system. Generally you will not use a steam cleaning system on the small parts but only on large units.

After thoroughly cleaning everything, place the parts in a baking oven and set at 250° until they are completely dry. Usually this takes 20 to 24 hours. After parts are dry, test for insulation breakdown with a 500 to 1000 volt *megger*, a device which applies a voltage and measures the leakage. Then connect the generator windings to a low voltage to warm the coils. By the way, when measuring the electrical resistance from insulated coils to ground or frame, you need at least one *megohm* of resistance before they are considered suitable for operation. Finally, operate the unit *at reduced power output* for a while to check its operation and the operation of its engine, which of course also has been thoroughly overhauled. Then you can apply full loading to the unit and it should operate okay. Keep an eye on it, however, and check carefully before depending upon it completely, or for long operational periods at sea.

TO STORE YOUR POWER PLANT

The following recommendations are made in case you plan to store or mothball your boat for a while. The work will be worthwhile and prevent later troubles. The most sorrowful words among boat owners are "I planned to do it, but I just didn't get around to it."

When taking a marine generator set out of service for 30 days or longer, proper storage methods must be used to prevent damage

Table 3-6. Troubleshooting AC Revolving Field Generators.

NATURE OF TROUBLE	CAUSE	REMEDY
Incomplete circuit between exciter and slip rings.	Slip ring brush shunt broken.	Check all slip ring brush shunts with an ohmmeter and replace broken brush shunts.
	Slip ring brushes not contacting the slip rings.	Replace slip ring brush spring which may have come off or broken; or replace brushes which may have become worn down to far to contact the slip rings.
	Insulating film on slip rings.	Clean slip rings with stone or fine sandpaper and blow out dust. DO NOT USE EMERY CLOTH.
	Open circuit in rheostat or voltage regulator resistance is high.	Check rheostat or regulator with ohmmeter and repair or replace.
Revolving field windings shorts.	Insulation or coils broken.	Rewind or replace with new rotor.
Revolving field windings open.	Original short circuit may have burned a coil or connections.	Test with an ohmmeter and if open replace with a new rotor.
AC stator winding shorted.	Insulation or coils broken.	Rewind or replace stator winding.
AC stator winding open.	Original short circuit may have burned a coil or connection.	Test with an ohmmeter and if open rewind or replace with a new stator winding.
Faulty load connections.	Open circuit or short circuit on line.	Check line and load connections and the load.

from corrosion, contamination, and temperature extremes. The Onan Company's recommended storage methods are:

1. *Fuel system*—For gasoline types only, drain entire engine fuel system by shutting off fuel supply and allowing engine to run out of fuel. Clean the flame arrester or air cleaner thoroughly. Do not service the air cleaner with oil. Cover or seal exposed flame arrester or air intake openings. Clean throttle linkage and governor linkage thoroughly. Lubricate metal ball joints with graphite. Do not lubricate any *plastic* ball joints.

2. *The oil system*—Drain engine lubricating oil while the engine is warm. Service the engine with proper viscosity and type oil according to your owner's manual. Be sure to tag the engine to identify the type and kind of oil you used. Next, remove the spark plugs if it is a gasoline engine, or remove the fuel injectors if it is a diesel engine. Pour two tablespoons of rust inhibitor oil (SAE 10 is a substitute) into each cylinder. Crank the engine by hand over several revolutions to lubricate the piston walls, pistons, and rings. Reinstall plugs or fuel injectors and be sure to lightly lubricate the spark plug threads, especially during this operation. Remove and replace the oil filter if one is used, and finally, clean the crankcase breather valve and breather tube flame arrester if one is used.

3. *The cooling system*—Considering air cooled type engines only, remove access panel and clean all cooling surfaces. Clean out air screens and all air ducts. When considering water cooled type engines you must drain the entire cooling system including the water cooled exhaust mainfold and exhaust line. Drain the radiator, heat exchanger, or keel cooler components, also the engine cylinder block and water pump. For those engines equipped with a closed type cooling system which has a radiator, heat exchanger, or keel cooler, you may fill these with a good quality antifreeze if freezing temperatures are expected. Drain only those components not protected from freezing such as exhaust lines, water pumps, water intake valves and tubes, and outlet lines.

4. *The electrical system and batteries*—Clean the generator brushes, the commutator and slip rings by wiping with a clean, dry, lint free cloth. Do not lubricate these parts. Remove the dust and dirt deposits in control box and junction boxes with a dry, low pressure air. Disconnect and remove batteries from the vessel. You can service the batteries by maintaining the liquid level in them and using a trickle charger to hold their voltage. Coat the battery cable connections with a good grease.

5. *Overall inspection*—Cover or seal all exposed openings such as the exhaust outlet, cooling passages, hoses, etc., and inspect the cooling system for deterioration and leaks, and repair any damage you find. If you cannot do all the required maintenance before using the boat the next time, tag everything stating what should be done to put it in proper operating condition when it is taken out of storage.

To be complete let's consider what to do when returning the boat power plant to service.

1. *General procedures*—Remove all protective wrappings. Wipe the oil film off all exposed engine parts and remove the plug from the exhaust outlet. Visually inspect the power plant for any damage and check to be sure that the carburetor and governor linkages are free. Remove the generator end bell band and check to be sure the brushes work freely in their holders. Check the tags to insure that oil of the proper brand and grade has been installed and check the oil level. Then install the battery but be sure it is fully charged and clean, and observe the proper polarity of the cable connections. Remember ground is negative. Make cable clamp connections bright and tight.

2. *Plugs and injectors*—Remove all spark plugs and clean and gap or replace them as necessary. Turn the engine over by hand several times with the spark plugs removed. Reinstall the spark plugs or if your engine is a diesel torque the fuel injectors and bleed the fuel system. If you find any evidence of moisture or contamination in the fuel tanks, replace the secondary filter and clean the primary filters.

3. *Cooling System*—Service the cooling system with clean, fresh water and prime the water pump and see that all air is removed from the cooling system. If antifreeze was left in the cooling system, check it and add water or antifreeze as required. If you have an air cooled system, check to see that all air passages and cooling surfaces are bright and clean.

4. *Operating the Power Plant*—Turn on the fuel, disconnect the electric fuel pump lead and electric fuel solenoid lead to its shutoff valve, if your unit has these. Jumper the fuel pump and electric fuel solenoid shutoff leads to the battery to prime the unit. Use the hand primer lever on units which have mechanical pumps. Once primed, reconnect the disconnected leads, being sure all loads are removed from the generator output lines, and start the generator engine. The initial start may be slow due to oil or rust inhibitor in the cyclinders. Excessive smoking and rough operation may occur at first until the oil or rust inhibitor is burned off. Then apply a 50 percent load after the engine finally settles down and runs smoothly. With this load connected, let the unit run for about one hour while you check its speed and voltage output. Also check for any fuel leaks, cooling system leaks, and exhaust system leaks. At the end of the hour is all is well, you can operate full power and your unit is back in service.

So we conclude this chapter on power plants. Remember that the finest electrical and electronic gear in the world, and the best and most desired comfort items are worthless if the primary supply doesn't work and work properly. Take care of it, and it will take care of you.

Chapter 4
AC And DC
Motor Operation
and Troubleshooting

Because there are so many types of ac and dc motors used on board larger craft, we include here some pointers on their operation, test, adjustment, and troubleshooting—courtesy US Army. This information may well be of interest mostly to those of you who are somewhat familiar with electrical and electronics systems. But there are some points of which an average person, not so well electrically informed or experienced, should have knowledge. You may find that your normal maintenance procedures and abilities will be enhanced by study of this section and then an examination of your own boating equipment. At the least, if you are one who doesn't normally dig into this sort of thing, you will acquire a better knowledge of equipment which is motor operated. Thus you will derive more benefit from it through a better understanding of its abilities and requirements, and be able to converse more readily with those who install and maintain such equipment.

DC MOTOR

Fundamentally, there is little difference in the construction of dc generators and dc motors, except in shunt-field windings and in the size of the field-coil resistance, which must be somewhat less for a generator. The brush angle, too, may be different, since motors are often required to reverse rotation. It is quite possible to convert a dc motor into a dc generator by means of a prime mover connected to the shaft, providing the direction of rotation of the armature remains the same. Otherwise it is necessary to reverse the polarity of the residual magnetism in the field poles. Usually the residual magnetism in the field poles of a motor will, as in generators, provide sufficient voltage to create a field.

Recall that a conductor carrying current in a magnetic field tends to move at right angles across the field. Therefore, if an electromotive force is impressed across the windings of an armature by means of brushes and commutator, and also across the field poles, a force is created sufficient to turn the shaft of the motor. The overall turning effect on the armature, that is, the combined force on the two sides of the loop, times the distance of the conductors from the axis (shaft center), is called the torque.

The connections of fields and armatures in motors are the same as in generators. The only differences between motors and generators are mechanical. A motor may be series-wound, shunt-wound, or compound-wound. There are also other ways of classifying dc motors—by speed rating and mechanical modifications. Physical characteristics of motors serve to classify as well. For example, motors are identified as being open, enclosed, drip proof, and so on. All of the foregoing types of motors are available with interpoles to improve commutation.

The characteristics of these common motors will be discussed in some detail in the following paragraphs.

The Series Motor

The field of the series motor is obtained by a low resistance coil connected in series with the armature. Any additional load placed on a series motor will cause more current to flow through the armature to produce the necessary torque. Since this increased current must pass through the series field, there will be a greater flux, which in turn will produce a large counter electromotive force at low speed. The motor speed will therefore greatly decrease. The characteristic of a series motor is that speed changes rapidly with torque, and when the torque is high the speed is low; or if the torque is low the speed is high. Never start a series motor without a load, or remove the load while the motor is in operation. The motor will gain speed until it

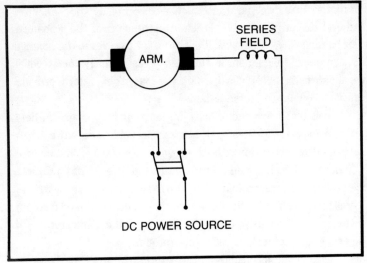

Fig. 4-1. Connection of a series dc motor.

goes so fast that it may be damaged. You can see how a series motor is connected in Fig. 4-1.

The Shunt Motor

In a shunt motor the field is across the line or in parallel with the armature, Fig. 4-2. The rheostat in series with the field winding is used for speed control. The field current stays the same, regardless of changes in the armature current. Therefore, when the armature current is doubled, the torque is doubled. The speed of a shunt motor changes very little with a change of load; the speed may increase slightly as the load decreases, but the main charactristic of the shunt motor is that it has an almost constant speed for all reasonable loads.

The Compound Wound Motor

Compound motors differ from the stabilized shunt types by having a more predominant series field. Like compound generators, compound motors can be divided into two classes, the differential and the cumulative. This depends on the connection of the series field with respect to the shunt field. Some diagrams of compound wound motors and a comparison chart are shown in Fig. 4-3. In the series type, the series field opposes the connected shunt field.

Therefore, this motor operates at practically constant speed. As the load increases the armature current increases to provide more torque. The series magnetomotive force increases, thus weakening the shunt field, and this reduces the counter-electromotive force in the armature without causing a reduction in speed.

The cumulative compound motor diagrammed in Fig. 4-3 (b) is connected so that its series and shunt fields aid each other. From this connection comes its name, the cumulative-compound type motor. A motor thus connected will have a very strong starting torque, but poor speed regulation. Motors of this type are used for machinery where speed regulation is not necessary, but where a great deal of torque is desired to overcome the application of heavy loads—such as on winches. Operating characteristics of the series, shunt, and compound motors are compared in Fig. 4-3 (c).

Limitations

Several different types of dc motors have been discussed and they have varied particular uses depending on their construction.

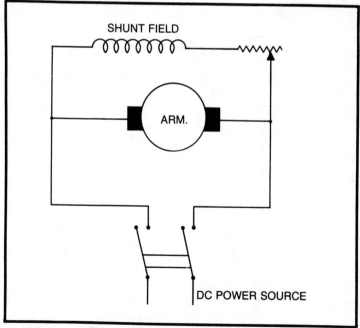

Fig. 4-2. Connection of a shunt dc motor.

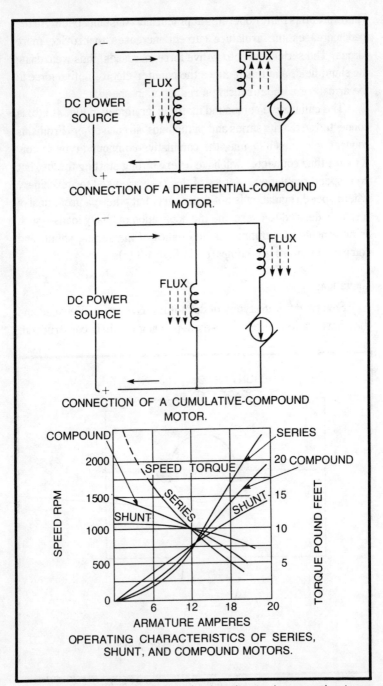

CONNECTION OF A DIFFERENTIAL-COMPOUND
MOTOR.

CONNECTION OF A CUMULATIVE-COMPOUND
MOTOR.

OPERATING CHARACTERISTICS OF SERIES,
SHUNT, AND COMPOUND MOTORS.

Fig. 4-3. Operating characteristics of series, shunt and compound motors.

Continued use of any dc motor depends upon the kind of load to be carried, the speed, and the torque. Remember that dc motors not adapted to the load, or of improper ratings, should not be used for even short periods of time due to possible damage by overheating, inefficient operation, or improper speed control. The location in which the motor is to be operated is also a big factor to be considered when selecting a machine for a particular job. A dusty atmosphere requires an enclosed motor—as does a high humidity atmosphere. A high temperature atmosphere necessitates a motor which has special insulation. We refer you again to Chapter 1 wherein we discussed the environment of the marine equipment. Motors must be specially designed for this use.

CONTROLLERS

We had mentioned controllers; now we will examine them in somewhat more detail as they are very important with large motors. Recall that a controller is a device for regulating the operation of electrical equipment. A controller for electric motors is simply a mechanism which conveniently and safely performs several or all of the following functions: connection to the power line, limiting of the starting current, control of acceleration, control of speed, and disconnect from the power line.

A manual type controller is one having all of its basic functions performed by hand. The basic functions are usually line closing, acceleration, retardation, and reversing. Manual control permits regulation of machines from only one position and is limited in the size and capacity of the equipment which can so be controlled.

The full magnetic controller performs all of its functions using electromagnets or relays. The power circuits to the motor are opened and closed by magnetic contactors (relays). These are, in turn, controlled by a pilot device which has a small voltage and current operating requirement. This pilot device may be manually operated by pushing a button or a master switch, or it may be automatically operated by a float switch or thermostat or other type of sensor. The magnetic controller (solid state or mechanical relay) makes it possible to control motors automatically and this has some advantages over the manual type of control. For example, the operator may accelerate the motor too rapidly with a manual type controller, with the result that the motor may require excessive current and this may cause circuit breakers to trip or fuses to blow. Also, this may burn out the starting resistance or resistances. With automatic controllers the starting resistances may be cut out at the maximum safe rate by the magnetically operated contacts of the controller. The operator need only press a button and the electromagnetic relays start the motor and bring it up to speed automatically in the proper time sequence to prevent damage to the motor or associated parts. The motor is stopped by merely pressing the stop button.

Some advantages to using an automatic controller are:

- Smooth accelerations, slowing down, and reversing of the motor.
- Control of the motor from one or more stations.
- Automatic control of the motor when the operator is not present.
- Operation of the motor from a distant point.
- Operation of high voltage type equipment (motors).
- Conservation of space by locating the controller in an out-of-the-way place and operating it with its pilot device. We will see how important this concept is when we examine automatic autopilots in a later chapter.

These types of controllers may be further divided into general classes, starters and speed regulators. The starter is designed for accelerating a motor to normal rotation speed in one direction or another. If it is designed to start the motor in either of the two directions of rotation, it is called a reversing controller. The speed regulator is designed to operate the motor at a given speed.

Controller Sizes

Controllers, either manual or magnetic types, which supply full voltage to the motor can be used to connect small dc motors of up to about two horsepower directly to a line. Reduced voltage controllers of either type are used to connect or operate smaller motors of up to one-half horsepower. Manual reduced-voltage starters and speed regulators of the faceplate type, with self-contained resistors, are nonreversing and are used with motors of up to about 25 horsepower. Separate devices are necessary for reversing service. Drum controllers with separately mounted resistors for starting or speed regulating duty may be used with motors of up to about 50 horsepower. Magnetic controllers are used for any size motor and can be obtained for nonreversing or reversing service and with other basic functions.

Slowing Down the DC Motor

The resistance in the armature circuit can be increased, or in the case of the adjustable speed dc motor, resistance is reduced in the field circuit to slow down a dc motor.

Another method is to apply dynamic braking for quick stopping of shunt and compound motors, and sometimes as a step in reversing service. When the motor circuit is opened, a dynamic-braking resistor is instantly connected in parallel with the armature. The shunt field remains energized. The motor, turning by inertia, then acts as a generator with the braking resistor acting as the load for the generator. Braking resistors are seldom designed to permit more than 150 percent load current at the instant the braking circuit is closed. Dynamic braking is seldom applied to series motors because the series field must be reversed to be effective. This complicates the control.

Another method of bringing motors to a quick stop is *plugging*. This is done by reversing the motor connections to the power line. It is used most often with series motors or heavily compounded motors.

AC MOTORS

Of all the various types of ac motors, the induction type is most popular. The induction motor is subdivided according to methods of starting and of construction. The majority of fractional-horsepower motors are operated on single-phase circuits. Universal type ac motors can be divided into three classes: the straight-*series* type, the series type with shifted brushes, and the compensated-*series* type. These motors are used mostly for drills and adding machines and will not be covered in this section. The popularity and wide application of the ac induction motor is principally due to its simplicity of construction. Rugged and reliable, it has constant-speed characteristics. For example, the speed is substantially independent of the load, within

Table 4-1. AC Motor Starting Characteristics.

AC Motor Starting Characteristics.			
(1) Motor Type	(2) Start Current Peak Ampl. RMS	(3) Duration of Start Surge in Sec.	(4) Load-Second % I + t Sec.
		2.0 sec.	.3
Series AC-DC	530%	.100	.5
Series AC-DC	200%	.400	.8
Series AC-DC	333%	.167	.5
Split Phase	600%	.116	.7
Split Phase	425%	.500	2.0
Capacitor Load	400%	.600	2.4
Capacitor No Load	300%	.100	.3
Capacitor Load	420%	.500	2.1
Induction	700%	.750	5.
3 Phase	350%	.167	.6
Cap. Start, Split Phase Run	290%	.083	.24

the normal working range. The polyphase induction motor is comparatively simple. Current is established by an emf across the stator. By transformer action, this induces an emf in the rotor. The secondary windings are short circuited upon themselves, either directly or through an external resistance, and are not connected to an external power source. The secondary winding is usually put on the rotor, and commutator or collector rings and brushes are not required except in the case of special applications.

The ac motors create a problem. The starting energy requirements are spread over seconds rather than milliseconds and vary considerably with the type of load (viscous or frictional) and with the inertia of the load. However, the peak amplitude of the starting current is generally with reason. Table 4-1 provides some typical figures, as observed on motors selected at random. Note that single-phase induction motors are the worst, usually having a starting winding which can draw seven or eight times the running current for the best part of a second. A 750-millisecond surge duration was observed on several of various horsepower ratings.

Induction motors usually are protected by a thermally acting device imbedded inside the motor. Little else can be done—a breaker which will handle the starting surge will not trip out soon enough on lesser overloads to prevent damage to the motor. Here a designer is forced to protect the power wiring rather than the device.

Operating Principles for AC Motors

An induction motor consists essentially of two units, the stator and rotor. The induction motor stator is like the stator used on alternators. The motor consists of a laminated cylinder with slots in its surface. The winding placed in these slots may be one of two types. One type, called the squirrel-cage winding, usually consists of heavy copper bars connected together at each end by a conducting end ring made of copper or brass. The joints between bars and the end rings are commonly made by an electric welding process. In some cases the rotor, including the bars, is placed in a mold, and the bar ends are cast together with copper. In small squirrel-cage motors the bars are aluminum, cast all in one piece. Some industrial applications require a motor with a wound rotor instead of the squirrel-cage type. In this second type of winding, the rotor is provided with a wound rotor instead of the squirrel-cage bars. The winding is similar to that used in the stator. The winding is generally connected in star (wye), and its open ends are fastened to slip rings mounted on the shaft. Brushes mounted on the rings are attached to a star-connected rheostat. The purpose of all this is to provide a means of varying the rotor resistance. You can determine the number of poles in a machine—if it is not stated on the faceplate and you cannot inspect it visually—by using the following formula:

$$P = \frac{120 \times f}{N}$$

P = poles per phase
f = frequency in Hertz
N = rated speed in rpm

An example would be a machine with a speed of 2400 rpm operating on 60 Hertz. The computation gives 3. Thus the machine should have three poles for each phase and if it is a three-phase machine it would have 9 poles.

When thinking of ac machines we have to think of *slip*. This is when the rotor of an induction machine is subjected to a revolving magnetic field produced by the stator windings. A voltage is introduced in the longitudinal bars of the rotor which causes a current to produce another magnetic field, which, when combined with the

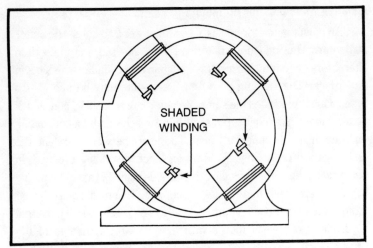

Fig. 4-4. Shaded pole ac motor.

stator field, causes the rotor to move to a position in which the field and induced voltage is a minimum. As a result the rotor revolves at very nearly the synchronous speed of the stator field. The difference in speed is just sufficient to produce enough current in the rotor to overcome the mechanical and electrical losses. If the rotor were to turn at the same speed as the rotating field, the rotor conductors would not be cut by any magnetic lines of force. No emf would be induced in them, no current would flow in the stator bars, and there would be no torque. The rotor would then slow down. For this reason, there must always be a difference in speed between the rotor and the rotating field. This difference in speed, the slip, is expressed as a percentage of the synchronous speed. For example, if the rotor turns at 1750 rpm and the synchronous speed is 1800 rpm, the difference in speed is 50 rpm and the slip is equal to 50/1800 × 100 or 2.78 percent.

In single-phase ac machines, the field, instead of rotating as in the two- and three-phase machines, merely pulsates. No rotation of the field takes place. However, a single-phase pulsating field may be considered to be two rotating fields revolving at the same speed, but in opposite directions. In this way, we find that the rotor will revolve in either direction at nearly synchronous speed, provided it is given an initial start in either one direction or another. The exact value of this initial rotational velocity varies widely with different machines but a velocity higher than 15 percent of the synchronous speed is usually enough to cause the rotor to accelerate to the rated speed. A single phase motor can be made self-starting if some means is provided to give the effect of a rotating field. There are several ways to do this.

The shaded pole machine has salient stator poles, a portion of each pole being circled by a heavy copper ring. The effect of the copper ring is to cause the magnetic field through the ringed portion of the pole to lag appreciably behind the field through the other part of the pole face. See Fig. 4-4. This produces a slight component of rotation of the field, enough to cause the rotor to revolve. As the rotor accelerates, the torque increases until the rated speed is obtained. Such motors have low starting torques and find their greatest application in small fan motors where the initial torque requirement is very low.

The split phase motor is usually a fractional horsepower machine and is used to operate such devices as washing machines, small pumps, and blowers. Much marine equipment uses split phase type motors. The motor has four main parts: the rotor, the stator, the mounting frame, and the centrifugal switch. Figure 4-5 shows a schematic. The winding of the rotor is usually of the squirrel-cage type consisting of copper bars placed in slots in the laminated iron core and connected to each other by copper end rings. The stator has two windings, the main, or running winding, and the starting winding. These are wound into slots on the iron stator core. The

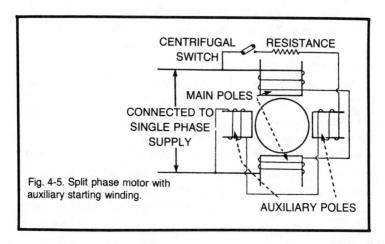

Fig. 4-5. Split phase motor with auxiliary starting winding.

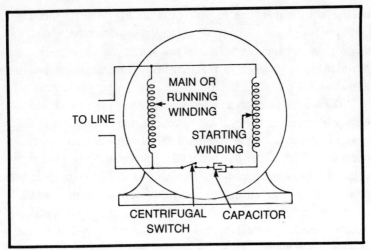

Fig. 4-6. Typical capacitor start ac motor connections.

main winding is connected across the power line in the usual manner and produces a magnetic field for the main poles. Between the main poles are auxiliary poles, the windings of which have a resistance greater than that of the main winding. Sometimes additional resistance is put in series with the auxiliary winding. As the ratio of resistance to impedance in the auxiliary winding is greater than in the main winding, the voltages in the auxiliary and main windings differ by about 90 electrical degrees. Thus these two sets of poles and their windings produce a rotating magnetic field which starts the motor. When the motor reaches a predetermined speed, the starting winding is automatically disconnected by a centrifugal switch inside the motor. You can usually hear the click when it disconnects.

With the development of high-capacity electrolytics and other type capacitors, a variation of the split-phase motor, known as the capacitor starting motor, became popular and is much used today. Figure 4-6 shows a schematic. Nearly all fractional horsepower motors in use today on refrigerator systems, oil burners, and similar applications use this type of motor. In this method, the starting winding and running winding have the same size wire, which gives the same electrical resistance but the phase is shifted 90 electrical degrees between them by means of a capacitor connected in series with the starting winding. Capacitor start motors have a starting torque comparable to their torque at rated speed and can be used in applications where the initial load is heavy. Again, here, a centrifugal switch is necessary to disconnect the starting winding when the rotor gets up to about 75 percent of its rated speed.

A variation of the capacitor-start motor is the capacitor-start-and-run motor. Examine figure 4-7. This is similiar to the capacitor-start motor except that the starting winding and capacitor are connected in the circuit all the time. This type of motor is quiet and smooth running in operation but can be used only where medium starting torque is required. Such applications include blowers, fans, oil burners, etc. The capacitor used is generally a paper insulated, oil filled type.

The direction of rotation of a three-phase, three-wire motor can be reversed by simply interchanging the connection of any *two* leads. See Fig. 4-8(a). The same effect can be produced in a two-phase, four-wire motor by reversing the motor leads of either phase A or B as shown in Fig. 4-8(b). To reverse the direction of rotation of two-phase, three-wire motor, simply interchange the outer two motor leads, 1 and 2 of Fig. 4-8(c). Three-phase, four-wire motors are generally not used. In a single-phase motor, reversing the connections of the starting winding in relation to that of the running winding will reverse the direction of rotation of the motor. Nothing can be done to reverse the direction of rotation of a shaded pole motor as it is a physical location which gives the motor its rotational ability. Some squirrel-cage motors can be reversed if the armature is re-

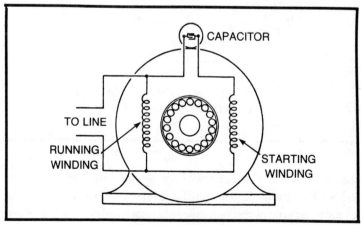

Fig. 4-7. Typical capacitor start-and-run motor connections.

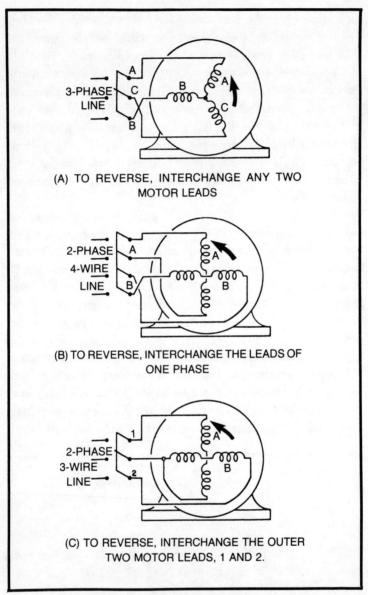

(A) TO REVERSE, INTERCHANGE ANY TWO
MOTOR LEADS

(B) TO REVERSE, INTERCHANGE THE LEADS OF
ONE PHASE

(C) TO REVERSE, INTERCHANGE THE OUTER
TWO MOTOR LEADS, 1 AND 2.

Fig. 4-8. Reversing direction of rotation of ac motors.

versed in the stator. This would primarily apply to fan type motors or other small motors of this type. To reverse the direction of rotation of any other type of ac motor, simply remove and reverse the entire stator field winding.

134

The repulsion induction type of motor consists of a wound rotor with commutator and brushes. The brushes are not connected to the supply line, but are short circuited. The principle involved in this method of starting may be best understood by examination of Fig. 4-9. Although the current through the stator is alternating, the arrows only indicate the direction of this current during a half cycle when the current goes in one direction. In Fig. 4-9(a), suppose the stator current is increasing and is in the direction indicated. The flux produced will induce voltages in the armature conductors as shown. These voltages are additive on each side of the brushes and therefore will send a high current through the rotor and the short circuited brushes. No torque will be developed, however, because half of the conductors under each pole carry current in one direction, and the other half carry current in the opposite direction. If the brushes are shifted 90 degrees as shown in (b), the emf in each path will be neutralized. Then no voltage exists at the brushes, consequently no current flows through the rotor, and no torque is produced. If the brushes are shifted to the position shown in (c), a resultant voltage will exist in each path, sending a current through the rotor as indicated in (d). Now all conductors under one pole carry current in one direction, and all conductors under the other pole carry current in the opposite direction. Then a torque develops, and the rotor rotates. If the brushes were shifted in the opposite direction from the position shown, the rotor would turn in the opposite direction. This method is used for starting single phase motors. For this purpose the rotor is provided with a commutator which is radial, or cylindrical, in design just like those used in dc electric motors. At start, the machine functions as a repulsion motor developing a high starting torque. As soon as the rotor reaches nearly full speed, a centrifugal device forces the short-circuiting ring into contact with the inner surface of the commutator. This short circuits the metal bars of the commutator to convert the motor into an induction type motor. At the same time that the centrifugal device shorts out the commutator, it also raises the brushes so that the wear on the commutator and brushes will be reduced. This kind of machine is used in blowers and other places where a high starting torque is desired.

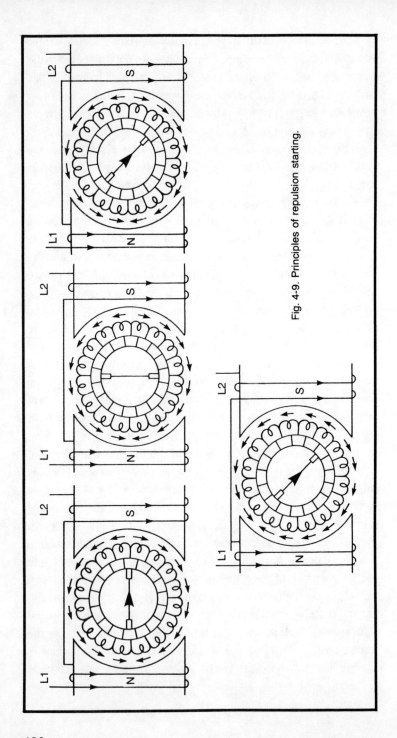

Fig. 4-9. Principles of repulsion starting.

136

Synchronous motors are not self-starting and must first be brought up to speed before they will operate. More care is required when starting a synchronous motor then with an induction motor. There are several starting methods used:

1. Where the dc exciter is coupled directly to the shaft of the synchronous motor and enough dc power is available, the dc exciter may be operated as a motor to bring the synchronous motor up to speed. Normally there is enough residual magnetism in the field poles of the synchronous motor to do this. The field of the synchronous motor is then excited (by the exciter-generator) and the motor synchronized as with an alternator.

2. If a separate dc motor with enough dc power is available, it may be used to bring the synchronous motor up to speed, after which the motor is synchronized as before.

3. If a separate induction motor is available it may be used to start the synchronous motor as in 2.

4. A synchronous motor may be started as an induction motor. The starting torque to bring the motor from rest to synchronous speed is obtained by means of a damper winding. These are separate windings placed in the slots of the rotating field poles which make it possible to insert external resistance producing high starting torques, as with a wound rotor type induction motor. First the field circuit is opened, but the field poles retain enough residual magnetism to maintain their polarity. Then the stator is connected to an ac supply at full voltage or reduced voltage by means of an auto-transformer. The stator winding develops a rotating magnetic field which induces a voltage in the damper windings. The reaction between the rotating field of the stator winding and the magnetic field of the damper winding exerts a torque that accelerates the motor. The stator winding also develops a voltage in the rotor field winding. The rotor field winding circuit is closed through a voltage dropping resistor, which prevents the development of excessive voltage in these windings when starting. The excessive voltage might puncture the insulation of the windings. After the motor comes up to speed,

the rotor field resistor is shunted out at the same time that dc voltage is applied to the field. This is necessary because if the motor should not have a dc field supply voltage, it would stop immediately.

Selection of AC Motors

It is very important to select and use the proper motor for the application, service, and location you require. The important ac motor characteristics that follow will help you choose the proper motor for your application.

1. The starting torque must be considered. For squirrel-cage motors of various operating characteristics, minimum values of starting torques, which are known as normal, have been established. With full voltage applied, the starting torques range from 510 percent of full load torque for 2 and 4 pole motors down to 105 percent for 16 pole motors.

2. The starting current is important. Normal starting currents were established for squirrel-cage motors. These range from 450 to 650 percent of the full load current, depending on the size and speed of the motor. You will want to make certain that your primary supply is capable of giving you the required starting current for any motors of this type (or other types) you may be operating simultaneously. A separate power plant may be required in marine use for some size motors.

3. It is important to consider slip, discussed earlier. Recall that it is the difference between the synchronous speed and the actual rotor speed under load, expressed as a percent of the synchronous speed.

4. The voltage and frequency used by the motor are important. Motor performances and guarantees are based on normal, or rated, voltage and frequency applied at the motor terminals. Satisfactory operation can be obtained at rated load and frequency, if the voltage applied is within the limits of 10 percent above or below the rated voltage. Motors for 220 volt circuits will operate satisfactorily on supplies of 208 or 199 volts but not in accordance with the

performance established at rated voltage. Operating, starting, and maximum torques of an induction motor will vary as the square of the applied voltage. Reduction in torques should not affect the usual application of poylphase induction motors because starting and maximum torques are not the limiting factors. However, where standard motors are used with such torque applications as would be required on hoists, cranes, elevators, and valves, the factor of reduction in torque should be given very careful consideration. Standard motors will operate successfully on frequencies within the limits of 5 percent above or below the specified operating frequency. The output, starting, and maximum torques will be increased slightly with a drop in frequency, and decrease with an increase in frequency.

5. Induction motors with mechanical modifications are made for special applications. The important ones are:

   (a) The splashproof motor is so constructed that dripping or splashing liquids will not enter the motor. However, since the motor is self-ventilated, and since moisture saturated air may be circulated through the motor, the windings are made moisture resistant. Motors of this construction are used to drive pumps and are used as components of machinery in such places as dairies, paper mills, and chemical plants.

   (b) The totally enclosed fan cooled motor has totally enclosed windings and rotor. Cooling air is circulated over the enclosure to carry away the heat. This motor is used widely where the air contains dust, as in grain elevators, coal handling plants, large foundries, and machine shops.

   (c) The explosion proof motor is similar to the totally enclosed fan cooled motor but is constructed to prevent any explosion within the motor from igniting gases or dust in the surrounding air.

   (d) The gear motor is usually built with a gear mechanism and a motor as an integral unit. In some cases, the gear unit is designed to permit the use of motors having the other mechanical modifications, as well as the electrical characteristics. This construction is often used to connect motors directly to low speed or high speed loads.

(c) The vertical motor has the shaft vertical to the working plane. Mountings are flanged, ring based, tripod based, or with machined end shields for mounting on the bolt circle of a machine.

6. The selection of a motor for a job is usually relatively simple and, with minor variations, can be based on similar jobs. However, to insure correct application, these important requirements should be kept in mind:

   (a) Starting or breakaway torque.

   (b) Accelerating time.

   (c) Frequency of starting.

   (d) Speed requirements.

   (e) Variation of load.

   (f) Special limitations imposed by the power supply.

   (h) Position of motor with respect to driven load.

   (i) Condition of surrounding atmosphere (temperature, humidity, clean or dust laden, or presence of gas).

   (j) Noise.

7. After determining the characterstics of the load, a suitable type of polyphase motor can usually be selected from a motor characteristics and selection chart. In the majority of cases, standard motors can be selected. However, there will always be some applications which are not covered by the standard types. Important special conditions may affect the choice of motor drives. High voltage may be a consideration. Reversing duty and dynamic braking may be required.

COMMUTATION BASICS

Good commutation of dc current and flow of ac current in generators and motors is indicated during normal operation by an absence of excessive sparking or burning about the commutator bars, collector rings, and brushes. Commutators are used on dc generators and motors, and on the starting windings of some ac motors, such as repulsion motors. When so used with ac motors,

140

they are called rotary commutators. Commutators are also used with the auxiliary machines which generate the dc current for excitation of the fields in ac generators and some ac motors.

The first requirement for good commutation and collection is continuous, close contact between the brushes, the commutator, and the collector rings. Thus, the surface of the commutator and the collector rings must be smooth and concentric, properly undercut, and finished; the brushes must be properly shaped and adjusted; and the armature and rotor must be well balanced.

Another requirement is the development of a uniform copper-oxide and carbon film (as distinguished from a pure copper surface) on the commutator and collector rings. This film is formed by normal oxidization, and by heating and ozone action on particles of graphite from the brushes and copper on the surface of the commutator or collector rings. It may vary in color from copper to straw, or light chocolate to black. The surface should appear highly polished and smooth, without color shading around the brush contacts. Green discoloration indicates the presence of chlorine fumes; blue discolorations denote sulfuric fumes. Gases, oil, oil vapors, and grease tend to cause a mottled, streaked, or gummy surface. An even film on the commutator or collector ring enables the brushes to function at a relatively low rate of wear. Like oil adhering to a bearing, it acts as a lubricant over the commutator surface. Abrasive particles in the air can cause threading and grooving of the film, resulting in a selective action and an ultimate decrease in efficiency or operation.

Successful commutation is not a function of the electrical circuit, or the brush, or the commutator alone. It is the result of the best electrical and mechancial brush-to-commutator conditions, which can be obtained only through proper inspection, cleaning, and maintenance.

Checks and Adjustments

1. Check all the bars on the commutator for flats, burn conditions, and looseness indicated by irregularly high and low bars. Such conditions cause brush chatter, resulting in fractured brushes.
2. Check for streaks and grooves.

3. Check for dragged copper on the leading edges of the bars and for filled slots caused by the dragged copper.
4. Check the commutator riser connections for thrown solder.
5. Check the mica for a pitted condition and the presence of oil, grease, dirt, minute particles of carbon, or copper embedded in the mica.
6. Check the commutator bars for looseness while the machine is in operation. Use a wooden pencil held on the brush tops to feel for an undue vibration indicating that the V-ring which holds the insulating mica in place is loose.
7. Check for high and low commutator bars. This irregularity in the position of the commutator bars is caused by differences in current conduction in the overloaded and underloaded coils of the armature at the commutator, causing some bars to wear faster than other. Also, after the machine has passed through a number of heat cycles, differences in expansion and contraction cause some bars to shift their position. Locating these poor connections may be difficult because of the difference in the resistances of the connections. The connections may not be poor enough to cause burned insulation or hot connections, but may cause unbalance in the coils.

Cleaning

1. Clean heavy accumulations of dirt, oil, or grease with a lintless cloth moistened with a safety type petroleum solvent or equivalent. This should be done while the unit is at rest.
2. Final cleaning and polishing are done while the unit is in operation. Hold a piece of dry canvas or other hard, lintless cloth, which has been wound around a stick against the commutator. A good commercial cleaner will improve the cleaning and polishing action and make use of the sandpaper unnecessary. Clean the back of the commutator with air pressure and vacuum suction. Do not use a lubricant on the commutator either during or after polishing.

3. Another, and simpler, method of polishing the commutator is to apply a light load to the unit for several hours, increasing the load as brush contact improves with operation. Continue until the unit is able to carry its full rated load.

The principle of close electrical contact applies to the ac collector rings as well as to the commutator. The same uniform copper-oxide and carbon film over the contact surface of the rings, for example, is necessary for efficient operation. With but few minor exceptions, the procedure for inspecting, cleaning, and resurfacing collector rings is identical to that of commutators. Brush failure is usually the result of one or serveral of the following conditions: a rough or eccentric commutator; high mica; vibration due to imbalance or loose bearings; or the improper adjustment of spring tension, brush position, brush angle, brush spacing, or brush staggering.

DC MOTOR PROBLEMS AND REMEDIES

Failure to Start

Cause	Cure
Open circuit in the control	Check for open. Replace open resistor or fuse.
Low supply voltage	Check with voltmeter and adjust.
Frozen bearing	Replace and recondition shaft.
Overload	Reduce load or get a larger motor.
Excessive friction in motor	Check for air gap, bent shaft, worn bearings, misaligned end bells; replace or correct.

Stops Running After Short Time

Cause	Cure
Failure of supply voltage	Apply proper voltage, replace fuses, reset the circuit breaker.
Ambient temperature too high	Ventilate motor space and motor with fans, etc. Check loading on motor.
Overload relays set too low	Adjust relays.

Attempts to Start but Circuit Breakers Trip

Cause	Cure
Motor field weak or absent	Check field and coils and connections.
Overload	Check meter readings against nameplate voltages, etc; replace motor with larger one.
Circuit Breakers Trip	Check sizes and use proper type and size.

Runs Too Slowly

Cause	Cure
Line voltage low	Check and adjust
Brushes ahead of neutral plane	Adjust brushes
Overload	Check ratings and replace motor if necessary; reduce loading.

Runs Too Fast Under Load

Cause	Cure
Weak Field (series type motor)	Check field and replace open coils, open resistors; tighten connections.
Line voltage too high	Measure and adjust.
Brushes off adjustment of neutral plane	Adjust.

144

Sparking at Brushes

Cause	Cure
Overload	Check meter readings against nameplate rating voltages and currents, and adjust; reduce loading.
Brushes off neutral plane	Adjust brushes.
Dirty brushes and commutator	Clean.
High mica on commutator	Undercut.
Rough or eccentric commutator	Resurface.
Open circuit in commutator	Replace or repair.
Grounded, open, or short circuited field winding	Replace or repair.
Insufficient brush pressure	Adjust tension springs.
Brushes sticking in holders	Clean holders, sand brushes.

Armature Overheats

Cause	Cure
Overloaded	Reduce loading.
Excessive brush pressure	Adjust and replace tension springs.
Couplings not aligned	Align couplings properly.
Bent shaft	Straighten or replace
Armature coil shorted	Replace or replace armature.
Armature rubbing or striking poles	Check for bent shaft, loose bearing, loose pole pieces. Repair or replace units.
Clogged air passages	Clean out thoroughly.
Repeated changes in loads which are heavy	Use larger motor.
Broken shunts or pigtails	Replace brushes.

AC MOTOR PROBLEMS AND REMEDIES

The failure of an ac induction motor to start may be caused by an open circuit breaker, a blown fuse, a low supply voltage, rotor or stator windings open or shorted, windings grounded, or simply an overload on the motor. Check each item and apply a suitable remedy.

If the ac motor produces excessive noise it may have an unbalanced load, a coupling misalignment, a loose lamination, or an air gap not uniform. You can check and balance the load, adjust the air gap by replacement of rotor bearings, and in the case of the lamination, dip the motor in a high temperature varnish and tighten bolts. Of course you tighten any loose couplings.

Overheating of any motor may be caused by overloading, and in the case of *induction type* ac motors, by electrical unbalance, an open fuse, restricted ventilation, short circuited rotor, open or grounded rotor or stator, or bad bearings. The bearings must not be overlubricated or dry, neither worn nor loose. In case of an unbalanced supply voltage you must balance the phases.

With an ac wound-rotor motor, you may have an open circuit in the rotor, cables, or controls, or possibly dirty slip rings, which can cause sparking.

The rules, causes, and cures stated for the other motors may also be applied to an ac synchronous motor, with the addition that if it fails to start, it could be that a field exciter current is being applied when it shouldn't. In this case, make sure the field contactors are open and that the field discharge resistors are connected until the motor starts. With this motor it may run too slow if the field is excited too soon; check the delays, tripping currents, and voltages to correct this. Also check for a low supply voltage and, again, that probable cause, overloading. If it fails to pull into step at synchronous speed, it may have no field excitation, open rotor coils, an inoperative exciter, or a faulty field contactor. A lack of field excitation can be caused by a grounded or open rotor coil, grounded or shorted slip rings, or no output from the field exciter. Also, it may pull out of step if the exciter voltages drop, or there are intermittent or shorted cables. This may also result from a reversed field coil or a low supply voltage to the motor. A fluctuating load may cause this motor to "hunt," that is, to vary its speed—but also, an uneven commutator can cause this. Overheating may be caused by an underexcited rotor or a reversed field coil, as well as the things mentioned previously.

The ac repulsion-induction motor needs the same physical checks mentioned earlier but it also has some individual problems and has some particular cures for its problems. A low supply voltage caused by leads of insufficient capacity will keep it from starting. A bad connection in the leads will reduce the voltage and cause this trouble. This machine, you will recall, has a centrifugal device as part of its makeup. If it is not operating properly, the machine may not start. Correct brush settings are very important to make this machine start. Locate the neutral plane by shifting brushes until there is no rotation when current is applied. Shift the brushes in the direction of the desired rotation 1 1/3 bars from neutral on four pole machines of 1/2 horsepower or smaller, and 1 3/4 bars on large four pole machines. On two pole motors set 1/3 bar farther than these settings. If the motor runs but shocks you when you touch it, you have a grounded stator coil or static discharge which you must overcome. The static can be reduced by proper grounding connections which are bright and tight.

The split phase capacitor start and transformer coupled motors have the same problems and cures as previously stated, but they also have some individual ones. They won't start if the capacitor is open or otherwise defective. It also has a centrifugal element as part of its structure, and if this is not working properly the motor will give you all sorts of trouble. The mechanism must be cleaned and adjusted throughly. Then if other troubles exist, check the other problems and solutions and follow through as previously stated.

In marine applications most motors are sealed and do not require attention, but the connection to them may need constant attention as the elements they are exposed to may cause real problems. Never take a motor for granted. Always check it out thoroughly and remember that if it has brushes, even if it is sealed, those brushes will wear and the connections and the springs may become weak and break. So if your motor has been operating a long time, disassemble it to be sure it will continue to perform. Other motors you may have of types discussed may be checked and serviced as we have explained. Usually there is a manual furnished by the manufacturer—which has a nasty habit of being lost when you need it the most—that should be taken care of and followed to get the best and most dependable operation from your electric motors. But enough on this subject. Let us progress on to the next chapter.

Chapter 5
Air Conditioning,
Electric Galley Stoves,
Lights, and Radio Beacons

A lot of equipment operating from the electrical system is used for safety, convenience, pleasure, and for assisting in convenient operation of the boat. Such things are the bilge pumps, blowers, air conditioning units, equipment, and pleasure items such as TV, radio, stereo, and recorders. Since we now have a good background concerning the wiring systems, batteries, and electrical generating power plants, let us begin to examine some of the gear which use electric current. We will save for later chapters the communications, radar, navigation, and piloting equipment, and other such devices as might fall more properly in the electronics chapters.

ELECTRIC STOVES

Although there are many types of flame operated stoves used on boats, the electric galley stove is ideal because it will operate on the power plant already installed and does not need a separate source of energy. Of course, if the electric power plant should fail, you have a problem. Therefore, if you are cruising for some time, a back-up cooking system using other than electrical power would be advisable. The type fuels used in these other systems are kerosene, natural low pressured gas, compressed natural gas (methane), and alcohol. Few, if any, use oil or coal.

It has been said that the electrical stove is the safest heat source. It is of the simplest construction and most convenient in operation. You just turn on a switch to have heat for cooking. The ovens are thermostatically controlled, and you can have a timer. You don't have to worry about spilled fuel from some storage tank or lines, and replacement of units is simple. Proper circuit breakers give immediate protection in case of malfunctions which could otherwise cause fire.

It may turn out that you do not have the capability on board for the power plant required for an electric stove, and if so will be restricted to dock-side power to operate it. This might be the one drawback. Some may argue that since you have to have fuel for the power plant and other equipment, that you might as well have it for cooking. True. But the power plant also would provide many more services for other electrical and electronic equipment, so the cooking stove becomes just a minor part of its capability.

Ship stoves have gimbals which keep the pots and pans upright when the ship rolls or pitches or yaws. It is of interest to know that there is an intersection of these three axes on the ship, the vertical, the longitudinal, and the transverse axes. See Fig. 5-1. If your stove is located as near as possible to this point, the gimbal action will be somewhat reduced, providing more stability for cooking utensils. Wherever the stove is located it should be provided with an exhaust fan or other means of ventilation. The long gimbal axes of the stove should run fore and aft as the pitch of the boat is generally less than the roll. Gimbal systems are discussed in a later chapter when we consider gyroscopes.

ELECTRIC HEATERS

Of course when considering heat from a stove, we think of the cabin heaters. The same arguments as for the electric galley stove hold in this case, with one possible addition. You probably will need an auxiliary power plant to provide the wattage necessary for electric heating of the cabin. You certainly will find, as you analyze the situation, that there will be a limit on the power the circuits can handle. This limits the size of the heater. Electric heaters, ranging from 500 to 1500 watts or more, and circuit breakers generally trip on 30 amperes at 110 volts (either from shipboard power or

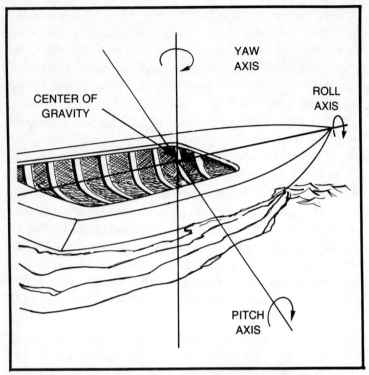

Fig. 5-1. Roll, pitch and yaw axes of a boat.

marinas). This means that a 1500 watt heater uses half the available power from a circuit, as each circuit can supply no more that 3300 watts (30 × 110).

Electric heaters are available in a range of sizes. Portable units have safety switches to cut them off if they tip over. Built-in heaters can be forced air units installed into bulkheads or under counters, or you may have perimeter or baseboard type heaters which do not use fans but radiant heating instead. Normally it is best to have the heater close to the floor to get the full benefit from rising heat. Again the advantages are on-and-off heat at the flick of a switch, thermostat control, and cleanliness.

DEHUMIDIFIERS

Another electrical device which is often advisable to have on board is a dehumidifier. This device removes moisture from the air when the relative humidity is high. You know how uncomfortable high humidity can be, especially with high temperature. It is sometimes possible to reduce the discomfort by providing some heat inside the cabin. If the dew point happens to be 80° (the temperature at which the air becomes saturated with moisture), increasing the temperature above this point will keep moisture from forming in the cabin. Of course it gets hotter this way.

But the real way to gain some relief from the heat and the humidity is to have a dehumidifier. These are readily available. Electrically operated, they will reduce moisture in a closed cabin, making the area quite comfortable. These units are rated in the amount of moisture they will remove from the air per day. This can be a pint, a quart, etc.; thus you can judge from manufacturer's literature just what size is required for the cabin and relative humidity of the area you plan to be in. These units require drainage, and they are usually mounted so the drain is overboard, thus posing no problem. The units, being like refrigerated air conditioners, require electric power and have thermostats, pump controls, and blower motor controls to govern their operation.

AIR CONDITIONERS

We are generally familiar with the refrigerated type air conditioners. They recirculate the air, removing moisture as they cool. They operate on electric power, of course, so a good power plant must furnish the necessary energy. As an introduction to these units, their operation and installation, examine Table 5-1 to obtain some idea about the size required. Notice that air conditioner sizes are rated in tons.

Now let us examine (by courtesy of Cruisair, MDC Development Corp.) some units which are designed for shipboard use. In Fig. 5-2 is shown a cooling unit, which has a high pressure blower built in, designed to feed into several ducts on board the ship. It has a capacity of 12,000 BTUs, which is relatively large. In Fig. 5-3 we can examine the condensing unit which gives coolant the conversion necessary to produce the cooling effect. To gain some idea of how the system works, examine Fig. 5-4 wherein the refrigerant flow-cooling cycle is graphically pictured.

We shall, a bit further on, explain the operation in detail. Next examine Fig. 5-5 to see how the motor section of the condensing unit

Table 5-1. How to Determine the Amount of Air Conditioning You Need.

In the capacity table below are listed the three general categories of cabin space. Take the area of the floor space of the cabin or stateroom to be air conditioned (multiply the length times the width). In the appropriate column of the table check the number of square feet closest to the area of your cabin. The first column on the left, opposite this figure, will tell you the capacity of the unit you need. If one end of the cabin is narrower than the other, take your measurement about in the middle for the average.

CAPACITY AND AREA DATA

SIZE	WATTS REQUIRED	CAP. IN TONS	BELOW-DECK CABINS	MID-DECK CABINS	ABOVE-DECK CABINS
1/2 Ton	935	1 1/3	270	200	135
3/4 Ton	1400	1	200	150	100
1 Ton	1775	2/3	140	100	70
1 1/2 Ton	2970	1/2	100	75	50
2 Ton	3420	1/3	70	50	35

The energy efficiency ratio (EER) is the amount of cooling you get for the amount of electricity used. To determine the EER of an air conditioner, divide the model's capacity (BTUs) by the energy it uses (watts). For example, 12000 BTUs divided by 1200 watts = 10. The higher the EER the more efficient the unit. Light companies recommend a minimum 7.5EER.

is connected. Notice the use of starting and running capacitors associated with the ac motor. We examined the use of these in the last chapter. A cooling unit which has a duct intake on its left is shown in Fig. 5-6. The rear covering of the heavy duty fan can be seen. Figure 5-7 shows the electrical wiring of this unit. Notice the wall mounted controls. A final diagram, which shows a slave blower attached to the basic system, is shown in Fig. 5-8.

We must not disregard some other ideas associated with the air conditioning of boats. One of these is to have the cabin heat exhanged into the sea water through appropriate cooling units which are submerged. This can be done by having the condensing unit for the refrigerant mounted so it is sea water cooled. With this method, used by Cruisair, there are no hot air discharges from the air conditioner; therefore, no such outlets need be established in any of the bulkheads.

Marine air conditioners are designed with several considerations foremost. They must be compact and physically shaped to fit into the irregular spaces on board. They must be able to operate on low voltages and not come apart at the seams in pounding seas. They must be ruggedly built. The water cooled condensing units must be able to withstand and operate efficiently in engine room temperatures as high as 140°F.

We have mentioned that air conditioners are rated in BTUs (British thermal units). We need to explain that this unit is that amount of heat required to raise the temperature of one pound of water one degree Fahrenheit. In air conditioning we are interested in reducing the temperature, or exhausing heat, and BTUs are used to express the ability to do this. (The word ton used in air condition-

Fig. 5-2. A 12,000 BTU air conditioning cooling unit. (Courtesy Marine Development Co.)

Fig. 5-3. Condensing unit for air conditioner. (Courtesy Marine Development Co.)

ing refers to the cooling of one ton of ice in 24 hours. It also means, to a refrigeration expert, 12,000 BTUs or 400 cubic feet/min.)

When we consider the size of air conditioners in cooling capacity we must rationalize desired capacity in terms of the available electric power. Most small air conditioners operate from 115 volts 60Hz, and this means a capacity of not over 1 1/3 tons for each unit. To exceed this capacity a larger motor is required because operation at 115 volts is not efficient. Thus 220 volts or 440 volts might have to be used. Thus we find that on boats, usually more units are used, each of which can operate on 115 volts 60 Hz.

Suppose you have one condensing unit and two cooling units, one in each cabin of a 36 foot Pacemaker pleasure craft. The disadvantage of this is that the cooling may not give the temperature desired for the different people occupying the cabins. They have to reach a compromise on the temperature to be set. If individual units are used, each person can set his own temperature and be com-

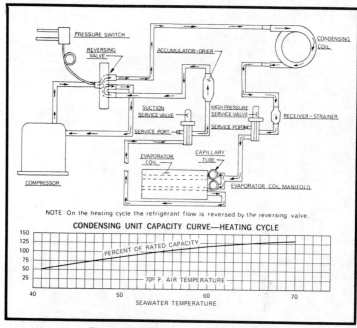

NOTE: On the heating cycle the refrigerant flow is reversed by the reversing valve.

Fig. 5-4. Refrigerant flow—cooling cycle.

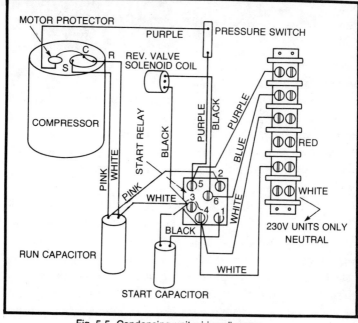

Fig. 5-5. Condensing unit wiring diagram.

155

Fig. 5-6. Type O cooling unit. (Courtesy Marine Development Co.)

pletely comfortable. In the first case a one ton compressor can operate a 2/3 and a 1/3 ton cooling unit if you have to consider cost and installation room and if the people concerned are able to reach an agreement on the cooling requirements.

Now let's consider another facet of air conditioning. It is well known that air conditioners extract heat from the air to give cooling. Why not use them also as heat pumps, which means that in cold weather you simply reverse the process and add heat to your cabins instead of extracting it. This is possible and heat pumps are available which work in both directions—to cool and to heat. But you must remember that a heat pump will not operate efficiently if the water temperature dips below 38° F, so you may find it more efficient and

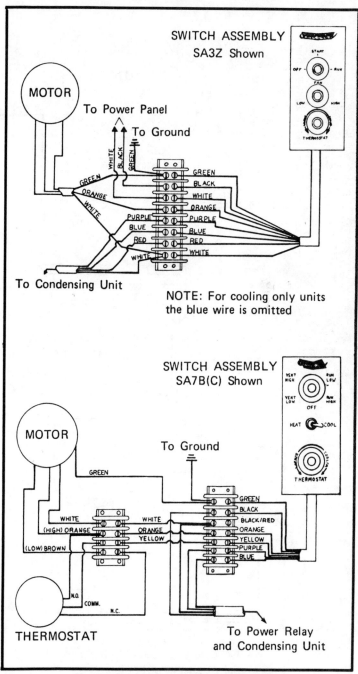

Fig. 5-7. Type O cooling unit wiring diagrams.

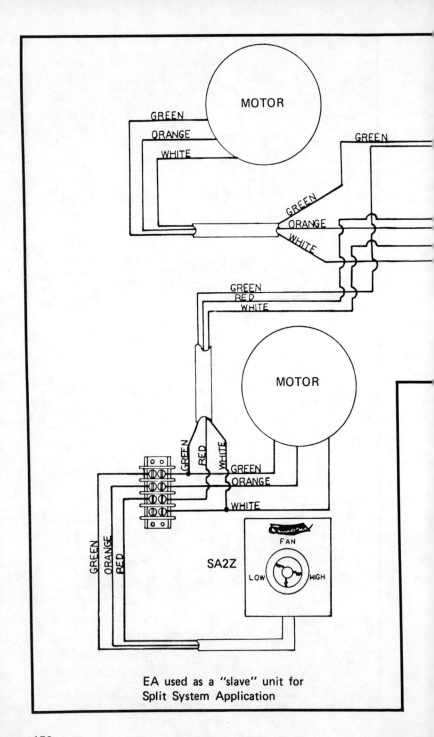

EA used as a "slave" unit for
Split System Application

158

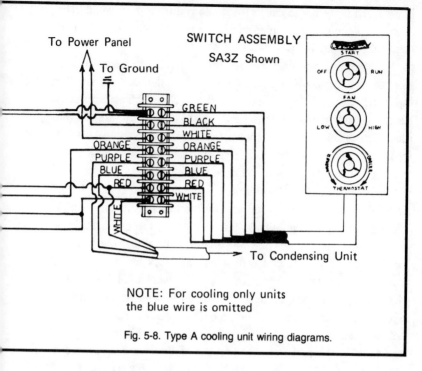

NOTE: For cooling only units
the blue wire is omitted

Fig. 5-8. Type A cooling unit wiring diagrams.

economical to use separate heating systems such as we have mentioned earlier.

As an added bit of information, note that when a heat pump is used in its heating cycle to warm a cabin space, it draws its heat from the outside water and sends it into the area to be warmed. Thus when the outside water is very cool, there isn't much heat in it, and the efficiency of the unit drops considerably. Now let us examine some more details of installations of air conditioning units.

Installation of Air Conditioners

In all installations the cooling unit must be installed so that the air outlet is at least three feet from the floor level. Ideally the cooling unit must be installed with the condensate drip pan positioned at the bottom of the unit so water dripping from the evaporator coil collects in this drip pan. The cooling unit drain must be installed so the drain tube makes an immediate 1 inch drop after leaving the drain fitting and must be routed from that point to continue downhill to a suitable drain location. It is recommended that the condensate be drained

159

overboard since it can cause rot if allowed to drip on wood. The quantity of the water involved on a hot humid day may be as much as several pints per hour.

The cooling unit must be installed so there is an adequate path for the air to circulate freely into the unit from the back and into the space being cooled. It is important that the cross sectional area of all discharge air ducts and grills be at least equal to the area of the discharge-air portion of the cooling unit involved. In some units the cross sectional area of the discharge-air duct must be at least twice the area of the discharge-air portion of the units.

The cross sectional area refers to the open area of a discharge air grill rather than the total area as determined by the overall measurement of the grill itself. For example, if the grill is made of expanded metal, perhaps only 50 percent of the area is open for the passage of air. The metal web itself will block air from passing through the 50 percent that is covered by the webbing. In such cases the total area of the grill must be doubled to achieve the required open area. In the return air duct, mount a piece of ordinary household wire screen as close to the cooling unit as possible to serve as an air filter. Use proper screen to prevent rusting. On a boat there is not so much concern about dirt and dust as there is about lint. Ordinary window screen does an excellent job of catching the lint without causing an inlet airflow pressure drop as the thicker and denser materials will do. Screen wire is the only recommended air filter material.

For all air discharge applications, wood or plastic frame grills are recommended. Aluminum frame grills will become cold and produce secondary condensation that will drip from the grill frame. If aluminum frame grills must be used, however, a heater strip can be installed behind the lower edge of the frame to prevent this condensation.

The switch assembly is an integral part of most units. On certain types of units, however, the switch is supplied as a separate item. When using the integral-switch cooling unit, *never* remove the switch assembly from the cabinet to install it in a remote location. On some cooling units the fan speed rheostat will overheat if installed away from its well ventilated cabinet position. The switch assembly for most units has a three position fan speed control which produces no heat at the switch assembly. On one unit, the Cruisair, the main switch assembly has three knobs and the plate is printed either for horizontal or vertical installation. The switch assembly mounts over the opening cut to receive it and is fastened from the front with four screws. Wiring from the three control switches terminates in a color coded terminal strip that must be securely mounted in a suitable place with two screws. This terminal strip is the electrical connections center of the system. These connections are typical for all such units that use 115 volt 60 Hz as primary power. Note, however, that the switch assemblies for cooling only and for heating and cooling together cannot be interchanged. The proper type for each system must be used.

The thermostat in the switch assembly has a 36 inch capillary tube leading from it to a temperature sensing bulb. This bulb must be located in the return air stream so it is exposed only to air returning from the area being cooled (or heated). If this detail is neglected, the thermostat will have little or no control over the operation of the system. Also available are 10 and 20 inch capillary tubes from most manufacturers.

The example we are using, Cruisair condensing units, are so designed that they can be installed in any location. This may apply to other types of systems as well. They are not affected by moisture, vibration, or ambient temperatures up to 140° F. No ventilation is required. The units can withstand the normal pounding encountered on a pleasure yacht in a heavy sea. All refrigeration components are hermetically sealed and all electrical components are spark proofed for maximum safety. So you can install this unit wherever you wish, wherever space permits. Just make sure the wood base is positioned at the bottom of the unit in a horizontal plane. Fasten the condensing unit securely to its base and mounting.

Cooling for the condenser is provided by the flow of seawater through the unit. The compressor in the condensing unit is cooled by the refrigerant gas returning to the compressor in a cold and un-superheated state. The condensing unit is sufficiently quiet to allow installation under a bunk or in a locker if no engine room space is available.

When installing the two copper tubes between the cooling unit and the condensing unit, several important factors must be considered. First, the tubing can be run in lengths up to 50 feet. It can run uphill, downhill, or sloping, as required, and it can have as many bends as necessary. Avoid sharp bends, of course, and do not use soldered elbows. The tubing should be insulated to prevent moisture from forming on the tubes and dripping off.

CAUTION: Always insulate the tubes *separately*. Never allow them to touch each other. On cooling only systems, only the largest tube need be insulated. On the heating and cooling systems, the two connecting tubes must be insulated separately. Be sure to insulate the connecting flare nut joints carefully to prevent dripping of condensed moisture from these joints.

Always use refrigeration grade, seamless, soft copper tubing. Never use neoprene, Teflon, rubber, or any other type hose or tube. The refrigerant used in Cruisair systems is monochlorodifluoromethane (WOW!). It is not compatible with any tubing except copper. We realize that some automotive units use neoprene refrigerant lines, but they use a different refrigerant. When the copper is connected to the cooling unit and the condensing unit, excellent flare joints must be used. This is essential to prevent refrigerant leaks. These flares must be of the 45 degree single flare type. Do not use a double flare on this kind of system. The flare must be large enough in diameter to fill the flare nut completely.

In the Cruisair system, a remote condensing unit has a seawater cooled condenser requiring a pump to provide a continuous flow of water through the condenser. Two basic types of pumps can be used. These are the centrifugal pump and the positive displacement rubber impeller pump. The centrifugal type has a longer life and is quieter in operation but it does have some characteristics which must be considered before using it. It is strongly recommended if you can use it after considering the following: The inlet of the centrifugal pump is below the water line at all times, either when the boat is at rest or under way in a rolling sea. This type pump produces no suction with air, so if the inlet is above the waterline, the pump will not operate unless it is primed each time it is to be used. Water hoses from the seawater thru-hull fittings to the pump, from the pump to the condensing unit, and from the condensing unit overboard must all be installed so they are self-draining. Thus if the boat is lifted straight out of the water, the pump and all associated plumbing must drain completely. *This is absolutely necessary*. If the plumbing system is not self-draining, it will not be self-purging. That is, it will not expel air. Whenever air gets into the system, such as can easily happen when the boat operates in a heavy sea or makes a sharp turn, this air will be trapped in the centrifugal pump itself. With air in the pump, no pressure can be produced to expel the air. The water flow then stops and the system is airlocked. If this happens, the outlet hose from the pump must be loosened to allow air to pass out of the pump so that water will flow in behind it. This re-establishes the pressure needed to provide a flow of water. Examine Fig. 5-9 for an installation of the condenser.

In some installations there are several condensing units on the boat. It is recommended that you use only one seawater pump in this type of installation, making sure it is large enough to provide water to all of the condensers involved. Examine Fig. 5-10.

Going back to Fig. 5-9, notice that the plumbing is self-draining and self-purging because the water flow is constantly uphill to the point marked 7, from where it flows constantly downhill to go overboard. If this boat were lifted straight up, all water in the system would drain out at points 1 and 8. An improperly installed system would be created if point 7 were allowed to drop below point 6. Under this condition, if the boat were lifted straight up, water would remain in the overboard hose between points 6 and 8. The system would not be self-draining and pump airlocking problems would result.

If all these considerations and cautions are accounted for in your installation, and they are considered critical to the successful installation of a centrifugal pump system, then you can use the centrifugal pump successfully. If you cannot meet the requirements, then the rubber impeller, positive displacement pump should be used. It has the ability to pump air as well as water.

In a conventional yacht, however, proper plumbing of the centrifugal pump is usually no problem. But in shallow draft boats, such as houseboats, the plumbing may be a significant problem. In shallow draft boats the positive displacement pump is recommended.

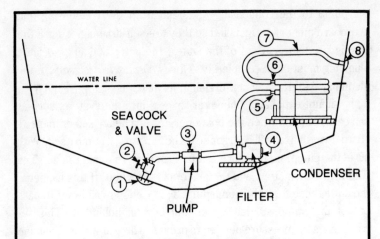

WATER LINE

SEA COCK
& VALVE

CONDENSER

FILTER

PUMP

1. Scoop type thru-hull fitting located no more than 6′ from the keel, ahead of the stuffing box, and aft of the forward engine room bulkhead.

2. Shut-off valve or sea cock.

3. Seawater Strainer. Large outside strainer may be used instead of side strainer.

4. Seawater pump. Must be below the waterline.

5. Condensing unit inlet (lowest of the two fittings).

6. Condensing unit outlet (highest of the two fittings).

7. High point in plumbing system. There can be only one high point in a self-purging plumbing system.

8. Overboard fitting. Install 1′ to 2′ above the waterline so that the discharge water will run quietly, but will be visible from on deck. Use a separate overboard for each condensing unit.

Fig. 5-9. Condenser installation.

Cooling System Operating Procedures

The following is a list of items to be checked before any cooling system is purged or started. Be sure that:

- The cooling unit is bolted securely in place.
- Cooling unit discharge cross sectional open area is equal to the face cross sectional open area of the air outlet portion of the evaporator coil, as a minimum. In some cooling units this area must be twice that of the unit outlet area.
- Cooling unit return air cross section open area is equal to the face area of the evaporative unit coil, as a minimum.
- Return air to the cooling unit is filtered through a screen wire filter.
- Switch assembly terminal strips are securely mounted in a dry place safely out of reach.
- Thermostat temperature sensing bulb is installed in the cooling unit air stream.
- Cooling unit condensate drain is in place and working. Test by pouring about two quarts of water rapidly into the cooling unit drip pan.
- Cooling wires are connected securely to the switch assembly terminal strip, color to color.

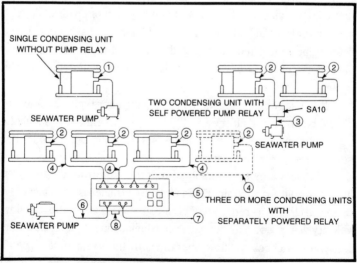

Fig. 5-10. Seawater pump wiring diagrams.

- Flare nut joints at the cooling unit are tight.
- Flare nut joints at the cooling unit are insulated to prevent dripping. Insulate well after testing for leaks.
- Wire harness to the condensing unit is securely connected to the switch assembly terminal strip, color to color.
- Power line from ship's panel is connected securely to the terminal strip of your system. And be sure that the proper size circuit breaker of the time delay type is installed.

Maintenance of Air Conditioning Units

In general the fan motors on cooling units are sealed bearing types and no lubrication is needed. Switch contacts are of the self-cleaning type and also require no maintenance. At the beginning of the boating season, however, check the cooling unit condensate drains for total or partial obstruction, by pouring water—about a quart—into the condensate drain tray. It should drain completely within about 30 seconds. If you have installed the piece of screen wire in the return air to the cooling unit duct, locate this screen and clean it if a visible buildup of lint has collected. In general the cooling units are sealed and require no winterizing.

The condensing unit is sealed and has no exposed parts or bearings and so does not need any maintenance. You might examine it for physical damage if it became loose on its mounting due to unusually rough seas. In case you find any sign of physical damage check it for leaks in both the oil and refrigerant lines. The gas charge refrigerant should not be changed or altered unless the unit was improperly charged initially or unless a leak is detected in the system.

If the seawater pump is the rubber impeller type, the impeller should be inspected after each 300 hours of operation. It should be replaced if worn. If the pump is the centrifugal type, a model PM series needs no maintenance.

The seawater system should be protected from debris by an inboard or outboard strainer. If an inboard strainer is used inspect it often and clean it as required. If your condensers are of the high flow velocity design you may not have scale buildup in salt or fresh water. But you can check for flow operation. In the wintertime close all thru-hull seacocks and loosen screws on the pump head to allow

Fig. 5-11. A running light on a yacht.

water to drain from the pump—if you do not have the self-purging system previously discussed or if you do not lift the boat straight out of the water. You can remove the hose from point 6 (Fig. 5-9) if you have a Cruisair system and allow the water to drain from the condensing unit. Then, if you desire, you can pump the system full of antifreeze of any type to prevent freezing.

MARINE LIGHTING SYSTEMS

Next we examine some important electrical devices—the electric lights on board, both fixed and portable types. Each boat is required to have running lights (Fig. 5-11) if it operates in international waters or has more than a given displacement. The running light requirement is shown in Fig. 5-12.

There is currently an attempt being made to standardize the running light requirements for vessels all over the world, and if a new treaty is adopted concerning this, the current lighting-system range on some vessels will be inadequate. New standards will be specified. The whole idea behind the lighting, as well as the idea of whistles and bells, is for greater safety at sea—to avoid collision. And with the ever growing number of boats one must agree that whatever is required to produce a safer passage for water borne vehicles is worthwhile. There are at present, requirements for one mile visibil-

LIGHTS REQUIRED ON BOATS UNDERWAY
BETWEEN SUNSET AND SUNRISE

VESSELS OF LESS THAN 65 FEET
USING INTERNATIONAL WATERS
(May be used on Inland waters)

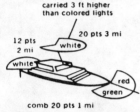

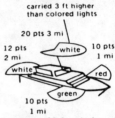

INTERNATIONAL: (1) Vessels 40 to less than 65 feet in length must carry 20 point white light 9 feet above gunwale as well as 3 feet higher than colored sidelights. (2) All vessels may display either separate colored sidelights or combined lanterns except vessels under sail alone 40 to less than 65 feet in length must display separate colored sidelights.

VESSELS USING ONLY INLAND WATERS
(including Great Lakes and Western Rivers)

LESS THAN 26 FEET

26 FEET TO NOT
MORE THAN 65 FEET

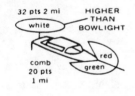

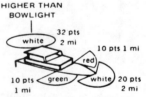

VESSELS UNDER SAIL ALONE

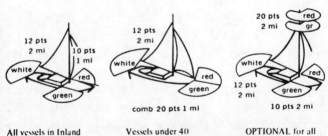

All vessels in Inland and International waters.

Vessels under 40 feet in International waters only.

OPTIONAL for all boats in International waters only.

EXCEPTIONS: (1) Western River Rules. Sidelights for vessels under sail must be visible for 3 miles. (2) Great Lakes. On the Great Lakes sailing vessels show a white light (in lieu of a stern light) upon that portion of the vessel which is being approached by another vessel.

LIGHTS FOR USE WHEN ANCHORED OR ROWING

POWER BOATS under 65 feet and all Sailing Vessels at anchor must display anchor lights except those under 65 feet in "special anchorage areas." An anchor light is a white light visible to a boat approaching from any direction, and is displayed in the fore part of the vessel.

ROWING BOATS: Rowing boats whether under oars or sail shall have ready at hand a lantern showing a white light which shall be temporarily exhibited in sufficient time to prevent collision.

IMPORTANT: LIGHTS MUST BE PLACED HIGH ENOUGH THAT THEIR LIGHT WILL NOT BE BLOCKED BY PERSONS OR PARTS OF THE BOAT OR ITS EQUIPMENT.

DEFINITION: "10 pts. 1 mi." means that the light can be seen through an arc of 10 points for a distance of 1 mile by another vessel.

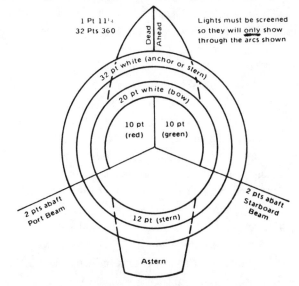

Fig. 5-12. U.S. Coast Guard lighting requirements.

ity and specified cut-off angle as shown in the Fig. 5-12. New standards would require two mile visibility if the treaty is signed.

To gain some understanding of what the electrical power and lighting relationship is, let us review some lighting terms. *Candlepower* is simply the measurement unit for light, just as meters and grams or inches and pounds are the units for distance and weight. The light *intensity* is expressed as the number of *candles* required to give the same amount of light that a certain bulb produces, that is, a 50,000 candlepower bulb produces the light of 50,000 candles. In order to understand what 50,000 candlepower of light can do as far as illuminating something is concerned, we must remember that this power may be diffused throughout a whole circle or it may be directed in a small arc by means of reflector mountings. With reflector mounting, a 50,000 candlepower light will cause the illumination of *reflective* objects out to about three-quarters of a mile. Raising the power to 75,000 candles gains an additional quarter mile, and raising the candlepower again to 110,000 candles gains an additional one-half mile. It takes 200,000 candlepower to illuminate a reflective object at two miles.

If we make a linear graph of these values we can gain some idea of power versus distance. (See Fig. 5-13.) Notice that the curve tends to flatten out. This indicates that after a given distance is reached, it takes a tremendous amount of light power to gain even a small increase in visibility on a reflective type object.

The kind of light that it produces is a function of the inside temperature of the light. We know that some light frequencies will penetrate the atmosphere better than others and some will penetrate water better than others. This means that you should consult the manufacturers to find out exactly what kind of light in both power and type you will need for your specific requirements, whether it be for running lights, search- or spotlights, or underwater lights.

Of course you must have available the battery or have electric power from a generator to power these lights, and if your electrical system, as calculated by the means discussed earlier (adding all appliance, etc., wattages), is running near full capacity without these lights, then you may want to make more primary electrical power available. It is proper, when planning your electrical installation, to make sure you have included all present and future lighting require-

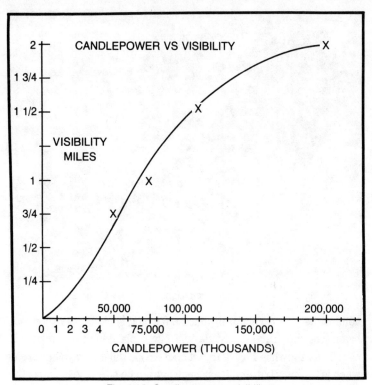

Fig. 5-13. Candlepower vs. visibility.

ments, and then add an increase of at least 15 to 25 percent additional power capability for things which you haven't thought of.

The Beam Gun Searchlight

It is always important to have some kind of portable light on board which can be used in case of failure of other lights, or in areas where fixed lights do not illuminate adequately. They can also be used to signal for help. Often such a light is used in the engine compartment to check the systems there or the batteries. A good portable light should be operable underwater in case it is dropped overboard or in case the owner wants to find something under the water when diving or swimming. An example of such a light is shown in Fig. 5-14.

This kind of unit is easily carried. It is waterproof. It has a beam intensity of 6,000 to 22,000 candlepower and it operates on a standard 6 volt lantern battery. It will operate up to 10 hours

Fig. 5-14. A beam gun searchlight. (Courtesy Chromalloy.)

continuously. It does not produce a flashing light, but a continuous beam. Its construction and the battery replacement are relatively simple, as shown in Fig. 5-15. Of course one must always be careful when installing a battery in any such light to be sure and maintain the sealing integrity of the unit.

Many of the portable kinds of lights use dry cell type batteries which are not rechargeable, and so the question arises, "When do I need to replace batteries?" We have a tendency to think that if we don't use them, they don't need to be replaced. Nothing could be further from the truth. Dry cell batteries will deteriorate and are affected by the temperature, humidity, and vibration. So it is a good idea to have some kind of test to use on batteries—aside from just turning the light on—to gain an idea of how much of a charge they might still have.

One must realize also that just because we get a new battery off the shelf of a store, this does not necessarily mean that the battery is in good condition. It may have been there a long time and may have had environmental changes which shortened its life. So the first thing we need to do when purchasing a dry cell battery is to examine the date on the side. If it has been on the shelf for 6 months to a year, do not purchase it. We have found a relatively simple test which gives

172

some idea as to the condition of the battery and, if the merchant will permit its use, will help you to select a good battery—but check only those which have a recent date of manufacture or a date far ahead which indicates that it should be "good until...."

The test we speak of requires a small, simple voltmeter with a scale of 6 to 10 volts. It may have others but we use only this one for this test on a 6 volt battery. From a radio parts store obtain a resistor of about 30 ohms, 2 watts. Test the battery by connecting the resistor across its terminal and measuring its voltage while you have the resistor connected. If the voltage does not drop appreciably at the end of a 15 to 20 second test period, the battery is in pretty good condition. It is usually safe to buy it. You will, of course, have spare batteries on board and these will have been subjected to the environment. Don't forget them. Don't assume just because they have never been used that they will perform satisfactorily. The same, of course, will be true of the batteries in any equipment. Be aware that batteries deteriorate, even if they are sealed. Wet cell batteries, which can be recharged, may deteriorate so that they will not take a charge. So you may be caught up in that dangerous situation where you might have thought: " I'll recharge the batteries at sea." Then, there you are in the middle of nowhere and your batteries won't take a charge. The dry cells may fail after a few minutes of operation, and the spares just have no life whatever.

Fig. 5-15. The ACR/L6 beam gun cutaway.

173

Test new batteries and charge your wet cells to be sure they are okay before you put out to sea. If you go often, then replace your dry cells every six months—and discharge and re-charge your wet cells at least once every three months. That way you will be assured of electrical power from these sources in an emergency.

If it should happen that your batteries fail, or you do not have portable equipment, but you do have a light bulb or light which will operate from a 6 or 12 volt source, you can usually get enough electrical power from the ship's batteries—even if they won't work any pumps or crank the engine or run electronic equipment. You can "tap" the battery halfway to get 6 volts—or across the outside terminals for 12 volts. This may be an emergency source of electrical power which can help you out. If your main batteries fail, sometimes you can disconnect them, let them rest for a while, and have them build up some reserve power. You may then be able to reconnect them and get a starting surge. It won't last long, so be ready for it. If the engine was flooded, for example, be sure it has dried out, etc.

There are many safety type lights which can be used as markers in case of distress or emergency. These have a high visibility at night and can even be seen some distance in daytime under certain conditions. These use a pulsed light which means that a tremendous amount of power can be generated in light for a few thousandths of a second and not run down a battery too quickly, nor require too large a battery supply. These light intensities can be as great as 250,000 *lumens*. A lumen is the amount of light on a surface one square foot in size at a distance of one foot from one candle. Thus the 250,000 lumens means that the light intensity is the same as 250,000 candles placed one foot from a one square foot surface. That is a lot of light. Safety lights may pulse much higher than the 250,000 lumens in some cases.

Speaking of light and the efficiency of production of light, Table 5-2 will give some idea of the relationship for a tungsten filament light of watts, output lumens, and efficiency.

There are filaments other than tungsten and the efficiencies for these may be higher than our table shows. But it has been found that most marine lights use the tungsten-carbide type of filament. This produces a reddish-orange light which has very good atmospheric penetration. You might want to write to General Electric Company

Table 5-2. Watts, Lumens and Efficiency of Tungsten Filament Lamps.

Input Watts	Output Lumens	Efficiency Lumens per Watt
25	260	10.4
60	835	13.9
100	1580	15.8
200	3640	18.2
500	10,050	20.1
1000	20,700	20.7
10,000	325,000	32.5

for their booklet *Sealed Beam Lamps*. This is a good primary reference on the subject and makes a good addition to your bookshelf.

We considered some examples of searchlights and spotlights and a representative example was one which was produced by Optronics. They make a 50,000 candlepower light which produces a white, sunlight type beam with good atmospheric penetration. It operates on 12.8 volts and requires about 5 amperes of current. Thus this light consumes about 60 watts of energy from your primary battery supply. Another representative type we examined produces 100,000 candlepower of light in a focused beam and requires 100 watts of primary power from the 12.8 volt source. This is the same as that (the 100 watts) used as an ordinary house light bulb of the same rating.

Illumination Markers

Lights will help to save lives. There are types of markers which can be floated in the sea which will produce strong flashes which can be seen for miles from aircraft. These are small self-powered units. They are easy to carry on board any boat. One type made by Chromalloy Electronics Division is shown in Fig. 5-16. This unit is easily carried on board in a non-corrosive mounting bracket and when needed is simply removed and thrown into the water. It rights itself and begins flashing a light of 250,000 lumens at peak brilliance. It can be used for a man-overboard marker, boundary marking of diving areas, underwater obstruction definition, and other similar kinds of uses. Its 6 volt battery will give about 50 hours of continuous operation. Its flashes of light can be seen through a hemisphere as it is nondirectional in operation.

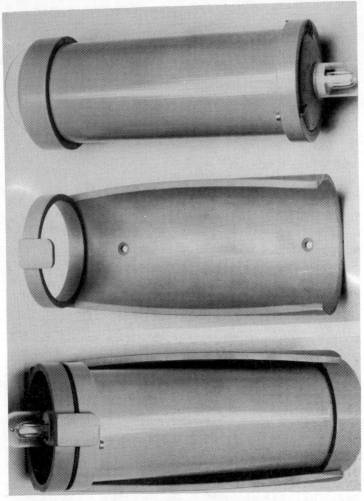

Fig. 5-16. ACR-SM2 illumination marker.

How do you maintain such a unit? It should have a monthly operation check. It is activated by means of a magnetic reed switch, built inside, when it is turned right side up. So you invert it and see if it flashes. You need to inspect its lens at least once a month to see if it is clean and to see that all condensation is removed. Its battery should be replaced at least once a year. When assembling, check all O-rings for nicks and cuts. Be certain to grease it with a silicone compound. Finally, after the battery has been inserted and top cap installed, assure that the locking swivels are properly seated in the

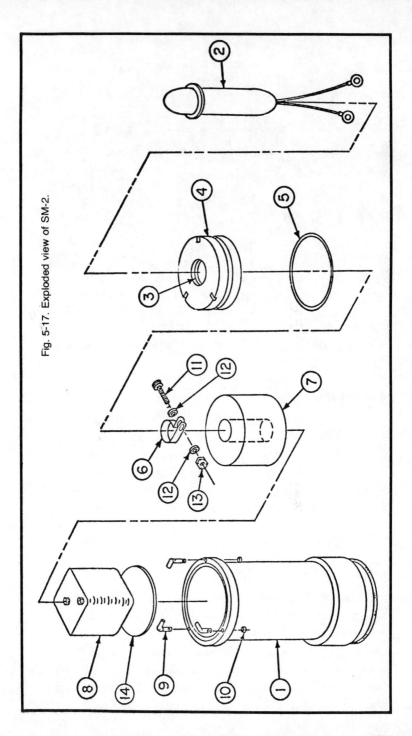

Fig. 5-17. Exploded view of SM-2.

177

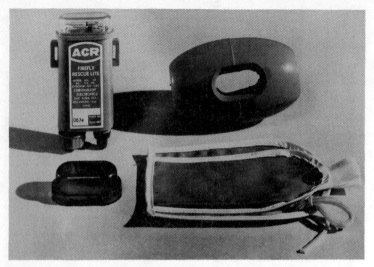

Fig. 5-18. Rescue light ACR/4F. (Courtesy Chromalloy.)

cap grooves. Then test it to see if it flashes. If it is okay, mount it upside down in its hanger. An exploded view of the unit is shown in Fig. 5-17.

Rescue Lights

There are several types of rescue lights available which will produce high intensity (250,000 peak lumens) light flashes and which can be viewed from as far as 7 or 8 miles from an aircraft at 1500 feet or more. These units use batteries which are rechargeable and which will provide flashes for as long as 9 hours' duration. The units are small, roughly 2 inches by 5 inches, and can easily be carried in one's pocket. The ACR/4F type unit is shown in Fig. 5-18. Another type of light is shown in Fig. 5-19.

Anticollision Light

This unit, Fig. 5-20, can be seen within a 2,000 mile *area* by an aircraft flying at 3,000 feet, under *good* weather conditions. The surface to surface visibility claimed is nearly ten miles. It operates from a 12 volt ±2 source, which means it can operate from the boat's regular battery supply, and because it has a small drain, a regular 12 volt car battery, for example, will give over 1,000 hours of operation.

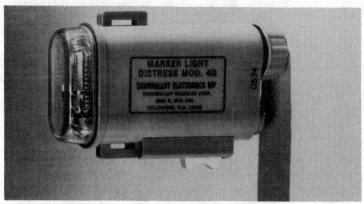

Fig. 5-19. The ACR/4G Firefly. (Courtesy Chromalloy.)

The specifications for this kind of light are informative. Its size is about $2 \times 4 \times 5$ inches and it weighs only 13 ounces. Its light output is 500,000 lumens per flash and it flashes at the rate of 60 per minute. It must be realized that in this kind of light the low voltage

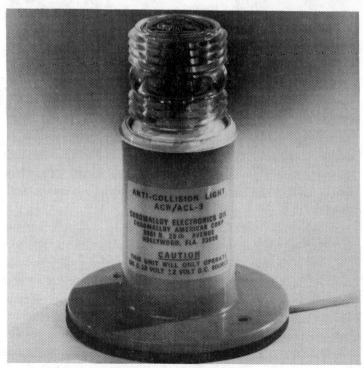

Fig. 5-20. The anticollision light.

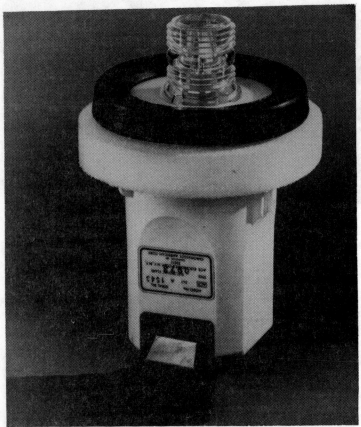
Fig. 5-21. The ACR/565 distress marker light.

source is converted to a high voltage inside the unit and this high voltage is applied to the flash tube. Time is necessary for the high voltage buildup and discharge, just as it is with your camera flash units.

The current drain for this unit is about 100 milliamperes from the 12 volt source and it is said to have at least 15 miles' visibility on a clear night. Shorter distances are obtained in case of fog or bad weather, but it does have good penetration of the fog or even water. It is shockproof, vibration proof, and waterproof. It will operate when completely submerged in water.

If it is desired to have a light with slightly less power for marker purposes in case of distress, the ACR/565, by Chromalloy, is an example of one which operates on a single 6 volt lantern battery, producing 350,000 lumens in flashes, and about 50 hours of operation with the battery. On a clear night it would have about 8 miles' visibility. Figure 5-21 shows the unit.

Finally we show in Fig. 5-22 an example of a *water activated battery* which can be stored almost indefinitely on a raft or in a life jacket. When its plugs are removed the water enters the unit and reacts with the copper halide and magnesium plates to produce the electricity required for its operation.

Radio Beacons

Because we have been discussing safety, marking, and distress signals in this chapter, we will include now a discussion of the radio beacon which is also an emergency type unit. These should be another vital part of your equipment if you are at sea or on large lakes and not just on small lakes where shores are always visible. These units radio a distress signal on monitored channels. One example is shown in Fig. 5-23. Radio Beacons operate on 121.5 and 243.0 MHz

Fig. 5-22. The water activated Chromalloy ACR/L-12A.

Fig. 5-23. A radio beacon. (Courtesy Simrad.)

simultaneously with a distinctive tone, sweeping across the audio range of 1300 to 300 Hz in accordance with RTCA regulations. This unit has a power of 200 milliwatts and will produce the signal for a period of 48 hours, approximately. It complies with the Federal Communications Commission regulation part 83.144 as a class B electronic position indicating radio beacon (EPIRB).

It is to be realized that to locate a ship in distress when only the emergency beacon acts as a locator source, the search craft must "home in" on the beacon signal. This means the signal should have clear and identifiable signals denoting that it is a distress call, and sufficient range so that it can be picked up by many sources. Thus triangulation or more multiple line marking can be obtained to determine its exact position. The Chromalloy unit shown has a range to an aircraft of 200 to 300 miles, line of sight. It operates in the VHF-UHF region with its special tone modulated signal.

The battery package is somewhat unusual. It is a magnesium battery which will operate for 48 hours even at below zero temperatures and a much longer time above this temperature. The battery package is said to have useful life of six years but FCC recommends replacement at 3 year intervals. It is possible to test the beacon by means of a switch and a light which shows when it is operating as it should. The indicator light is a light emitting diode which consumes very little power. Of course you need to test such a unit frequently, and it would probably be a good idea to keep a log of the test dates and times of test. Every so often it might be a good idea to get a radiation field check when in harbor, measurement of the actual power it is putting out into the atmosphere. This can be accomplished by trained technicians who have the sensitive radiation measuring equipment necessary.

Of course, any such device floating in water can have its radiation pattern varied by the waves around it. The larger the waves the more its signal will rise and fall so that when high its signal radiates far and when in the trough its signals can be blanketed out by the seawater. An intermittent signal thus might be received by a distant station, and if it too is rolling or yawing, the actual fix might be difficult. In this case it could be economical to have several such beacons and have them all operating simultaneously in a given location where the help is needed. The probability exists then that a more continuous signal be sent and received.

If you have a radio beacon, you do not have it in the water, as in the case of capsized boat or sinking vessel, you will want to operate it on a deck as free from any obstructions, wires, and masts as possible, and get it as high as possible. If you go to a raft, then you'll have to tether it to the raft with its lanyard and let it float. When servicing the unit, replacing the battery, etc., you will, of course, follow the manufacturer's instructions. The water seal is most important. At the same time you can make some tests to be sure that all is proper. These tests are:

- Check the antenna vinyl tube covering for any signs of chafing, wear, cracks, or other damage, or signs of resultant corrosion beneath the tubing. Clean and repair or replace as necessary.
- Check the antenna socket at the cap surface for any signs of looseness or corrosion.

It must be realized that just having such a unit on board is not enough. When it is needed, it is too late to do the cleaning necessary

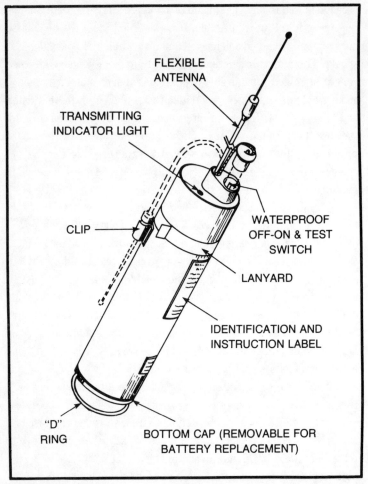

FLEXIBLE
ANTENNA

TRANSMITTING
INDICATOR LIGHT

CLIP

WATERPROOF
OFF-ON & TEST
SWITCH

LANYARD

IDENTIFICATION AND
INSTRUCTION LABEL

"D"
RING

BOTTOM CAP (REMOVABLE FOR
BATTERY REPLACEMENT)

Fig. 5-24. The ACR/RBL-12 emergency position indicating radio beacon and major parts designations.

to have the antenna make good contact and thus give a strong, clear signal. A corroded antenna might reduce the transmission to a few hundred yards. Don't take chances with it. Check your antenna and its connections and the battery often. Figure 5-24 shows the major parts of this beacon.

In concluding this important chapter which involves much on safety and safety devices, we remind you that one weak link in a chain renders the chain useless. If you don't do your part, all the safety devices in the world can't help you.

Chapter 6

Servo Systems
and Automatic Pilots

To relieve the tedium of steering and to make certain that a boat continues on its proper course, an automatic pilot is often used. These systems are used more on craft like the 58 foot cruiser shown in Fig. 6-1 than they are on smaller pleasure boats. But automatic pilots can be found in a size and a complexity from the very simple to the very complicated and are adaptable for any size boat. Commercial vessels use them to relieve the helmsman or to follow a specific course.

BASIC SYSTEMS

Simple versions of the control mechanism may be compared to the power steering system of an automobile in that they permit manual steering with just a fingertip effort. The true automatic pilot is one that has a reference so it can steer a particular course with respect to this reference. The North Pole is commonly used. Its direction is sensed either by a magnetic compass or a gyrocompass. Both of these are used in modern autopilots as we shall learn in this chapter. There are some limitations on magnetic compass units and systems on which we need to be informed.

But it is also possible to have an autopilot system which can steer the boat by signals transmitted for navigation (loran), or by satellite reflected signals using the thoroughly modern positioning

Fig. 6-1. A large motor yacht has an autopilot. (Courtesy Hatteras.)

satellites now in orbit around the earth. Autopilots can also have a radar or sonar type sensing unit. With the radar one might steer along a shoreline a fixed distance away and the automatic system will keep it at that distance, no matter how the shoreline may change or whether you can see the shore through bleak weather or dark nights.

Steering a boat using loran signals is not a new idea. This was first accomplished in aircraft way back in World War II and it does permit an infinite number of courses to be selected, as the captain chooses. Long range loran signals are not affected by the curvature of the earth as radar, UHF, and VHF signals are. Thus great distances can be traveled around the curvature of the earth following this type of automatically controlled course.

It is not inconceivable to have a star measuring unit on board which will give star position data. When this is fed into a shipboard computer and thence to an autopilot, it can cause any given course to be followed by any size vessel. The main problem here is that the measurements must be made from a "stabilized" platform, one which doesn't pitch or roll or yaw, but instead remains parallel to the earth's surface at all times. So the larger vessels may use this kind of system, but in general the smaller boats and yachts won't have the stability in themselves to permit the use of this kind of system.

In the systems to be examined, we will be most concerned with the magnetic compass and the gyrocompass as sensors and reference determining devices. Before we get much further into the subjects of autopilots, let us examine some of the limitations of using a magnetic compass as a reference on a steel hulled ship.

Engineers have been aware for some time that magnetically sensing automatic pilots, generally speaking, may not do a good job of steering steel hulled vessels. The problem is particularly severe in cases where the compass is located in the steel pilothouse of the vessel. The problem with a magnetic compass sensor in this situation is that the vessel will yaw from side to side on all headings, but particularly severely on northerly and southerly headings. This will be the case regardless of what the compass-error-angle to rudder deflection angle ratio may be. No matter how well the compass is adjusted or how finely tuned the ratio, yawing will occur.

The reason is that the compass is fooled and it thinks the magnetic field of the ship is the earth's magnetic field. You see, a steel hull is like a big, hollow piece of iron. It is magnetized by the earth's relatively strong magnetic field and becomes, itself, a magnet. It will assume the same polarity as the earth's field and that polarity will change, relative to the ship, as the ship changes position in this earth magnetic field. Now the problem is that the ship does become magnetized in a particular direction and then, due to something called hysteresis—a tendency to remain magnetized in a given direction—it does not readily change the direction of its magnetization even though the ship may change its position with respect to the earth field. There is actually a delay in time before the ship's field changes to correspond to the earth's field. Eventually, of course, the magnetic field of the ship will coincide with the earth's field, but it will not do this instantly as the ship changes position. There will be a delay.

The result of this delay is that an improperly located magnetic autopilot compass, which is responsive mainly to the ship's magnetic field, will not respond instantly to changes of the ship's heading because the ship's field doesn't change quickly. Thus the ship will fall off course but the automatic pilot won't know it. Finally the angle of the ship's magnetic field will become great enough with respect to the earth's field that the compass will sense a change in the ship's field. When this field changes, it will do so rapidly, and the autopilot system will operate to correct the ship's heading. But of course this changes the ship's heading again and so yawing results.

On northerly and southerly headings, the length of the ship is parallel to the earth's field. You must recall that any magnet will orient itself more readily to its length than to its width, so the ship magnetizes easily in this direction.

Well, how do we solve this problem? It is solved by first getting the compass away from the steel pilothouse and the hull so that it can sense the earth's field and not the ship's field. This can be accomplished to some degree by mounting the pilot compass above the pilothouse of the ship. The higher it is mounted, the less it will be affected by the ship's field. But the best solution would be to use a gyrocompass sensor which does not depend upon the earth's magnetic field for its operation. Magnetic compass systems are usually used with small boats and vessels, which have little steel in their hull, so that a proper mounting of the compass can be accomplished. Then it won't be sensitive to any but the earth's magnetic field.

The autopilot systems we will examine here are proven and reliable, and through the assistance and cooperation of the manufacturers we are able to give you a good insight into the operation of this equipment. Now, since we need to be on the same background footing as we begin this examination, we will begin by a review of what an automatic control system consists of and how it works. We will also examine how the transducers, the synchros and selsyns work. These are some key units in such automatic control systems.

A BASIC CONTROL SYSTEM (SERVOMECHANISM)

A servo mechanism means slave unit. This says that this device or system will respond to commands given it. Its output is usually mechanical motion of a desired kind with tremendous speed and power if necessary. In practice the complexity of these control systems will vary according to application, but basically, each will follow an arrangement similar to that shown in Fig. 6-2.

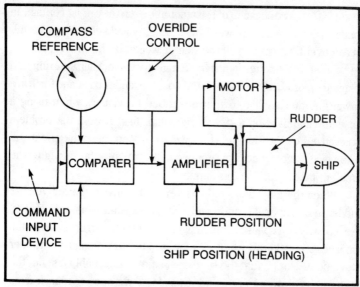

Fig. 6-2. Basic block diagram of control system.

There will be some kind of reference input which, in this application, is from a compass. There will be a dial or knob to set the desired heading into the unit. Usually, an electrical signal will go to a comparator unit. This unit, which may be an integral part of the gyrosensor system (a transducer), will compare the ship's heading to the desired heading, and if the ship is not going correctly, an error signal will be generated. This signal may be of positive or negative polarity to indicate the direction of the error. It may be an in-phase or out-of-phase signal, which will give the same information. Knowing the error direction, the amplifier is able to turn the rudder to make the correction.

The amplifier has a second duty. It must be able to release electrical power in proportion to the size of the error so there is sufficient electrical power to move the rudder with electric motors. In some systems the electrical signal from the amplifier will operate hydraulic valves which in turn release high pressure oil to move pistons and thus obtain the necessary rudder moving power.

It is usual to find electric motors on the smaller boats and hydraulic units on the larger boats and commercial ships. But be aware that hydraulic units may be found on even very small boats as we shall see in the following examples. Electric motors having high torque are heavy because of the amount of iron they must contain. In many cases, hydraulic power is less weighty and still very powerful. In any event, regardless of the size or weight of the rudder, it must be moved fast enough and far enough to correct all steering and heading errors without causing the boat to wander back and forth in a yawing motion similar to that described previously when using a magnetic compass on a steel hulled ship. In that case the problem was caused by the sensor. Here we are saying the same effect will take place if the rudder isn't moved fast enough or far enough. The problem takes place in the output.

When the amplifier sends power to the device that moves the rudder in a proper direction and a proper amount—as specified by the polarity (or phase) and magnitude of the error signal—the amplifier must know when to stop sending the signal for rudder movement. Notice that the rudder will move reasonably fast but the boat will be slower to respond; therefore, we need feedback from the rudder to the amplifier to tell the amplifier that, indeed, the rudder has been placed in the desired position for a return to the correct course. We will also find that the amplifier must know when proper course is reached. This is accomplished through feedback as we shall see.

When the rudder has moved in the amount and direction specified by the error signal, a rudder position feedback signal from a potentiometer or synchro zeroes out the input signal from the comparer. In Fig. 6-3, the electrical bridge input will be balanced off center. As the boat turns, the heading change is noted by the compass sensor and this signal goes to zero, leaving an unbalanced condition due to the deflected rudder transducer (potentiometer). Now, as this signal is opposite in polarity due to this change, it will cause the rudder to move back to neutral and zero out this feedback signal as it does so. With the boat again on course and the rudder in neutral position, the automatic pilot will do nothing until the boat begins to wander off course again due to sea motion, wind, etc. Then the whole steering operation starts all over again. With a tight control servo system autopilot the boat never does get much off course. The smallest error in direction is sufficient to cause a correction, so as far as the ship is concerned it follows a straight line

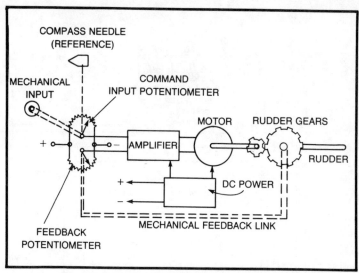

Fig. 6-3. Expanded block diagram of control system.

from one point to another. This is economical in fuel, time, effort, and in steering.

All automatic pilot systems have an override system so that, when necessary, you can take over the wheel and override the control system. This is considered to be a safety feature and may be necessary in some cases of bad weather or very unusual conditions.

Now examine Fig. 6-3 for further insight into the control mechanism. As you see, the amplifier is the big unit in the system considering all the signals and power furnished to the motor. You can see in Fig. 6-4, a schematic of the Encron 77 autopilot, that solid state design is used. The motor is in the upper right-hand corner of the diagram.

In this system the motor is designed with a clutch, and the control mechanism engages it in such a way that right or left movements are accomplished for the rudder. Notice also that there are other factors that are used in setting the operation of the autopilot. The boat speed is important to operation of this circuit. Its control is just below the rudder feedback potentiometer. At the top center is the switch for course change. This system operates on 12 volts so it is compatible with most small-boat battery supplies.

Now let us become more advanced for a moment. In Fig. 6-5 is shown a block diagram of an electrohydraulic system which is used in

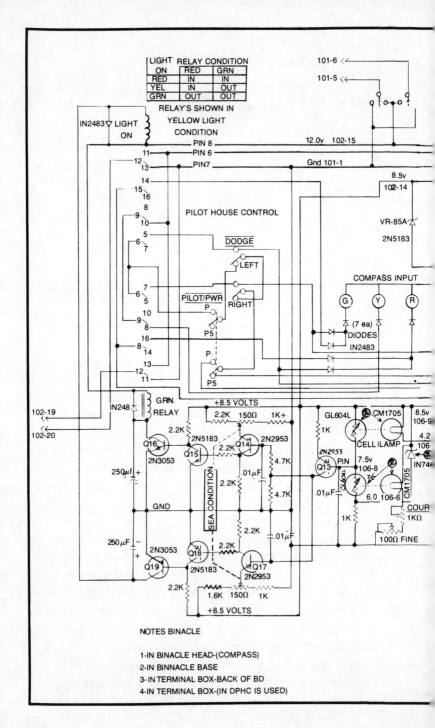

LIGHT	RELAY CONDITION	
ON	RED	GRN
RED	IN	IN
YEL	IN	OUT
GRN	OUT	OUT

RELAY'S SHOWN IN
YELLOW LIGHT
CONDITION

101-6

101-5

IN2483 LIGHT
ON

PIN 8   12.0v 102-15
11 — PIN 6
12
13 — PIN7   Gnd 101-1

14   8.5v
15   102-14
16
8
9   VR-85A
10
5   PILOT HOUSE CONTROL   2N5183
6
7   DODGE
LEFT
7
6
5   COMPASS INPUT
PILOT/PWR
P   RIGHT
10
9   G   Y   R
8
P5
16   (7 ea)
8
14   DIODES
13   IN2483
12
11   P
P5

102-19   GRN.
IN248   RELAY
102-20   +8.5 VOLTS
2.2K   150Ω   1K+   GL604L   CM1705   8.5v
2.2K   106-9
Q16   2N5183   Q14   2N2953   1K   CELL   LAMP   4.2
2N3053   Q15   2.2K   4.7K   106
250μf +   2.2K   .01μF   4.7K   2N2953   IN74
                                          Q13   PIN   7.5v
GND   SEA CONDITION   .01μF   106-8
                              2.2K   6.0   106-6
250μF -   2N3053   2.2K   .01μF   1K   COUR
+   Q18   Q17   1KΩ
Q19   2N5183   2N2953   100Ω FINE
2.2K   1.6K   150Ω   1K
+8.5 VOLTS

NOTES BINACLE

1-IN BINACLE HEAD-(COMPASS)
2-IN BINNACLE BASE
3-IN TERMINAL BOX-BACK OF BD
4-IN TERMINAL BOX-(IN DPHC IS USED)

192

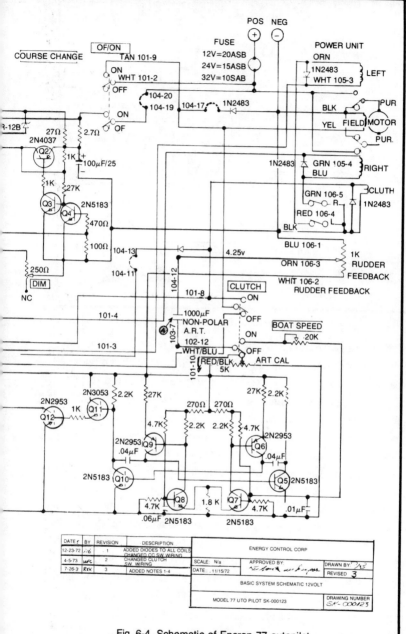

Fig. 6-4. Schematic of Encron 77 autopilot.

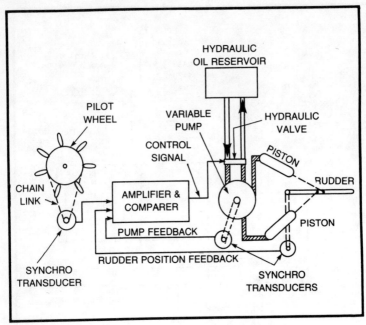

Fig. 6-5. Ship servomechanism (power steering).

ship steering. The amplifier in this case controls a hydraulic valve which in turn controls the direction of oil flow through the pump so that it reaches the proper piston for the correct rudder displacement. Notice the two feedback synchros. This simply means the amplifier uses ac power and signals rather than dc signals as in the previous example. Notice how the pilot wheel is geared to the command input transducer through a chain linkage.

With a system such as this we can derive a mathematical model which then can be solved to show exactly how well the autopilot will steer the ship. The solution of the mathematical model will also tell us how much gain to put in the amplifier, how powerful the piston system must be, etc. So before ordering parts and building the system, we know exactly how it will perform in a given boat.

With small boats, there are enough adjustments on a so-called standard autopilot system to account for the differences in tonnage, displacement, and speed of the boat. Recall the speed control on Fig. 6-4. But when you are concerned with large yachts and ships, the control system must and should be designed for that ship specifically. The mathematical model enables a designer to do this.

194

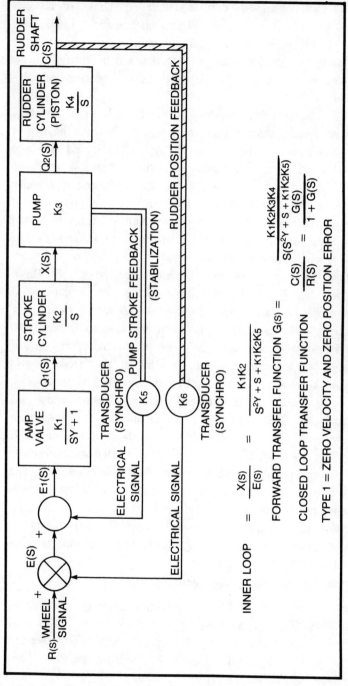

Fig. 6-6. A mathematical model for Fig. 6-5.

$$\text{INNER LOOP} = \frac{X(S)}{E(S)} = \frac{K_1 K_2}{S^2 Y + S + K_1 K_2 K_5}$$

$$\text{FORWARD TRANSFER FUNCTION } G(s) = \frac{K_1 K_2 K_3 K_4}{S(S^2 Y + S + K_1 K_2 K_5)}$$

$$\text{CLOSED LOOP TRANSFER FUNCTION} \quad \frac{C(S)}{R(S)} = \frac{G(S)}{1 + G(S)}$$

TYPE 1 = ZERO VELOCITY AND ZERO POSITION ERROR

We will not show the derivation of the equations of operation of this system. For those readers who are mathematically inclined, the procedure is quite straightforward and standard. Some may question the second integration in the outer feedback loop, but it was found that this gave the required stability rather than producing an instability.

The transfer functions show the system to be a type 1 system. Control systems go from type zero to type 3. The lower the number the more inherent errors it has. The type 1 system will have zero velocity and zero position errors and this will give very smooth steering. Just for the record, if you are purchasing an autopilot system you might want to ask what type it is. The type 0 system has a zero position error but the rudder movement will usually be slower than the input command lever movement. If the movement of the rudder is made to be too fast, there will be "hunting," or movement back and forth, around the desired position for a few seconds. This is not desirable. Neither is a too slow response with no "hunting." A slow response, however, is probably better than a too-fast, or "hunting," response because this latter type uses up hydraulic fluid rapidly or consumes electrical power continuously, and that is costly. On type 0 systems you can avoid hunting by reducing the gain of the control amplifier as you can with the type 1 systems.

The type 1 system, as stated, has a zero position and a zero velocity error. It is the best all-around system for boats. The rudder follows immediately and smoothly the command lever movement. It may overshoot its final position once or twice, but it will settle down quite quickly and stably into the commanded angle of deflection. The type 2 system is a zero acceleration type of system. It is much more complicated as it has zero position, zero velocity, and zero acceleration errors. This type of system may be required for fast objects like guided missiles and space ships, generally it does not apply to boats as far as steering is concerned.

AUTOPILOT QUESTIONS AND ANSWERS

Here are some of the most frequently asked questions about autopilots. "What is the main reason for using them?" This is to provide steering while you are away from the helm or to reduce the tedium on clear days and with safe courses. If you are alone it can steer the boat while you fish or whatever.

"How complex an autopilot should I have?" This depends on the size boat as we previously indicated. Almost any size boat can be equipped with an autopilot of some sort. On boats from 30 to 60 feet, the cost is relatively minor. On smaller boats it may be high, depending on the displacement of the boat. But the cost also depends on the type of autopilot so it will pay to shop around to find the right one for your needs.

"Is the installation difficult?" Not especially. A linkage must be attached to the rudder and an electric or hydraulic drive device installed to move the rudder. The directional reference sensor must be mounted so it will not be influenced by the magnetic field of any metallic objects on the craft, especially if the sensor is a magnetic compass. The amplifier must be shock mounted and should be placed in an inclosure and supplied with electrical power. The drive device must receive electrical or hydraulic power too.

"What is the difference between a hunting and a nonhunting autopilot?" The hunting autopilot moves the rudder all the time to keep the boat on course, so it consumes energy all the time. In a sense the rudder vibrates all the time. This will create an S-type wake. A nonhunting type autopilot is on only when making a course correction and so consumes less power. Most autopilots are of the nonhunting type. The sensitivity of an autopilot can be from 1/2 degree to 5 degrees, meaning that this amount of course error must appear before a course correction is made. As you can imagine, a boat with autopilot control will really steer a slightly wavy course over a straight line course you plot on the chart.

Just how wavy the course is depends on the sensitivity of the autopilot correction. In the case of a hunting autopilot, the rudder moves constantly, but the boat tends to remain exactly on the straight line course. But the consumed energy is the price you pay for this. A sensitive (1/2 degree error) type autopilot will be close enough for all practical purposes, and it does little hunting.

SYNCHRO (TRANSDUCER) BASICS

We need to understand the synchro (also called a transducer) transformer at this time because it is used as a sensor to set the course. It is also used as a feedback element sensor to monitor the rudder position at all times and send back the signal representing this position to the main amplifier or to the system comparer.

197

The synchro is built like a small motor, having a rotating armature and a fixed field inside a case very much like a small electric motor. The difference is that due to the type of wiring and the method of connecting the two units (two units are almost always used) together, we get a transmitter-receiver effect. Although the armature could rotate like a motor, it only turns back and forth in use. It simply turns in exact correspondence with the transmitter input armature's rotation or angular displacement. This means that if we place a dial on the transmitter shaft and turn it ten degrees, the receiver shaft will also turn ten degrees and stop. If we reverse the direction of the transmitter shaft rotation, the receiver shaft will also turn in the opposite direction. So we get an exact duplication of the transmitter shaft position and angular displacement from the receiver even though the two units may be physically separated and are connected together only by electrical wiring.

You will find such units, also a type called selsyn, much used in ships. They maintain bridge-to-engine-room signals and send back information confirming that the throttle, rudder, or whatever has been moved or set the amount specified. You will also find that if properly connected—that is, so the receiver shaft is geared to the rudder, for example—selsyn units can also send a signal representing rudder position. They do this by means of magnitude and phase of the ac voltage supplied.

The magnitude of ac voltage output from such a receiver is proportional to the amount of rudder displacement in either direction, neutral rudder being zero, as shown in Fig. 6-7. The phase, when compared to a reference, is what specifies which direction the rudder has moved. Left rudder, for example, would be out-of-phase compared to the reference. Right rudder would be an in-phase voltage compared to the reference. Thus this unit can send back rudder position information which can be compared to the voltage and phase of the input command sensor in an appropriate amplifier and the result will be an error signal, if they do not cancel. This error signal will cause the rudder to move in the correct direction to cause error signal zero.

A synchro has three field windings and they are usually marked S1, S2 and S3 (S for stator). When connecting two units together for mechanical position feedback as in the case of the captain to engineer

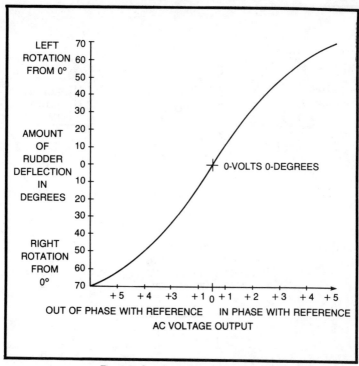

Fig. 6-7. Synchro transmitter output.

signal, the transmitter terminals must be connected exactly to the same terminals on the receiver unit. Meantime, the rotors, which have a single winding, are simply connected to the same source of ac voltage. This can be 110 volts, 60 Hz, or sometimes 110 volts, 400 Hz. In Fig. 6-8(a) we see a diagram showing the circuit hookup for physical remote data transmission as discussed. The input is a physical rotation of the transmitter rotor, and the output is a physical rotation of the receiver rotor in the same direction and amount. The receiver is often called a control transformer in the literature, and when used to give an error signal it is used as in Fig. 6-8(b). It does not rotate electrically; it must be turned physically, as by a rudder connection.

AUTOPILOT INSTALLATIONS

As you can imagine, when installing an autopilot it is necessary to zero the command transmitter with the reference axis of the boat, and then to adjust the receiver, or feedback synchro, so it causes the

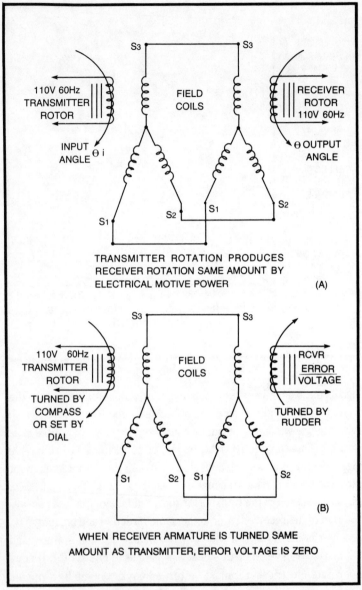

Fig. 6-8. Connecting a synchro transmitter to the receiver.

rudder to go to neutral position—when the command transmitter input is the same as the ship heading.

If we imagine the simplest case now, that of using a magnetic compass delicately geared to a transmitter synchro, we can also imagine having a dial knob that will turn the compass housing to establish neutral rudder for any particular course heading. Then, anytime the ship heading goes off this course, the compass needle, which is holding the transmitter armature motionless, lets the stator, which is affixed to the ship itself, rotate, and thus creates an input course-error signal. Immediately the rudder will be made to bring the ship back to the desired, and preset, heading.

The Remote Pilot Control Unit

We need to mention another feature of this kind of steering system which isn't of the automatic steering concept. As can be visualized, we can install a small hand held unit with a dial, which we can turn by hand, to steer our boats. This takes all the strain and muscle out of steering because the electrical devices in the control system will do the rudder moving for you. All you really need to do is set in a course error by turning the small dial in your hand, and this will then be like the signal from the automatic pilot—in fact it may be the override part of the system. When this steering unit is attached to the end of a long flexible cord, you can move about anywhere and steer your boat while enjoying the pleasures of boating. This part of a control system comes as an integral part of the system on some automatic pilots and can be added easily on others.

We need to mention here that, actually, steering on any but the smallest pleasure craft is mechanically assisted in some manner. Usually, for larger craft, the system is hydraulic, in which a slight turn of the wheel opens a valve forcing pressurized hydraulic fluid into cylinders to move the rudder. This kind of system is much the same as the power steering system used on automobiles. On smaller craft you may find that the wheel is geared to the rudder and must be rotated many degrees to effect a course change. The number of degrees of rotation of the wheel compared to the number of degrees of movement of the rudder is called the *steering ratio*, and it is normally dependent upon the gearing ratio between the wheel and the rudder. It is governed by the sensitivity in a power system or automatic pilot system. Direct drive through gears to create rudder movement by sheer muscle force often requires strong arms and results in real fatigue.

The Dampened Sensor

If we think about magnetic compasses usually found in stores, the rapid and erratic movement of a ball with a dial inside a small plastic bowl comes to mind. These are flotation suspended, with the liquid acting like a gimbal system, and gravity keeping the compass dial band relatively level. The ball, however, can slide from side to side; it can rotate quickly and hunt before settling down. It is, in general, pretty unstable.

The sensor for an automatic pilot cannot be permitted to do this. If it did, it would cause the rudder to swing wildly in an erratic manner to follow the sensor gyrations. Because of this requirement, that it not hunt, the compass, or the directional element of the autopilot, must be dampened. This can be accomplished by using a thick liquid with a magnetic compass so that the sensitive element will not respond to small, quick movements of the boat but will tend to respond more slowly and average out all movements and directional changes to give the final heading readings. This way the rudder will move more slowly to steer the boat. This is all right because a boat's response, except for the very fast planing hulls, is usually slow. First the rudder is moved, then, rather gradually, the boat turns in the direction called for by this deflection. On the ships it takes a finite time to get a response to the rudder movement, and turns for the very large ships cannot be made in less than a several mile radius.

The previous statement, which has some bearing on autopilot control, also has great implication on course collision avoidance. You just can't maneuver a large ship the way you can a car. This means that in our ever more crowded sea lanes, it is necessary to know the whereabouts of all vessels around you, large and small, when they are close and when they are a long way off. We will discuss this in more detail in a later chapter.

But at this point, we want to make it clear that the boat's response is a big factor in setting up the autopilot system. In one boat, a movement of the rudder 10 degrees may cause a very gradual turn; in another, a quick turn. So an autopilot system must be adjusted for the particular boat it is in and with the kind of responsiveness which makes for pleasure, convenience, and safety as well.

Not let us begin an examination of several actual autopilots for marine use.

THE SPERRY 8T AUTOPILOT

This is a dc operated system for 12, 14, 24, or 32 volts. It has three basic parts and a remote attachment. A navigational 8 inch illuminated magnetic compass, Fig. 6-9, furnishes directional reference for the system. The controller assembly, which is mounted directly over the compass, consists of a toroidal coil magnetometer with brushes and slip rings mounted inside the assembly housing; a heading selector dial marked every 5 degrees from 0 to 360, and illuminated by the compass; and a prism that is used to view the lubber line and compass card. A dimmer control is located on the front side of the compass binnacle, and a cable is provided for connecting the compass to the amplifier.

A fully transistorized control amplifier assembly is fitted with an adjustable mounting bracket and can be positioned for operating convenience. The assembly is shown in Fig. 6-9. Switches and controls on the front panel of this control amplifier include a power switch, mode switch, weather control, and a rudder control. A cable is provided for connecting the control amplifier to the relay panel or junction box.

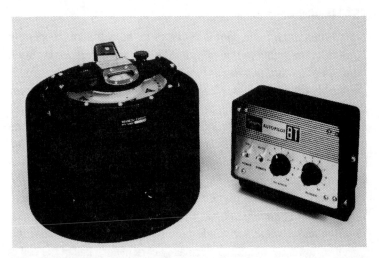

Fig. 6-9. Sperry 8T directional reference and control panel. (Courtesy Sperry Marine Systems.)

Fig. 6-10. Sperry 8T electric steering engine. (Courtesy Sperry Marine Systems.)

The electric rudder positioning equipment is shown in Fig. 6-10. The steering engine is provided with an electric clutch, follow-up, or feedback, potentiometer, and adjustable limit switches.

8T Technical Operation

When the 8T autopilot is operated in the automatic mode, the controller assembly on the compass detects any difference between the vessel's actual heading and the selected heading. This controller assembly contains a center tapped coil wound on a ring shaped core. When the selected heading, as indicated on the heading selector dial, and the actual heading, as indicated on the compass card, are the same, the magnets of the compass are parallel to a line joining the midpoints of each half of the coils. A 1 kilohertz excitation voltage is applied across the coils from the amplifier, and because of the symmetry of the coil-magnet arrangement, the resultant average signal between the center tap and ground is zero when the actual heading and the selected heading are the same. This is because the net flux flowing through the Permalloy core of each half of the coil is zero.

When the coil is rotated relative to the magnets, the net magnetic flux flowing in the core of each half of the coil changes, making the net flux flowing in the core of one half of the coil positive and in the other half negative. This is comparable to raising the dc level of excitation of one half of the coil and lowering the dc excitation of the other half. Thus the average signal level of the center tap relative to ground will be greater than or less than (minus) zero, and an error signal will exist.

The ac heading error signal from the center tapped coil of the compass controller assembly is applied to a potentiometer which has been factory adjusted for the proper rudder ratio setting for the craft it is to be used in. This heading error signal is then stepped up by a transformer, peak demodulated by diodes, and filtered by resistors and capacitors so it is a dc output. Thus if the average heading error signal from the center tapped coil is zero, the output of the demodulator is zero.

A 30 volt potential is applied as excitation across the rudder feedback potentiometer. When the potentiometer wiper is in the middle of its movable range, corresponding to rudder amidships, there is no voltage between it and ground. However, when the rudder is moved off center, the potentiometer wiper is also moved from its center position, and a voltage appears between the wiper and ground. The polarity of the voltage is determined by the direction of movement from the center position.

The dc heading error signal from the demodulator is series added to the dc signal from the rudder feedback potentiometer and then applied to the operational amplifier. The proportion of the rudder feedback signal that is summed with the heading error signal is adjusted by the rudder control on the control amplifier panel. This control is adjusted for the desired amount of rudder displacement for a given heading error. Diodes are used to limit the magnitude of the input signal to the operational amplifier.

The output of the operational amplifier is applied to the weather control on the control amplifier front panel, and this is adjusted for the desired sensitivity of the system, that is, the amount of heading error tolerated before rudder is applied. From this control potentiometer, the signal is applied to the demodulator amplifier. When its output is positive, a transistor will conduct, energizing a reed relay which energizes a switching relay which, in turn, energizes the motor armature (or control solenoid of the hydraulic system, if used). If the signal from the operational amplifier is negative, another transistor conducts so that the relays are energized, and the armature (or other solenoid) is energized. For left rudder the output of the operational amplifier will be positive; for right rudder, the output will be negative. The magnitude of the operational amplifier output ranges from 0 to plus or minus 10 volts.

8T Autopilot Steering

When the selected heading is the same as the vessel's actual heading, the heading error signal from the demodulator is zero. If the rudder is amidships there will be no signal from the rudder feedback potentiometer. Thus there will be no output from the operation amplifier; neither of the switching circuits will be energized; and the rudder will not move from the amidships position.

When the selected heading is different from the vessel's actual heading, there will be a heading error signal from the demodulator. If the rudder is amidships, there will be no signal from the rudder feedback potentiometer. The resultant output from the operational amplifier will energize one of the switching circuits, and the rudder will move until the signal from the rudder feedback potentiometer cancels the heading error signal from the demodulator.

The rudder is then displaced from the amidships position by an amount corresponding to the amplitude of the feedback signal necessary to cancel the heading error signal from the demodulator. As the vessel begins to turn toward the selected heading, the difference between the selected heading and the actual heading becomes less. Therefore the amplitude of the heading error signal becomes smaller. When the decreasing heading error signal is summed with the feedback signal, the net result applied to the operational amplifier is no longer zero, but of a polarity that causes the rudder to return toward the amidships position. When the actual heading is the same as the selected heading, the rudder will have returned to its original amidships position.

Although we have not discussed its use, there is an optional rate filter network available for use with the control amplifier. This network causes the feedback signal to be applied longer than the command input signal so the rudder will overshoot its desired position before settling in. What the rate network does, really, is to anticipate the amount of steering required to keep course variations from becomming too large. It also improves the course-keeping performance on some vessels.

8T Autopilot Remote Control Operation

When the 8T Autopilot is operated in the remote steering mode, the compass heading error signal is not used. The 30 volt potential is applied across both the rudder feedback and the remote controller potentiometers. When each potentiometer wiper is in the middle of its movable range, the signal between each wiper arm and ground is zero. During the remote control mode of operation, dc signals from a remote controller and feedback potentiometers are summed by resistors and amplified by an operational amplifier. The weather control and the rudder control are bypassed for this mode of operation, but the switching circuits function just as they do during the automatic mode.

When the rudder is amidships, there is no signal from the feedback potentiometer. If the remote controller is positioned to zero, there is no signal from the controller, there is no input to the operational amplifier, and the rudder does not move from its amidships position. If the remote controller is positioned for right rudder, a signal will be applied to the operational amplifier, and as the rudder moves, a signal of increasing amplitude (having the opposite polarity of the signal from the remote controller) is generated by the feedback pot. The rudder will continue to move until the amplitude of the feedback signal cancels the remote controller signal. When this occurs, the rudder will stop moving and remain stationary until the remote controller is repositioned manually.

8T Electric Steering (Mechanical Helms).

The electric steering engine shown in Fig. 6-10, used with 12-, 24- or 32-volt dc supplies, is coupled to the existing steering wheel by a chain and sprocket, Fig. 6-11. When the power switch on the control amplifier front panel is positioned to on, a relay in the relay panel is energized, which energizes the electric clutch and the field coil of the motor.

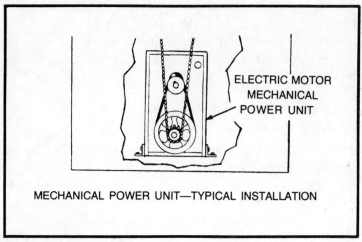

ELECTRIC MOTOR
MECHANICAL
POWER UNIT

MECHANICAL POWER UNIT—TYPICAL INSTALLATION

Fig. 6-11. Mechanical electric steering engine installation. Uses an electric motor.

The electric clutch couples the motor armature with the shaft of the electric steering engine so that motions of the armature will be transferred to the vessel's steering system. When the clutch is de-energized, the motor armature is no longer mechanically connected to the wheel and the steering system functions manually.

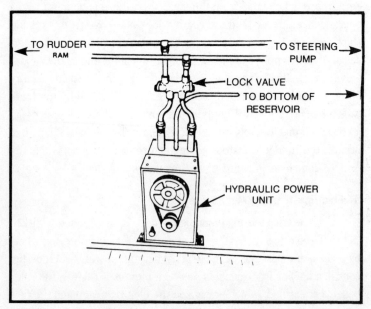

TO RUDDER
RAM

TO STEERING
PUMP

LOCK VALVE
TO BOTTOM OF
RESERVOIR

HYDRAULIC POWER
UNIT

Fig. 6-12. Hydraulic installation.

8T Hydraulic Steering

Hydraulic rudder positioning equipment, Fig. 6-12, is controlled either by thyristors (ac systems) or by switching transistors (dc systems). When the power switch on the control amplifier is positioned to on, a bypass valve is energized. This blocks the flow of oil from one side of the hydraulic cylinder to the other side through hydraulic lines and prohibits manual steering. The bypass valve, when de-energized, permits the flow of oil from one side of the cylinder to the other so the vessel can be steered manually.

When a thyristor or switching transistor conducts, one of the solenoids of the control valve, Fig. 6-13, is energized, thus directing oil flow from the pump to the proper side of the hydraulic cylinder. When the power switch is positioned to off, or when rudder position is not being changed, oil flowing from the pump is directed back to the sump through the control valve.

When the Sperry 8T Autopilot is operational, a bypass valve prevents free movement of the power output piston. Then, signals from the control amplifier energize one of the control valve solenoids

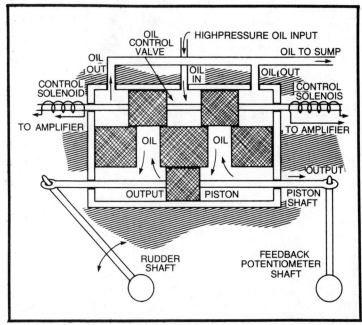

Fig. 6-13. Hydraulic control valve. The oil transfer valve is electrically operated.

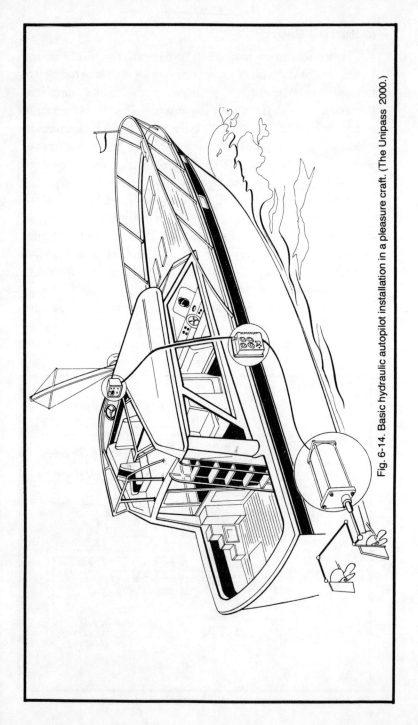

Fig. 6-14. Basic hydraulic autopilot installation in a pleasure craft. (The Unipass 2000.)

causing oil from the pump to flow into one side of the power output cylinder. The cylinder piston moves to force oil out of the other side of the cylinder, back through the control valve and into the sump.

The piston and a separate rudder feedback are connected to the rudder by a mechanical link. As the rudder is moved by the piston, the wiper arm of the feedback potentiometer also moves, thus applying dc voltage to the control amplifier for feedback purposes. Figure 6-14 shows a very basic hydraulic installation in a pleasure craft fishing boat.

THE SPACE AGE ELECTRONICS COMMAND PILOT

The primary elements of this basic system, less the steering motor, are shown in Fig. 6-15. To the left is the sensor and its base, and beside it is the command panel. Notice that trim can be set into the autopilot system. This is to correct anything which might cause the rudder to assume other than its neutral position when you want it to be neutral, or you may have to have the rudder offset somewhat so that the boat goes exactly straight away.

The sensor for this system is called an Electronic Polar Locking Unit. This means the bearing can be set with respect to the North Pole; thus, it has compass characteristics. This unit sends a signal to the translator (amplifier) unit porportional to the heading error.

The rudder angle transmitter (synchro type) also sends rudder angle information to the translator unit, and when the translator has

Fig. 6-15. Sensor and control panel of Space Age Electronics. Command Pilot model autopilot.

211

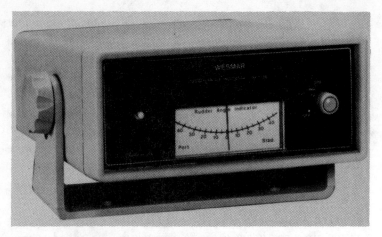

Fig. 6-16. Rudder angle indicator. (Courtesy Wesmar.)

both messages, it compares them in a proportional manner to come up with a proper electrical correction signal for an electric motor which moves the rudder. This electric motor is linked to the rudder shaft by either a chain or by a cable drive.

This autopilot makes no attempt to correct short duration errors. These may well be cancelled by the next wave or natural movement of a boat at sea. But should the heading error persist for a few seconds, *then* the autopilot will apply appropriate rudder angle correction. This damping or delay, in response, will make for a smoother ride and cause less power to be consumed in the actual steering of the ship.

THE WESMAR R1200 RUDDER ANGLE INDICATOR

The rudder angle indicator (Fig. 6-16) can be of use when docking or when using an autopilot system so you will know the system is working correctly and not over-controlling the rudder, causing burned out motors or excessive wear on moving parts. The rudder is the output of the autopilot system and we want to know at all times what the output is doing.

Installation

The rudder transducer produces the electrical signal indicative of the rudder position (Fig. 6-17). Its output may be fed only to the rudder indicator or it may be fed to this *and* to the autopilot system.

In the autopilot the signal gives rudder position feedback information.

Installation of the Wesmar rudder angle indicator involves location, wiring, and calibration. The rudder angle indicator should be located where it can be viewed from the pilothouse. Avoid areas where the temperature is likely to exceed 120° F. The front panel is splash resistant, not waterproof. So locate the indicator where it won't be exposed to direct wetting such as from rain or from sprayed water during boat washings. It can be mounted on a bulkhead, countertop, wall, or overhead, for example.

Calibration

Next you must calibrate the angle indicator. Remove the console's two front panel screws and the six rear panel screws. Remove the front panel and circuit board partially from the enclosure, exposing two adjustment pots. Turn the vessel's wheel until the rudder is

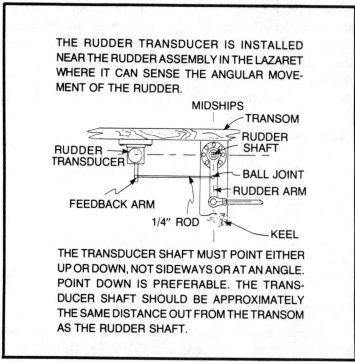

THE RUDDER TRANSDUCER IS INSTALLED NEAR THE RUDDER ASSEMBLY IN THE LAZARET WHERE IT CAN SENSE THE ANGULAR MOVEMENT OF THE RUDDER.

MIDSHIPS
TRANSOM
RUDDER SHAFT
RUDDER TRANSDUCER
BALL JOINT
RUDDER ARM
FEEDBACK ARM
1/4" ROD
KEEL

THE TRANSDUCER SHAFT MUST POINT EITHER UP OR DOWN, NOT SIDEWAYS OR AT AN ANGLE. POINT DOWN IS PREFERABLE. THE TRANSDUCER SHAFT SHOULD BE APPROXIMATELY THE SAME DISTANCE OUT FROM THE TRANSOM AS THE RUDDER SHAFT.

Fig. 6-17. Rudder angle transducer installation.

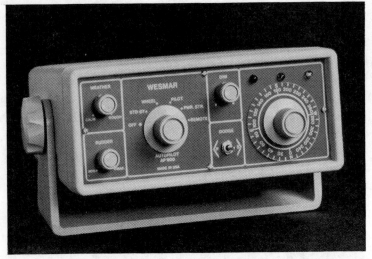

Fig. 6-18. Wesmar control panel and amplifier AP 900 autopilot.

amidships. At this point turn the AP 900 function switch to the wheel mode. Turn the power on. With the rudder amidships, adjust the zero pot for a 0 meter reading. Turn the wheel starboard until the rudder is at a 35 degree angle in the water. At this point make sure the meter needle swings in the right direction. If the meter reads in the port direction, simply switch the two wires coming from the circuit board up to the meter terminals. Be sure the unit is turned off when making this change. With the needle swinging in the right direction, adjust the gain pot so that 35 degrees is indicated on the meter scale. This completes the installation and calibration of the indicator. Replace and secure the front panel and circuit board in the enclosure.

The green light indicates that the unit is on and receiving power.

If using a second indicator as a remote station, it is installed and wired in the same manner as the first unit. A remote indicator is calibrated as was the first.

THE WESMAR AP 900 AUTOPILOT

An examination of the unit shown in Fig. 6-18 will provide still more knowledge about this equipment for your boat. Also, the more you become familiar with various systems the better able you will be to understand their capabilities and limitations, maintenance and installation advantages and disadvantages, and special requirements, as applied to your own boat.

The system is compatible with any type of steering system and can be installed on nearly any size vessel. It has many unique features valuable to commercial fishermen and workboat captains. Among them is a steer-by-lights mode which allows programming a course while steering manually. A dodge control allows you to easily avoid obstructions in the water without having to reset the main course bearing. The optional remote hand control, Fig. 6-19, is a miniconsole that gives you total control of your autopilot from any location aboard your boat. Figure 6-20 shows the ease of control

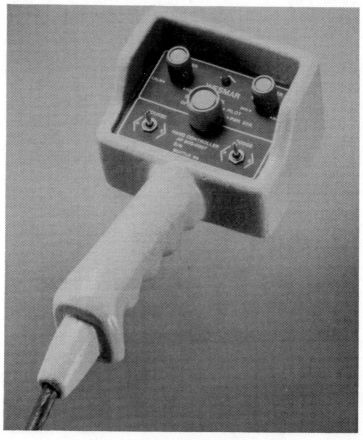

Fig. 6-19. Wesmar's AP 900 remote control unit.

possible during fishing maneuvers or other work operations. This can result in greater efficiency and increased catches for fishermen. On long runs a good autopilot will save both fuel and valuable time by keeping you on course in any sea condition.

The Saturable Core Magnetic Compass

The saturable core compass shown in Fig. 6-21 weighs only 16 ounces, yet replaces the sluggish mechanical floating disc compass used in earlier autopilots. Sensing the earth's magnetic field electronically, it uses no moving parts as do conventional compasses. Thus course change response is instant, giving immediate feedback to the autopilot. This instant feedback into the AP 900's solid-state computer-type logic system permits precise control of the vessel. The compass is permanently housed in a waterproof enclosure and

Fig. 6-20. Using the remote control unit for the AP 900. (Courtesy Wesmar.)

can be installed up to 250 feet from the AP 900 autopilot operations console. Recent field tests with the system have shown that it performs exceedingly well in any sea condition. The solid-state compass will compensate for full 80 degree pitch and roll.

Control Settings

Refer to Fig. 6-18, which shows the autopilot control panel. We will examine what the various dials and switches are used for and, in doing so, will learn about the types of controls common to most autopilots.

OFF. In this setting the autopilot is nonfunctional and dc power is off.

STD-BY. This mode automatically adjusts the course set dial on the right of the panel to the course being manually steered. In this position the WEATHER control has no effect, as the exact course will be automatically set in. In the STD-BY mode the autopilot is standing by to take over the steering of your vessel. As you steer onto a new course, the autopilot is automatically rotating the course set dial to this new course. When you are on course a yellow function light will be lit. With WEATHER and RUDDER set to the approximate desired settings, simply switch to the PILOT mode and the autopilot will take over the steering function.

WHEEL. In this position the dc power is on. The course sensing circuits are the only active circuits. All other drive and feedback circuits are inactive. This position is used by the technician to calibrate the system; however, to the operator this position offers a mode for steering the vessel by lights on the panel.

To use this mode the operator sets the course set dial to the course to be steered. Once this is set and the WEATHER control is set (as explained under weather), the yellow function light should light up. If the vessel falls off to port the green function light will come on, and the yellow function light will go off. The operator must then steer the vessel to starboard by applying starboard rudder as discussed under weather. The WEATHER control will set the area of width of on-course control. If the vessel veers to starboard, the red light will come on and you must apply port rudder.

PILOT. While in the PILOT mode, all sensing and control circuits are activated, and the autopilot is steering the vessel on the course set-in by the course set dial (see STD-BY). In this mode of operation, the helmsman or operator can change course by changing the dial setting. The vessel may also be dodged to the port or starboard by simply pressing the DODGE switch to port or starboard. Rudder will then be applied as long as the DODGE switch is activated, or until a limit switch stops the rudder movement. When the DODGE switch is released, the rudder returns to neutral and the boat picks up its original course under autopilot steering.

PWR-STR. In this mode of operation the autopilot will hold the rudder at any position desired. This is essentially an electric steering mode with changes in course and rudder angle being made by pushing the DODGE switch.

REMOTE. The remote mode position transfers console control to any remote station. Thus all control is transferred to the remote hand control when it is plugged in. Examine Fig. 6-20 again.

WEATHER. The WEATHER control is used during varying sea conditions to set the yaw, or null, area for the course steered. Examine Fig. 6-18 and note that when the WEATHER control is rotated to minimum, it is set for CALM seas. In this position, the width of the null, or no steering area, is approximately plus or minus 1-1/2 degrees. With the control rotated to ROUGH, the null area is about 15 degrees, plus or minus. In good weather, the control should be rotated towards CALM but not to a hunting condition. In rough seas the WEATHER setting is turned clockwise to open the course width, or null area. In this condition the course made good will be an average of the vessel's movement. The WEATHER control should be set so that the yellow function light (over the course set dial) will be lit through normal oscillation of the bow. In other words, the red and green function lights will blink occasionally. The proper setting of the WEATHER control in heavy weather is as far clockwise, or as much rudder, as possible without causing the vessel to yaw.

RUDDER. The RUDDER control establishes their angular displacement. This is an important control function which keeps the vessel from yawing. Should the rudder be small and nonresponsive, should the vessel have an apparent dead rudder, or should the boat be in a following sea or perhaps just moving slowly, rotating this control clockwise provides more rudder for a fixed off-course deviation. Always turn the RUDDER control clockwise until the vessel yaws, then rotate the control counterclockwise a small amount until the yawing stops.

DODGE. The DODGE switch is activated when the mode switch is set on PILOT or PWR STR, and can be used to steer around objects or for continuous electric steering. When in the pilot mode, and the switch is pressed either port or starboard, the rudder will be applied until it is released or a limit switch is activated. Once released in the pilot mode, the vessel will return to the original course. When the DODGE switch is pressed in the PWR STR mode, rudder is again applied, but when the switch is released, the vessel will not be returned to the original course. This is useful because it allows you to electrically steer your craft for docking, circling a school of fish, or perhaps picking up crab pots.

COURSE SET DIAL. The course set dial, on the right in Fig. 6-18, will automatically set in a heading when in the STD-BY mode. In other modes, the operator must dial the desired course. The heading is controlled by the saturable core compass which is shown in Fig. 6-21.

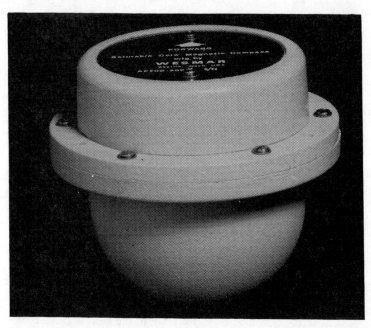

Fig. 6-21. Saturable core compass. (Courtesy Wesmar.)

DIM. The DIM control is used to vary the intensity of function lights and back lighting.

LIGHTS. The function lights are provided to show how the autopilot is functioning as well as to aid in setting the WEATHER and RUDDER controls. An additional benefit is that they can be used to steer the vessel. The red light indicates you are off-course starboard, the yellow light indicates the correct heading, and the green light indicates off-course to port. These are the controls on the main panel and they are easy to use and understand. Other autopilots have similar type controls, and they should be as inclusive as these.

Functional Description

Next we want to examine Fig. 6-22, which shows the basic components of the system in a block diagram form. In this figure we see how the various components form the system.

In Fig. 6-23, for the benefit of many like myself who appreciate the design diagrams, is shown the technical approach. The numerical values applied to the various elements would be derived from elements being considered. As we had pointed out previously, a diagram such as this is very useful to determine beforehand that the system will work. The computer solution to the design equations depicts operation of the system before it is built and helps the designer eliminate any problem areas.

In Fig. 6-24 we begin to examine general placement of system components, and we now want to consider other important requirements.

Installation Requirements

Locate the console within convenient reach of the wheel and steering compass. Avoid installing the console in areas that are very damp, poorly ventilated, or hot, where temperatures rise above 120° F. The console can be mounted on a bulkhead, overhead, or on a panel top. The trunnion mount provided must be securely fastened to the selected location. If you are planning to install a remote rudder angle indicator or a remote digital compass close to the console, be sure to leave room for this additional equipment.

Route the power and control cable to the amplifier, interconnecting matrix, or junction box, by using the shortest and most

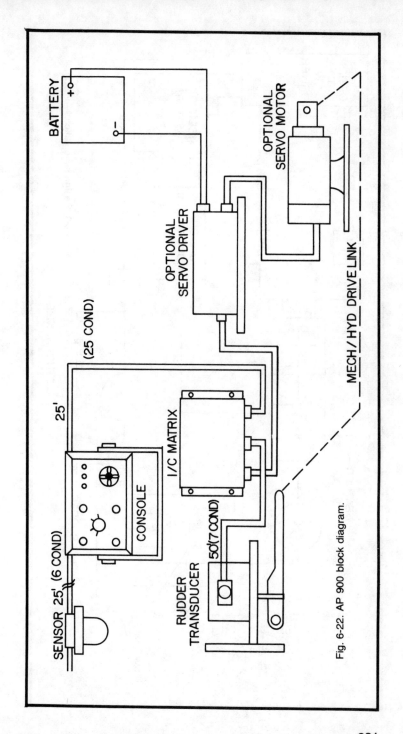

BATTERY

OPTIONAL SERVO MOTOR

OPTIONAL SERVO DRIVER

MECH / HYD DRIVE LINK

(25 COND)

25'

I/C MATRIX

CONSOLE

SENSOR 25' (6 COND)

RUDDER TRANSDUCER

50'(7 COND)

Fig. 6-22. AP 900 block diagram.

221

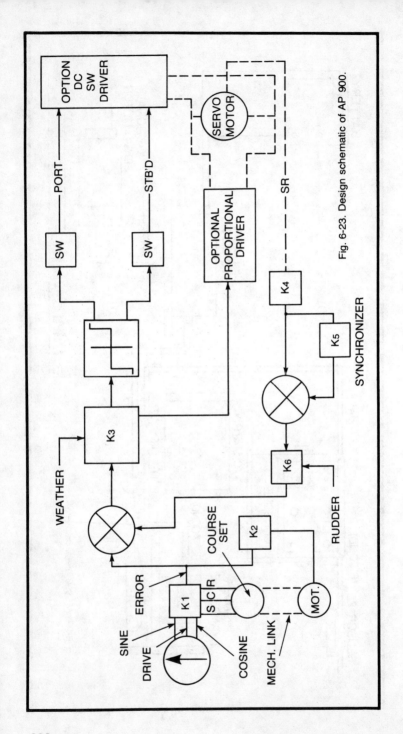

Fig. 6-23. Design schematic of AP 900.

222

direct route. Keep the cable as far as possible from other power cables, electronic equipment, unshielded antenna and signal cables. Fasten down the cable so it cannot sway or be pulled on. Leave a slight bit of slack so that normal tensions and compressions won't break fittings.

The amplifier, or matrix, depending on system used, probably is the junction box for the system. It should be located close to the console (which usually contains the amplifier), say within 20 feet. It should be accessible. The engine room may be a good location for this. Attach the junction box, or matrix, to the bulkhead firmly and securely.

Here are some general wiring rules—of course, manufacturers will usually supply wiring instructions with their own equipment, but here are some guidelines most often recommended. Remember that the marine environment is always very harsh on wiring and electrical connections, so follow these procedures:

- Always determine the correct length of wiring needed and cut to that length. Do not coil or leave slack unnecessarily.
- Strip off the end of wires to be connected 1/4 inch from the end of the wire.
- Use a spade lug for the 18-22 size wire to fit a 4-6 size stud.
- Crimp and solder the wire onto the lug.
- Attach wire to matrix as directed or so that it is firm and mechanically secure.
- Make certain that plug connections are tight and firm and have no strain on cables.

INSTALLATION OF THE RUDDER TRANSDUCER

The rudder feedback transducer is always installed near the rudder to detect the angular movement of the rudder. It must be mounted securely in position. The transducer shaft must point either up or down, parallel to the rudder shaft, and never be mounted so it points sideways or at any angle. It is preferable to have it pointing downward. The transducer shaft should be approximately the same distance out from the transom as the rudder shaft, and the same height from the hull as is the quadrant, or rudder arm. Once the transducer is securely mounted, connect the rudder transducer

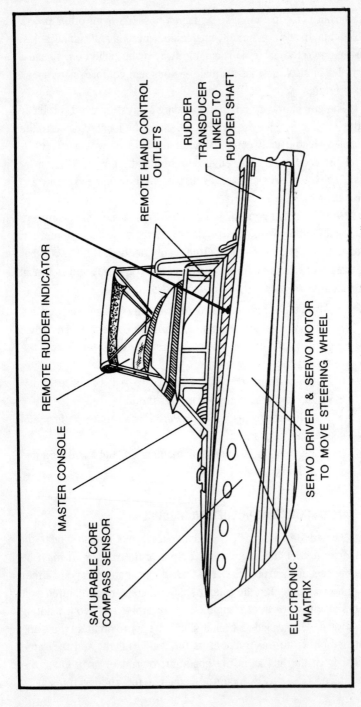

REMOTE RUDDER INDICATOR

REMOTE HAND CONTROL OUTLETS

RUDDER TRANSDUCER LINKED TO RUDDER SHAFT

MASTER CONSOLE

SATURABLE CORE COMPASS SENSOR

SERVO DRIVER & SERVO MOTOR TO MOVE STEERING WHEEL

ELECTRONIC MATRIX

Fig. 6-24. General installation locations for an autopilot.

feedback arm to the transducer shaft. Then connect it carefully to the quadrant (rudder) arm as shown in Fig. 6-25.

At this point you must determine exactly where is the amidships rudder position. Amidships is not necessary having the rudder parallel with the keel line; it is the rudder position steering the vessel straight ahead. Once you are sure of amidships rudder, tighten ball joints down on steel rod so that the quadrant or rudder arm and the transducer arm are parallel.

When done, the rudder feedback arm must follow the movement of the rudder quadrant smoothly and easily without binding.

INSTALLATION OF THE SATURABLE CORE COMPASS

So that the AP 900 compass will be free from any magnetic interference, locate it at least 4 feet from any other electronic equipment or strong magnetic fields. Any large dc conductors within 3 feet of the compass must be paired (+ and − wires twisted together).

Possible compass locations include lockers, cupboards, and bulkheads. On steel vessels it may be necessary to install the compass on the mast to overcome strong magnetic interference. If

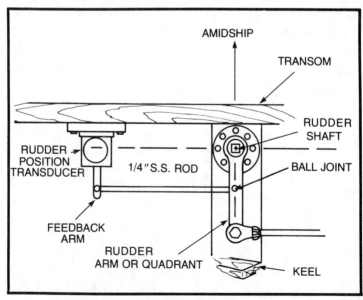

Fig. 6-25. Autopilot feedback transducer installation.

possible, the compass should be on the keel line and in the center of vessel movement. The location should be relatively free from vibration as with conventional compasses.

Secure the compass mounting bracket with 4 brass (preferably chrome plated brass) screws or bolts.

The mounting bracket does not have to line up with the vessel's keel line; however, the arrow on the compass must be aligned with the keel line of the vessel. When you are sure the arrow lines up with the keel line, secure the compass in its mounting bracket using the brass screws. Connect the compass cable into the back of the console. Route the cable to the compass. Keep the cable as far as possible from power cables, other electronic equipment, and unshielded antenna and signal cables.

INSTALLATION OF SERVO DRIVER AND MOTOR

All autopilot systems require a servo driver and motor to convert the electronic logic information into mechanical action. The servo driver takes the small electronic signal from the console and amplifies it to sufficient power to drive the servo motor clockwise or counterclockwise. The servo motor receives this amplified electrical signal and converts it into mechanical or hydraulic torque to move the rudder port to starboard.

Locate the servo driver and servo motor (mechanical or hydraulic) within 3 feet of each other. Mount the driver (a bulkhead is often a good position) and secure with screws or bolts. The driver is connected with cable to your dc power source (usually your battery).

Table 6-1. Cable Gauge vs. Length and Voltage.

Length (Feet)	Supply Voltage 12V 24V 32V			Length (Feet)	Supply Volts 12V 24V 32V		
2	14	14	14	18	12	10	6
4	14	14	14	20	10	10	6
6	14	14	14	22	10	8	6
8	14	14	10	24	10	8	6
10	14	12	10	30	8	6	4
12	14	10	8	40	8	6	4
14	12	10	8	50	8	6	2

The distance between the driver and power source determines the size of cable needed. Use Table 6-1 to determine cable size.

Mechanical Servo Motors

See Fig. 6-26 for basic ideas concerning where and how the mechanical servo motor can be installed. The most common location places the servo motor drive sprocket in line with a sprocket mounted on the steering wheel shaft. It should be accessible for maintenance. Servo motor assemblies are weather resistant, not waterproof, so locate them where they won't be splashed on or submerged.

Servo motors usually have a mounting bracket so they can be mounted on the side or end on the deck, overhead, or even in a corner. A shelf or bracket, if the servo motor is to be mounted on one, must be of sufficient strength so as not to flex under full load torques.

Unless already present, a sprocket must be installed on the pilot wheel shaft. Table 6-2 is a general guideline for selecting the correct size sprocket.

Speed of rudder movement is determined by the size of the sprocket at the pilot wheel. For proper autopilot operation, rudder speed should be between 8 and 20 seconds hard-over to hard-over (about 15 seconds is best). For a large hard-to-steer vessel, slower rudder speeds can be obtained by installing a larger sprocket at the pilot wheel, thus increasing the delivered torque but decreasing pilot performance.

It is advisable that the required torque be determined. To do this, tie one end of a cord to a spoke on the pilot wheel, the other end to a hanging type fish scale. Pull the free end of the fish scale at a right angle from the point of attachment to the wheel. When the wheel just starts to move, read the indicated load. Repeat this procedure four times to determine the average load. Multiply the average load (in pounds) by the distance (in inches) between the center of the wheel and the point where the cord is attached to obtain the torque (in inch pounds) required to steer the vessel. Then multiply this by a factor of 3 to obtain an approximate figure for steering under the worst conditions. If this figure exceeds 200 inch-pounds (torque delivered by average servo motor), install a larger

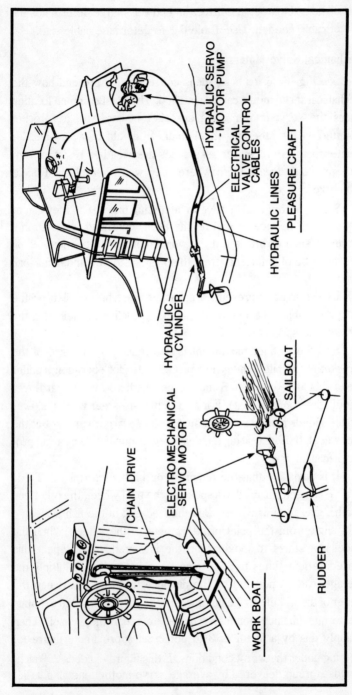

HYDRAULIC SERVO
- MOTOR PUMP

ELECTRICAL
VALVE CONTROL
CABLES

HYDRAULIC LINES

PLEASURE CRAFT

HYDRAULIC
CYLINDER

CHAIN DRIVE

ELECTRO MECHANICAL
SERVO MOTOR

WORK BOAT

SAILBOAT

RUDDER

Fig. 6-26. Servo motor installation ideas.

Table 6-2. Sprocket Wheel Size vs. Steering Wheel Turns.

Steering Wheel Turns Hard-over to Hard-over	2	2 1/2	3	3 1/2	4	4 1/2	5	5 1/2	6	7
Steering Wheel Sprocket Size: No. 41	35 teeth	32 teeth	29 teeth	26 teeth	24 teeth	22 teeth	20 teeth	18 teeth	16 teeth	5 teeth

sprocket which will deliver the required torque. Should your vessel require over 1000 inch-pounds torque, get a higher torque servo motor assembly.

The AP 900 servo motor output speed is 22 rpm. There need not be any relative ratio between sprocket size and boat speed as this function is controlled by the rudder control on the master control console.

Once the servo motor position is determined and the servo motor sprocket and pilot wheel sprockets are aligned, secure the servo motor. Connect the two sprockets with roller chain. Be sure each sprocket is secured by a setscrew and a keyway. Enough slack should exist in the chain to prevent possible binding but excessive slack will decrease autopilot control and cause defective steering.

After the unit is mechanically secured, attach the interconnecting cable from the servo drive assembly to the terminals on the servo motor assembly. With most installations, do not lengthen these wires. Connect the power cable from the driver to your dc power source.

Hydraulic Servo Motors

The hydraulic servo steering assembly (driver and motor) is normally located in the engine compartment, near the hydraulic lines which connect the cylinder to the rudder. In the hydraulic system all the air must be bled from the system if the autopilot is to perform properly. Air which is left in the system will cause the rudder to move after the autopilot has stopped applying corrective rudder. As this compressed air moves the rudder, a yawing situation will occur, which cannot be corrected by adjusting the rudder control at the master console. If you have this kind of yawing problem, check your system for air in the lines.

So, with the above in mind and the location of the servo motor assembly determined, drain the steering system sufficiently so that minimum fluid is lost when cutting the lines to install the autopilot

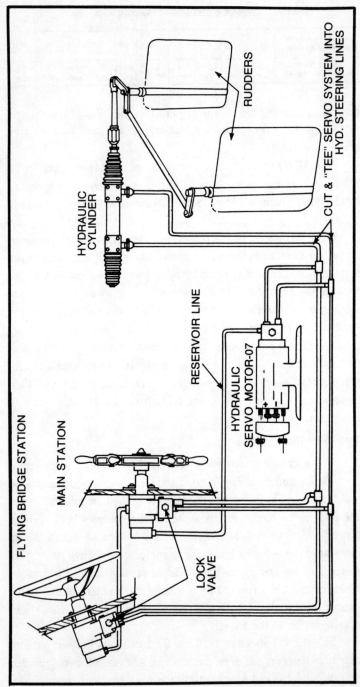

FLYING BRIDGE STATION

MAIN STATION

LOCK VALVE

RESERVOIR LINE

HYDRAULIC SERVO MOTOR-07

HYDRAULIC CYLINDER

RUDDERS

CUT & "TEE" SERVO SYSTEM INTO HYD. STEERING LINES

Fig. 6-27. Typical boat hydraulic system without autopilot. Note where cuts are made for tee installations.

system into your present power steering system. To connect the hydraulic servo motor into your steering system (see Fig. 6-31) you must cut and modify the existing hydraulic lines. Be sure to cut the lines with a standard wheel-type tube cutter. Do not cut these lines with a hacksaw. A hacksaw produces small filings and chips which are impossible to remove from the lines, and these chips and filings will damage the steering system.

In the installation you will use standard tube fittings of the flare-type, not the compression type. Insert the tees into the lines at the points indicated and connect to the output ports of the servo motor. It does not matter which lines connect to which ports as the motor rotation can be reversed. Be sure that all pipe threads and connections are sealed with a good sealing compound. Make sure the servo motor pump bleed line is connected to the bottom of the system reservoir.

The desired hard-over-to-hard-over rudder time is about 10 seconds, but it may be longer or shorter than this, from 5 to 20 seconds, and still be okay.

Once the unit has been installed and fitted, loosen one of the hose connections at the cylinder and turn the wheel hard over until it is difficult to turn, building up pressure to force all the air out of the lines. Once the air bubbles stop flowing, tighten the hose connection. Repeat this process in the opposite direction. Continue the process over and over until no air bubbles escape. Then you know your lines are air free. Be sure, of course, to keep the reservoir full at all times; check this often.

INSTALLATION OF THE SOLENOID VALVE

A solenoid valve assembly, consisting of a driver and valve as shown in Fig. 6-28, is used on vessels which already have an engine driven power steering system. This solenoid assembly controls the vessel's power steering system.

If, in the case of an engine driven hydraulic system, a solenoid valve isn't already installed, it should be installed "in series" between the hydraulic pump and the steering helm unit. This is done by cutting the lines and connecting as shown in Fig. 6-28. You connect the pressure line from the pump to the P port on the valve. Connect the T port on the valve to the helm steering unit. Connect the A port

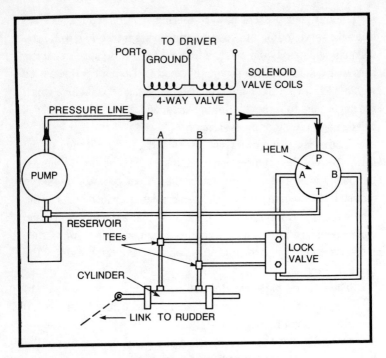

Fig. 6-28. Solenoid valve assembly.

on the valve to one steering line going to the rudder cylinder. Connect the B port to the other line going to the cylinder. Use *only* high pressure, double wire braid hoses with machine fittings attached. Of course you then have to bleed the air from the system as described earlier.

After the solenoid driver and valve are mechanically secured and hoses connected, attach a connecting cable from the driver to the solenoid valve and connect the power cable to the dc (it may be an ac) power source, depending upon the kind of system you are installing.

CALIBRATION OF AN AUTOPILOT

Once installation is complete an autopilot must be checked and calibrated. This is normally done by qualified technicians who will follow the factory instructions in checking the electrical outputs of the amplifiers and other parts of the system. Actually, of course, these technicians will probably make the autopilot installation in your boat unless it is a small craft in which case much can be done by you personally. In some systems the technical checkout and calibration is very simple, so shop around for the size and type autopilot you need. When buying, you should seek the dealer's advice. Explain the size craft you have and how you use it.

DOCKSIDE CHECKOUT OF THE AP 900

With this system, which we are using for an example, the following dockside procedure should be completed before you cast off. The procedure can well apply to any autopilot system. After you have started the engines and you allow time for them to warm up, do the following (Fig. 6-18):

1. Turn the mode switch to STD-BY. One of the function lights should be lit. The course set dial should rotate until a null or yellow light condition is attained.
2. Set WEATHER to approximately 8 o'clock.
3. Set RUDDER to approximately 8 o'clock.
4. Turn mode switch to PWR STR, press DODGE switch and observe if the rudder is moving. Using the DODGE switch, return the rudder to 0 or amidships.
5. Turn mode switch to PILOT. PILOT may apply rudder automatically until a null condition is achieved. Now rotate the course set dial and note that the autopilot applies the correct rudder.
6. Switch the mode switch back to STD-BY.

This completes the dockside test of the autopilot. The system is now in standby and you can cast off. After you have manually steered the vessel out of port and wish to have the autopilot take over, simply switch the dial to the PILOT mode, adjust the WEATHER and the RUDDER controls for the speed of the vessel and the current sea conditions, and then settle back and enjoy your cruise. The use of the WEATHER and RUDDER controls is illustrated in Fig. 6-29.

PREVENTATIVE MAINTENANCE OF AN AUTOPILOT

The preventative maintenance of any system is important. For the autopilot it should be performed at least every six months. Some points to check are:

- Check all plug and socket connections making sure they are clean and tight.
- Check all terminal wiring connections in all junction boxes, making sure they are secure.
- On electro-mechanical systems which use a wheel chain type drive, check that the drive chain is sufficiently tight and oiled.
- On hydraulic steering systems make sure that all hydraulic connections are tight and not leaking. Also check all fluid levels.
- Check the rudder transducer seals, making sure that no condensation has accumulated inside the rudder transducer.
- Check the rudder linkage to rudder arm, making sure that all ball joints are tight and greased.
- Check remote hand control bulkhead connectors, making sure no pins are bent or corroded or that the cable is frayed, cracked or split.
- Check all remote accessories for secure wiring and their proper operation.
- Check master console for moisture condensation and firm mounting. Make sure that all cabinet seals are tight. Check all internal and external connections.
- Check the electronic compass, making sure that the mounting screws are tight so compass cannot vibrate or turn.
- Check all cables and connections.
- Remove the top cover on the compass. Check to see that screws are tight on each connecting lug and that no corrosion is present.
- Perform the dockside checkout as previously explained, and, if possible, make a short run with the craft under autopilot control to check its accuracy and overall operation.

AUTOPILOT PROBLEMS AND SOLUTIONS

In Table 6-3 are listed some of the troubles common to autopilots. Your system may differ somewhat in physical appearance or in the method of control setting, but it will, in general, have the same characteristics as any other system. Thus these procedures can be applied to your system with a little thought as to what is being

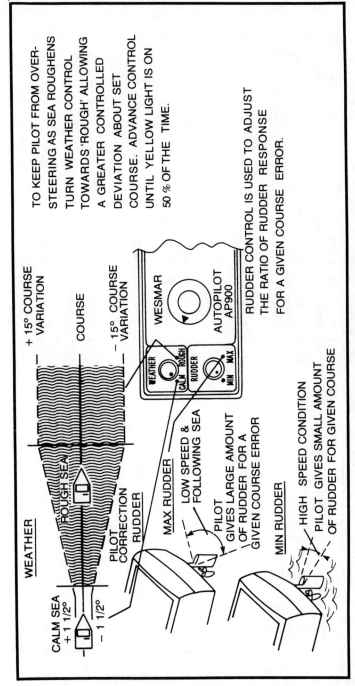

TO KEEP PILOT FROM OVER-STEERING AS SEA ROUGHENS TURN WEATHER CONTROL TOWARDS 'ROUGH' ALLOWING A GREATER CONTROLLED DEVIATION ABOUT SET COURSE. ADVANCE CONTROL UNTIL YELLOW LIGHT IS ON 50 % OF THE TIME.

+ 15° COURSE VARIATION

COURSE

– 15° COURSE VARIATION

WESMAR

AUTOPILOT AP900

RUDDER CONTROL IS USED TO ADJUST THE RATIO OF RUDDER RESPONSE FOR A GIVEN COURSE ERROR.

WEATHER

ROUGH SEA

WEATHER   CALM ROUGH   RUDDER   MIN MAX

CALM SEA
+ 1 1/2°
– 1 1/2°

PILOT CORRECTION RUDDER

MAX RUDDER

LOW SPEED & FOLLOWING SEA

PILOT GIVES LARGE AMOUNT OF RUDDER FOR A GIVEN COURSE ERROR

MIN RUDDER

HIGH SPEED CONDITION PILOT GIVES SMALL AMOUNT OF RUDDER FOR GIVEN COURSE

Fig. 6-29. Weather and rudder control adjustments. (Courtesy Wesmar.)

Table 6-3. Autopilot Troubles, Causes and Solutions.

Symptom	Area of Malfunction	Probable Cause	Corrective Action
Course set dial will not automatically null to course heading in STD BY.	Resolver drive motor not turning.	No drive signal to motor. Check for approximately 6 volts across motor with red light on in STD BY.	If voltage is present defective motor, replace. If voltage is not present, replace amplifier.
	Resolver drive motor turning. Reducer not turning.	Broken drive belt.	Replace.
		Reduce binding on panel.	Loosen mounting bracket & realign.
		Dial rubbing on panel.	Move forward.
		Course set knob binding on dial.	Loosen & move forward.
No power. Fuses not blown.	Power input lines.	Corroded connection.	Clean & replace.
		Broken power wire.	Replace with correct size.
	Vessel's battery.	Boat's battery low.	Replace or recharge.
	CKT breaker.	Boat's circuit breaker off.	Turn on.
	Servo driver.	Servo driver cable loose.	Tighten.
		Servo driver cable has open wire.	Replace.

Symptom	Area of Malfunction	Probable Cause	Corrective Action
Blown fuse in servo driver.	Console.	Console interconnect cable defective.	Replace.
		Console function switch defective.	Repair or replace console.
	Driver power fuse blown.	Short in driver.	Replace
		Too heavy torque load.	Change steering ratio.
		Short in servo motor.	Check resistance & replace.
	Console power fuse blown.	Possible short in console.	Remove each circuit board.
		Possible short in accessories.	Eliminate each accessory one by one until defective unit is found. Repair or replace.
Blown fuse in master control console.	Voltage regulator.	Defective.	Replace if defective.
	Reference regulator board.	Defective reference regulator or component.	Replace or repair defective component.
	Control amplifier.	Defective component on control amplifier board.	Replace or repair defective component.
Rudder moving in wrong direction.	Servo motor.	Motor wires reversed.	Reverse.
Rudder going hard-over to port.	Servo driver.	Defective starboard transistor.	Replace.
	Control amplifier.	Defective comparator.	Replace.

Continued on page 238.

Table 6-3. Continued.

Symptom	Area of Malfunction	Probable Cause	Corrective Action
	Sense amplifier.	Wrong course error signal.	Repair or replace.
Rudder going hard-over to starboard.	Servo driver.	Defective port drive transistor.	Replace servo driver.
	Control amplifier.	Defective comparitor.	Replace.
	Sense amplifier.	Wrong course error signal.	Repair or replace.
Rudder goes port but not starboard.	Servo driver.	Defective starboard drive circuit.	Replace servo driver.
	Rudder transducer.	Starboard limit switch open; defective.	Replace.
		Starboard limit cam moved to engage switch.	Recalibrate.
Rudder goes starboard but not port.	Servo driver.	Defective port driver.	Replace servo driver.
	Rudder transducer.	Port limit switch open.	Defective. Replace.
		Port limit cam moved to engage switch.	Recalibrate.
Rudder will not return to amidships.	Control amplifier.	Loss of feedback signal.	Replace.
		Defective rudder synchronizer.	Replace.

Symptom	Area of Malfunction	Probable Cause	Corrective Action
Erratic steering while underway.	Amplifier.	Noise	Replace or isolate noise problem.
	Battery.	Weak battery.	Recharge or replace.
	Servo driver (proportional).	Defective.	Replace servo driver.
Excessive yaw.	Rudder control.	Too much rudder being applied causing an oversteering condition.	Turn rudder control until yaw diminishes.
		Not enough rudder being applied causing an understeering condition.	Turn rudder control until yaw diminishes.
	Weather control.	Not enough sensitivity; vessel drifts too far off course.	Turn weather control CCW.
	Rudder of vessel.	Dead rudder. No effect when autopilot gives rudder. Happens even during manual steering. But rudder moves.	Add shingle to rudder for more rudder response.
Slipping servo motor clutch.	Mechanical servo motor.	Excessive load on drive motor assembly.	Change gearing.
	Control amplifier.	Oil spilled on clutch face.	Replace.
	Master control console.	Binding in steering system.	Repair. Continued on page 240.

Table 6-3. Continued.

Symptom	Area of Malfunction	Probable Cause	Corrective Action
Unable to narrow course width.	Control amplifier.	Defective.	Replace.
	Master control console.	Defective rudder pot.	Replace
	Remote hand control.	Defective cable wiring or weather pot.	Replace hand control.
No weather adjustment.	Control amplifier.	Defective amplifier.	Replace.
	Master control console.	Defective weather control	Replace console.
	Remote hand control.	Defective cable or defective component.	Replace remote hand control.
No rudder adjustment.		Defective amplifier.	Replace.
		Defective rudder control	Replace console.
	Remote hand control.	Defective cable or defective component.	Replace remote hand control.
Rudder response slow or erratic.	Servo driver.	Defective.	Replace driver.
		Defective drive circuit.	Replace driver.
	Control amplifier.	Defective.	Replace.
Lights off or blinking.	Light itself bad. Amplifier trouble.	Burned out light, or defective, cable bad or unplugged. Voltage off, fuse or circuit breaker off.	Replace.

checked, how it is being checked, and what it is about the system that causes the malfunction.

A TRIM PLANE CONTROL SYSTEM

Now that we are somewhat familiar with the automatic control systems concept for boats, let us spend a few moments examining one of the simplest possible systems applicable to small craft. This is the trim plane system, designed to stabilize boats when they are in motion. The planes are hydraulically operated and will operate independently in response to a manual lever. An installation is shown in Fig. 6-30, with the small hydraulic pumping unit appearing in Fig. 6-31. Operation of the unit is relatively simple. The control lever deflection will cause deflection of either trim plane independently, or will raise or lower them both together. This will raise or lower the boat stern as necessary. Of course it is possible to correct for height and listing at the same time.

Movement of the control lever causes hydraulic oil to be fed into the cylinders shown in Fig. 6-30, and this causes a compression of

Fig. 6-30. A trim plane installation. (Courtesy Bennett Marine.)

Fig. 6-31. A trim plane hydraulic unit. (Courtesy Bennett Marine.)

springs in the cylinders as it positions the deflection of the planes themselves. Complete removal of oil pressure will let the springs position the trim planes in an upward position, one we imagine would not frequently be used. In the rest, or neutral control lever position, oil is under pressure in the cylinders pushing against the springs and effectively locking the trim planes into neutral position. If the hydraulic motor is caused to reverse direction, oil is withdrawn from either or both cylinders causing the springs to push the planes upward. When the hydraulic motor runs forward, the oil is forced into the cylinders, together or independently, to move the trim planes downward.

Figure 6-32 shows the general schematic layout of this system. Feedback for this system is the pilot who senses response of the boat to control signals as he adjusts the control lever to produce the response desired in trim and lift. A change in speed will require a new control lever setting, as the forces are dependent on the water flow around the boat. Thus a larger deflection is required on the trim planes for slower speeds.

Moving the control lever makes the hull react in the direction the lever is pushed, exactly like an aircraft joystick. Push forward on the lever and the bow comes down (actually the stern comes up, lowering the bow). Pull back and the bow comes up. Push the lever forward toward the port bow and the port bow lowers; the same for starboard. Give no thought to the position of the trim planes—no more so than an aircraft pilot concerns himself with the position of the ailerons and elevator when flying. You would find that the trim planes act like a combination of these aircraft elements.

Most boats level out to the optimum planing angle with no trim when the fuel supply is low, when only one or two passengers are aboard, and when the boat is running with wide open throttle(s). By sighting the horizon relative to the bow rail or bow staff, you will usually find what the most efficient planing angle will be. This is not true of all boats, however, as a few will not "lay out" even under the speed and loading conditions mentioned. Usually a boat is planing most efficiently when half of the radius at the base of the stern is

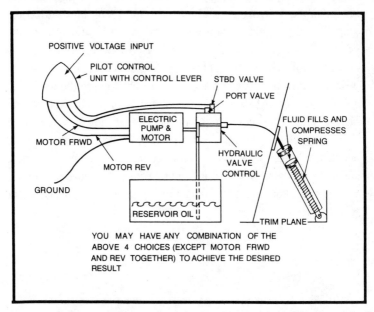

Fig. 6-32. A trim plane control system. (Courtesy Bennett Marine.)

underwater. This will be about 4 to 5 degrees inclined angle from the at-rest position in the water for most boats under 35 feet, and less as the boat length increases.

You can also sense the ideal attitude of your craft by listening to the reduced laboring of the engines, the increased tachometer readings, and the reduced wake astern.

When beginning to use a trim plane control system it is best to push the control lever in short half-second bursts. The reaction is not immediate as it takes a few seconds for the boat to work over. But be careful not to overtrim as, then, the bow will dig in and you can have trouble.

In heavy following seas or when running an inlet, best maneuverability is obtained with a bow-high attitude. To be sure the planes are full-up in the zero control lever position, pull back the lever for a few seconds. You will then have the heavy going seaworthiness safety that was designed into this kind of system and into the hull of your boat.

Now notice one other feature which makes trim plane control systems different from the completely automatic systems we began with in this chapter. In this system, there is no automatic return to neutral of the control planes when you put the lever into neutral and stop the oil pressure. Once you adjust the lever for a bow-high position, you must then use a bow-low position to bring the bow down to a lower position. Just returning the control lever to neutral will not return the control planes to neutral. You are the feedback, and feedback is required to position or change the position of the trim planes. This is not necessarily a disadvantage, for once you set a running speed for your boat with a given load, you can trim the craft and just let it run and enjoy it. But heed this caution: When running wide open most boats do not require trim unless loaded. Do not overtrim fast boats when running wide open, as the bow may dig in causing the boat to veer.

Chapter 7
Gyrocompass Systems
and the Sperry Autopilot

We have examined several types of compass systems so far and gained some idea of why a simple undampened magnetic compass is not really suitable for automatic control applications of a boat. The reason is that its erratic and quick movements would cause undue rudder movement and hunting, and this would expend energy and wear out motors and other parts. It would not necessarily serve to keep a craft on course, which is the prime requirement of such automatic control systems.

But we have also learned that a magnetic compass that is satisfactorily dampened—be it floated in a thick liquid or dampened by other means—might be used on small craft control systems. Since its changes are slow, perhaps too slow, it does not cause the rudder to move excessively, so it doesn't cause unnecessary expenditure of energy or wear of parts, but it also does not keep the craft very close to a planned course line. Since it senses changes slowly, and adjusts slowly, the craft does not correct its heading as fast as we would like, and so yawing will occur, or an oscillation about the planned course line. This, of course, might not be too bad if the damping were not any more than necessary. It is possible that, with a very properly dampened compass designed to work in a specific autopilot system, there might not be yawing at all, and a fine course-following capability would result. But the compass must be dampened if it is to work in this kind of system.

The third kind of compass which we have learned about is that using the flux-gate principle. This type has no moving magnetic parts, although it does depend upon the earth's magnetic field for its indication and output. It is fixed to the boat, and when the various angles of magnetic flux of the earth cut across its sensory element, an electrical output is obtained indicating the ship's heading with respect to the magnetic field of the earth. This sensor requires no dampening and it does not oscillate, or have erratic movement, since it has no moving parts. It is a fine type sensor for most autopilots used in smaller craft that do not have steel hulls.

THE GYROCOMPASS

Now we will examine the gyrocompass, which provides directional information for large ships and which also makes a fine sensing element for automatic steering of these vessels, including steel hulled versions. Since the gyrocompass is not dependent on the earth's magnetic field for its orientation, the kind of vessel it is in makes no difference in its operation. It has fine accuracy and is thoroughly reliable. It will be found in most undersea craft and military type vessels, as well as those larger ships used in international commerce and pleasure voyages. The gyroscope is specially mounted in a fluid-filled binnacle which is sealed and designed for deck mounting. It is shock mounted to make it immune to the ship's vibrations and poundings. The fact that the sensitive element is fluid mounted, or floated, insures isolation of the north seeking element from any physical effect which might disturb its operation or accuracy.

Figure 7-1 shows the Sperry gyrocompass binnacle. Notice the indicator dial showing headings from north. Now examine the completed unit in its cabinet mounting, which houses much of the system's electronics (Fig. 7-2). Notice the gimbal arrangement for the sensitive binnacle at the top of the cabinet. The connections for sensing the directions and for supplying electrical power are applied through the gimbal joints. There are no exposed cables or lines. The gimbal arrangement keeps the sensing element in a level position regardless of the pitch or yaw of the vessel.

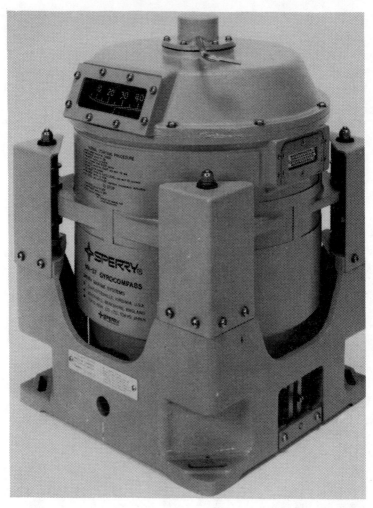

Fig. 7-1. The Sperry gyrocompass binnacle. (Courtesy Sperry Marine Systems.)

GENERAL GYROSCOPE OPERATION

The method of operation of this type compass is that a wheel rotor will turn about some axis until the wheel plane is parallel to the earth's meridian plane and the axle of the rotor is parallel to the earth's North-South Pole axis. It will hold this position when mounted in a suitable gimbal system as long as the rotor is turning. The ship's heading will then be measured from the mounting struc-

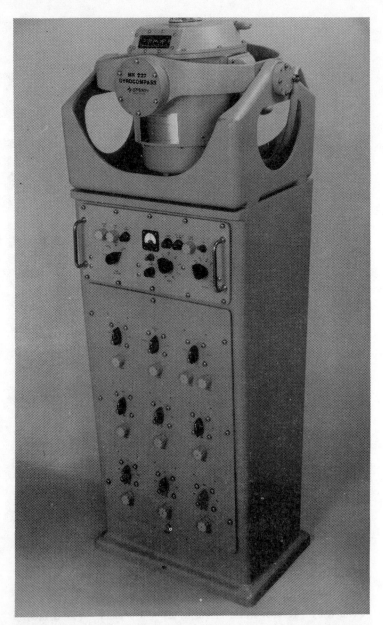

Fig. 7-2. The complete console of the Sperry gyrocompass. (Courtesy Sperry Marine.)

ture, fixed to the ship, to the axle of the rotor, in degrees. For example, if the ship is going due north, then the angle between the ship's longitudinal axis and the rotor axle will be zero. The sensitive element, encased in its binnacle, is shown in Fig. 7-3.

This unit provides not only for normal manual steering but also for autopilot steering of the ship. We will examine this further, but first we need some gyroscope background. Examine Fig. 7-4, which shows the main stations to which the gyroscope sends reference information.

It is necessary, before proceeding further, that we understand how the gyroscope is made to align itself automatically so that the rotor axle is parallel to the earth's North-South Pole axis and the rotor plane is parallel to the earth's meridian plane.

Fig. 7-3. Sensitive gyroscopic element and its gimbal system. (Courtesy Sperry Marine.)

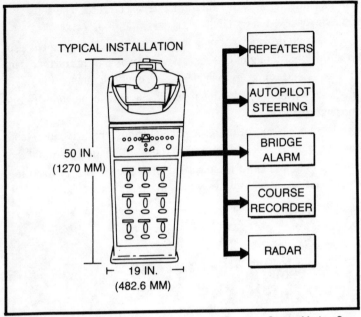

Fig. 7-4. Gyrocompass system block diagram. (Courtesy Sperry Marine Systems.)

PROPERTIES OF THE GYROSCOPE

If a heavy wheel rotating at high speed is supported in rings, as shown in Fig. 7-5, it becomes a true gyroscope. The supporting rings provide three mutually perpendicular axes which allow the spin axis of the wheel to point to any direction. As shown in Fig. 7-5, the axes are known as the spin axis, horizontal axis, and the vertical axis. The assembly is balanced about all axes. Now two properties of this rotating wheel can manifest themselves. They are gyroscopic inertia and gyroscopic precession.

Inertia, the First Property

Gyroscopic inertia, or rigidity in space as it is sometimes called, is that property of a gyroscope which makes it try to keep the spin axis always parallel to its original position. This happens when the wheel is rotating. The property is explained by Newton's law of motion, in that a rotating wheel will continue to rotate at a constant speed in the same direction unless it is acted upon by an outside torque.

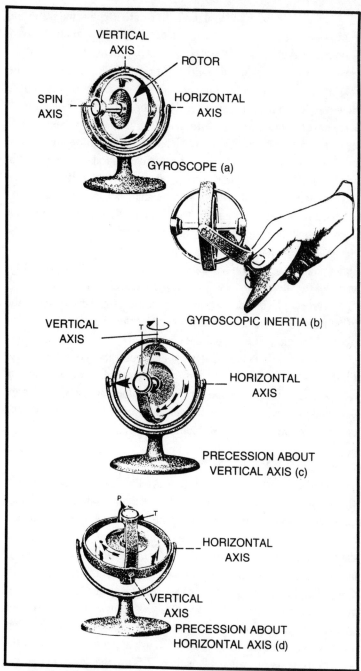

VERTICAL
AXIS

ROTOR

SPIN
AXIS

HORIZONTAL
AXIS

GYROSCOPE (a)

GYROSCOPIC INERTIA (b)

VERTICAL
AXIS

T

HORIZONTAL
AXIS

P

PRECESSION ABOUT
VERTICAL AXIS (c)

P

T

HORIZONTAL
AXIS

VERTICAL
AXIS

PRECESSION ABOUT
HORIZONTAL AXIS (d)

Fig. 7-5. Gyroscopic properties. (Courtesy Sperry Marine Systems.)

Thus, the rotating wheel tends to rotate in the same plane and resists any torque which tries to change its plane of rotation. Gyroscopic inertia may be illustrated by slowly tipping the base of the gyroscope as shown in Fig. 7-5(b). If the wheel is not rotating, the bearing friction will cause the wheel to tip when the base is tipped. However, if the rotor is spinning, the rotor will remain in its original plane or rotation as shown. Note the angle between the base gimbal and the rotor plane in this figure. This is typical of the angle measured by the ship (base) to the rotor which is parallel to the earth's North-South Pole axis when it is aligned as a compass. If we assume some directions here, we *could* say the ship was heading southeast. But back to the rotor; the rotor will continue to maintain its original plane of rotation no matter how much the base of the gyroscope is tipped about, as long as it continues to spin with sufficient velocity. Although bearing friction still affects the gyro wheel, it affects it to a much lesser degree than when the gyro wheel was stationary.

Gyroscopic inertia depends upon the angular velocity, the weight and the radius at which the weight of the rotor is concentrated. Maximum effect is obtained, therefore, from a wheel rotating at high speed with its principal weight concentrated near the rim. All rotating machinery—electric motors for example—will exhibit this resistance to change of plane of rotor phenomenon, and when forced to change direction, such machinery will have a larger than usual bearing friction and wear problem.

Precession, the Second Property

Precession (turning about an axis other than the spin axis) is that property of a gyroscope which causes the spin axle to change direction when a torque is applied to the gyrowheel. Precession may be illustrated by applying a torque to the spinning gyrowheel about the horizontal axis as shown in Fig. 7-5(c). The torque force is down, labeled T, and it does not cause the axle of the rotating wheel to turn down. The applied torque meets with resistance and the gyrowheel, instead of turning about the horizontal axis as it would if it were not spinning, turns or precesses about its vertical axis in the direction indicated by the arrow P. Similarly, if we apply a torque about the vertical axis, as shown by P in Fig. 7-5(d), the gyro wheel will precess (turn) about the horizontal axis. The rate of precession (how fast it turns) will be such that the resistance of the gyro wheel to the applied force will be exactly equal to the applied torque at any instant, and no movement in the direction of the applied torque will take place. So, if you attempt to push the rotating wheel down, it turns! If you attempt to turn it, it swings up. It moves always in a direction 90 degrees away, in the direction of rotation of the rotor.

THE GYROSCOPE AS A GYROCOMPASS

Before a free gyroscope can be converted into a gyrocompass, the mounting structure must be changed slightly. Figure 7-6(a) shows the gyro wheel mounted in a gyrosphere, and this gyrosphere is supported in what is called the vertical ring assembly. The gyro-sphere is supported in what is called the vertical ring assembly. The gyrosphere and vertical ring are, in turn, mounted in a base called the phantom yoke assembly. Now assume that the vertical ring and phantom yoke follow the gyro wheel about the vertical axis as it turns in azimuth.

With no further additions, the gyroscope as shown in Fig. 7-6(a) will, neglecting friction, maintain its position in space (the axle of the rotor pointing in any direction but holding that same direction all the time) so long as no outside forces are exerted on it. To make the gyroscope into a gyrocompass, the gyroscope rotor axle has to be made to seek and maintain a true north direction. Because north is the direction represented by a horizontal line in the meridian plane from the point of observation to the North Pole, some means have to be provided to cause the gyroscope to do three things: (1) make the gyrowheel plane parallel to the meridian plane, (2) make the axle nearly horizontal, and finally (3) make the rotor maintain its position once this is reached. The axle will then be parallel to the earth's North-South Pole axis.

Seeking the Meridian

The first step in making the gyroscope into a gyrocompass is to make the gyro wheel seek the meridian. To do this, a weight is added to the bottom of the vertical ring, as shown in Fig. 7-6(b). This causes the vertical ring to be pendulous about the horizontal axis. Actually a weight is not used in the Sperry gyrocompass, but the same effect is obtained. Figure 7-6(b) is used to explain the principle involved, not to show actual construction of a gyrocompass.

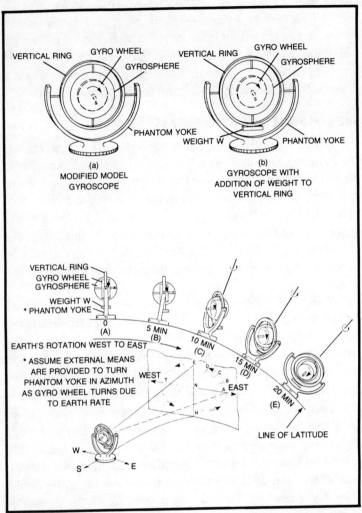

Fig. 7-6. Effect of weight and earth's rotation on the gyroscope. (Courtesy Sperry Marine Systems.)

Seeking North

To see how the gyro wheel axle points north, let's start with the gyro wheel at the equator, the axle horizontal and pointing east-west, and the gyro wheel spinning clockwise, viewed from the west (point A in Fig. 7-6(c)). The gyro wheel and vertical ring are vertical and no torque is created by the added weight. At this point both properties of the gyroscope, gyroscopic inertia and gyroscopic pre-

254

cession, are brought into play. As the earth rotates, the axle, and therefore the vertical ring, become inclined to the horizontal as shown at B in Fig. 7-6(c). Weight W is raised against the pull of gravity and consequently causes a torque about the horizontal axis of the gyro wheel. This torque causes a precession, or turning, about the vertical axis in the direction indicated at (C) in Fig. 7-6(c). The gyro wheel then has moved out of its original position, when the axle was pointing east-west. As the end of the gyro wheel that was first pointing east (which will now be referred to as the north end of the axle) continues to rise, the torque on the gyro wheel caused by the weight becomes greater because the moment arm through which the weight acts gets longer due to the greater tilt. Because the speed of precession is directly related to and proportional to the tilt, the gyro wheel turns about a vertical axis as shown at D (in azimuth) at an increasing speed until its axis is on the meridian at E.

At the meridian, the tilt, the torque caused by the weight, and the precession are all at maximum. It should be noted here that it is the righting couple applied to the tilted axle by the pendulous weight that causes the gyroscope to precess past the meridian. The kinetic energy of precession, being entirely negligible, plays no part here. After the north end of the gyro wheel axle crosses the meridian, the higher (north) end of the tilted axle is to the west of the meridian. As a result the earth's rotation reduces the tilt at the time. As the tilt becomes less, the speed of precession in azimuth decreases. Finally the axle becomes horizontal, pointing north, and precession to the west stops; the weight on the vertical ring causes no torque about the horizontal axis because it is hanging straight down. At this point, the axle has precessed as far west of the meridian as it was east originally.

As the earth continues to rotate, the north end of the axle starts to dip. Weight W is raised on the opposite side of the horizontal axis in the opposite direction to what it was originally. Precession takes place in the opposite direction carrying the gyro wheel axle back across the meridian to its original position. At this point, the cycle is repeated and will go on indefinitely unless something is done to stop the oscillations. The oscillation about the meridian may be clearly understood by referring to F in Fig. 7-6(c) which shows the movement of the gyro wheel axle projected on a vertical plane. The ellipse in the figure is the result of a displacement of the gyro wheel axle only a few degrees from the meridian. If the axle were pointing east-west at the beginning of the cycle as it was at (A), precession would take place through 180 degrees in each direction, and at one extreme the axle would point east, at the other, west. In any case, the gyro wheel would never come to rest because there is no force tending to restore the axle to the horizontal position until it has passed the meridian.

The ratio of the movement about the horizontal axis (caused by apparent rotation) to the precessional movement about the vertical axis, caused by swing of the weight, determines the shape of the ellipse. If the weight is increased, the speed of precession will increase and the ellipse will be flatter. If the weight is decreased, the speed of precession will decrease and the ellipse will change in shape to where it would, theoretically, be almost circular. The time, in minutes, required for one complete oscillation, is called the period of oscillation. For any given wheel size and speed at a certain spot on the earth the period will be nearly the same regardless of the angle through which the wheel axis oscillates. The period can be changed by changing the amount of weight on the bottom of the vertical ring. With such a gyroscope modified by hanging a weight on the vertical ring, the first condition required to make a gyroscope into a gyrocompass, that of making the gyro wheel axle seek the meridian, has been fulfilled. However, some means must be provided for suppressing these oscillations so the gyro wheel will quickly come to rest with its axle level in the north-south position.

Suppressing the Oscillation

To suppress the oscillations of the gyro wheel about the meridian, a small weight W_1 is restrained by the vertical axis bearings. When the gyro wheel axle tilts due to earth rate, the vertical axis is no longer vertical; the force of gravity, however, still pulls straight down on the weight. This allows the torque to act about the vertical axis and causes the spin axis to precess back toward the horizontal.

Now, with both weights, the gyro wheel will begin to tilt due to earth rate if it is off meridian and precesses in azimuth toward the meridian and downward toward the level position. As a result of the leveling action of weight W_1, the gyro wheel axle does not have as much tilt when it reaches the meridian as it had with only weight W. Because the gyro wheel axle is not tilted as much, the torque produced by weight W is not as great. Therefore, the gyro wheel axle will not precess as far to the west of the meridian as it was east of the meridian when it started.

After reaching a point where the axle is level and as far west of the meridian as it is going due to the action of weight W, earth rate is still causing the north end of the gyro wheel axle to tilt downward. As

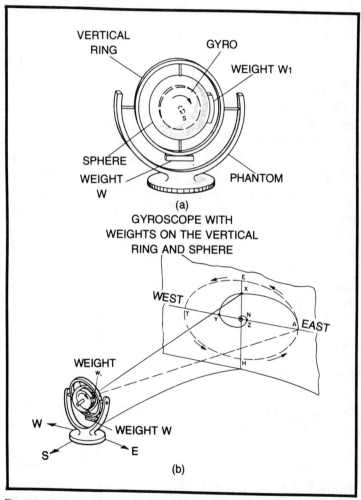

Fig. 7-7. Effect of both weights on the gyroscope. (Courtesy Sperry Marine Systems.)

257

a result, the forces due to the weights are reversed and the torques are created which precess the north end of the gyrowheel axle to the east and up. The gyro wheel, during this half of the cycle, is not precessed as far to the east as it was to the west. Thus, added weight W_1 causes the movement of the north end of the gyro wheel axle to be reduced each successive oscillation; the north end of the gyro wheel axle will thus follow a spiral path, as shown in Fig. 7-7 (b), instead of an elliptical path as previously described.

A careful consideration of the action of the two weights will make it apparent that the only position of rest that the gyro wheel can find will be with the gyro wheel axle horizontal and on the meridian. In other words, the free gyroscope has been converted into a true meridian-seeking gyrocompass. The gyrocompass period can be changed by varying the weight W, and the speed with which it settles to a level position (damping percentage) can be changed by varying the weight W_1.

An instrument such as that described will indicate true north only as long as it is at the equator and not transported over the surface of the earth. When this gyrocompass is moved, acceleration on the weights (because they are gravity-sensitive) will cause torques on the gyro wheel, and the effect of change in latitude from the equator will result in false indications. The gyrocompass in its present stage does not fulfill requirement (3), that of maintaining the true north level position other than at the equator. Some means must be used to eliminate the effect of accelerations on the unbalanced weights hanging on the gyrocompass and to adjust for the changes in latitude. This is accomplished in a rather unique way in the Sperry MK 37 gyrocompass as we will now explain.

SPERRY MK 37 GYROCOMPASS

The MK 37 gyrocompass differs in construction from elementary gyrocompass used in the previous discussion of gyrocompass principles. It was noted that a weight added to the bottom of the vertical ring caused the gyro wheel to precess in azimuth. The effective action of this weight depended upon the gyro wheel axle tilting due to the earth rate. The weight then applied a horizontal torque to the gyro wheel which caused a precession in azimuth. While in the preceding discussion this weight was placed on the vertical ring, the same action would result if the weight had been placed on the gyrosphere. The resultant torque would still be horizontal because the force of gravity is down and the resultant torque is perpendicular to the applied force.

The use of a weight added to the bottom of the gyrosphere produces undesirable disturbances in the gyrocompass during accelerations. If the pendulous weight could be eliminated by using a more appropriate means of producing horizontal torque, the gyro wheel would be balanced and accelerations would not cause the gyro wheel to move from the meridian. A better method is used to produce torques about the horizontal axis proportional to the axle tilt without destroying gyrowheel balance.

Liquid Ballistic and Damping Control

In the MK 37 gyrocompass, gravitational torques to make the gyro wheel axle seek north are provided by a liquid ballistic. The ballistic consists of two interconnected brass tanks, partially filled with a refined silicone oil, mounted on the gyrosphere assembly as in Fig. 7-8. This ballistic system is employed because it is substantially free of roll acceleration effects. The small bore of the tubing connecting the two tanks retards the free flow of fluid between the tanks.

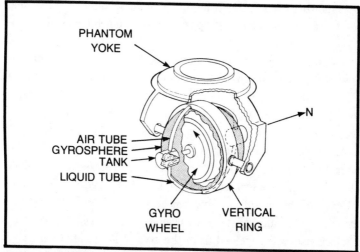

Fig. 7-8. Ballistic system of the Sperry MK-37 Mod 1 gyrocompass. (Courtesy Sperry Marine Systems.)

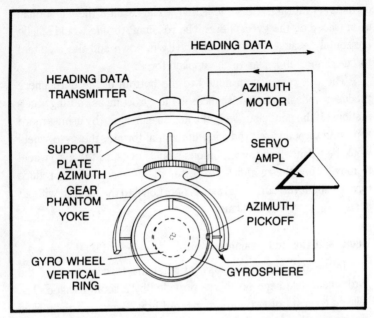

Fig. 7-9. Simplified diagram of follow-up system on gyrocompass. (Courtesy Sperry Marine Systems.)

Because the time it takes for the fluid to flow will be long compared to the roll period, roll acceleration errors will be minimized.

It should be noted that the primary difference in theory of operation of a ballistic construction is that the resulting torque action for the same tilt direction is opposite that of the pendulous gyrocompass.

Consider the difference between the action of the bottom-mounted weight and the ballistic method of control. With the axle tilted and the gyro wheel not spinning, the bottom-mounted weight would tend to level the axle. On the other hand, with the use of ballistic control, the initial tilt would cause the fluid to flow to the lower tank unbalancing the gyrosphere even more and increasing the tilt angle. Thus the direction of the torque is reversed as a result of using a ballistic control and the torque would move the north end away from the meridian. This can be resolved by reversing the direction of rotation of the gyro wheel so that it will rotate counterclockwise when viewed from the south. To achieve damping, weight W_1 must then be added to the west side to reverse direction of the vertical torque as well.

The Follow-Up Control

It was stated earlier for simplicity that the vertical ring and the phantom yoke were made to follow the gyro wheel in azimuth. The reason and means of doing this are now considered.

A gyro wheel without followup could rotate until the spin axis was aligned with the horizontal axis. This is called gimbal lock and the gyro wheel will lose one axis of freedom and can no longer be considered to be a gyroscope. So, to keep the phantom yoke and vertical ring aligned in azimuth with the gyro wheel, a conventional followup system, as shown in Fig. 7-9, is used.

A followup pickoff, Fig. 7-10, which detects movement of the gyro wheel, has an E-core pickoff mounted on the vertical ring and an armature on the gyrosphere. A signal is obtained proportional to the gyro wheel movement from its null position and, after amplification,

Fig. 7-10. Sensitive element of gyrocompass with drive and pickoff units in top foreground. (Courtesy Sperry Marine Systems.)

drives the azimuth motor. The motor positions the phantom yoke to maintain alignment of the vertical ring with the gyrosphere at all times.

With the addition of the movable phantom yoke element, another support of a fixed type must be provided for the gyrocompass assembly. This support plate assembly is mounted to the ship through the binnacle assembly and shock mount. The azimuth motor is positioned on the support plate, and the gear on the motor shaft meshes with the azimuth gear attached to the phantom yoke.

Correcting for the Latitude Error

As you recall we said that the tilt of the ballistic causes the horizontal torques which precess the gyro wheel in azimuth. We said that the horizontal earth rates affect a gyro wheel when located anywhere except at the Poles. Horizontal earth rate also causes the gyro wheel to tilt. The torque developed by the tilted ballistic will be just enough to keep the gyro wheel precessing at a rate equal and opposite to the vertical component of the earth's rate. The higher the latitude, the greater must be the tilt of the spin axis to keep up with the higher vertical earth rate.

Now, as a result of this tilt, the dampening weight produces a vertical torque which causes the north end of the gyro wheel to settle eastward from the true meridian in north latitudes, and westward in south latitudes. This displacement from the true meridian, increasing with latitude is called the latitude error. In the Sperry MK 37 gyrocompass this latitude error is corrected by applying an opposing vertical torque to the gyrosphere of a magnitude to just cancel this steady torque produced by the damping weight. The gyro wheel settles with a tilt, but with no latitude error.

An E-core type torquer (which is like a synchro) produces this torque. An ac current is introduced into the control field windings of the E-core torquer on the vertical ring. The eddy current induced in the gyrosphere produces a torque on the gyrosphere and thus the counteracting vertical torque is created.

Making Speed Error Correction

A speed correction is required to compensate for the northerly or southerly component of the ship's speed. The northerly component developed a torque about the gyrosphere which causes a westerly error. A southerly course causes an easterly error.

A signal proportional to the northerly component of the ship's heading is produced by the speed correction resolver (synchro resolver) in the binnacle and supplied as an input to the compensator unit. This signal is modified proportional to the ship's speed by the speed-knots control, then combined with the latitude correction signal and applied to the E-core torquer on the vertical ring.

Control Steering

Now that we have an understanding of how the unit operates, we will examine how a ship is steered using this kind of control

Fig. 7-11. Universal gyropilot steering control console. (Courtesy Sperry Marine Systems.)

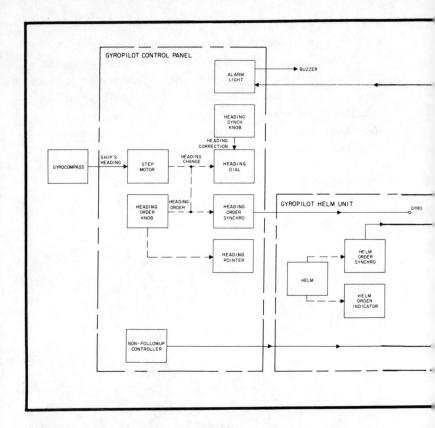

steering device, the gyropilot. There are three types of steering controls which may be selected by a mode selector switch on the helm unit, Fig. 7-11.

We also refer you to Fig. 7-12, which is a block diagram of the overall operation and will be of help in the discussion to follow.

Now, the three possible types of control are:

(1) GYRO. The automatic steering by means of the heading selector components on the gyropilot control panel.

(2) HAND. The hand-electric steering by means of the steering wheel assembly on the gyropilot helm unit.

(3) NFU. This is the non-followup steering by means of the non-followup controller switch module on the gyropilot control panel. In this mode the rudder does not follow the movement of the wheel, but it can be positioned at any displacement desired. Essentially you signal left and the

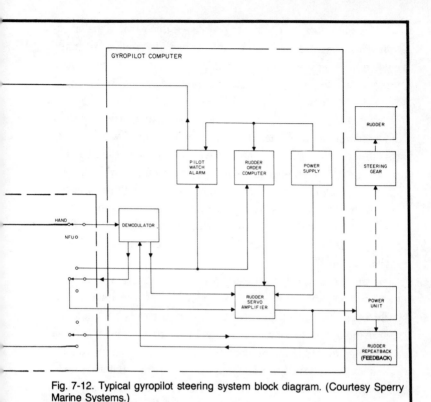

Fig. 7-12. Typical gyropilot steering system block diagram. (Courtesy Sperry Marine Systems.)

rudder moves left until the limit switches stop it or you return the control to neutral. To get the rudder back to neutral you must then signal right and watch the rudder indicator and when the rudder is at neutral, position the signal switch to off.

Gyro Mode of Steering. Here the steering system is slaved to the gyrocompass by means of a step motor. A heading error signal is generated in either of two ways:

(1) The ship deviates from a selected heading
(2) The selected course is changed by means of the heading order control

In either case, a synchro signal (heading error) is generated and routed to a demodulator in the gyropilot computer where it is converted to a dc error signal and routed to the rudder order computer.

The rudder order computer processes this error signal in accordance with the setting of the controls on the gyropilot computer panel (the integrator, weather, rudder multiplier, rate multiplier, gyro rudder limits, etc.) and routes the resulting rudder order signal to the rudder servo amplifier.

Within the rudder servo amplifier, the rudder order signal is compared with a demodulated rudder feedback signal which represents the rudder angle. Any difference between where the rudder is and where it is supposed to be results in an output which is the rudder error signal and this is applied to one of the valves (transfer valve hydraulic) solenoids in the power unit. This causes the rudder to be moved until the error signal is wiped out and the rudder is then properly positioned in accord with all the information mentioned previously.

Hand Steering by Wheel. When the steering wheel is rotated by hand, an error signal is generated by the helm order synchro. The synchro signal (rudder order) is routed to a demodulator in the gyropilot computer assembly where it is converted to a dc signal and routed to the rudder servo amplifier. Within the rudder servo amplifier the rudder order signal is compared with the demodulated rudder repeat back (feedback) signal as in the gyro mode, and again, the difference in signals represents a rudder error in position, and the difference results in a signal to the amplifier which causes the rudder to move to wipe out this error. The rudder order computer and its controls are inoperative in this mode.

Hand Steering by Panel Control. This unit is only used for special systems in which a standard wheel type helm unit is not used. When the control is rotated a dc potentiometer signal is applied directly to the rudder servo amplifier helm input. This signal is compared with a demodulated rudder feedback signal and the resultant output signal is applied to the solenoids of the hydraulic power unit or electric steering unit.

Non-Followup Steering. In the NFU mode the power unit directional valve solenoids are directly connected to the non-followup controller module on the gyropilot panel and the gyropilot computer is inoperative. When the non-followup controller handle is held in either left or right position, the rudder movement continues until the rudder limits are reached. When the handle is released, the rudder stops at its present position. To return the rudder to amidships, the handle must be held in left or right positon until the rudder reaches amidships as indicated by the rudder angle indicator, then the steering handle is released.

If the mode switch is in hand or gyro, placing the non-followup controller handle in left or right will cause the rudder to respond immediately (NFU override feature). To achieve normal NFU operation, however, the mode switch must be placed in NFU before the non-followup controller handle is released. If this procedure is not completed, rudder control will be taken over by the steering mode selected by the mode switch location when the controller handle is released.

Power Distribution

Figure 7-13 is a simplified power distribution diagram for a dual gyropilot steering control system. The port and starboard control systems have separate power sources and circuit breakers and are independent. The lighting circuit has its own circuit breaker and power source. The gyropilot helm unit circuit breaker panel contains all of the circuit breakers for the gyropilot helm unit, gyropilot control panel, and gyropilot computer.

Heading Selector Components

The heading selector components visible from the outside of the panel include a fixed index (lubber line) that represents the fore-aft axis of the vessel, a repeater dial that displays the gyrocompass heading under the lubber line, and a heading pointer that points to the selected heading. (When the vessel is on the selected heading, the heading pointer and lubber line are aligned.) A heading order control is used to position the heading pointer when a change in heading is desired. A heading synch control is used to synchronize the repeater dial with the ship's gyrocompass on starting.

Within the panel are a step motor that is controlled by the gyrocompass, synchro(s) that supply heading error data to the gyropilot computer, and an integrator reset switch that automatically resets the integral function in the rudder order computer when the change in selected heading is greater than 10 degrees.

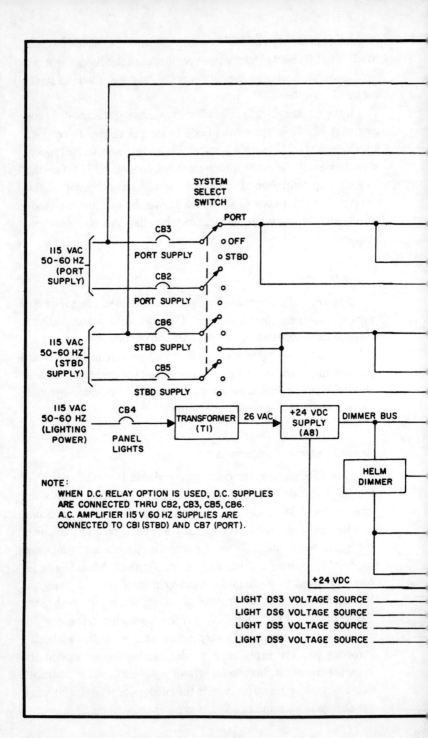

SYSTEM
SELECT
SWITCH

PORT

CB3

o OFF

115 VAC
50-60 HZ
(PORT
SUPPLY)

PORT SUPPLY

o STBD

CB2

PORT SUPPLY

CB6

115 VAC
50-60 HZ
(STBD
SUPPLY)

STBD SUPPLY

CB5

STBD SUPPLY

115 VAC
50-60 HZ
(LIGHTING
POWER)

CB4

PANEL
LIGHTS

TRANSFORMER
(T1)

26 VAC

+24 VDC
SUPPLY
(A8)

DIMMER BUS

HELM
DIMMER

NOTE:
WHEN D.C. RELAY OPTION IS USED, D.C. SUPPLIES
ARE CONNECTED THRU CB2, CB3, CB5, CB6.
A.C. AMPLIFIER 115 V 60 HZ SUPPLIES ARE
CONNECTED TO CB1 (STBD) AND CB7 (PORT).

+24 VDC

LIGHT DS3 VOLTAGE SOURCE _____
LIGHT DS6 VOLTAGE SOURCE _____
LIGHT DS5 VOLTAGE SOURCE _____
LIGHT DS9 VOLTAGE SOURCE _____

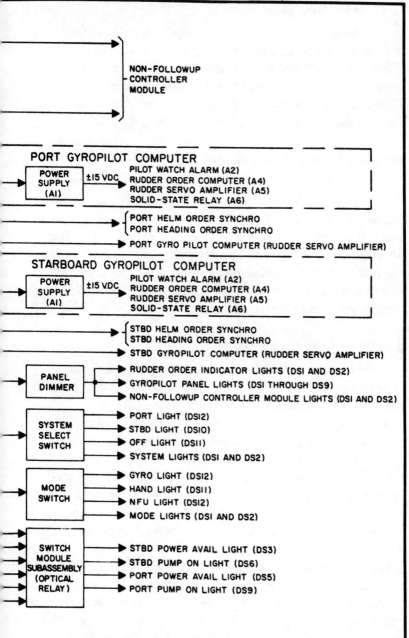

NON-FOLLOWUP
CONTROLLER
MODULE

PORT GYROPILOT COMPUTER

POWER SUPPLY (A1) ±15 VDC
PILOT WATCH ALARM (A2)
RUDDER ORDER COMPUTER (A4)
RUDDER SERVO AMPLIFIER (A5)
SOLID-STATE RELAY (A6)

PORT HELM ORDER SYNCHRO
PORT HEADING ORDER SYNCHRO

PORT GYRO PILOT COMPUTER (RUDDER SERVO AMPLIFIER)

STARBOARD GYROPILOT COMPUTER

POWER SUPPLY (A1) ±15 VDC
PILOT WATCH ALARM (A2)
RUDDER ORDER COMPUTER (A4)
RUDDER SERVO AMPLIFIER (A5)
SOLID-STATE RELAY (A6)

STBD HELM ORDER SYNCHRO
STBD HEADING ORDER SYNCHRO

STBD GYROPILOT COMPUTER (RUDDER SERVO AMPLIFIER)

PANEL DIMMER
RUDDER ORDER INDICATOR LIGHTS (DSI AND DS2)
GYROPILOT PANEL LIGHTS (DSI THROUGH DS9)
NON-FOLLOWUP CONTROLLER MODULE LIGHTS (DSI AND DS2)

SYSTEM SELECT SWITCH
PORT LIGHT (DS12)
STBD LIGHT (DS10)
OFF LIGHT (DS11)
SYSTEM LIGHTS (DSI AND DS2)

MODE SWITCH
GYRO LIGHT (DS12)
HAND LIGHT (DS11)
NFU LIGHT (DS12)
MODE LIGHTS (DSI AND DS2)

SWITCH MODULE SUBASSEMBLY (OPTICAL RELAY)
STBD POWER AVAIL LIGHT (DS3)
STBD PUMP ON LIGHT (DS6)
PORT POWER AVAIL LIGHT (DS5)
PORT PUMP ON LIGHT (DS9)

Fig. 7-13. Simplified power distribution system. (Courtesy Sperry Marine Systems.)

269

Turn Rate Indicator Meter

Gyropilot control panels may be equipped with an instrument that displays the vessel's rate of turn in degrees per second. The instrument is calibrated in 0.1 degree per second increments between 1.0 degree per second left and 1.0 degree per second right. The instrument is controlled by a turn rate interface unit that generates a dc signal proportional to the ship's turning rate.

Panel Mounted Helm Control (Optional)

The panel mounted helm control consists of a control switch that positions a potentiometer and a control dial that is calibrated in 5 degree increments and is back-lighted by two lamps. When the switch is turned to the selected position, a dc signal from the potentiometer, which acts as a rudder order signal, is generated. The rudder will move to the ordered rudder angle and stay in that position until a new order is entered. This optional unit is used only when no gyropilot helm unit is fitted.

Gyropilot Computer Control Panel

The gyropilot computer control panel, which is located behind a hinged cover, contains the following controls for the gyropilot computer and is operational only in the gyro mode:

Integrator switch. This is a manual on-off switch that can hold or reset the integrator circuit when in the off position. In the on position the integrator is enabled and computes a rudder offset signal to counter the effect of wind and current on ship's heading. Integrator reset is performed automatically by a cam-operated switch in the heading selector whenever a heading change of more than 10 degrees is ordered. The manual switch should normally be placed in the on position.

Weather ADJ potentiometer. This control is calibrated in increments between 0 and 5 degrees to control the sensitivity (amount of heading error permitted before sensitivity is automatically increased). The system operates at reduced sensitivity until the ship yaws beyond the setting, at which time the sensitivity is automatically increased to bring the ship back to the selected heading. The potentiometer should be set to 0 degree in calm seas for maintaining the best heading. In rough seas, where there is considerable yaw, the potentiometer should be set to correspond to the approximate number of degrees of natural yaw motion from the base heading.

Rudder MULT potentiometer. This multiplier control has settings between 1 (minimum gain) and 3 (maximum gain) which vary the gain of the summing amplifier in the rudder order computer to provide operator control of the rudder ratio. The higher settings cause the ship to respond more quickly to heading error by ordering larger rudder angles. The rudder multiplier may have to be set to a higher value at low ship speeds for best performance.

Rate MULT potentiometer. This multiplier controls the heading rate gain level for optimum heading keeping and heading changing. This control provides a 2-to-1 adjustment of the rate gain level over an internal rate level which is set during installation and sea trials.

Rudder limit potentiometer. This control sets the limit of rudder movement, right or left, between 5 and 45 degrees in the gyro mode only. If there is a rudder offset from the integrator, the rudder will be limited equally to either side of the offset position.

Pilot Watch Alarm (Optional)

The pilot watch alarm contains circuits that control an alarm lamp and audible alarm on the gyropilot control panel. The alarms operate when power fails or heading error has exceeded a preset magnitude (1 to 10 degrees as set by an external alarm potentiometer) for a preset time interval (1 to 30 seconds as set by the time delay calibration potentiometer). A battery charging circuit provides a means of charging a 5 volt, rechargeable nickel cadmium battery in the gyropilot control panel. This battery makes the alarm system independent of other power.

The Digital Compass Repeater

Information from the gyrocompass is required at various other stations for information or for equipment. The gyropilot control panels may be equipped with a digital compass repeater which receives serial data from a master station compass repeater and displays it on four readout tubes. The brightness of the readout tubes is controlled by a repeater dim potentiometer.

The Rudder Angle Indicator

We have seen an example of this kind of unit in previous pages. The gyropilot helm units may be equipped with a rudder angle indicator that is installed above the rudder order indicator. This way you know what you want the rudder to do, and if it is doing it. The rudder angle indicator consists of a linear scale and a pointer driven by a belt from a synchro. The synchro is controlled by an external rudder angle transmitter. The scale markings are added when the unit is installed if the standard scale used does not match the rudder angle transmitter used in the particular installation.

Chapter 8
Marine
Communications Systems

In this chapter we will examine some marine communications systems. We will try to gain an insight into the kinds of systems by first thinking through a slight bit of theory of operation and then we will examine the equipment itself. We want to know how it works, how to maintain it, and also how to get the most reliable communication from its use. We want to know where the weak points are and what to do about them.

RELIABILITY

The reliability of communications equipment might be called the prime requirement for marine use. Even with all the gear shown in Fig. 8-1, an unreliable system can be nearly as dangerous as having no gear. It is true that without navigation equipment operational you may not be able to continue on course or determine where you are. But in the event of failure of everything else, at least with the power source and the communications equipment, you can radio for assistance to perhaps save lives or the boat.

So we consider this an important chapter and will try to give as much good information on the subject as possibly can be put together. Read and reread it and think of what it has told you. Then try to follow the rules and your reward may be your own life.

Fig. 8-1. Antennas on a pleasure craft.

TYPES OF COMMUNICATIONS SYSTEMS

There are presently three types of communications systems most applicable to boats: the VHF gear, which is relatively short range, line-of-sight communications; the citizen's band gear which operates in the high frequency range; and the specifically designated equipment for marine operation, the single sideband radiotelephone systems. Of course we do not rule out emergency radio operation with amateur radio communications.

The 2-megahertz (MHz) band and the very high frequency, frequency modulated (VHF-FM) maritime mobile band are the only systems that provide distress frequency coverage. For this reason, the Coast Guard does not encourage the use of citizen's band equipment when it is the sole means of communications on your boat. The Coast Guard is now using VHF-FM as its primary short range means of voice communications. Coast Guard search and rescue (SAR) stations are now equipped with VHF-FM equipment as are a large percentage of the small SAR boats.

A wide range of frequencies is used for communications. We can best give a quick insight into the range of them by using a band designation as follows:

Kilohertz range (HF)

- 1619 to 1712
- 2003 to 2784
- 3258 to 3261
- 4069.2 to 4428.6
- 6147.5 to 6455
- 8207.6 to 8796.0
- 12,379.0
- 13,379.0 to 13,175.5
- 16,477.0
- 17,269.0 to 17,321.5
- 22,653.5 to 22,692.0

Megahertz range (VHF)

- 156.750 and 156.800
- 161.800 to 162.000

The specific designation for each frequency in the above listed bands is given in the U.S. Government Rules and Regulations, Volume IV, December 1971 (or later), Part 81; Stations on Land in the Maritime Services and Alaska-Public Fixed Stations and Part 83; Stations on Shipboard in the Maritime Services. This booklet is available from the Federal Communications Commission, Washington, D.C., and should be a part of every boatowner's library. This volume will also specify what the types of communications are on each channel and technical specifications for such transmissions types.

DISTRESS COMMUNICATIONS

At this point we include international distress information which one must know to gain immediate recognition of an imminent disaster. The telegraph code signal for SOS is three dots, three dashes, and three dots.

Many times it is possible to transmit through a severe storm situation using code rather than voice communication, but usually only commercial ships will have the equipment and a trained operator to communicate with code. It is important, even when actual communication is impossible, to keep sending the signal so that direction finders can zero in on the signal to determine your location. In some sea conditions drifting and movement with high winds will continuously change your position. The direction finders must be able to follow this movement.

There are watches on 500 kilohertz, and all ships using this band must have receivers tuned to this frequency except when the operator is communicating. There is a watch on 143 kilohertz, and on the Great Lakes, there is a watch on 2182 kilohertz for ships using the 1605 to 3500 kilohertz band. There is also a watch on 156.8 megahertz in the VHF band.

In radiotelephone systems, where code is not applicable, then the word *mayday* is to be used in groups of three and followed by the call sign of the vessel in distress.

Always have available the position to the best known coordinates, the type of distress being experienced, and the kind of help needed. The formulation of this message in simple terms, spoken clearly without panic, is essential to sending the message through interference.

Distress Frequencies and Range

Now let us consider information concerning the U.S. Coast Guard and emergency or distress information. Consider the 156–162 MHz band first, where frequency modulation (FM) is used, and the average ship-to-ship range is 10 to 15 miles and ship-to-shore range is 20 to 30 miles. This range, of course, is dependent upon the height of the antennas, the power used, and the conditions. Most all U.S. Coast Guard stations and all VHF Public Coast stations maintain a continuous guard on channel 16 (156.8 MHz), the VHF distress frequency. Also, there are regularly scheduled weather broadcasts on 162.55 or 162.400 MHz. The severe weather warnings are broadcast on 156.8 MHz. When purchasing equipment, remember that the FCC recommends the use of 12 channel gear due to the large number of channels in this VHF band.

In the lower frequency band of 2 to 4 MHz, single sideband amplitude modulated signals are used. The daytime range is from 50 to 150 miles, but nighttime range is unpredictable because skywave propagation changes with variations in the ionosphere. The Coast Guard maintains a continuous watch on 2182 kHz, and routine broadcasts are sent on 2670 kHz. Remember that, although the Citizen's Band can be used for communication from 2 to 15 miles, you cannot consider channel 9 to be a substitute for the authorized marine distress frequencies. There are no official marine information or weather broadcasts on any of the CB frequencies.

Distress Information to be Stated

If your boat is in trouble, then state:

- Who you are, the vessel's name and call.
- Where you are, the position in latitude and longitude or some specific reference.
- What is wrong, the nature of the trouble.
- Kind of assistance desired, rescue, medical advice, etc.
- Number of persons on board and if any are injured.
- Description of your vessel, length, type, cabin, masts, power, color of hull, superstructure and trim details.
- Your listening frequency and schedule.

If you observe another boat in trouble, then state:

- Your position, bearing, and distance from boat in trouble.
- Nature of the trouble.
- Description of vessel in trouble.
- Your course, speed, and what you are going to do.
- Your radio call sign, name of your vessel, listening frequency and schedule.

RADIO STATION LICENSES AND OPERATOR LICENSES

It is important to know that the radio station itself is not licensed but instead the vessel. No examination or personal appearance is needed to do this. The FCC's form 502 is used and processing it costs $4.00. A CB radio must be licensed separately using FCC form 505. A restricted radiotelephone operator permit is required for the operator. Use FCC form 753-A ($4.00) to get this. Again, no exam is required.

If you have licensed your boat and sell it, the license goes with the boat. You must get a new license for a new boat, and be sure to notify the FCC when and to whom you made the sale of your old boat. It is good news to know that if your boat was licensed for the old type communication (DSB) you will not have to apply for a new license or modification of your present license to use the new VHF equipment. The FCC has ruled you may add this equipment without any paperwork. But on item 18 of form 502, request a modification and list the new frequencies. If you add radar, list the radar frequencies. This modification of your license will not change the expiration date of that license, so normal renewal dates must be followed. Finally, note that you do not need to log all transmissions, but you must maintain the ship's radio log, and you must log all distress signals. You also need to state on the radio log that the original installation met the FCC requirements and note any changes to the equipment. A licensed technician must make these entries. Remember, also, that it is the owner's responsibility to see that his station is operated within the FCC rules and regulations at all times. In the owner's absence, anyone operating the station must have a valid FCC operator's license.

Again, for a moment here, let us talk about the operator's license. To use the shipboard radio station, the operator must have a valid license. For small noncommercial vessels this license is called a restricted radiotelephone operator permit. Application for this license is made by filling out FCC form 753 and mailing it to the nearest office of the FCC. Your marine dealer usually has these forms. There are no technical questions or examinations. The license must be carried by the operator or be visibly posted near the radiotelephone installation.

It is permissible for the licensed operator to let nonlicensed passengers *speak* over the radiotelephone. The licensed operator, however, must initiate and conclude the transmissions by identifying the stations and making suitable log entries.

A SUMMARY OF THE FCC REGULATIONS

Prevent Interference

Always make calls first on your VHF radiotelephone. If the station is out of communications range, then call on the SSB radiotelephone. To minimize the interference with other stations, always monitor the channel before calling.

Procedure

The operator must announce his call sign whenever trying to contact another station (even if the contact is not completed) and when finished with the conversation. On some frequencies, air time is limited to three minutes. On ship-to-shore conversations the call signal should be given every 15 minutes during extended conversations. When calling a station, limit air time to 30 seconds. If an answer is not received, wait two minutes before calling again. With permission of the FCC (and if a matter of safety is involved), one can operate without a call sign. In such cases, the operator must announce the name of the vessel and operator's name, stating that the station is being operated under special temporary authorization.

Emergencies

The primary function of the radiotelephone is to provide for the safety of the vessel in an emergency situation. Safety and distress transmissions have priority over all others. This is the reason for monitoring 2182 kHz (or VHF channel 16) at all times when not transmitting on this or other channels.

OPERATING THE SINGLE SIDEBAND TRANSMITTER

Operating a single sideband radiotelephone is quite similar to operating conventional AM equipment. After the desired channel is selected, press the microphone button and begin speaking. Speak in a normal tone of voice with the microphone held close to the mouth.

Do not shout. Transmitters incorporate an automatic circuit that adjusts for variations in voice level. Shouting is not only unnecessary, it does not increase transmitter output, and it may garble the signal so that intelligibility is reduced.

Remember that no carrier is being transmitted until you speak. Even though the microphone button is pressed, no signal appears on the air until the operator begins speaking. Thus, one cannot acknowledge a transmission from another station by merely blipping the button.

Operating Positions

Select a convenient operating location for the radiotelephone. Mounting brackets are often reversible. Thus, the radiotelephone may be mounted on any flat surface, vertical or horizontal, or perhaps hung from the overhead. The location selected should allow at least one inch of space around the cabinet for ventilation. Avoid installing the equipment a long distance from true ground, such as on flying bridges. Such locations complicate or prevent proper antenna loading and may make the use of an antenna coupler mandatory.

FCC Requirements (Not Applicable for Export Users)

In most cases, before an SSB radiotelephone can be licensed for a vessel, the owner must also have a VHF radiotelephone installed.

The owner must also have a ship station license and be in possession of a valid operator's license before using the transmitter. Finally, the owner is required to have a current copy of FCC Rules and Regulations, Part 83, on board the vessel. Part 83 may be ordered from the Superintendent of Documents, U.S. Government Printing Office, Washington, D.C.

Monitoring

One should always monitor the distress and calling frequency (2182 kHz or channel 16 on VHF) when underway so that the vessel can provide assistance if necessary. Note also that anything one hears on the air is considered private and it is unlawful to relate these conversations or to use the information in any way.

Violations

If the equipment is operated in violation of the rules and regulations, there is a possibility that the owner will receive an official notice of violation. Upon receipt, it is necessary to reply to the notice within 10 days. The response should explain why the violation occurred and what is proposed to prevent its future occurrence.

The Radio Log

A radio log must be kept for all radio transmissions, even if no contact is made. An examination of a log sheet will show the type of information required. The operator must also indicate the times when maintaining a watch on 2182 and/or VHF channel 16. Any emergency signal which one hears should be entered, and if any safety or urgency messages or transmissions are initiated, they should be noted accordingly. Always keep the log in the 24 hour time system.

Any technical work performed on the radio that may affect the operation of the transmitter must be entered and signed off by the licensed technician performing the work.

The radio log must be maintained for at least one year. If the logs contain notations regarding emergency communications, the owner is required to keep them for at least 3 years, or longer if requested by the FCC.

SENDING A DISTRESS CALL

Be certain to know the difference between distress, urgency, and safety communications. In an emergency, make the call first on VHF channel 16, then, if unsuccessful, on 2182 kHz, the medium frequency (MF) distress channel. This frequency is usually set up on the channel 1 position.

Speak slowly and clearly into the microphone: "Mayday—mayday—mayday. This is (vessel name and call sign)." Repeat this call three times. Pause, listen, and repeat again if necessary.

If within range, you can usually make direct contact with the U.S. Coast Guard. Give the name of the vessel, location, nature of the distress, and the type of assistance required.

If the operator has repeated the call several times and cannot contact the U.S. Coast Guard, he will probably be called by a nearby ship offering assistance. If completely out of range on 2182 kHz, the operator can switch to one of the high seas channels to contact a distant shore station who will either relay or patch directly into the U.S. Coast Guard over the telephone line.

Remember that distress, urgency, and safety transmissions have priority, in that order.

PROPAGATION OF RADIO SIGNALS AT SEA

An operator will soon learn that the propagation characteristics of medium and high frequency radio telephone signals are extraordinary. Unlike VHF, the signals which radiate from these lower frequency bands are capable of traveling far beyond the horizon. For this reason, you will also hear more interference than on the VHF band. However, this is a small price to pay for the ability to communicate 1,000 miles or more.

Characteristics of the 2 MHz marine band are usually quite stable and predictable. During the day a range of up to 50 miles on amplitude modulated equipment is normal. At night, stations from a much greater distance will come in and cause interference. On the higher frequency bands, it is not unusual to hear stations coming in from enormous distances.

Generally, the operating location of the vessel is of minor importance. The ability to get through is a function of the operating frequency and the propagation conditions.

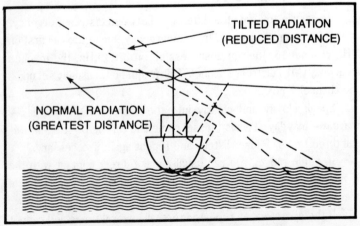

Fig. 8-2. Radiation pattern effect from rolling boat.

Transmissions from a seagoing craft may be more difficult than transmissions from a land based station. The rigidity of the antenna system will be different. The ground wave along salt water may receive more attenuation, but the line of sight should be better at sea, without the hills and mountains of land terrain. It is likely there may be some effect on propagation when a boat is rolling or pitching. Examine Fig. 8-2.

The radiation pattern from a vertical dipole antenna is doughnut shaped. If the boat is rolling, the doughnut tends to dip and rise, and that may cause fluctuations and fading in a signal received from the boat. The radiation pattern of a horizontal quarterwave antenna is also doughnut shaped, with the strongest signal broadside to the length of the antenna. Thus, the antenna whipping in the wind, combined with rolling, yawing and pitching of the boat will change the plane of the doughnut, thus causing fading reception at a distant station. This is particularly true when the received signal is directly from the boat antenna and not from the ground wave radiation.

When the transmission frequency is lowered, there is a pronounced ground wave signal, which is that signal traveling along the water and ground itself. Of course the sky wave signal at some frequencies (not VHF) travels upward to the ionosphere layers and then is reflected back to earth many miles away, often 1,000 or more, to give a longer range, much as broadcast stations obtain at night. But this signal fades and may not be reliable.

The ground wave will often give good solid reception, but it attenuates fast and so is good for only a relatively short distance. So when establishing communications, especially over long distances, use the sky wave and experiment with various bands and channels to find out which is the most reliable and solid for that time of day or night and that particular range.

The FCC requires that the antenna system be set up so that it produces vertical polarization, except in those cases where it grants permission to do otherwise. This means that the antenna itself should be placed so that it is vertical. One reason for the FCC requirement is that the electromagnetic wave portion of the signal—which is the component that actually cuts across the antenna—produces the received signal. So both the transmitting and receiving antennas need to have the same polarization. If you think

Fig. 8-3. A modern seagoing ship has little room for antennas.

about it for a moment, you note that the vertical antenna may also have less trouble from a sea reflection than a horizontal antenna would.

When the antenna is said to have vertical polarization, the electric field aligns itself with the vertical direction of the antenna. But the magnetic field, which is always present when an electric field is created, will be perpendicular to the antenna and the electric field. This magnetic field must also be perpendicular to the receive antenna to generate a good signal in it. You can imagine that if the antenna is for low frequencies, and happens to be mounted between two masts, you will have a horizontally polarized signal attempting to transmit with vertically polarized antennas elsewhere. Permission is necessary from the FCC to use this arrangement. Sometimes the mounting of such an antenna is difficult, especially when the atmosphere above the ship's superstructure is cluttered, as in Fig. 8-3.

With all transmission systems, a good ground is essential. If the ship is metal hulled this may pose no problem. Ground through the hull. But if the ship is plastic, wood, or of other nonconducting materials, you will need at least 12 square feet of good conducting metal, such as copper or brass (may be fine meshed screen), below the waterline to make good contact in the water. The metal should be corrosion resistant to the extent possible. The connection to it should be welded or soldered, physically strong and electrically perfect.

All this brings to mind some differences between a salt water grounding system and the clear water of some lakes. It is to be noted that the clear water doesn't permit the ground wave to travel as well, so communication by this ground wave may be limited. More line-of-sight communicaton will be used in this situation, but, for long distances, the ship may have to have an artificial ground plane for its antenna or be fitted with a counterpoise system in addition to the bonding of all the metallic structures on board to form a ship ground.

SINGLE SIDEBAND EQUIPMENT REQUIREMENT

The FCC has ruled that starting in 1977 the conversion to single sideband communication equipment for the lower frequencies will be accomplished. For some boat owners this means obtaining the newer type equipment. But the reason is important. The communicating ability of the double sideband and single sideband equipment is about the same, but as far as crowding the airwaves, the single sideband equipment requires only half as much space. That is why it is required.

Adding Channels

The operator will soon gain experience with the SSB radiotelephone and its characteristics. One may then wish to have additional channels installed to avoid interference or to achieve more range. Usually a factory representative can accomplish this for you without having to remove your system.

Noise

Single sideband radios are considerably more susceptible to electrical noise than are VHF radiotelephones, which are frequency modulated. It may be necessary to turn off the ignition when receiving very weak signals. If this is inconvenient, a marine electronics dealer can install a noise suppression system on the electrical system to minimize or possibly eliminate this noise.

Routine Care

Given reasonable care, an SSB radiotelephone will provide many years of trouble free service. Like any other piece of electrical equipment, however, it should be checked routinely to insure peak performance.

We discussed reliability of some shipboard equipment with an old salt and one of his maintenance concepts was interesting. He said, "Well, the radar is used to locate channels (by determining positions of the buoys) and to avoid collisions. I use my loran to navigate from one place to another, and I use my automatic direction finder to find out where I am or to get my position. Of course my loran can give that to me, too. What most people don't know is that they need to turn on their equipment often and let it dry out. If they don't, sometimes it won't work." So we took this to heart and promised we would pass along the information given.

RANGE FOR VHF, UHF AND RADAR

We need to examine the range equation for the line-of-sight equipment now available. It is true that in some cases a phenomenon called ducting occurs in the atmosphere which tends to lengthen the distance over which communications or radar signals can be obtained. This occurs when a signal is trapped between two layers of atmosphere or between the surface and a layer. But this can be uncertain and should not be counted on over, say, 7 percent of the total range past the horizon. There is a formula which relates the distance for line of sight to the horizon:

$$R = \sqrt{2h}$$

where: R = statute miles
h = height, in feet, of the antenna above water

The range for radars may be increased slightly if there is a radar reflector high up on the mast of another boat. In fact, this height could be added to your own height in determining the range. The nomograph of Fig. 8-4 can be used to determine line-of-sight range geometrically, that is, by sight.

Refer to Fig. 8-5 for an expansion of the short mileage range. Notice that the increase is linear from 5-1/2 miles to 9-1/2 miles. It begins to flatten out somewhat above this figure. The nomograph will give values above this expanded portion.

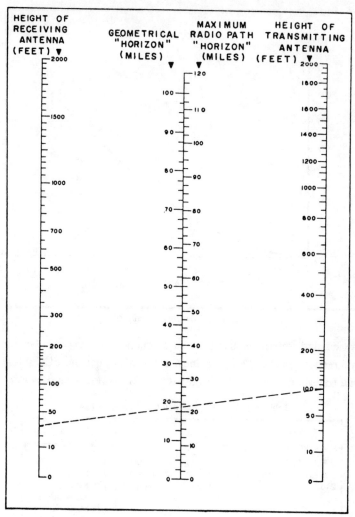

Fig. 8-4. Line of sight transmission ranges and skywave ranges.

SPECIFIC CHANNEL INFORMATION

Although we have designated, in general, the frequencies used in marine communication, we now present some specific frequencies and their use. They may be used if there is no interference with their primary function as safety channels.

Examine Table 8-1. These are the lower frequencies. Now examine Table 8-2 for the ship frequencies in the VHF channel

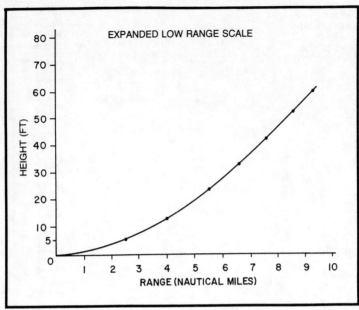

Fig. 8-5. Expanded low range scale of Fig. 8-4.

region, and note that you talk on one frequency and the Coast Guard will respond on another frequency. Be advised that the FCC rules and regulations require that you have a VHF-FM capability before

Table 8-1. Marine Frequencies and Areas of Use.

Frequency	Use	Areas
2003 kHz	Ship-to-ship—Operational	Great Lakes only
2082.5 kHz (SSB)	Ship-to-ship—Operational	All areas
2142 kHz	Ship-to-ship—Operational	Pacific coast area south of latitude 42° N. on a daytime basis only
2182 kHz	Distress—Safety—Calling	All areas
2203.0 kHz (SSB)	Ship-to-ship—Operational	Gulf of Mexico only
2638 kHz	Ship-to-ship—Operational	All areas
2738 kHz	Ship-to-ship—Operational	All areas except Great Lakes and Gulf of Mexico
2830 kHz	Ship-to-ship—Operational	Gulf of Mexico only

they will license you for operation on other frequencies, and the regulations state that you must use the VHF when you are within range of its satisfactory operation. Usually this means you use it during approaches to, and while in, harbors, and when sailing along coastlines.

When communications has been established, there is a time limit for each communication. It is three minutes between two ship stations in the medium frequency (MF) band. This band is 2003 kHz to 2830 kHz. So you must make your talk quick and accurate, just as aircraft crews do. Remember also that you have a call sign and you must identify yourself with it at the beginning and at the end of each transmission.

With each communications system purchased and installed will be included information on channels and operation of the equipment. You will want to study and be familiar with this information. If you are still in doubt as to operation of your radiotelephone equipment, you may obtain from the FCC a small booklet which gives the pertinent facts. Write to the Radio Technical Commission, P.O. Box 19087, Washington, D.C., and reqest their booklet on radiotelephone.

Table 8-2. General Channels.

Channel	Purpose	Band	Note
Ch. 1	Ship to Shore TELCO	4 MHz	(note 1)
Ch. 2	Ship to Shore TELCO	4 MHz	(note 1)
Ch. 3	U.S. Coast Guard	4 MHz	(note 2)
Ch. 4	Ship to Ship	4 MHz	(note 3)
Ch. 5	U.S. Coast Guard	6 MHz	(note 2)
Ch. 6	Ship to Ship	6 MHz	(note 3)
Ch. 7	Ship to Shore TELCO	8 MHz	(note 1)
Ch. 8	Ship to Shore TELCO	8 MHz	(note 1)
Ch. 9	U.S. Coast Guard	8 MHz	(note 2)
Ch. 10	Ship to Ship	8 MHz	(note 3)
Ch. 11	WWV Time & Weather	10 MHz	Receive Only

Note 1

Telephone shore stations New York (WOO), Ft. Lauderdale (WOM), Mobile (WLO), Oakland (KMI) and Honolulu (KQM). Secondary channels (-2) recommended. The frequencies of 4419.0 (ship receive) and 4120.4 (ship transmit) are assigned to Tampa and New Orleans. Galveston and Corpus Christi are assigned 4425.4 and 4126.8. None of these Gulf coast stations are operational as of summer, 1975.

Note 2

Coast Guard Shore Stations Washington D.C. (NMH), New Orleans (NMG), San Francisco (NMC), Honolulu (NMO) and (6 MHz only) Kodiak.

Note 3

Simplex, others are duplex.

ANTENNAS

It really doesn't make much difference whether you have a high priced or low priced, complicated or uncomplicated communications system if it does not establish the communication you need and desire. The real secret to good radio communications is to get the signal to the antenna and then away from that antenna so others can receive the signal with sufficient intensity to reproduce your message. We need to examine antenna systems for a moment and learn about some of them.

Too often the captain or owner assumes that, because there is a wire in the air connected to the transmitter, he has done all that is necessary to establish communications. He then forgets about the antenna except to raise or lower it, as the case may be. But let us look at the antenna situation on board a craft. Figure 8-6 shows a clean installation of antennas. First, the antenna is a metallic structure so that it can permit the flow of electric currents along its length. Second, it is usually enclosed in some kind of plastic material so that corrosion will not take place along its length and reduce the flow of these currents. Third, it must be a specific length or have a means of making the transmitter think it has this length through the use of loading coils. When properly designed energy is transferred from the antenna into space.

In an antenna the current flow is on the surface of the metallic radiator, unlike normal electrical current, as for lighting, where the flow is through the wires. Thus, with an antenna, any pitting or corrosion on the surface impedes current, so the system does not radiate efficiently and your range is reduced. This also applies to all connections to the antenna and with the cables used.

There is more. The transmitter itself "looks" at the antenna in terms of a certain amount of resistance (to current flow), capacitance, and inductance. The capacitance is the electric current stress between the antenna and other metallic objects such as the deck, cabin, other antenna structures, the ground or water, and anything else which will absorb radio frequency energy. Even people are absorbers.

Inductance is the self hindering effect caused by a magnetic field generated in any conductor carrying current. Because the antenna is a conductor carrying current, it has this inductance. Inductance

Fig. 8-6. Simple uncluttered antenna system forward of cabin on pleasure craft. (Courtesy Hatteras.)

produces this "back pressure" only when rf energy is present. This differs from resistance in concept but it has the same effect of reducing current flow. It can be tuned out whereas resistance cannot. When a transmitter is properly adjusted, its antenna system properly tuned, and the antenna in a fixed position with respect to everything around it, most all hindering effects are cancelled out so that only a small amount of resistance remains. Then, the system is ready to operate efficiently.

But imagine that after all tuning is performed and the craft is at sea and the antenna is vertical, that a wind rises to cause bending of the antenna, or cause it to swing sideways, as may be the case with some horizontal antennas. Then the relative distance to all conducting surfaces changes. Some detuning takes place because of this, as the capacitances and inductances of the system change, and so the radiation is somewhat reduced. The system is less efficient than it was when the antenna was still and in the position it was tuned in. Figure 8-7 shows this effect.

Of course the plane of radiation will also change as we discussed previously. So you begin to see why communication during adverse

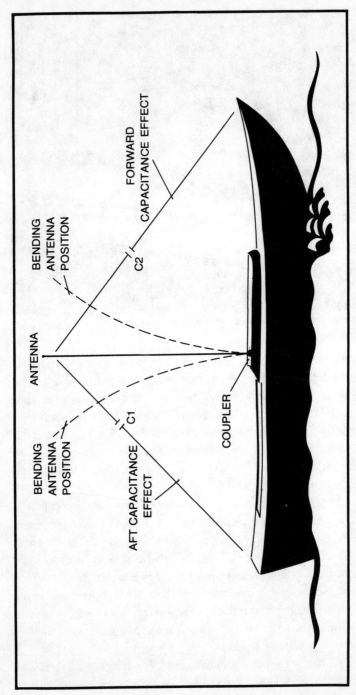

Fig. 8-7. Effect of bending antenna makes C1 and C2 variables.

BENDING
ANTENNA
POSITION

FORWARD
CAPACITANCE EFFECT

C2

ANTENNA

BENDING
ANTENNA
POSITION

C1

AFT CAPACITANCE
EFFECT

COUPLER

292

weather becomes difficult. For you who might be interested in the mathematics of the antenna systems, we can refer you to our book *A Guide to Radio and TV Broadcast Engineering Practice*, TAB No. 523. The networks for antenna matching are discussed at an engineering level in this work. "So what," you say. "The antenna bends. What can I do about that?" Well, let's consider some answers. First, use a rigid type antenna or one which is strong enough so that it won't bend under normal operating conditions. Be sure it is coated and that corrosion does not take place along its length. Check it for cracks and breaks in the coating. Be sure that all connections to the antenna and the transmitter are tight, waterproof, and corrosion proof. Check the fittings often and be certain that everything is bright and tight and making good hard physical contact; also make sure that no wires are broken. With horizontal antennas, get them tight and strong and as high as possible away from all other wires, masts, and other conductive items.

Range vs. Power

Once we get the antenna properly set up and start transmitting, we need to examine the range situation compared to power. We have been asked: "Will it do us any good to increase our power from 10 to 15 watts? If we double the power will our range of communication double?" Unfortunately the answer to the last question is no. The range increases as the square root of the power, so doubling the power doesn't represent a large increase in range at all. Often, more efficiency in the antenna system will do more to increase the range than doubling the transmitter power.

If you are purchasing an antenna, it has an important specification called standing wave ratio (SWR). This may perhaps be 1.5 to 1, or 2 to 1, or 3 to 1. This is important to you. The standing wave ratio is simply the back pressure ratio impeding the flow of energy. Therefore, the lower the back pressure ratio, the more efficient the antenna system will actually be. If you could get a 1 to 1 standing wave ratio you would have the ultimate in efficiency of your antenna system. In practice, a 1.2 to 1 or 1.5 to 1 is considered good. Fig. 8-8 shows a power and an SWR meter.

It is important that you have a technician using the proper equipment measure the standing wave ratio of your communications

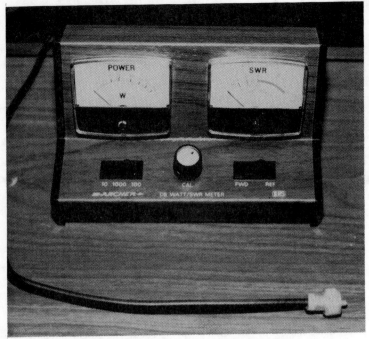

Fig. 8-8. Radio Shack SWR and power meter.

system after it is installed on your boat. The standing wave ratio is affected by all the factors previously stated about antennas, and the only way you can learn if your antenna system is actually performing well is to have this measurement performed under actual operating locational conditions.

Let us examine the range equation for the range versus power of your transmitter. We assume the antenna is doing its best under your conditions and that everything else is okay except that you have a choice of increasing your power or buying a piece of equipment with double the power of another set you might be considering. The range equation may be stated as:

$$\text{Range} = 2\sqrt{P_t/S_{min}}$$

Where: R is range in meters

P_t is the power transmitted in watts

S_{min} is the required receiver power in watts.

Let us consider an example. Suppose you have a system of 10 watts power and you will be communicating with a receiver which has a minimum sensitivity of 10^{-7} watts. Then this equation indicates you will have a range of:

$$\sqrt{1 \times 10^{8}} \text{ meters}$$

The square root of this is 10^4 meters or, considering 2,000 meters per mile, a 5 mile range. Now let us double the *power* transmitted to 20 watts. The range becomes:

$$R = \sqrt{20 \times 10^7}$$
$$= \sqrt{2 \times 10^8}$$
$$= 1.41 \times 10^4 \text{ meters}$$
$$= 7 \text{ miles, approximately.}$$

The range has not doubled. Although you have made some gain by doubling the transmitted power, you must not consider that just doubling the power doubles the range. It DOESN'T.

When a technician measures the efficiency of your antenna system he will check not only standing wave ratio but also field strength. You can obtain a field strength indication yourself as it is checked by a simple instrument which has an antenna and a meter dial. With this field strength instrument you can see how far away you can get and still produce an indication, thus establishing a rough idea of how well you're transmitting. These simple meters only pick up signals very near the antenna.

The following is some theoretical information to calculate the microvolt field strength from some different types of antennas.

Radiation-field measurements should not be made at distances less than 0.6 wavelength from the antenna, as the presence of the induction field in the vicinity of the antenna will introduce errors. The strength of the induction field varies inversely as the third power of the distance from the transmitter.

For general coverage antennas, field strength measurements are ordinarily taken at a number of points around the antenna (usually from 10 to 30), at distances ranging from 0.6 mile to 6 miles, using professional field strength meters.

By comparing actual field strength with the computed field strength, irregularities in the design of an antenna system may be

---

*An output of 150 watts is recommended for AME (A3H) mode of transmissions. Europeans have standardized on 400 watts (100 watt carrier) for AME. AME receives both AM and SSB signals.

detected. For instance, with a given antenna and radiated power, a certain field strength may be expected at a given distance from the antenna. If measurements show a discrepancy of more than 20 or 30 percent between the estimated and the actual field strength, trouble in the antenna system is indicated.

The nature of the terrain between the transmitter site and the measuring point affects the value of the signal strength at the measuring point; this fact should not be overlooked when making a comparison with the calculated value.

The power radiated from a resonant and matched antenna may be calculated in the following manner: measure the antenna rf current under full-power operating conditions at the resonant frequency; square this value of current, and multiply the result by the surge impedance (Z_0) of the transmission line; the result is equal to the power (P_t) supplied to the line.

Multiple Antennas

On boats, there may be a very small space between the various antennas used for navigation, communication, direction finding, and purposes. The proximity of these antennas to each other may cause some degradation of performance in the operation of the various equipment. Notice again Figs. 8-1 and Fig. 8-9.

If these antennas, the vertical types, are spaced less than a wavelength apart, and are anywhere near the resonant frequency of, say, the communications signal, a directivity pattern may be established. This can be checked out by taking a sensitive field strength meter around the boat, at a good distance away and in a clear area—say, at sea—where the water makes a flat unobstructed surface. If the readings vary significantly as you circle the boat at a fixed distance, you can tell in which directions with respect to the boat axis the readings are high and in which direction they are low. A plot will show you the directivity pattern.

You may find that you cannot communicate very far off, perhaps, the bow or the stern, while there is a good distance to the port or starboard. You may find that the directivity pattern is a figure 8 instead of a doughnut, or it may be a heart shaped pattern. In any event one should know his radiation pattern so that, if necessary, he can turn the boat in a direction to get maximum radiation for help or other vital type communications.

Fig. 8-9. Antennas close together may cause degradation of performance.

It may be, also, that the effect and proximity of other antennas near the one you are using may be causing a loading effect on your transmitter so that you show a very strong signal going out by your meters, yet you cannot communicate very far. The check for this is to remove the other antennas and adjust your transmitter for maximum output and most efficient antenna operation, and then to reinstall the other antennas and see if the loading (meter readings) changes appreciably. If it shows a marked change, you do have a radiation problem.

Ground Planes

Proper grounding is an important installation detail that is often overlooked. There are two ground systems to be considered: bonding equipment together and to the earth, and the antenna ground plane. Each requires separate consideration even though there is an interrelationship.

Ideally, all units of a system—the control, radio, coupler or antenna tuner, and antenna ground plane—must be at the same rf ground potential. Seldom is this ideal achieved. The installation and tune up problems are usually proportional to how close to the ideal condition you are able to come. The ideal, of course, is that there is no rf potential difference between any units of the system.

Sometimes ground loops will cause trouble. A ground loop is more than one ground path for a given unit or between units so that when an rf potential difference does exist, circulating currents may be generated, and these cause trouble by inducing currents and voltages into the control circuits.

Ground connections involving dissimiliar metals can set up an electrolysis action, especially when they are exposed to the salt water environment. This may cause future degradation of performance even through everything was normal at the time of the installation. The electrolysis action can eventually corrode so much that there is no ground contact at all. So every effort should be made to waterproof every joint and connection and make them mechanically and electrically as perfect as possible.

Always remember that the vertical antenna always starts at its electrical ground plane, whether you put the conductor you call the antenna there or not (see Fig. 8-10). So, in an installation you first determine the antenna ground plane. That is where the antenna coupler must be located. This may differ from where someone may want you to put the coupler, but that is where it must go for proper operation of the antenna.

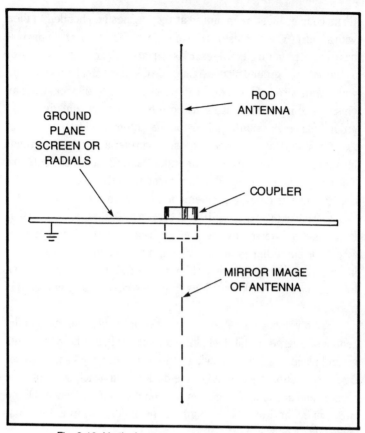

Fig. 8-10. Vertical antennas ground plane concept.

On fiberglass or wooden boats, the hull grounding plane system should have several hundred square feet of surface, with about 100 square feet being the absolute minimum. This is about a 10 foot by 10 foot screen. It is important to know that small porous bronze plates, which are sometimes advertised as having a large surface area, really are not suitable. Large surface areas claimed for small plates refer only to dc applications and not to rf applications. To have an effective radio ground, the system must be physically large. In fact, the larger the better.

But there are some marginally acceptable alternatives to the optimum ground plane system. If a fiberglass or wooden hull boat has two rather large engines that are well bonded together, they may be used as an alternative grounding system. But remember, the antenna coupler must be mounted at the engines and bonded to them with a short (6 inch or less) strap of wide surface area. Or, if the boat has a metal tower on it of at least 100 square feet area, it may be used as the antenna ground plane. Again, the coupler must be bonded to it with a wide strap of not more than 6 inches. Stacks and metal booms on some commercial vessels also can be used very effectively as a ground plane, or counterpoise, for the antenna system.

On fiberglass or wooden boats, it is preferable to have a ground plane screen imbedded on, in, or under the deck below the antenna. The coupler is then bonded to that screen. As the size of the screen is reduced, the tune-up problems for a system may increase. It is best to have at least a 10 by 10 foot screen or copper plate at 2 MHz. If you use any lower frequencies, increase the size. Use copper screen or any other good conducting material. In some cases this may be replaced by a series of long wire radials which spread out from the coupler in all directions to form a circular fan-type ground plane.

But if you have a metal boat and the antenna is mounted in the center of a large metal deck, the antenna will see the deck as its ground plane regardless of where the waterline may happen to be. Again, the coupler is bonded to the deck with a 6 inch strap of wide copper, and a lead-in is run from the coupler to the antenna. Of the two connecting items, the length of the ground strap is the most important. Keep it short.

How do you know when you have a ground plane problem? It is not difficult. When some part of the radio is "hot" from stray rf when it is keyed, then the antenna coupler is probably not located at the ground plane. It is probable that you have a long lead from the coupler to the ground plane. This lead then functions as part of the antenna instead of as a ground. The equipment cabinets become part of the antenna and will be radiating signals. When you key the transmitter you are, in effect, holding on to a part of the antenna.

When a radio tunes funny or appears to be unstable or goes into oscillation on some frequencies, the ground plane is almost invariably at fault. There is no "cookbook" way to correcting all the problems that might arise from this situation except to find the true antenna ground plane and put the coupler in that position. Experimenting with different ground systems will sometimes be a cure. Be careful, however, that some experimental hookup doesn't just change the problem to another frequency. Check all bands, if you experiment, to be sure all are clean and pure.

Transmission and Reception

Always remember that an antenna is a two way device. If it transmits well it will receive well. The pattern in transmission will be the pattern in reception. So if you have a navigation receiver on board that seems to be insensitive to a station, execute a 360 degree turn while monitoring the frequency. There will most likely be headings where the station comes in quite strong and others where it nearly fades out. Once you determine you best reception direction, you can always position the boat at that angle to obtain best coverage of any station. It might be that other antennas on your craft are causing the pattern which makes the reception of signals from some directions difficult. This can be checked out by a capable and experienced technician.

Frequencies, Distance and Types of Antennas

We are spending much effort to include here as much on antennas and antenna systems as we can without writing a complete book just on this subject, but that is how important the antenna system is. We hope that, with the inclusion of all this information, both the technician and the owner might be assisted in understanding how antennas work, what problems may exist, and where to improve a specific antenna system. So if we seem a little redundant, we simply requrest that you bear with us in this effort to give you as much good information as possible.

The choice of a working frequency depends on the time of day and distance to be covered. Modest transmit power on 2, 4, and 8 MHz provides fairly regular day and night service over moderate ranges from 250 to 1,000 miles. To increase the range and talk long distances by daylight requires high power and operation on 12, 16, and 22 MHz.

To determine wavelength you use:

Wavelength in meters = 300,000,000/freq. in cycles

For example, the wavelength of the signal on 2 MHz would be:

300,000,000/2,000,000 = 150 meters.

Recall that MHz is millions of cycles per second and kHz is thousands of cycles per second.

If the radiotelephone output circuitry has sufficient tuning range, a plain wire or whip system theoretically can be used to 22 MHz. However, a 22 MHz quarterwave antenna is only about 11 feet long. Such a short antenna has to be located at the transmitter if the coupler is built into its output stage. The ground connection has to be directly beneath the equipment. This may not be practical. An antenna this short is not the most efficient and may be hard to tune on some lower frequencies. It also might be screened by other objects on board the craft.

One way to get around the problem is to use a longer antenna. An antenna that is an odd number of quarter waves long will resonate in the harmonic mode instead of in the fundamental mode. For example, a 32 foot antenna will operate on its third harmonic at 22 MHz. Other harmonic combinations are possible with antennas of different lengths. But the single sideband channels are not all harmonically related, so a single antenna cannot be made to operate most efficiently over so great a frequency spread when using the simpler radiotelephone sets. To eliminate the problem, some radios are simply limited in upper frequency to channels of 4 or 8 MHz. This permits fundamental mode operation with a 30 foot, or shorter, antenna.

Some radiotelephone sets are made with split output circuits. Two antennas are used, each one designed to work on bands related to the two outputs. You see many craft with more than one vertical antenna. The antenna for the low frequencies may have a built-in loading coil to help it resonate. The higher frequency antenna may have little or no loading coil built-in. Such antennas are designed to resonate at a frequency just above the highest one at which it is to be used. For example, dual antennas may be designed so that one resonates at 3 MHz and the other at 12 MHz.

Trap Antenna

A trap antenna provides a simple means of electrically adjusting the length of one radiator so that it will cover the SSB spectrum. The antenna has one or more built-in wavetraps, which are simple coil and capacitor circuits. At each SSB frequency, the corresponding trap resonates, blocking off the length of antenna beyond, progressively shortening the antenna as frequency rises.

If the trap antenna is located close to the radiotelephone, a conventional wire lead-in can be used. Or, provided the radiotelephone has a coaxial connector output, the trap antenna can be connected by coaxial cable. This can be of any reasonable length. It can be routed down below or wherever convenience dictates without deterioration of performance, either by loss of transmitter power into the hull or by pickup of noise from the boat's machinery.

Trap antennas are available to cover all channels. However, because the traps electrically shorten the antenna with each rise in frequency, the working portion at 22 MHz is just a smidgen of the radiator down at the bottom. Unless the antenna is situated in the clear, the same chance of screening and interference by nearby objects exists as with an ordinary short antenna.

Antenna Tuners

The maximum frequency coverage with a single antenna is afforded by an L- or pi-network tuner taking the place of the simple loading coil output circuit. Such tuners are built into some sets or provided in a separate box which can be located away from the radio. Tuners are capable of matching antennas of practically any length and configuration. When tuners are external they also permit using the most favorable antenna location. External tuners are connected by coaxial cable and control wiring, so the radio transmitter must be especially built for them.

Whip antennas (unloaded forms may be preferable) made of insulated rigging spans or special wires aloft will all operate well with a tuner. The tuner may be mounted on the deckhouse or on the mast in any location that will palce it immediately adjacent to the lower end of the antenna. A good ground, as directly under the tuner as possible, should be used. If the tuner is located on an elevated structure, such as a bridge or tower, a very heavy ground lead, even several of them, should be used. Metal superstructures, railings, and any other metal objects should be bonded into the ground circuit, top and bottom. Ground connections for tuners on masts are sometimes made by connecting to the standing rigging and grounding the chain plates. All intervening turnbuckles and shackles must be bonded across with heavy cable. The upper rigging and the tuning unit may be "hot" with high voltage rf at some frequencies, so installing the tuner aloft is not the best practice. Better to design the system so the tuner is close to the ground connection.

Installation of a Trap Antenna

Through the courtesy of SGC, Inc, we give examples of some trap antenna systems, the ATM-8, and ATM-10.

The ATM-8 antenna system is an extremely efficient marine whip antenna. It uses resonant inductors (center loading configuration) on the 2, 4, and 6 MHz marine bands. This antenna is simply an extension of the same technique used for years on the 2 to 3 MHz band. It was customary to resonate these whip antennas at approximately 2.850 MHz by means of a center loading coil. The antenna then resonated as low as 2 MHz by adding a series, base loading inductor inside the radiotelephone. Antenna resonance could then be moved around by selecting taps on this loading coil. The taps, of

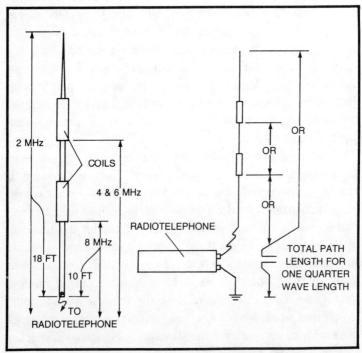

Fig. 8-11. Three band trap antenna, the ATM-8.

course, are connected to the bandswitch to establish antenna resonance on each frequency. This same scheme is used with the ATM-8, on not only the 2 MHz band, but also the 4, 6, and 8 MHz bands as well. See Fig. 8-11.

The ATM-10 trap vertical antenna (fed with open wire GTO cable) is really a modern day version of this basic antenna. However, the center loading coil is divided into sections which are resonated with a capacitor to form a trap. Thus, various resonances are established to permit the same antenna to radiate on 4, 6, and 8 MHz, in addition to the 2 MHz band. Physically the ATM-8 consists of a 3.3 meter, heavy, gold-anodized base pipe, two coils of phenolite (covered with white vinyl), and a 2 meter detachable whip section with static discharge ball. Only stainless steel hardware is used on the antenna. The total length is approximately 6 meters and it weighs approximately 7.9 pounds.

The ATM-8 has three natural resonant frequencies, i.e., 2850, 4100, and 6210 kHz. The 8 MHz band is radiated by means of the feedwire used to connect the antenna to the radiotelephone, in addition to the 10 foot base pipe section. All the bands must be resonated by using the loading coil in the radiotelephone. More important, technicians often overlook the concept of *total path length* in an installation. Keep in mind that most radiotelephones are designed to load a quarter wave or shorter vertical whip or wire antenna. On a typical 2 to 9 MHz installation, the ideal total path length is 27 feet and this includes a 10 foot base pipe section of the antenna. The length of 27 feet is a quarter wavelength at the 8 MHz transmitting frequency and is the maximum *total path length* which can be tolerated.

However, even though the feed line is only 15 feet long, and the base pipe section is 10 feet long (making a total length of less than one quarter wave at 8 MHz), there is no assurance that the radiotelephone will be able to load the antenna properly. Total path length means exactly that. It also includes the length of ground strap between the radiotelephone and true ground in the bilge. If this happens to amount to 10 or more feet (this is not at all uncommon), there is no way the antenna will load up on 8 MHz except by series tuning the feed wire. This is extremely inefficient and results in greatly reduced transmitting range.

The quarter wavelength antenna must work against a counterpoise to radiate. Thus, the total quarter wavelength or total path length starts at the true ground and continues up past the radiotelephone to the tip of the antenna (or just below the loading coil, as the case may be). Thus, the longer the ground lead, the further the radiotelephone is moved up the quarter wavelength. Obviously if the radiotelephone was at ground potential, everything would be perfect. Equally obvious, if the radiotelephone is located near the top of the quarter wavelength, very little energy is going to be radiated and the radiotelephone will be "hot" with rf. Thus, when installing the ATM-8, it is absolutely mandatory that the ground lead be kept short and fat and have as much surface area as possible. This precludes the use of wire and makes use of ground *strap* mandatory.

It can be seen that the requirements for the 2 MHz antenna and the 4, 6, and 8 MHz antenna are diametrically opposite. In other words, the 2 MHz antenna requires a large ground plane but can tolerate a long lead length to ground. On the other hand, the 8 MHz antenna needs very little counterpoise area but, by the same token, cannot tolerate a long ground lead. This is the basic reason why SGC, Inc., strongly recommends the use of two antennas, a 2 MHz radiator, and a second, coax fed, trap vertical antenna for the 4, 6 and 8 MHz bands.

However, if a single antenna is mandatory and if it is not possible to meet the requirements of the total path length (less than 27 feet), there are two tricks which will assist you in resonating the antenna. One is to simply insert a capacitor in series with the 8 MHz clip lead to series tune the antenna. However, a preferable method is to connect a 27 foot length of 14 or 16 gauge wire to the radiotelephone. Stretch out the wire and "bury" it out of sight and out of the way. This wire will act as a quarter wave counterpoise for the radiotelephone. Although the radiation will not be as efficient as from the ATM-10 coax fed trap vertical, at least the radiotelephone will not be "hot" with rf, and you will be able to load the antenna normally. This technique can also be used on the 4 and 6 MHz bands, if necessary, by cutting additional wires which are physically a quarter wavelength at the operating frequency.

If the antenna is series tuned with a capacitor, use a value between 25 and 200 pF. Select the highest value that permits the clip to be positioned two to three turns from the "hot" end of the loading coil. The coil can then be used to trim the antenna into exact resonance. The Centralab "door knob" style of capacitor works very well for this application. Some persons use the 1,000 volt DM-19 mica capacitors and have experienced no problem with breakdown.

Wooden or plastic hulls will require more attention and grounding work with the ATM-8 antenna. On frequencies of 4 MHz and above, the ground (engine, tanks, keel or ground plates, etc.) below the radiotelephone have a reduced value as a counterpoise. Metal objects directly under the antenna are far more important. These objects (radar, pedestal, lifelines, railing, etc.) should be bonded together with a 2 to 3 inch wide copper strap and connected to the radiotelephone to provide a counterpoise for the antenna. Considerable improvement in the radiated signal strength can be obtained on small wooden or plastic hull vessels by covering the top of the wheel house with copper or bronze screen and tack soldering the joints together to make a continuous sheet. Paint this with no-slip latex compound, which will cover and conceal the screen. Bond the screen to the radiotelephone by connecting it with a short, direct copper strap.

One handy instrument which is seldom found in the marine electronics shop is a grid dip meter. If there is a problem loading the antenna, it can easily be analyzed by removing the ground and antenna lead from the radiotelephone and connecting a two or three turn link to these wires. Then couple the grid dip meter to the link (antenna and ground) and tune it through the various bands. It will be easy to see the resonant frequencies of the antenna. If they are below the nominal designed resonances for the antenna, it will not be possible to load the antenna without series tuning, shortening the ground path, etc. Thus, the grid dip meter can be very valuable in analyzing problems of antenna loading.

AM AND SSB CHARACTERISTICS

We have discussed, to some extent, that amplitude modulation (AM) equipment will become obsolete, and single sideband (SSB) equipment has been used since 1976. A brief technical explanation of the differences in the two modes of transmission is in order. Be aware that the reason for going to SSB operation is to conserve

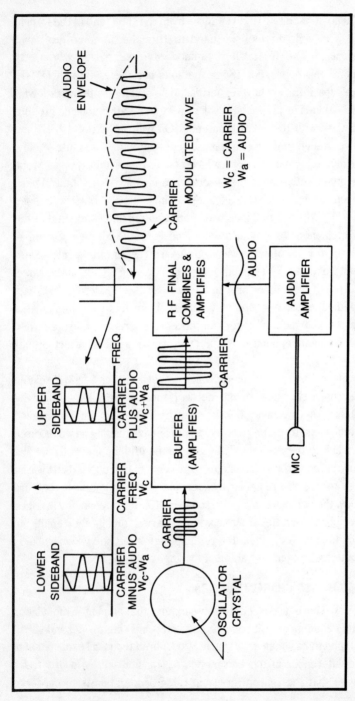

Fig. 8-12. AM signal with two sidebands.

some of the precious frequency space over which electromagnetic siganls may be sent. Only half as much (even less than that) is required for SSB as is required for AM transmissions.

When you key the microphone of an AM transmitter, you create a carrier wave in space which is a vibration on a specific channel to which your equipment is tuned. When you speak into the microphone, you cause a variation in that carrier wave so that it covers more air space, both above and below that which the carrier itself would normally occupy. Examine Fig. 8-12. Here you see that if you send out a 1,000 cycle tone on your 2103 kHz carrier you will create an upper and a lower sideband, one being the sum of the carrier and 1,000 cycles, the other being the difference between the carrier and 1,000 cycles. But notice that the information on each sideband is identical. All this information is always sent as an amplitude modulated signal.

When using single sideband, then, it is only necessary to have circuitry which will remove one sideband, say the lower one (in our example 2102 kHz). By leaving the one at 2104 kHz, you have a signal that contains all the necessary information you want to com-municate. Notice here that this is true SSB. If you examine the situation you will see that the carrier actually contributes nothing to the intelligence. It is necessary to have it present in the receiver to re-create the modulation, or intelligence; but with modern crystals you do not need to transmit it. If you have a crystal oscillator in the receiver tuned exactly to the transmitting carrier, then you can send only the sideband and re-create the intelligence at the receiver. This is known as single sideband suppressed carrier transmission. Figure 8-13 illustrates.

If you tune in a sideband signal on a normal receiver it will sound like gobbledegook. The reason is that the carrier is missing. The detection process in an AM receiver is the exact opposite of the modulation process at the transmitter—also true for SSB and SSB supressed carrier receivers. Recall in the AM system the carrier was mixed with the audio to produce sidebands. The identical mixing process must be repeated in the receiver to convert the sideband back to audio. Since no carrier is supplied with a supressed carrier SSB signal, the receiver must reinsert it for sideband detection. With an AM receiver that has a code oscillator, this can easily be

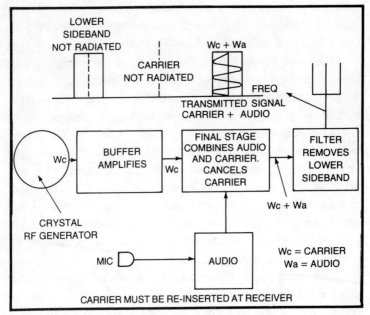

Fig. 8-13. Single sideband suppressed carrier has no lower (or upper if this is chosen for elimination) sideband or carrier transmitted. The signal output $W_c + W_a$ exists only when you talk.

done by switching on the receiver beat frequency oscillator (BFO) used for code reception. In this way a carrier may be supplied to the received sideband and the mixing of this signal with the sideband frequency will enable the recovery of the audio intelligence. Regular SSB type receivers do this automatically.

SSB SYSTEMS AND DEFINITIONS

We need to define the terms *simplex* and *duplex*. These terms relate to frequencies used for the transmission and reception on marine radiotelephones. Simplex is used for ship-to-ship transmissions, although this may not always be the case. It simply means that transmission and reception occurs on the same frequency on both ends of the communications circuit. When only one frequency is used, it is necessary to speak to your party, then to say "over" or "go ahead" and then to listen for them. You cannot speak at the same time: one party must talk and the other listen, and vice versa.

The term duplex is really somewhat incorrect; however, it is commonly used in marine service. Duplex means the ability to talk and listen at the same time, much the same as you do on landline telephones. Virtually all shore telephone stations are set up for full duplex operation by utilizing two channels. The operation of a land-line telephone is essentially duplicated on large passenger carrying vessels. However the smaller vessels do not have this elaborate and expensive capability. Even though the same two duplex channels are used, it is still simplex operation since a party cannot talk and listen at the same time. Thus with simple radiotelephones, the term *two frequency simplex* is more technically correct than the commonly used word: *duplex*.

Now we examine some of the communications equipment used in marine operations, for small craft, pleasure boats, yachts, commercial ships, and work boats of any other type used in offshore operations. Each must have good reliable communications with other vessels, to shore, and sea stations, and with aircraft. Some of this equipment is shown in Fig. 8-14, ranging from a relatively small unit at the top to the larger 180 watts peak emitted power (PEP) of the Europa One SSB systems.

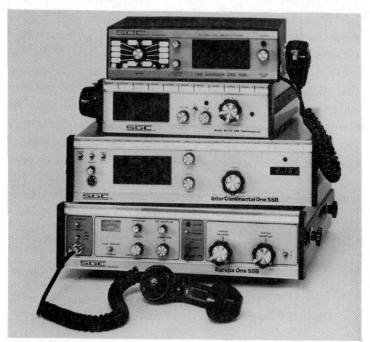

Fig. 8-14. Types of communications equipment. (Courtesy SGC.)

Fig. 8-15. The SGC SSB radiotelephone model 711. (Courtesy SGC.)

Let us examine first the model SG 711 SSB radiotelephone, which is second from the top in Fig. 8-14, and which is shown in large reproduction in Fig. 8-15. Notice that this is a relatively small unit for its operational power of 100 watts PEP. This unit can operate both in the SSB and in the normal AM mode and supplies a full 50 watts output power for AM transmissions. The unit can be programmed for simplex or duplex on any channel from 1.6 to 9.0 MHz. It is relatively easy to install using a Simpson 260 meter. In the simplest case you simply connect the antenna and adjust the coil taps for a maximum reading on the Simpson meter while whistling into the microphone. One coil adjusts resonance and the other the antenna impedance so that if you have some experience with this kind of equipment you can quite easily make the installation. The range of this unit is said to be on the order of 1,000 miles on the 6 and 8 MHz frequencies. It is expected that many of these units may be in operation toward the 1980s and, of course the AM capability have not been used since 1976.

To get an idea of what specifications a radiotelephone system has, examine the following technical data for this unit.

Frequency Range   1.6 to 9.0 MHz

Channels   11, simplex or split frequency

Input Voltage	13.6 volts dc (24 or 32 or 115/230 optional)
Circuitry	All solid state, single up-conversion superheterodyne. 10.7 MHz i-f
Operating Modes	A3j, USB supressed carrier (LSB or USB/LSB optional). A3H (AM equivalent) A3A, reduced carrier (-16 dB)
Environment	$-30°C$ to $+60°C$, up to 95% relative humidity
Weight	14 lbs (6.4 kg)
Size	3.5″ × 12″ width and depth
Certification	Type accepted by FCC under parts 81, 83, 87, 89 and 91

Receiver

Sensitivity	0.5 microvolts produces 1 watt of audio with a signal-to-noise ratio of better than 20 dB
AGC	Fast attack (2 msec) slow release (2 sec) less than 6 dB audio change between 4 microvolts and 0.1 volt
Clarifier (tone)	No less than plus or minus 200 Hz
Selectivity	2.1 kHz at -6 dB, 4.0 kHz at -60 dB (2:1 shape factor)
AM reception	Reinserted carrier or envelope detector optional
Audio Output	5 watts with less than 5% distortion

Transmitter

Power Output	Nominal 100 watts PEP on all modes
Performance	Meets all FCC requirements
Stability	Plus or minus 20 Hz
Response	400–2400 Hz plus or minus 3 dB
Microphone	Hand held carbon
APC	Automatic Performance Control optimizes performance, prevents overmodulation, and protects the transmitter from damage

Of course the receiver is part of the unit. Notice that it has an output of 5 watts so that signals may be heard over a high sea environment noise situation.

SHIPBOARD INSTALLATIONS

The installation of a radiotelephone system is quite simple for an experienced person if the antenna and counterpoise, or ground system, have been previously installed and meet the requirements for the unit. Now we go into some detail concerning a typical installation. This is especially for those who are technically inclined and who, like most of us, like to get into the real gory details of equipment testing and adjustment. The information which follows is representative and gives a good background for other types of systems.

Even though the antenna coupler circuitry of the SG 711 is quite simple, it is capable of loading virtually *any* type of antenna system. This output circuitry practically eliminates the need for a remote antenna coupler if the antenna is direct and the equipment can be located close to it and the ground plane. There are only two instances when an antenna coupler is required: when a considerable amount of feed wire must be routed inside the superstructure of the vessel, and when it it not possible to get a satisfactory ground on the radiotelephone itself. A typical instance might be when the radiotelephone is located on the flying bridge, well above the water-line of the vessel and well above the ground plane. In such a case, mount the coupler down near the ground plane and feed the antenna from that location.

There are several basic rules to remember when working with the simple self-contained coupler in the SG 711. They are:

1. The ground, or counterpoise, forms the other half of the quarterwave Marconi antenna used in most marine installations. Thus, if the ground, or counterpoise, is inadequate or defective, the antenna current will be incomplete and the equipment will not produce the required antenna current.

2. The basic coupler is designed to feed antennas which are one-quarter wavelength or *shorter* at the operating frequency. It will feed longer antennas, however, by series tuning.

3. The length which constitutes a quarter wavelength is the total distance form true ground (ground plane) up through the radiotelephone and on to the extreme end of the radiating portion of the antenna.

Normally a radiotelephone system such as this is adjusted at the factory for a reactive output. This should be checked, of course.

Bench Testing Before Installation

Before you attempt to make the shipboard installation, you should practice loading the equipment in the shop. It takes a bit of experience before you can become proficient in installing the set and loading the antenna. With a little experimentation, you will quickly get the feel of the loading circuitry and be able to recognize what is normal and what is abnormal.

The radio has been previously programmed so that the loading coil is connected to the ceramic wafer switch by means of the clips attached to the coil. These clips serve to short out unused portions of the coil. Also, taps have previously been connected to the 12 ohm point on the impedance matching autotransformer.

Construct a dummy load consisting of a 100 watt 115V light bulb in series with a 200 pF mica capacitor rated at 2 kV or more. This load will very closely simulate the action of the marine antenna except that it exhibits a constant impedance of approximately 100 ohms. More important, it will provide a very illuminating (no pun intended) visual presentation of the loading action of the antenna coupler. Connect this dummy load between the red and black terminals on the rear apron of the SG 711.

Metering. When loading the radio, have a Simpson 260 attached to the test point on the rear apron. This meter will then read relative rf antenna current. One word of caution. Don't use an inexpensive multimeter or the overload protected version of the Simpson 260. In addition to being VOMs, they make excellent field strength meters and their antenna current readings will be completely erroneous.

Normally, a second meter would be attached to the regulated 75 volt line. However, you seldom carry two VOMs around in your tool box. It is relatively simple to move the meter leads back and forth and switch scales.

Loading. Normally, you would start the loading of the highest frequency channels first and work down to the lowest. However, for this illustration, let's experiment with loading the lamp on 2182 kHz.

One handy trick to save a lot of fiddling with the coil clips is to use an EZ Hook or Clip-Ez (Pomona Electronics). Once the correct tap is located with the test clip, the regular clip can be fastened to the coil in the normal manner.

Start the loading procedure by switching to 2182 kHz. Slide the clip down the coil until a definite peak in receiver noise is noted. Temporarily attach the clip to the loading coil at this point. Depress the PTT button and note that the carrier causes the bulb to glow dimly. Say "ahhh" into the microphone and note that the bulb indicates very little modulation and the meter measuring antenna current (connected) to the rear apron test point moves only slightly. This condition is caused by flat topping. This can be verified with an oscilloscope. Flat topping, in this case, is caused by underloading the final.

Start moving the tap on the autotransformer from the 12 ohm tap to a higher point. Note that with each impedance increase, the bulb becomes brighter and the modulation increases. Note also that the antenna current meter shows pronounced upward kicks as you "ahhh" into the microphone. With the impedance matching leads on the 100 ohm tap, the bulb will be quite bright and the antenna current, shown on the Simpson 260, will read up-scale noticeably with modulation. Once again the oscilloscope can be used to confirm that the modulation is normal without flat topping.

At this point, a slight improvement in upward modulation can be obtained by moving the tap on the loading coil (usually in the direction of less inductance). This tap should be optimized for the greatest difference between the carrier reading on the rf meter and the higher reading obtained with modulation. Note that with a slight change in the loading inductance, the carrier reading may drop, but the modulated reading will be higher. This is the correct conduction as it indicates the modulation depth is at maximum. On a supressed carrier channel, the same tuning procedure would be followed by making the adjustments for a maximum meter reading with modulation. Note that it is particularly important that this dynamic loading procedure be followed either by speaking "ahhh" into the microphone or the more complicated method with the two-tone generator. If you simply load for maximum carrier antenna current, flat topping will invariably result.

During these tests, you should occasionally move the meter over to the regulated 75 volt line to observe the effect of the loading on the power supply voltage. When the impedance matching tap is on the 12 ohm point, the power supply voltage will be quite steady. However, as the tap is moved progressively to a higher impedance, slight downward kicks with modulation will be noted. With the tap on the 100 ohm point, and a substantial "ahhh", the meter should kick down 5 to 10 volts. This is the normal fully loaded indication.

As a further experiment in familiarizing you with the proper loading of the SG 711, connect two or three additional 100 watt bulbs in parallel with the dummy load bulb. Repeat the progressive increase in loading. This time, you should note that the rf meter reads higher (because of the lower impedance) and that the regulated 75 volt line loads down much more heavily.

The indication of the meters should be carefully noted and you should mentally correlate these to the indication of the dummy load lamps and oscilloscope. Remember that the only test equipment you will have on board the vessel (or will need) is the Simpson 260. Once you understand how flat topping and normal loading appears on the meter, the task of loading the SG 711 on the boat is greatly simplified.

After you have installed a few units with nothing more than a Simpson 260, it will be obvious that there is no need for a two-tone generator, tune-up switch, or other paraphernalia. Voice modulation provides the simplest and best method of loading the antenna.

Protection

By grossly detuning the loading coil on some frequencies, you may note that the protection circuitry kicks in. When this happens, the regulated voltage will kick down violently and the power converter may stall (as evidenced by a high pitched whistle). Release the button immediately as the overload has been transferred from the final transistor to the power converter transistors. Sustained operation in this overload condition can cause damage to the power converter transistor.

There is one point that many persons find confusing. Before installation, the radio is programmed so that all taps are connected to the 12 ohm point on the autotransformer. On this tap, the protection circuit may shut down the radio when using either the dummy lamp or the antenna. The confusion arises from the knowledge that the transmitter cannot be overloaded on this low impedance tap. This is essentially correct except that the protection circuit protects against every possible condition that could damage the final, i.e., excessive drive, collector voltage and current, SWR, etc. When the taps are on the 12 ohm point, the transmitter may be grossly underloaded. Thus, the collector will have excessive high voltage, causing the protection circuit to kick in. However, when the tap is moved higher in impedance, the shutdown action will cease. This effect is quite noticeable on 2738 when feeding a 100 watt (100 ohm) dummy lamp. The protection circuit will not trip on the 50 or 100 ohm tap of the autotransformer. However it will probably do so when the load is connected to the 12 ohm point as soon as the transmitter is modulated.

The overload protection circuitry can be a bit annoying when you're making the first few installations. However it should be a welcome sound. Whenever this shutdown occurs, this circuitry has just saved you the job of replacing the final transistors.

Once you get the feel of normal loading, you should start with the highest frequency and proceed to load the radio into the dummy load (lamp) on all channels. With this practice, the tuning on board the vessel will be greatly simplified and will be accomplished in a minimum of time.

Antenna Loading

If time permits, try a further experiment in the workshop. Ground the radio to a conduit, pipe, metal molding around the workbench, or any other large metal area. Connect a 15 to 20 foot piece of wire to the antenna post. Stretch out the wire so the far end is clear of large metal objects. The SG 711 will load this wire on all frequencies between 4 and 8 MHz. Other sets of equivalent design will also load the antenna in this manner although some may require a coupler or antenna tuner.

Practice loading this wire on the 4-, 6-, and 8-MHz bands, starting with 8 MHz. Reset the autotransformer tap to the 12 ohm point. Slide the clip down the coil for maximum noise pickup in the receiver. Energize the transmitter and proceed to load the antenna in the same manner as was previously done with the dummy lamp. Once you feel the antenna is properly loaded, hold a 40 watt fluorescent lamp near the far end of the antenna. The lamp should light brightly, indicating good radiation from the antenna. Repeat the same procedure on the 4- and 6-MHz bands. The bulb should light progressively brighter on the lower frequencies.

Notice that the loading and radiation will be very similar if the 15 foot antenna is used as a feed wire for the 2- to 3-MHz marine whip antenna. If the whip is located in such a place that the feed wire is very short, the 15 foot wire can be connected as a stub at the base of the antenna. Then rf between 4- and 8-MHz will excite this wire and ignore the 2- to 3-MHz antenna.

Miscellaneous pointers for when you are making an installation are:

- When working with multiband marine antennas, the impedance can vary between 10 and several hundred ohms, depending upon the frequency and many other factors.

- The antenna current will be inversely proportional to the base impedance of the antenna. At 2182 kHz, you may require a 12 ohm tap and the antenna current may read about full scale of the 2.5 volt range of the Simpson 260. On the other hand, it is not unusual to use the 100 ohm tap on 8 MHz and the meter will read less than 1 volt. In either case the antenna will be working equally well.

- If you are in doubt about antenna performance, hold a 40 watt fluorescent lamp up to the radiating portion of the antenna. It should always light up (although this may be hard to see in daylight) if the antenna is radiating. On 2 MHz it will not light up on the feed wire (except on 2182) since the high voltage point is on the tip of the antenna.

- If the antenna feed wire is shorter, or the antenna resonance high, it may not be possible to resonate the loading coil on 2182 and lower frequencies. In such cases, remove the ferrite loopstick from a defective transistor radio (which you usually always have around somewhere), break in half and epoxy the two pieces at the "cold" end of the loading coil. Place them so the magnetism does not cancel. You will want a strong magnetic field. This addition will produce a large inductance increase only at this end of the coil where it is needed.

- If the loading coil seems to want even less than zero turns on the 8 MHz (and possibly 6 MHz) band, break the clip lead wire and insert a 100–200 pF series capacitance. Select a value which produces correct loading with only a few turns of loading coil. This series tuning, in effect, electrically shortens the antenna length and increases the resonant frequency of the antenna.

- The 50 ohm point on the autotransformer is simply an assigned impedance. The 50 ohm point can be reassigned two tap positions either way to permit other impedances to be loaded. For example, in a base station, it is almost mandatory to move the 50 ohm point two tap positions toward the ground end. This will permit the autotransformers to match impedances as high as 400 ohms.

- If the antenna does not load, and the usual tricks don't seem to work, check the adequacy of the ground. Also check the resonant frequency of the antenna with a grid dip meter. If the meter indicates the antenna is resonant below the desired frequency, there is no way the SG 711 coupler will load this antenna without series tuning.
- If connecting additional metal surfaces to the SG 711 causes the antenna current to change (either up or down), then there is insufficient ground surface on the radio.
- Of course, if you try everything and cannot come up with a solution, then call your appropriate factory representative. He is always glad to assist.

A final word about antennas. Note that antennas that are fed with coaxial cable are commonly referred to as 50 ohm antennas. Common antennas of this category are dipoles, trap verticals, and mobile antennas. However, the impedance of these antennas is seldom 50 ohms.

The standing wave ratio on the coax line feeding the antenna should be measured. It will provide an excellent indication of the antenna performance if you are familiar with how to interpret the reading. For example, it is possible to have a reading of 2.5 to 1 on an antenna which is radiating perfectly. This is because of properly grounded Marconi antenna will have an impedance of approximately 20 ohms and the standing wave ratio is then $50/20 = 2.5$, using the differences in impedance between the coax line and the antenna. For a dipole with 50 ohms impedance and fed with a 50 ohm line, the SWR would be $50/50 = 1$. So check what the antenna impedance is supposed to be.

RECEIVER INTERFERENCE

Even though much communications equipment operates FM, which means a reduction of static and interference, and most units have squelch controls, which keep the equipment silent until a reasonably strong signal is received, sometimes interference can be a problem, not only with communications equipment but also with navigation equipment—to be discussed in the next chapter. We need to spend a moment on this subject, but first let us consider the use and identity of the squelch. We quote *Boating*'s Ken Englert for a good description and recommendation.

> The radiotelephone's squelch is probably the most useful yet least understood control on a marine radio. It affects the operation of the receiver only—it has no effect when your radio is transmitting.
>
> Noise is present naturally in the atmosphere and can be heard on any radio channel that is not in use. The squelch eliminates, by blocking out, this annoying background noise, while allowing voice communications to pass. This gives you the luxury of not having to listen to bothersome racket, without missing any transmission on the channel being monitored.
>
> Many boatmen do not understand the proper setting of this control. The squelch is adjusted only when no one is transmitting on the channel by rotating it to just slightly beyond the point where the noise disappears. The radio now silently listens for another radio to begin transmitting. When another vessel or station keys his microphone transmit button, the squelch circuit instantaneously senses the transmitted signal and turns your radio's audio back on for the duration of the transmission.
>
> It is important not to advance the squelch control too far, or more than necessary to just eliminate the undesired noise—an improper setting can cause weaker radio signals not to be heard. For best results the squelch should normally be set whenever the channel is changed."

When we consider noise itself, it may come from three sources: the equipment itself, in noisy controls or switches; it may be atmospheric; or it may come from other electrical equipment on board. We recognize that there is interference from other radios and other equipment external to your own boat but aside from a channel change we will not attempt to nullify that as it is not under our control.

If you get a loud scratchy noise when adjusting volume controls or switches, you have dirty controls which need to be cleaned. There are many good aerosol cleaners on the market obtainable from radio parts stores and these can be effectively used to clean the noisy control. You simply open the equipment so that you can spray the element. In the case of volume controls be sure to get some spray inside the case by spraying down the lugs—and then work the control vigorously with the equipment off. This usually tends to reduce the noise caused by bad or intermittent contacts inside these elements. If you cannot reach the interior of the volume control because of its sealing, and it remains noisy, then working it vigorously sometimes will smooth the inside parts out and reduce the noise. If this doesn't help then replace it.

Sometimes signals are lost when the boat motor is caused to speed up because it may then radiate signals from sparking so strongly that these will override your signals at your receiver and cause blocking. Then you can't receive any signals at all. Noise of this kind is eliminated by proper electrical filtering of the engines and by checking equipment as discussed in an earlier chapter of this book.

Proper twisting of the lines carrying ac, and isolation of these lines away from antenna cables may also help to solve this problem. Here are some ideas for relief from this kind of trouble.

- Noise generated by the ignition system will appear as a slow popping sound in the receiver and, when the ignition switch is turned off or with the engine running at a high idle speed, will immediately disappear. This type of interference may be reduced through the use of resistor-type spark plugs and by installing a 0.1 mF coaxial capacitor to ground from the ignition coil *primary* lead, not the coil-to-distributor lead. This capacitor should be as close as possible to the coil. Shielded ignition kits can also be used but should be used with the caution previously mentioned.
- Generator and Alternator. This type of interference is characterized by a high pitched whine that does not stop immediately when the ignition switch is turned off with the engine running at a fast idle. Make sure that the generator commutator and alternator slip rings are clean and that the

Table 8-3. VHF Channels.

CHANNEL DESIGNATION	FREQUENCY (MHz) SHIP	FREQUENCY (MHz) SHORE	TYPE OF TRAFFIC	FUNCTION SHIP-TO-SHIP	FUNCTION SHIP-TO-SHORE
6	156.300	—	Safety	Yes	No
7	156.350	160.950	Int'l. Only	Yes	Yes
7A	156.350	156.350	Commercial	Yes	Yes
8	156.400	—	Commercial	Yes	No
9	156.450	156.450	Commercial	No	Yes
10	156.500	156.500	Non-Commercial	Yes	Yes
11	156.550	156.550	Commercial	Yes	Yes
12	156.600	156.600	Commercial	Yes	Yes
13	156.650	156.650	Port Operations	Yes	Yes
14	156.700	156.700	Navigational	Yes	Yes
15	156.750	156.750	Port Operations	Receive Only	Receive Only
16	156.800	156.800	Weather Pending	Yes	Yes
17	156.850	156.850	Safety and Calling	No	Yes
18	156.900	161.500	State Control	Yes	Yes
18A	156.900	156.900	Int'l. Only	Yes	Yes
19	156.950	161.550	Commercial	Yes	Yes
19A	156.950	156.950	Int'l. Only	Yes	Yes
20	157.000	161.600	Commercial	No	Yes
21CG	157.050	157.050	Port Operations	Yes	Yes
22CG	157.100	157.100	Coast Guard	Yes	Yes
23CG	157.150	157.150	Coast Guard	Yes	Yes
24	157.200	161.800	Coast Guard	No	Yes
25	157.250	161.850	Public Correspondence	No	Yes
26	157.300	161.900	Public Correspondence	No	Yes
27	157.350	161.950	Public Correspondence	No	Yes
28	157.400	162.000	Public Correspondence	No	Yes
65	156.275	160.875	Int'l. Only	Yes	Yes

Channel			Use	Int'l
65A	156.275	156.275	Port Operations	Yes	Yes
66	156.325	160.925	Int'l. Only	Yes	Yes
66A	156.325	156.325	Port Operations	Yes	Yes
67	156.375	—	Commercial	Yes	No
68	156.425	156.425	Non-Commercial	Yes	Yes
69	156.475	156.475	Non-Commercial	No	Yes
70	156.525	—	Non-Commercial	Yes	No
71	156.575	156.575	Non-Commercial (Marinas)	No	Yes
72	156.625	—	Non-Commercial	Yes	No
73	156.675	156.675	Port Operations	Yes	Yes
74	156.725	156.725	Port Operations	Yes	Yes
77	156.875	—	Commercial	Yes	No
78	156.925	161.525	Int'l. Only	Yes	Yes
78A	156.925	156.925	Non-Commercial	No	Yes
79	156.975	161.575	Int'l. Only	Yes	Yes
79A	156.975	156.975	Commercial	Yes	Yes
80	157.025	161.625	Int'l. Only	Yes	Yes
80A	157.025	157.025	Commercial	Yes	Yes
83CG	157.175	157.175	Coast Guard Aux.	Yes	Yes
84	157.225	161.825	Public Correspondence	No	Yes
85	157.275	161.875	Public Correspondence	No	Yes
86	157.325	161.925	Public Correspondence	No	Yes
87	157.375	161.975	Public Correspondence	No	Yes
88	157.425	162.025	Int'l. Only	Yes	Yes
88A	157.425	—	Commercial	Yes	No
WE$_1$	—	162.550	NOAA Weather	Receive Only	Receive Only
WE$_2$	—	162.400	NOAA Weather	Receive Only	Receive Only

NOTE: The letter A after certain channel numbers denotes simplex operation in the United States.
Int'l. denotes duplex useage in International Service and is not used in the United States.

brushes are in good condition and making proper contact. At the generator/alternator armature terminal, install a 0.5 mF coaxial capacitor to ground form the armature lead. Make sure that the area of contact between the capacitor body and generator/alternator frame is clean and that the capacitor is securely fastened. Install metal brad shielding on the field and armature lead between the generator and voltage regulator. Ground both ends of the braid.

- Voltage Regulator. The voltage regulator can produce a ragged, rasping sound that does not immediately stop when the ignition siwtch is turned off with the engine running at a fast idle and is usually heard in conjunction with generator/alternator whine. Install 0.20 mF coaxial capacitors to ground from the battery and armature leads at the voltage regulator. Make sure that the capacitor bodies are well grounded. *Do not* install capacitors in the field lead.

- Instrumentation noise is generated by engine instruments and is usually in the form of hissing or cracking sounds. Gauges employing rheostats are likely to produce the most trouble. A low-pitched clicking sound is generally caused by the oil pressure sender. The clicking rate will vary as the oil pressure varies with engine speed. The offending gauge or gauges can be isolated by disconnecting the hot leads from the gauges and then reconnecting the leads, one at a time, to their respective gauges. After the lead is reconnected, jar or vibrate the gauge. If your hear noise in the receiver when this is done, connect a 0.25 to 0.5 mF capacitor between the hot lead and ground.

CHANNELS AND FREQUENCIES

Finally, in this big and all important chapter on communications, we consider it appropriate to include some channel and frequency information which may be of benefit to you. This information is included through the courtesy of SGC Communications, Inc., and Harris Communications, Inc.

Table 8-4. High Seas Telephone Service.

Oakland (KMI)

Ship RX	Ship TX
4371.0	4072.4
4399.8	4101.2
4425.4	4126.8
8738.4	8204.4
8735.2	8201.2
8748.0	8214.0
13161.5	12382.5
13151.0	12372.0
17307.5	16512.5
17304.0	16509.0

New York (WOO)

Ship RX	Ship TX
4390.2	4091.6
4403.0	4104.4
4425.0	4126.8
8757.6	8223.6
8754.4	8220.4
13175.5	12396.5
13172.0	12393.0
17321.5	16526.5
17318.0	16523.0

	Ship RX	Ship TX
Ft. Lauderdale (WOM)	4422.2	4123.6
	4428.6	4130.0
	4415.8	4117.2
	8796.0	8262.0
	8792.8	8258.8
	8805.6	8271.6
	8808.8	8274.8
	13140.5	12361.5
	13137.0	12358.0
	13186.0	12407.0
	17286.5	16491.5
	17325.0	16530.0
	17269.0	16474.0
	17339.0	16544.0
Mobile (WLO)	4412.6	4114.0
	8808.8	8274.8
	13186.0	12407.0
	17339.0	16544.0

Table 8-5. Popular High Seas Channels.

U.S. Coast Guard	Ship RX	Ship TX
	4393.4	4094.8
	6521.8	6207.2
	8760.8	8226.8
International Ship/Ship	4136.3	4136.3
	4139.5	4139.5
	4434.9	4434.9
	6210.4	6210.4
	6213.5	6213.5
	6518.6	6518.6
	8281.2	8281.2
	8284.4	8284.4
	12421.0	12421.0
	12424.5	12424.5
	12428.0	12428.0
	16565.0	16565.0
	16568.5	16568.6
	16572.0	16572.0

Table 8-6. Popular European Channels.

Bermuda	4422.2	4123.6
Bermuda Radio (VRT)	8789.6	8255.6
	13119.5	12340.5
	17290.0	16495.0
England	4422.2	4123.6
Portishead (GCN)	8789.6	8255.6
	13168.5	12389.5
	17314.5	16519.5
Holland	8776.8	8242.8
Shevenigen (PCH)	13154.5	12375.5
	17300.5	16505.5
Italy	4396.6	4098.0
Rome (Roma Radio)	8764.0	8230.0
	13147.5	12368.5
	17293.5	16498.5
Greece	4422.2	4123.6
Athinai Radio (SVA)	8796.0	8262.0
	13168.5	12389.5
	17314.0	16519.5

Table 8-7. Popular South Pacific Channels.

	Ship RX	Ship TX
Hawaii	4415.8	4117.2
Honolulu (KQM)	8751.2	8217.2
	13154.5	12375.5
	17272.5	16477.5
Tahiti	4383.8	4085.2
Mahina Radio (FJA)	8764.0	8230.0
Fiji	4377.4	4078.8
Suva (3DP)	8796.0	8262.0
Am. Samoa	4396.6	4098.0
Pago Pago (KUQ)	8783.2	8249.2
Soloman Islands	13142.5	12368.5
Honiara Radio (VQJ)	8738.4	8204.4
Fr. Polynesia	4383.8	4085.2
Noumea (FJP)	8764.0	8230.0
Australia	4371.0	4072.4
Sydney (VIS)	8757.6	8223.6
	13112.5	12333.5
	17265.5	16470.5
New Zealand	4409.4	4110.8
Wellington (ZLW)	8770.4	8236.4
	13168.5	12389.5
	17293.5	16498.5
Singapore	4377.4	4078.8
Singapore Radio (9VG)	8757.6	8223.6
	13112.5	12333.5
	17293.5	16498.5
South Pacific Emergency	6204.0	6204.0

Chapter 9

Marine Navigation Equipment

It would be difficult to say which is the most important, the communications equipment or the navigation equipment. Without the first you cannot communicate in times of emergency or distress. You cannot radiate a signal which will enable direction finders to locate you. You cannot receive the information as to your location from such sources.   But,   both kinds of equipment are important and can be omitted.

NAVIGATION SYSTEMS

In this chapter we will examine some types of navigation equipment including loran, Omega, and some direction finding (homing) equipment, including the omni range (which if you have a copy of our book *Aviation Electronics Handbook*, TAB No. 631 you may already be familiar). We will also examine, to some extent, the age old princicples of celestial navigation using a modern electronic calculator for solutions to navigation problems. We will consider the use of satellites for position determination so that you will become familiar with how they are used for this purpose. There will be other things as well, but these are the main points of this chapter.

A good captain will always have his communications equipment and his navigation equipment close by and ready for use, just as a motorist has his windows and mirrors for viewing and his speedometer and odometer for car movement information. Figure 9-1 shows one arrangement whereby the captain can handle the wheel and easily view the scope of his navigation equipment at the same time.

In some cases, as shown in Fig. 9-2, the loran receiver is mounted below deck, amidships, in the lounge where it can be comfortably viewed. The reference calculations and chart lines can easily be made and drawn using the adjacent table top as a base.

The choice for location of such equipment is often a compromise between what the skipper would like to have, and what the technician says will be best for the safety and security and overall operation of the equipment.

In researching for this work, we consulted some old salts around the water. We asked them about this navigation problem using such equipment. They said there were some problems, perhaps the largest being the effect of water and sea air on the equipment when it was mounted on the flying bridge, where the captain wanted it mounted. Moisture got into the equipment and eventually troubles developed.

Also mentioned was the lack of grease on the rotating antenna equipment of radars. They said that once such equipment was installed, everyone seemed to think that it was considered to be

Fig. 9-1. A navigation receiver fastened to cabin top can be seen easily by captain.

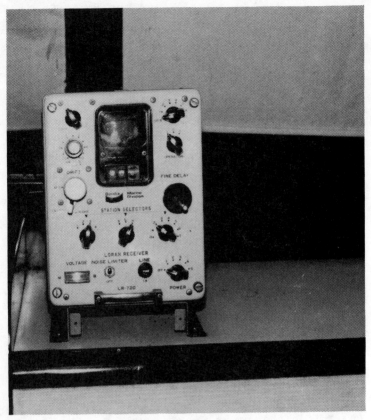

Fig. 9-2. Loran receiver in ship's lounge.

there permanently and that no further maintenance was required on it. Well, you know about rotating machinery and salt air and water and no grease.

But there was much satisfaction in these discussions from the fact that, in general, the equipment seemed to be well made, and was well installed so that even in high seas and high gales it performed well. We again emphasize that it will pay to have good equipment from reputable manufacturers installed by reputable firms and technicians. Sometimes, if you try to save a few bucks, it can prove most costly later on.

One problem case concerning navigation equipment was explained to us. It had to do with electrical interference. It seems that a high powered, and very large and beautiful yacht had some new navigation equipment (loran) installed, and then the craft was taken 100 miles out to sea for a test run using the equipment. What a beautiful sight. That craft was moving gracefully and swiftly through the water. The navigation equipment was turned on, and low and behold, the scope pulses would not settle down and there were light flashes of interference, the like of which had never been seen before.

Back to the harbor she came, and the checkout began. Nothing could be found that was incorrect in either the ships wiring, electrical power sources, or in the new navigation equipment. The equipment worked perfectly at the dock, and on the test bench, and another trial was ordered. Again failure.

Days went by and the engineers and technicians were about to loose all their hair, as well as their minds. Finally, one bright young chap said "I'm going to check the engines and their equipment and connections from the ground up." He did this in spite of the fact that they had been checked a dozen times and all the filtering and suppression equipment possible was on them. As a matter of course in his step-by-step check, he removed one spark plug and gapped it. It was twice the gap it should have been. He shouted, and a moment later everyone was pulling the other plugs, changing the gaps and reinserting them into the head. It turned out, that was the problem. A Thunderbolt ignition system with overgapped spark plugs had rendered that expensive navigation equipment useless.

Once the correction was made, another trial run was conducted and a lot of people celebrated the return of their sanity. Everything worked perfectly, as it was supposed to, and the great beautiful vessel left for ports unknown.

You just cannot take anything for granted in electrical or electronics systems. Check everything and do this twice, even three times. Have someone else check the same things. It becomes possible for a person to be so intent on finding things the way he imagines them to be that he just can't see the tree for the forest. Methodical, sure, step by step systematic procedures are the ones that always result in success.

So, now let us progress to an examination of the navigation equipment as to how it works, what it does, and how we can use it. The more we know about it, the better we understand its capabilities

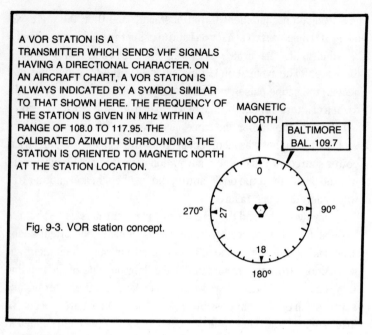

A VOR STATION IS A TRANSMITTER WHICH SENDS VHF SIGNALS HAVING A DIRECTIONAL CHARACTER. ON AN AIRCRAFT CHART, A VOR STATION IS ALWAYS INDICATED BY A SYMBOL SIMILAR TO THAT SHOWN HERE. THE FREQUENCY OF THE STATION IS GIVEN IN MHz WITHIN A RANGE OF 108.0 TO 117.95. THE CALIBRATED AZIMUTH SURROUNDING THE STATION IS ORIENTED TO MAGNETIC NORTH AT THE STATION LOCATION.

MAGNETIC NORTH

BALTIMORE
BAL. 109.7

Fig. 9-3. VOR station concept.

and limitations, and its maintenance requirements, the better we can use it. We start with a discussion of the omni system.

OMNI NAVIGATION EQUIPMENT AND CONCEPTS

The Narco OM410 is designed specifically for marine navigation. The receiver utilizes aircraft VOR stations for accurate navigation, and is more reliable than other types of direction finding methods. VOR is an abbreviation for VHF (*V*ery high frequency) *O*mnidirectional *R*ange. The terms omnirange, omni, and VOR are often used to mean the same thing. Examine Fig. 9-3.

Omni is designed for use as an accurate landfall navigation system along coastlines and inland waterways. Since omni receives VHF signals, its range, like all VHF communications, is affected by the height of the station and the height of the antenna on the boat. The omni can be used most effectively to establish a radio range to avoid shoal waters or to locate an inlet or offshore buoy.

In discussing VOR navigation, there are several terms whose definitions may help to explain the principles of omni.

- *Bearing.* In omni, a bearing (Fig. 9-4) is the direction of a line from the receiver *to* the station being received. In omni navigation, magnetic bearings are used exclusively, since VOR stations are referenced to magnetic north.

- *Radial*. In omni, a radial is the direction of a line *from* the station being received, to your boat. Radials are always read with reference to magnetic north and are the opposites of bearings. For example, if you are due east of a station being received, the direction of the line from your boat *to* the station would be a 270 degree bearing. Your boat would be on the 90 degree radial, the line from the station to your boat.

- *Heading*. Heading is the direction in which the boat is pointed as indicated by the craft's magnetic compass. In omni, the boat's heading has no effect on the signal being received.

- *Course*. The course is the line on the chart which the navigator intends to follow to reach his destination. He may plot his course in relation to true north, but it is more likely that it will be in relation to magnetic north. (In VOR navigation, only magnetic courses are plotted.)

- *VOR Signal*. Operation of omni is based on a phase difference between two signals, a reference phase and a variable phase. The reference phase is omni-directional and radiates from the station in a circular pattern, the phase being constant through 360 degrees. The variable phase rotates and changes as it rotates around the station. See Fig. 9-5.

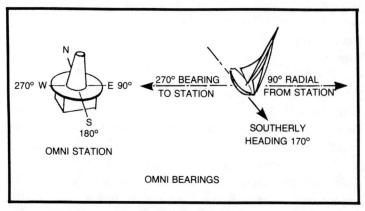

Fig. 9-4. Omni bearings.

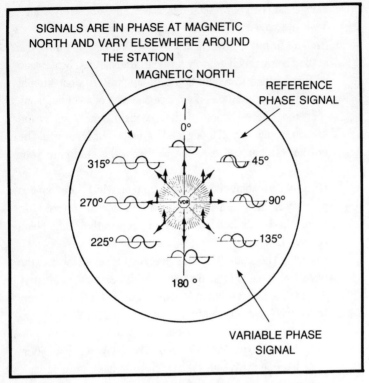

Fig. 9-5. Omni phase rotation.

Magnetic north is the reference point for measuring the phase difference between the two signals. At magnetic north, the two signals are exactly in phase. At other points around the compass, the phase difference varies accordingly. The omni receiver automatically resolves the difference and displays it in magnetic degrees.

The FAA maintains hundreds of omni stations within range of the coasts of continental United States, Hawaii, Bermuda, the Caribbean Islands and Europe. However, these aircraft omni stations are not indicated on marine charts, so it is necessary to obtan aircraft sectional charts at a local airport.

You may wish to use marine charts in omni navigation by determining the latitude and longitude of each station along the coast line and locating the position of these stations on the marine charts that will be used for navigation. Transparent azimuth rings can be purchased to be applied to the charts directly over the top of each station marked on the marine charts. The ring would be oriented to magnetic north at the station's position.

A further convenience would be to write the station frequency and the three letter code for each station in the center of the azimuth ring for each station on the chart.

The OM410 receiver shown in Fig. 9-6 is equipped with low level audio which may be wired to a headphones jack. You may then use headphones to receive the code signal from the station. However, the receiver is equipped with a crystal frequency synthesizer which assures reception of the proper station. Some VOR stations broadcast aircraft weather reports which may be heard through headphones.

When the VOR station can be used as a homing beacon and the boat steered on a fixed course toward the station, the bearing line will remain constant regardless of wind, current, or erratic steering.

The line cannot change. What can change is the position of the boat relative to the bearing line. As long as the boat remains on the bearing line, the indicator on the omni receiver remains centered. If

Fig. 9-6. Narco omni receiver.

Fig. 9-7. Narco omni receiving antenna. This antenna is to be located at the mast head in a horizontal position. The antenna rods may be oriented in any direction, usually aft.

the boat drifts or is steered off course, the indicator shows the deviation. Omni always tells the navigator whether his boat is on or off course regardless of the heading. The Narco omni antenna with its self contained amplifier is shown in Figure 9-7.

Using the OM410 Receiver

1. Clockwise rotation of the upper right knob (Fig. 9-6) turns the receiver on. The instrument face illumination will indi-

cate that you have power to the receiver. If audio has been installed, further rotation of the knob increases volume. Pulling the knob out enhances the station identification code and supresses voice.

2. Select the station frequency by means of the lower right concentric knobs.

3. Observe the needle deflection and the TO/FROM window. Action indicates the signal is being received. The TO/FROM signs appear in place of the OFF sign.

4. Turn the OBS knob slowly until the needle approaches center. Observe the needle and make intermittent adjustments of the OBS knob until the needle rests on center or averages around center.

5. A strong reliable signal will show a full window indicating TO or FROM. If the window indication is partial, the signal may be usable but unreliable. Continued monitoring of the signal may provide a full indication after a period of time. This is caused by varying atmospheric conditions. An OFF indication in the window with needle near center will show no signal being received. The window will also indicate OFF when the OBS reads 90° to the bearing line. In this case the needle will show a firm full deflection.

6. When a centered needle and full TO or FROM indication has been obtained, read the number at the top of the OBS dial. The numbers are every 30°. Zeros have been eliminated. There are divisions every 5° so you should be able to interpolate to the nearest degree. The number you read will be the magnetic compass line running between your boat and the station being received. The direction of the station on that line will be indicated by the TO/FROM window.

Some other considerations when working with an omni:

- A TO indicates the reading is a bearing *from* your boat *to the station*.
- A FROM indicates the reading is a radial *from* the station *to your boat*.
- The 180° reciprocal of the number is shown on the OBS dial by the small numbers on the inner perimeter of the dial.

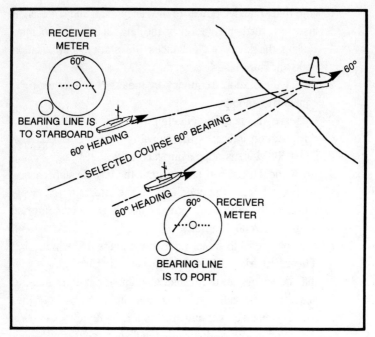

Fig. 9-8. Course position rule.

- A reversed reading can be obtained by rotating the OBS dial 180° which will cause the TO/FROM indication to reverse.
- Use omni bearings to plot your position as you would any other bearing information.

Course Position Rule

With omni, the navigator can visualize the relative position of his boat to the selected bearing line by memorizing this rule: *When the boat is steered to the heading shown on the omni bearing indicator, the needle will point in the direction of the selected line.* For instance, if the selected bearing is 60 degrees and the needle is deflected to the left side of the indicator, the selected bearing is to *port* while the boat is on the 60 degree heading; see Fig. 9-8.

It is important to visualize the boat as being on the same magnetic heading as the selected bearing because the direction of the needle deflection is actually independent of the boat's heading. It does not matter whether the selected line is a bearing *to* the station or a selection radial *from* the station. The position of the needle will indicate whether the selected line is to port or to starboard, as long as the boat's heading is the same as the selected line.

Navigating by Omni

A practical navigation problem shows how omni can be used to make a landfall. Assume that the weather conditions are bad, and only an approximate position, well offshore of a sea-buoy, is known. The navigator has the task of locating the buoy marking the entrance to an inlet. He checks his chart and locates an omni station within range of the buoy. Then he draws a bearing line through the buoy to the station, noting that the bearing to the station is 150 degrees. The navigator selects the station on the frequency selector and turns the omni bearing selector knob until the indicator needle centers. The bearing now reads 110 degrees *TO* the station, indicating that the boat is on a line south of the 150 degree bearing to the station as shown in Fig. 9-9.

The navigator now resets the omni bearing selector to the 150 degrees bearing line and notes how the needle is fully deflected to the left. He then directs the helmsman to steer northerly, parallel to

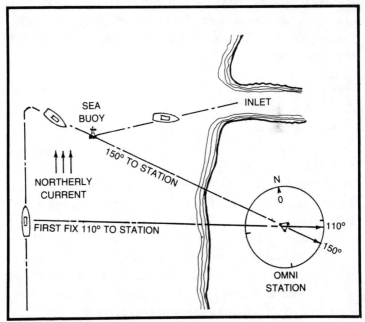

Fig. 9-9. Omni navigation example.

the coast, to stay outside the buoy. As the boat approaches the 150 degree bearing, the needle begins to move toward the center. What is happening is that the phase signals are beginning to come together. When the needle finally centers, the navigator knows he is on the 150 degree bearing line even though the boat is still headed north. At this point the navigator directs the helmsman to steer southeast toward the station on a course of 150 degrees.

However, as the boat proceeds on the 150 degree bearing and heading, the navigator notes that the needle on the omni dial starts to move to the right, indicating that the boat is slipping off the line to the north, apparently due to current. He directs the helmsman to correct his heading to offset the current and bring the boat back on the course, and the needle back to the center of the dial.

Once the seabuoy is located and provides a fix, the navigator gives the helmsman the compass course to the mouth of the inlet, taking into account the effect of the northerly set of the current.

Thus the omni navigational system can be a useful method of plotting precise fixes, or as a homing device for making landfalls or finding coastal buoys. However, like any electronic device, omni does not replace the need for a navigator skilled in dead reckoning or celestial navigation. As such, omni is an aid to navigation, not a complete system that will solve all problems in the demanding task of coastal navigation.

Checking out the Omni System

Turn on the receiver by means of the upper right hand knob. The internal lighting should be visible. Then:

1. Select a VOR station frequency by rotating the lower right hand knobs.
2. Rotate the lower left knob until the needle averages center. If the station is within usable range, the flag window should read TO or FROM. The magnetic compass direction TO the station or FROM the station is indicated by the reading in the window, and the large numbers at the top of the dial. The reciprocal of the direction is indicated by the smallest numbers on the dial under the larger numbers.
3. A strong signal will be indicated by a full flag in the window, while a partial flag in the window, while the needle centers,

indicates that you have a marginal signal which may not provide a reliable bearing.

4. In some instances the needle may waver around the center mark. This may be caused by aircraft near the station or some other disturbances. To get the best reading under these conditions, make small adjustments in the dial, and observe the needle for brief periods of time to get the best average around the centerline.

5. Distances that signals may be received are influenced by the height of the station, height of the antenna on the boat, weather, and interfering terrain between the station and your boat. It is possible, therefore, to receive signals at one place and not at another even though the distance to the station is unchanged. Usual receiving distance is about 30 miles when the antenna on the boat is 25 feet above the water.

6. Accuracy should be within 2°, which represents one mile 30 miles from the station. Occasionally inaccuracies in excess of 2° may occur from weak signals or unusual terrain conditions which may distort the signal.

Troubleshooting Tips

Notice first that the antenna has an active amplifier built in and this must have power applied to it. This is done through the same cable which brings down the signals to the receiver. Some other things to keep in mind:

- The most common cause of antenna trouble is traced to a poor conductor, either at the antenna, in the antenna lead, or at the receiver.

- There should be continuity through the center conductor to the shield. This should be a resistance ranging to several hundred ohms. This continuity check should not show an open or a short. Radio is off for this test, of course.

- To test the antenna amplifier performance, the sensitivity of a weak signal put through a TV type balun into the antenna system with no more than 100 feet of cable should exceed the same signal injected directly into the receiver. The ends of the antenna should be shorted together during the balun test, to prevent resonance.

- Approximate line voltage (A+) is supplied to the antenna from the receiver through the center conductor to the antenna. Check for DC voltage between the center conductor and the shield at each connector, while the radio is turned ON. If no voltage is apparent, check at the radio and inspect each conductor for a defect.

LORAN NAVIGATION SYSTEMS

Loran is a system of navigation which provides accurate fix information over a much longer range than the omni system just discussed. Loran, which stands for LOng RAnge Navigation first came into being during World War II, when it was used to provide invisible radio paths over enemy territory so that the bombers could be steered accurately to their targets. Basically it consists of sending out a pulse from each of two stations which are located in two different geographically located positions. Or sending the pulses, delayed, from one station in such a way that the receiver "thinks" it is receiving two stations geographically separated.

Since radio waves travel at a fixed speed, it is possible to measure the difference in time of arrival of two pulses from these different station locations. As you could imagine, if one station is closer to you, its pulse will arrive first. The pulse from the more distant station will arrive a few millionths of a second later. The time difference between these two arrival times is the means of determining where you are along a grid of time difference lines plotted for the base stations. Actually, a third station, or pair of stations, is required to give you a fix, as we shall see.

The equipment used in the system of navigation, aside from the stations, is the receiver on your boat. This has an oscilloscope type presentation and dials for adjusting the received signals as indicated in Fig. 9-10.

The signals from the two stations are received as pulses on two separate baselines on the oscilloscope. The dials are adjusted for superposition of the pulses one on the other, or positioned one below the other. Then the reading of the time difference is obtained from reading the dial numbers.

344

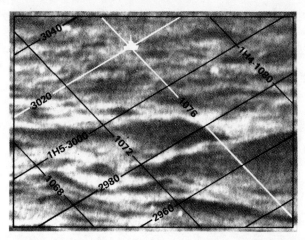

Fig. 9-10. KONEL KL155 loran A receiver. Two pulses from loran A stations adjusted for synchronization, and a sample grid. Chains of loran stations along the coast broadcast precisely synchronized pulses at various repetition rates. The difference in the time of receipt of paired station pulses varies with the distance from the transmitting stations. A line of position, or delay line, is indicated on the loran A chart for a given difference. By taking fixes on two loran A pairs, the line of intersection will give your ship's position.

In automatic systems, the pulses are positioned automatically and the reading, in clear numbers, is shown on the scope face. You then go into your charts, find the time differences that correspond to your numbers, and opposite these you will find listed your coordinates.

Loran has two systems: The A system, which uses 1900–2000 kHz frequencies, and the C system, which is the low frequency system using 100 kHz. This low frequency system can be used by submerged vessels as well as surface craft. The systems are worldwide, as you can see by inspecting Fig. 9-11.

When tuning your receiver to loran stations, you must select both the channel and the pulse repetition rate of the stations you desire.

The grid systems from the stations shown in Fig. 9-11 radiate over nearly all the oceans using both skywave and ground wave phenomena. You must know which station you are tuned to in order to know which chart of time differences to look at when you have adjusted your loran receiver. But this is not difficult. You know which ocean you are in, so you will have a log of the station frequencies in

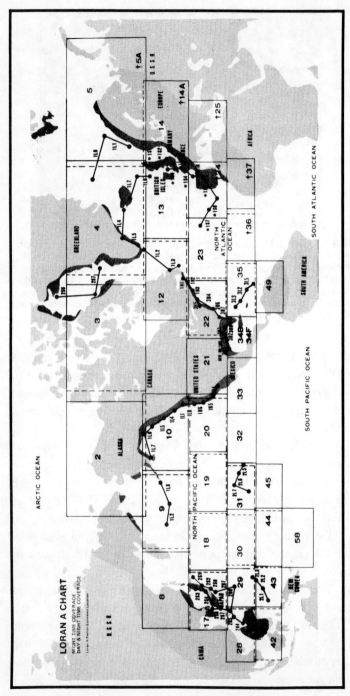

Fig. 9-11. Loran A station locations. (Courtesy Morrow Electronics.)

346

that area. Thus you will tune to the stations which are nearest your position to get your fix. Of course if you can't receive stable signals for any reason, you can select other stations and tune for these, then use the appropriate chart referring to them.

Now we will explain in more detail what loran is and about some of the phenomena of radiation associated with it. Then we want to examine in more detail the adjustment of a loran receiver for position information. Remember there are the two types of loran, the loran A, and the loran C systems. We will consider the loran A system next.

Principles of Loran

Unlike radar, which uses very high frequencies of millions of kilohertz, loran A operates on a frequency of about 2000 kHz. This is the region of the radio spectrum just above the commercial broadcast band used in the United States. The much shorter waves of radar travel along nearly equivalent optical paths and are therefore limited in their range by the curvature of the earth. The longer waves of loran, on the other hand, travel not only over the surface of the earth, but travel skyward and encounter the electrically ionized region of the upper atmosphere, which is called the ionosphere. Signals reflecting from it may return to earth many hundreds of miles from the sending antenna as shown in Fig. 9-12. This is what makes the long range of loran possible. With present techniques, the distance limit is about 700 nautical miles by day and some 1,400 miles by night, although unuseable signals may be received much further than this at night.

Operation of the loran system can be summarized in the following five items:

1. Radio signals consisting of short pulses are broadcast from a pair of special shore based transmitting stations.
2. These signals are received aboard ship on a specially designed radio receiver.
3. The difference in time of arrival of the signals from the two stations is measured on a loran indicator (dials or a scope digital display).
4. This measured time difference is utilized to determine directly from special tables or charts, a line of position on the earth's surface.

5. Two or more lines of position, determined from two or more pairs of pulses from transmitting stations, are crossed to obtain a loran fix.

Thus loran differs from the usual radio direction finding for it measures difference in time of arrival of radio waves, rather than the direction of the arrival. Loran, therefore, may use simple straight wire antennas rather than loops or complicated direction finding antenna arrangements.

Operation of loran involves measuring to a microsecond (millionth of a second) the time of arrival between the reception of pulses. One station of a loran pair emits pulses at a constant interval. This station is known as the master station (M).

Several hundred miles away a second transmitter, the slave station (S), emits a corresponding series of pulses which are kept accurately synchronized with those from the master station. The time difference (T) between the reception of a master pulse and the corresponding slave pulse establishes the loran line of position.

The line adjoining the two transmitters is called the *base line* and its perpendicular bisector is called the *center line*, as shown in Fig. 9-13. If both the master and the slave pulse were transmitted simultaneously, they would be received simultaneously on the centerline, and the corresponding time difference would be zero. On either side of the center line the pulse from the nearest station will arrive first. The farther the receiver is removed from the center line, the greater will be the time difference between the reception of the two pulses. On the base line extensions the interval will reach a maximum.

In an actual loran system the master and slave pulses are not transmitted simultaneously. Each slave pulse is delayed by a carefully controlled amount so that the corresponding master pulse is always received first. This eliminates any ambiguity in identifying the pulses, and gives time differences which increase continually from a minimum value at the slave station to a maximum at the master station.

A given line of position means a given, and constant, time difference. Each loran line of position is a hyperbola having the transmitters as focal points.

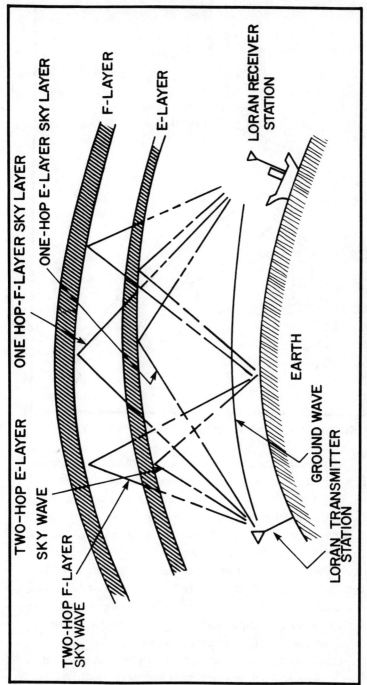

Fig. 9-12. Ground and sky waves. (Courtesy Raytheon Marine.)

349

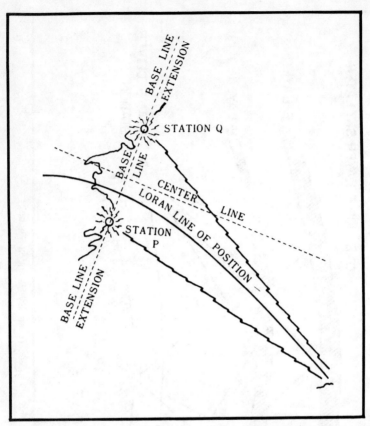

Fig. 9-13. Base line and center line. (Courtesy Raytheon Marine.)

The lines of constant time difference for each pair of stations are all precomputed, taking into account curvature and eccentricity of the earth and other factors, and are made available to the navigator in the form of loran tables and loran charts. Therefore, the navigator need not concern himself with the detailed theory of the method of establishing the time difference at the stations or the calculations of the lines. He merely has to follow a methodical measuring procedure aboard his ship, then to go directly to the charts or tables and interpolate between plotted or tabulated lines of position to determine the exact line corresponding to the measured time difference. We shall have an example on how to do this.

Loran shore transmitting stations are usually arranged so that the two stations of a pair are separated by 200 to 400 miles. But, under some unfavorable geographic situations, this separation may have to be reduced to as little as 100 miles or extended as much as 700 miles.

Station Pairs

Loran stations are located so that signals from two or more pairs of stations may be received in certain areas, and thus a loran fix is obtained by crossing two or more lines of position, as shown at X in Fig. 9-14. To economize on station installations, one station is often made common to two pairs (three stations, then, are used). Usually the master station is common to two other stations and is double pulsed, the slaves being single pulsed. Double-pulsed stations, however, send out two entirely distinct sets of pulses, one set paired with the pulses from each adjacent station. Therefore, from an operating viewpoint, a double pulsed station can be considered as two separate stations at the same location.

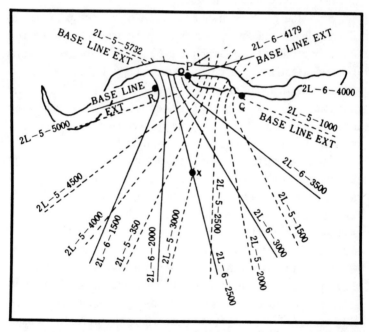

Fig. 9-14. Lines of position. Two lines of position from two pairs of loran stations provide a loran fix. P is a double pulsed master station common to both pairs. Q and R are slaves. Lines with prefix 2L5 are formed by P-Q. Lines with prefix 2L6 are formed by P-R. (Courtesy Raytheon Marine.)

The average error of a loran line of position depends on the location of the navigator. It amounts to about one tenth of a mile in the area between a pair of transmitters, but not exceeding two miles throughout at least three quarters of the total night time service area of a pair of stations which are separated by the usual 200 to 400 miles.

Loran Range and Signal Paths

The range of loran stations; the type of signal received, ground wave or sky wave or both; and the accuracy of the resulting time difference measurement are affected by the path over which the radio waves travel. A portion of the radio energy travels out from the transmitters parallel to the earth. This is known as the ground wave. Another portion of the radio energy travels upward and outward, encountering electrified layers of the atmosphere (known as the ionosphere) and if conditions are favorable, is reflected back to the receiver. Reflections from the ionosphere are known as skywaves. Refer back and examine Fig. 9-12.

Since the groundpath and the various skywave paths are of different lengths, a single transmitted pulse may be received as a series, or a train of pulses as shown in Fig. 9-15. As the ground wave path is shortest, the ground wave, if received, will always be the first pulse in the train. The one hop E layer reflected pulse is next and secondary pulses (multiple hop E layer and all F layer reflections) follow in time of reception. Sky wave reflections beyond one-hop E are considered too unreliable to be used for accurate navigation.

The loran indicator will give a reading (this is the receiver) no matter what ground wave or skywave pulses are matched. But, to get the correct reading, the proper pulses must be selected. We will tell you about that in a moment. This is the critical part of loran operation, the selection of the proper pulses on the receiver scope screen. This selection must be very carefully performed.

If ground waves can be received from both stations of a pair, they should be used, and a G put after the noted time difference to indicate its nature, e.g., $T_G = 2130$ G. Even weak ground waves are to be preferred to strong skywaves because sky waves are subject to variations in timing, changes of shape known as *splitting*, and fading, all caused by variations in the ionosphere—the height and density of these layers.

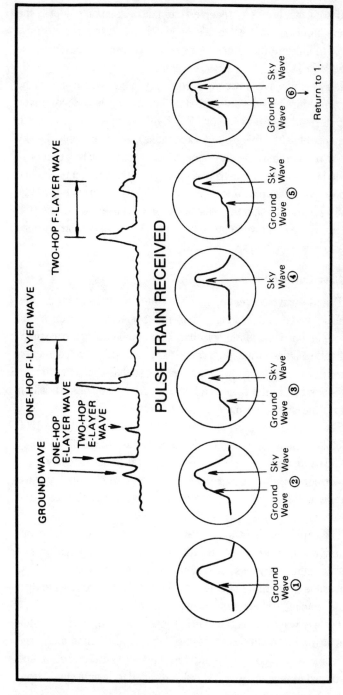

PULSE TRAIN RECEIVED

Fig. 9-15. Scope shows sky wave waveforms under fading. The pulse train appearing on the cathode ray tube scope is shown when the receiving signal includes both the ground and sky waves. (Courtesy Raytheon Marine.)

353

If no ground wave is received from either station of a pair, the two one hop E sky waves should be matched and an S put after the reading to indicate its nature. A skywave correction must then be applied.

If a ground wave is received from only one station of a pair, the usual procedure is to ignore it, match the two one hop E sky waves (you determine that they are one hop E by the time of arrival, which is immediately after the ground wave pulse), and then apply the sky wave correction. In some instances, however, a special correction is provided for matching the ground wave from one station to the one hop E sky wave from another station. Such time difference readings should be marked SG, if the master skywave is used, or marked GS if the master ground wave pulse is used. These corrections, where necessary, are of course tabulated.

Sky Wave Corrections

The sky wave corrections compensate for the fact that the one hop E sky wave path is longer than the ground wave path. Loran lines-of-position in tables and on charts are computed on the assumption that the signals travel the ground path. The sky wave correction reduces a sky wave time difference reading so that a single system of lines-of-position in the tables and charts can be used. Essentially it converts the sky wave time to ground wave time.

Sky wave corrections are tabulated to approximately the 1500 mile limit of usable loran signals. No corrections are tabulated closer than 250 nautical miles from a transmitting station because sky wave behavior here is too uncertain. Never attempt to extend sky wave coverage and corrections into areas not covered by the tabulated values.

The listed values of the skywave corrections are average values derived from many observations. Individual readings on sky waves are inherently less accurate than readings on ground waves. The average of several sky wave readings will be more reliable than a single reading. Whenever possible use ground waves.

The sky wave corrections, in microseconds, are entered on the charts at the intersections of lines of latitude and longitude, in the same color as the corresponding loran lines. The sign before the correction denotes whether it should be added to or subtracted from the observed reading. Interpolation between the tabulated values should be made whenever the sky wave corrections are changing rapidly. Failure to interpolate may cause appreciable errors.

How to Use Loran Table

Two methods may be used to fix a ship's position using a loran A receiver. One method is to use the loran chart with the values obtained in loran measurements, the other is to use the loran table. Separate loran tables are published for use in different waters. They are separated and color coded depending on the loran transmitter stations pairs. Each of these tables contains a small chart, sky wave corrections, and a calculating table for longitude and latitude.

The calculating table consists of upper and lower sections. The upper section gives time difference (T) entered in microseconds in the columns. The lower section gives latitudes and longitudes with their time differences in the vertical column.

Latitude and longitude coordinates for a ship's precise position may be obtained from the table by applying the corrections given under the mark Δ in the table to the latitude and longitude readings obtained from the table.

Example: The value of loran measurements are $2S3T_G = 1860$ (read: "from station 2S3 the ground time difference T_G is 1860 microseconds"), and $2S4T_G = 3806$ when the measurements are made at an estimated position of a ship at 41° 35′ N and 136° 36′ E. To find the precise position of the ship, open the tables for 2S3 and 2S4. Find the time differences nearest to the given time differences in the time difference column. See Table 9-1. Find the longitudes

Table 9-1. Partial Loran Table.

2S3-1860		
Lat.	Δ	Long.
41°36′N 41°23′4N	− 20 − 18	136°E 136°30′E
2S4-3800		
42°0′ N 41°0′ N	136°26′ 8E 136°21′ 5E	+ 27 + 22

Table 9-2. Rewritten Loran Table

2S4-3806	
Lat.	Long.
42°0′ N	(+ 0′ 27) × (Y) + 136°21′ 5 = 136°23′ 1E
41°0′ N	(+ 0′ 22) × (Y) + 136°26′8 = 136°28′1E

$$TG - T = Y \quad \text{or} \quad 3806 - 3800 = + 6 = Y$$

under the time difference columns which correspond to the latitudes nearest the estimated latitude. Tabulate the latitudes and longitudes obtained with the corrections given under the Δ marks.

For 2S3, the values of the table given as $T = T_G$ may be used as they are. For 2S4, however, the values of the table must be rewritten as shown in Table 9-2. Thus, the position of the ship may be plotted as shown in Figure 9-16 (a). For comparison, Figure 9-16 (b) gives the same fix using a loran chart.

Matching two one hop E skywaves is usually more reliable than matching a ground wave to a sky wave. When matching two sky wave signals, variations of sky wave travel time caused by ionospheric fluctuations will affect both signals by comparable amounts. Errors will be caused by the variation in the difference of the two corrections but will tend to cancel each other out. This is not true when matching a groundwave to a skywave since only one signal travels via the ionosphere.

Identification of Sky Waves and Ground Waves

The identification of ground waves and sky waves is the principal operational problem in loran and must be solved correctly if satifactory results are to be obtained. In making the identification the following should be considered:

- The ship's location relative to the stations, and the type of signals that might be expected.
- The appearance of the signals under observation.
- The spacing of the pulse under observation, relative to other pulses in the train.

The problem of identification will be solved almost automatically most of the time if observations are made at frequent intervals. It will then be possible to see how conditions are changing, and it will be possible to have a good idea as to what type of signals to expect before even looking at the scope. In addition, any temporary mistakes in identification will be made more obvious by the sudden discrepancy with respect to previous loran fixes.

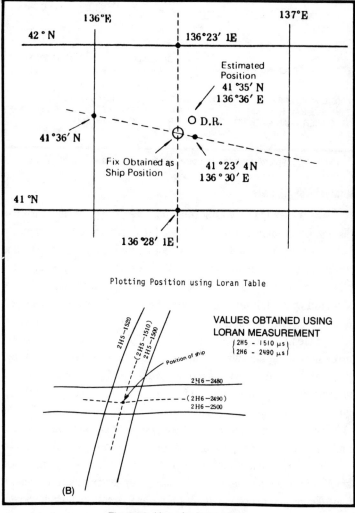

Fig. 9-16. Use of a loran chart.

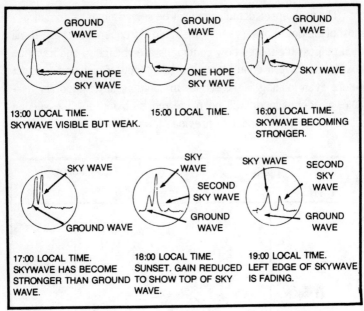

Fig. 9-17. Typical variation in appearance of signals with time of day.

Analysis of Signals

Sky waves have two inherent characteristics that can be used to distinguish them from ground waves. First, sky waves are subject to fading. At times this fading may be quite rapid, completing an up and down cycle in less than a minute. At other times the cycle of fading may be extremely slow and a sky wave may appear very steady, like a ground wave, for several minutes. Second, sky waves are subject to splitting, which consists of breaking into two or more humps, which fade more or less independently. Splitting may be a source of error in making sky wave readings, since the leading edge of the pulse (the left edge) may be momentarily faded down into the noise, and the pulse apparently is shifted over several microseconds. In general, the greater the distance to the transmitter, the steadier the sky waves. The one hop E sky wave generally is much steadier than multiple hop E sky waves or F-layer sky waves.

In contrast to sky waves, the ground wave is generally steady in amplitude and is always free from splitting, although if it is weak, it may flicker from noise. Also, there are occasions when violent rolling of the boat may cause the ground wave amplitude to vary somewhat. In this case, however, all signals should vary more or less together. A typical variation in appearance of ground and sky waves with local time is shown in Fig. 9-17.

Now let us examine some equipment. One type of loran receiver is shown in Fig. 9-18. Note the station selector dials. You could set 2S3 for one of the stations of the previous example of plotting. The readout gives you a number; then set 2S4 and get its readout. Use the readouts as in the example. Pulses appear in the left window and the time difference in the window in the center.

The installation of such a receiver and a typical location appears in Figs. 9-19 and 9-20.

To gain a feel for this kind of equipment, refer to Fig. 9-18 again while you examine Table 9-3. You will learn what the various types of controls do in adjusting the equipment. Notice under item 7 that reference is made to Figs. 9-21, 9-22, and 9-23, the adjustments for operations one, two, and three.

Now, before turning the power to ON, set the knobs on this equipment as follows:

OPERATION	set to	1
GAIN	set to	maximum
DRIFT	set to	center
ATTENUATOR	set to	off
NOISE LIMITER	set to	off

Fig. 9-18. Gemtronics GT 2205 loran receiver.

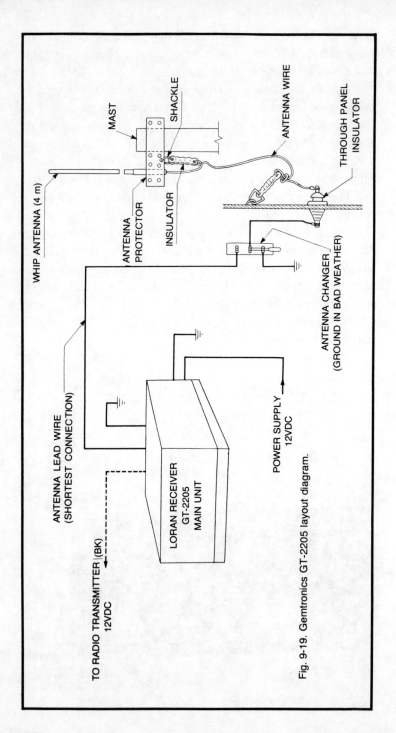

Fig. 9-19. Gemtronics GT-2205 layout diagram.

WHIP ANTENNA (4 m)

MAST

SHACKLE

ANTENNA PROTECTOR

INSULATOR

ANTENNA WIRE

THROUGH PANEL INSULATOR

ANTENNA CHANGER (GROUND IN BAD WEATHER)

ANTENNA LEAD WIRE (SHORTEST CONNECTION)

LORAN RECEIVER GT-2205 MAIN UNIT

POWER SUPPLY 12VDC

TO RADIO TRANSMITTER ((BK) 12VDC

Now set the STATION SELECTOR to the desired loran station. Adjust GAIN for both MASTER and SLAVE to find two pulses at a position (a) (b) (c) or (d), as shown in Fig. 9-24.

The pulses *must* be recognized as to which is the master and which is the slave. The length of a line from the master pulse to the slave pulse is *longer* than the length from the slave pulse to the master pulse. Notice the dashed lines on (a) and (c) of Fig. 9-24. Starting at the pulse position on the upper base line, going to the end of the screen and continuing along the lower base line to the second

Table 9-3. Knobs and Indicators for the Gemtronics GT2205 Receiver.

Name		Function
POWER		Power on off
STATION SELECTOR	Channel (1, 2, 3)	Selection of loran frequencies.
	BASIC (H, L, S)	Selection of basic recurrence rate.
	SPECIFIC (0-7)	Selection of specific recurrence rate.
GAIN		Adjustment of the gain. GAIN of MASTER and SLAVE adjust the strength of receiving signal on the upper and lower traces.
ATTENUATOR		Decreases the signal about 1/30.
MASTER KEY		Shifting the received pulse to left or right.
DRIFT		Stopping the movement of pulse, and pulling for AFC.
SLAVE KEY		Shifting the lower line pedestal, for "OPERATION" on Fig. 9-21. Overlapping the slave pulse to master, for "OPERATION" on Fig. 9-22. Superposing two pulses, for "OPERATION" on Fig. 9-23.
OPERATION		Changing the display.
NOISE LIMITER		Reduction of interference.

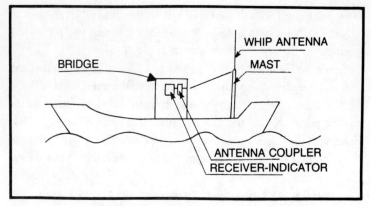

Fig. 9-20. Installation sketch. (Courtesy Raytheon Marine.)

pulse gives one line length. This can be roughly measured. Now, if the controls are changed you might get the picture shown in (c), and here you can again determine the length of the dashed line in the same manner. This line should be shorter than the first, so you would have to readjust your controls till you get the representation in (a). The master pulse in this figure is shown as (M) and the slave as (S).

Adjust the master key to set the master pulse on the upper pedestal as shown in Fig. 9-21 (a). Refer back to that figure. Notice also by referring back to Figure 9-21 (b) that the slave pulse is set on the lower pedestal by means of the SLAVE key.

Now adjust the two gain controls to get the same height. When the gain cannot adjust them to the same height, set the ATTENUATOR to ON. Then make this adjustment.

Now set the OPERATION SWITCH to 2; the picture on the CRT should be that shown in Fig. 9-22 (a). Adjust the slave key to set the slave pulse under the master pulse as show in Fig. 9-22 (b).

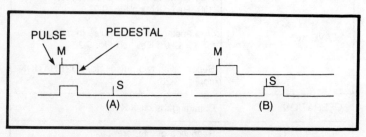

Fig. 9-21. How to adjust operation 1.

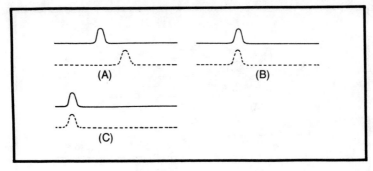

Fig. 9-22. How to adjust operation 2.

Finally, move the pulses to the left hand end of the scope face using the MASTER key to obtain the picture shown in Fig. 9-22 (c).

Set the OPERATION SWITCH on 3 to establish the pulses on a line as shown in Fig. 9-23 (a). You *superimpose* the two pulses using the SLAVE key, keeping them equal in height with the GAIN controls.

Carefully superimpose them at the left hand slope of the pulses as shown in Fig. 9-23(b). You will notice that there are two kinds of superimposing speeds available, depending upon how the SLAVE key is pushed in each way. Notice Fig. 9-23(c). If you want a slow speed of 1 microsecond/second, push carefully to the medium position. While in the case of the rough adjustment, push to the full, and pulse and digits run about five times faster than they do in the slow position. The reading of the indicator is ground wave time difference in microseconds. See Fig. 9-25.

Now adjust DRIFT to superimposed pulses so they stand completely still, then pull the knob to transfer to automatic frequency control (AFC). This must be done to make the automatic

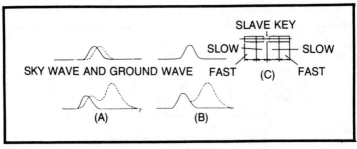

Fig. 9-23. How to adjust operation 3.

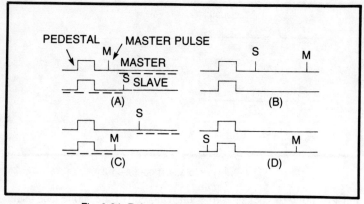

Fig. 9-24. Relation of master and slave pulses.

tracking stable. You transfer to automatic tracking by setting the OPERATION switch to AUTO. Then you'll have a constant readout of position time-difference as the boat moves.

THE RAYTHEON NA-110 RECEIVER

Automatic tracking is easily accomplished in this receiver. It is a loran A unit, and its operating controls are shown in Fig. 9-26. Operation is as follows:

1. Turn the POWER switch to ON. Check to see that the white pointer of the LEVEL meter deflects within the green marker of the scale. If the pointer fails to deflect within the marker, turn the POWER switch to OFF and adjust the power supply voltage until the pointer will deflect within the marker. (When the pointer deflects outside the green marker, the power supply voltage is below 10V or above 35V or 45V and a volt change switch is set to 32V.) If excessive voltage or current is applied to the

Fig. 9-25. Indication of time difference in microseconds.

receiver indicator, the fuse will blow to protect the internal circuit.

2. Set the CHANNEL switch to the desired position.

3. Set the BASIC PRR switch to the desired basic pulse repetition rate position.

4. Set the SPECIFIC PRR switch to the desired specific pulse repetition rate position.

5. Turn the OPERATE switch to position 1. Set the ATTENTUATOR switch to OFF. Check that the AFC, ATC and INTERFERENCE REDUCER switches are in the OFF positions. Turn the GAIN A and GAIN B controls fully clockwise (cw) until the signal and noise appear in large amplitude on the cathode ray tube. Then turn them counterclockwise (ccw) until the signals on the upper A and

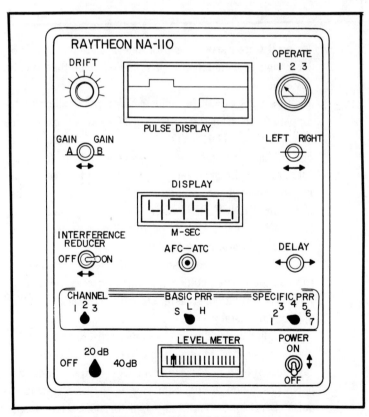

Fig. 9-26. Raytheon model NA-110 loran controls.

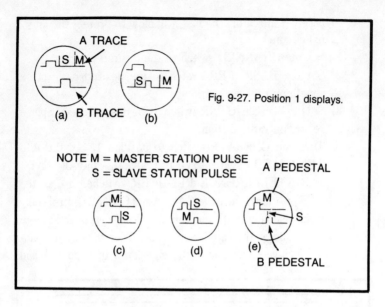

A TRACE

(a) B TRACE   (b)

Fig. 9-27. Position 1 displays.

NOTE M = MASTER STATION PULSE
S = SLAVE STATION PULSE

A PEDESTAL

(c)   (d)   (e)

B PEDESTAL

lower B traces provide appropriate amplitudes. A pair of loran signals should then appear stationary on the cathode ray tube.

6. If the signals cannot be adjusted to provide appropriate amplitudes by using the GAIN A and GAIN B controls, turn the ATTENUATOR SWITCH to 20 or 40 dB. If the base line fluctuates up and down excessively on the cathode ray tube, or if the loran signals sway slowly, radio reception is interfering with the loran signals. In this case, turn the INTERFERENCE REDUCER switch to ON and adjust the GAIN A and GAIN B controls again until the signals provide appropriate amplitudes.

7. Identify one of the two pulses appearing on the cathode ray tube as the master station pulse and operate the LEFT-RIGHT lever until the master station pulse is placed on the upper A pedestal.

To distinguish the master station pulse from the slave station pulse, first observe the two pulses on the cathode ray tube. If both pulses are on the A or B trace, then the pulse positioned at the right side is the master station pulse. See Fig. 9-27(a) and (b). If the pulses are placed separately on the A and B traces, the pulse on the A trace is the master station pulse, provided it is to the *left* of the pulse positon on the B trace as in Fig. 9-27(c). If the pulse on the A trace is to the right of the pulse on the B trace, then the pulse on the B trace is the master station signal, the condition at Fig. 9-27(d).

8. After placing the master station pulse on the A pedestal, operate the DELAY lever until the slave station pulse is placed on the B pedestal *at the left end* of the pedestal. (See Fig. 9-27(c)).

9. Check to see that the master and slave station pulses are placed on the left half of the A and B pedestal respectively; then, turn the OPERATE switch to position 2. The cathode ray tube should then display only the A and B pedestals spread over the scope as the upper and lower traces, which include the master and slave station pulses enlarged as shown in Fig. 9-28. Adjust GAIN A and GAIN B controls again until the master and slave station pulses provide the same amplitude. See Fig. 9-28(b). Operate the DELAY lever so that the lower pulse is positioned directly beneath the upper pulse. Then, throw the LEFT-RIGHT lever into the LEFT position until both pulses are positioned at the extreme left end of cathode ray tube scope as in Fig. 9-28(c).

10. To make the receiver automatically track the slave station signal with the master station signal, turn the AFC-ATC lever switch to ATC. This starts automatic tracking circuit operation and quickly brings both signal waveforms into

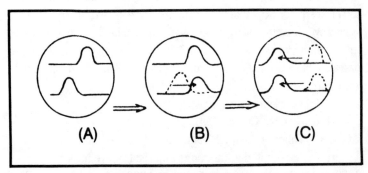

Fig. 9-28. Position 2 displays.

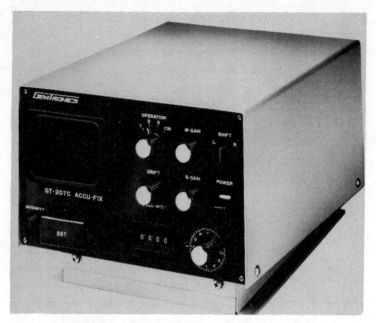

Fig. 9-29. Gemtronics GT-207C loran C receiver.

their overlapped condition even when there exists a difference of the order of ± 30 microseconds between both waveforms.

LORAN C NAVIGATION

In the previous discussion we learned that loran A systems operate in the 2000 kHz frequency band. We now examine the loran systems that operate at a very much lower frequency of 100 kHz and which have pulse *groups* to identify the signals. The reason for the lower frequency is that the ground wave is extended, and the accuracy of using the ground wave maintained. There is much information available on the use of sky waves at extreme distances and also loran C tables of time differences vs. latitude and longitude from the

Defense Mapping Agency,

Hydrographic Center Depot,

5801 Tabor Avenue, Philadelphia, PA, 19120

It is to be noted that the range of loran C systems is from about 1500 nautical miles daytime to about 2300 miles nighttime. The accuracy of the vessels line of position may be within 100 feet on a repeatable basis with some of the better equipment. One type receiver, the Gemtronics, is shown in Fig. 9-29.

In installations it is advisable to have the antenna above all other antennas and rigging wires and away from metallic masts if possible. Also, the receiver should be located so that it is adequately protected from the weather. This means that a remote indicator of the time difference may be of help in some installations, and this is available. One such unit is shown in Fig. 9-30.

Now let us consider some technical aspects of the loran C system, courtesy of Simrad, Inc., and then see how we would adjust a typical loran C receiver, such as the one illustrated, to receive these pulses and determine our position.

The radio carrier frequency used in the loran C system is 100 kHz. The radiated energy from the loran C transmitters is concentrated in groups of pulses, each pulse containing the 100 kHz carrier frequency and lasting about 200 microseconds. A single pulse is

Fig. 9-30. Remote loran C indicator. (Courtesy Gemtronics.)

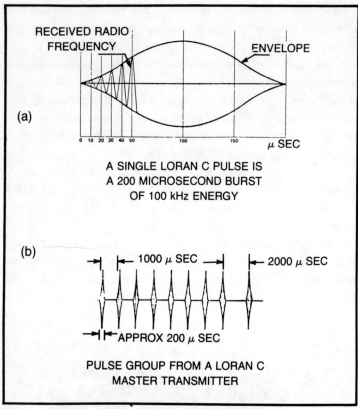

Fig. 9-31. Loran C energy and pulse. (Courtesy Simrad.)

illustrated in Fig. 9-31(a). Each pulse group is composed of eight pulses (plus a ninth identification pulse for the master). A typical pulse group is shown in Fig. 9-31(b).

Such a pulse group is radiated from the master transmitter at predetermined intervals (pulse repetition rate) for the respective loran C chains. Each pulse group from the master station is received directly by an operating loran C receiver within the area of the chain as well as by receivers at the slave stations.

The receiver at the slave station is used to synchronize the slave transmissions with the master transmissions. These stations thus transmit pulse groups locked in frequency to that of the master station. The pulse group transmission within a typical loran C chain, consisting of master and two slave stations, can therefore be illustrated as shown in Fig. 9-32.

370

As mentioned, the loran C receiver receives a pulse group from the master station first. Then it receives a pulse group from slave station 1, and so on. The transmission of the slaves is delayed so that their pulse groups always arrive later than those of the master regardless of receiver location. The delays also insure that the slaves are always received in the same order, that is, no overlap.

The time duration measured from the beginning of the leading edge of a pulse group transmitted from a master station, until the leading edge of the next pulse group from the same station is defined as the pulse repetition rate, abbreviated PRR. In the loran C system there are 48 possible PRRs consisting of six basic PRRs, each with the possibility of being varied by eight specific PRRs. The basic PRRs are identified by SS, SL, SH, S, L, and H, the specific PRRs by the figures 0 to 7. A particular chain (of station) may thus be indicated on a loran C chart as SL3 and the station pair (master/slave) by the slave stations type designator: W, X, Y, etc. (slaves).

The basic PRRs are identified as stated above and so the indication SL3-X-16600 on a loran C line of position contains the following information:

SL   Basic pulse repetition rate
3   Specific pulse repetition rate
X   Station pair information, master/slave X
16600 Loran C LOP for a time difference of 16,600 seconds
        (LOP is line of position).

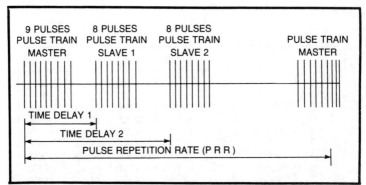

Fig. 9-32. Pulse group transmission within a typical loran C chain. (Courtesy Simrad.)

The pulse repetition frequencies for the basic PRRs are:

H   33-1/3 pulse groups/second
L   25 pulse groups/second
S   20 pulse groups/second
SH   16-2/3 pulse groups/second
SL   12-1/2 pulse groups/second
SS   10 pulse groups/second

Table 9-4 shows how the basic and specific PRRs are combined to give the 48 possible PRRs. In 1975, the U.S. Coast Guard changed the method for designating the chain PRIs (pulse repetition intervals). The new designations are four digit numbers which indicate the actual PRI. The easy coast chain is now identified by the number 9930 which means the PRI is 99,300 microseconds.

With this as a background, then, we can next examine the adjustments for a typical loran C receiver. If you will refer back to Fig. 9-29, which shows the front panel controls, we need to identify one or two units on this panel and then we will explain how to adjust this receiver. The chain plug (SS7) is a plug-in unit which gives your frequency coverage for one basic and one specific rate. The DRIFT control stops the received pulses on the CRT. The time difference fine dial superimposes the two pulses at OPERATION 3 or at CM. The time difference course thumbswitches (4 digit display) shifts the pedestals, the received pulses, and overlaps the slave to master pulse.

Table 9-4. Loran C Pulse Repetion Rates.

Specific PRR		BASIC PRR					
		SS	SL	SH	S	L	H
	0	100,000	80,000	60,000	50,000	40,000	30,000
	1	99,900	79,900	59,900	49,900	39,800	29,900
99	2	99,800	79,800	59,800	49,800	39,800	29,800
	3	99,700	79,700	59,700	49,700	39,700	29,700
	4	99,600	79,600	59,600	49,600	39,600	29,600
	5	99,500	79,500	59,500	49,500	39,500	29,500
	6	99,400	79,400	59,400	49,400	39,400	29,400
	7	99,300	79,300	59,300	49,300	39,300	29,300

Operation of Loran C Receiver

1. Set the knobs as follows prior to turning set on.
   OPERATIONS set to 1
   M-GAIN set to maximum
   S-GAIN set to maximum
   DRIFT set to center and push-in positions

2. Turn the power switch to POWER. The receiver will be operational after 10 to 20 seconds, and the picture will appear on the CRT.

3. Adjust M-GAIN and S-GAIN to find the master and slave pulse trains. The master group can easily be distinguished since it has 9 pulses, while the slave group has only 8 pulses. See Fig. 9-33(a).

4. Adjust the SHIFT key so that the master group is on the upper pedestal, as shown in Fig. 9-33(b). The slave groups are selected to keep the intersecting angle of two LOPs as perpendicular as near to the vessel as possible. See a chart (not included here) for time difference information of LOPs near your estimated position.

5. Set the time difference course to get one of the slave groups, for example X, on the pedestal of the lower trace as in Fig. 9-33(c). The four digit dial in the lower right hand corner of the receiver is the time difference course setting unit.

6. Adjust the M-GAIN and the S-GAIN to get the same height.

7. Set OPERATION to 2 and adjust the time difference course control to set the first pulse on the lower trace under the first pulse on the upper trace, both of which are to appear on the left hand side of the CRT. They should be overlapped by the SHIFT key and then confirm that the 9 pulses of the master group are on the upper trace. Be careful about this.

8. Set the OPERATION switch to 3 and adjust the time difference fine dial (lower right hand corner) and GAIN control for the two pulses, master and slave, to be superimposed while keeping them at equal height with the

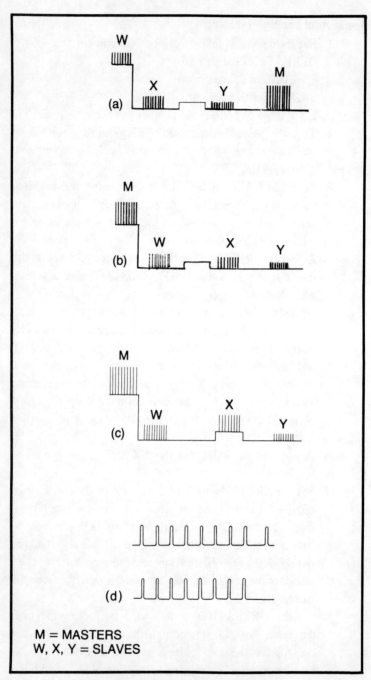

W

X   Y   M

(a)

M

W   X   Y

(b)

M

W   X   Y

(c)

(d)

M = MASTERS
W, X, Y = SLAVES

Fig. 9-33. Pulses and pedestals (loran C).

GAIN control. These pulses should be superimposed at the left hand slope as shown in Fig. 9-34(a). If this adjustment is not available for out of scale of the time difference fine control, then adjust time difference course control and repeat the procedure for the time difference fine.

9. Set the OPERATION switch to CM and superimpose the left hand side three waves of master and slave pulses by the time difference fine as shown in Fig. 9-34(b). When the AFC is ON, the figure sometimes shifts from its most suitable position. In that case, adjust its position with the DRIFT control. When the AFC is off and the position is not good, shift it with the SHIFT key until the reading is good.

Reading of time difference course is time difference in 10 microsecond steps and time difference fine indicates 1 microsecond steps divided with the 0.2 microsecond steps on the dial. For example, if the indicator shows the reading, as in Fig. 9-34(c), the time difference is 12347.0 microseconds.

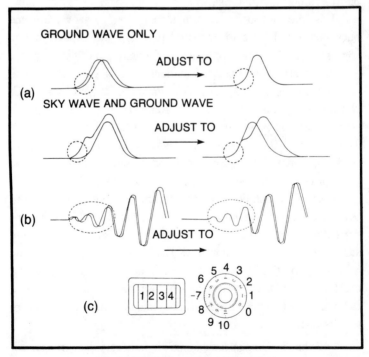

Fig. 9-34. Matching pulses and readout.

375

CAUTION. When the 9th pulse of the master train either disappears or drifts, the loran C system is in trouble. Do not believe the measured values.

OMEGA NAVIGATION SYSTEMS

The third type of system we want to discuss is the Omega system which uses still lower frequencies, but operates in the same general manner that the loran systems do. The Omega system, however, does not compare pulse arrival times. Its frequency is much too low for that. It compares the phase differences of two or more signals to establish the lines of position and thus is very accurate.

Because the accuracy of such navigation systems as we have been discussing is better for ground wave coverage, this system is an effort to improve position information over longer ranges than the other systems have. The Omega system's useful range is stated to be from 5,000 to 7,000 miles.

It is true that such a system is costly, but in answer to some questions asked, it is to be noted that now the Omega system covers about 75 percent of all navigable waters on this globe.

There are to be 8 planned stations for total coverage. These are: Norway, station A; Trinidad, station B; Hawaii, station C; North Dakota, station D; and Japan, station H. The other stations in planning are the Argentine, station F, and La Reunion, station E. They are probably operations as you read this work. Liberia, station G, is another to be completed and it is planned that this station will replace Trinidad, station B, and will assume its call.

Coast Guard stations can give information regarding where to telephone to get more information on the Omega stations that are currently operating. Examine Fig. 9-35 for a look at one example of an Omega receiver and indicator. The best way to give you good information on this system is to include at this point, through the courtesy of the Micro Instrument Co., Marine Division, some of the questions most commonly asked about this system and the answers to those questions.

- What is Omega navigation? It is a very long range, all-weather, day or night system of electronic navigation utiliz-

Fig. 9-35. Omega receiver and indicator. Position fixing is extremely simple without having to turn knobs which may have been left accidentally misadjusted. Once set, the receiver automatically tracks two lines of position. (Courtesy Micro Instrument Co.)

ing very low frequencies to establish accurate positions of ships.

- How does it work? Phase measurements are automatically made between signals produced by pairs of Omega transmitting stations. These phase measurements are read out as lines of position on all Omega receivers. Omega navigation charts then permit plotting of the ships position.

- What is the useful range of these signals? Typically from 5,000 to 7,000 miles. A ship departing from Maine can select three Omega stations (B, C, and D) and sail through the Panama Canal, all the way to Hawaii without ever changing stations.

- Who are the typical users of Omega? Military orgainzations were the initial users. However, with the introduction of commercial receivers, Omega is now being used by fishing boats, private yachts, and many commercial ships.

- What is the advantage of Omega? The Omega system provides a unique combination of daytime and nighttime coverage, long range use, high accuracy, freedom from skip error, and coverage under overcast conditions. In addition, it is the only electronic navigation system available in many parts of the world. Satellite and inertial systems can be used of course but are expensive.

- How does the cost compare to loran? At the present time receivers are available at the same prices of good loran receivers. Some models are more expensive depending upon their construction, features, etc.
- What coverage does Omega have? At present, as of this writing, with five stations in operation, coverage includes all of the Northern Hemisphere except the Indian Ocean, the South Pacific to latitude 45 degrees south in the area between Hawaii and the Americas, and much of the South Atlantic around South America.
- What accuracy does Omega have? Position accuracies average plus or minus 1 mile daytime, and plus or minus 2 miles nighttime. Receiver resolution is 1/100 of a lane, equivalent to 480 feet, far in excess of the loran system accuracy.
- How do the VLF frequencies help Omega? They permit long ranges using direct waves or ground waves. These are only slightly affected by atmospheric or ionospheric conditions
- Is daytime coverage really as good as nighttime coverage? Yes, because, unlike loran which depends upon nighttime sky waves for its long range, the Omega receiver used only VLF (Very Low Frequency) direct waves and is therefore very accurate during daytime and nighttime coverage.
- Are any Omega stations ever off the air? Yes, occasionally. A station going off the air for a few minutes will generally not affect position fixing. For longer station interruptions selection of an alternate station will provide normal operation. A chart recorder constantly monitors signals and shows any station interruptions.
- Will an Omega receiver work dockside or ashore? Yes, but precautions must be made to prevent noise from the 60 Hz power line from causing interference. The basic 10.2 kHz frequency used in Omega is the 170th harmonic of the power line and due to the high sensitivity of the receiver the shore antenna must be outdoors and well away from any power line.
- Will the receiver track signals I cannot hear? Yes, the receiver easily detects and tracks signals that may not be

heard. Therefore, even for very faint signals, the receiver can be operated satisfactorily. Proper operation is monitored on a chart at all times.

- How much operator skill is required? Very little. Once the basic principles are understood, an accurate positioning fix can be made in a few minutes by persons with little or no navigational experience.
- What is involved in the initial setup? At port, the instrument is first synchronized with a selected Omega transmitter. Next, stations are selected to give two or three lines of position. Then, the digital display is set to the correct starting position. After these initial adjustments, the receiver will track the selected stations for thousands of miles, normally, without any further adjustments.
- How difficult is the receiver synchronization? Very simple. When any one specific transmitter's audio tone has been identified in relation to the receivers sync light, a push button is released, and the receiver is synchronized to all stations.
- Is fully automatic synchronization available? Yes. In this case the operator does nothing. Just turn the receiver ON and push the auto button. That's all.
- How quickly can position fixes be made? This depends on navigators knowledge and experience. Normally accurate fixes, using the PPC tables, take only a few minutes.
- What charts will I need with the Omega system? You can obtain all charts for this system, along with the PPC tables from the U.S. Naval Oceanographic Office, or from most chart dealers nationwide.
- Why are the PPC tables required? Due to the long distance between Omega transmitters, a ship may be receiving signals from sunlight (day) and dark (night) transmitters. This causes certain small and predictable phase errors, which are printed in the PPC tables to correct Omega readings.
- Should the Omega receiver be kept on at sea? Yes. It should be kept on at all times as it is a tracking receiver. If turned off for a period of time due to any cause, the receiver must be set up again (synchronized).

- What does the digital display do? It provides an electronic readout of the two lines of position. The numbers on the readout slowly change as the ship moves through the water. A position fix is readily made by the intersection of the two lines of position numbers on the Omega chart.
- How many lines of operation are necessary? Two lines of position are required to establish a fix. A third line is useful to confirm that fix. Above that, the additional lines of position serve no useful purpose.
- What does the chart recorder do? The chart recorder serves several functions. It acts as an auxiliary line-of-position readout, a monitoring for Omega transmitter station operation, a permanent record of the voyage, and as an indicator of system operation at all times.
- Is the receiver installation difficult? No, it is quite simple. A whip antenna with coupler is mounted high up on the ship, or in sailboats, an insulated backstay is used. The Twinax cable is routed to the receiver which is mounted in any position— typically near the chart table. A good engine ground, or plate ground is made, and then when the receiver is connected to a power source it is ready to use.
- What if the ship has a positive ground? You can obtain a receiver which will operate with either a positive or negative ground.
- What if the ship's power fails? The receivers have provisions for three power sources: ac, dc, and internal battery. If any should fail, the others will automatically take over operation.
- What about latitude and longitude readings? It is planned, and may be true as of the time of your reading this work, that receivers will have been designed to give latitude and longitude readings instead of the line of position readings.

And so we leave this system with somewhat more knowledge about it than perhaps we had before reading the questions and answers. Since new developments are always being made, it is always wise to check around and see what's new and how it operates as time progresses.

A CELESTIAL NAVIGATION COMPUTER

We now turn to a modern way to use an old method of navigation. It is always possible to use star charts and the traditional navigation instruments: the sextant, the Nautical Almanac, and the chronometer to determine the ship's position. This has been used for centuries by sailors and navigators. What is of the most value about this system is that it is independent of any outside source for its information, or its accuracy. *You* do the navigating, using stars, the sun, and planets which will not vary with time from their prescribed motions, and so, if everything else failed, you could use the old method and find your way around this planet Earth.

The classical method of navigating is well known and presented in numerous texts (available in libraries), but there are some calculations involved, which can be difficult, in determining position by celestial observations. It is to reduce the effort of these computations and to increase the accuracy that we use electronics line Galaxy 1 Computer. In Fig. 9-36 you can see the labeling of the various push buttons. Now, before we go through a specific example of how to use this instrument, let us take a short review of some celestial mechanics (painlessly of course) and refresh ourselves on some basics of obtaining position information from celestial bodies.

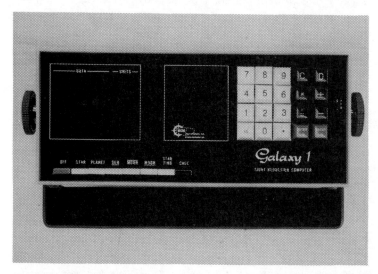

Fig. 9-36. Galaxy 1 sight reduction computer. (Courtesy Micro Instrument Co.)

Review of Celestial Mechanics

At every point on the surface of the earth, there is a point called the zenith vertically overhead on the celestial sphere. Conversely, for every celestial body there is a corresponding geographical position (GP) on the Earth's surface. If an observer were to measure the altitude of a body to be 90°, that body would be directly overhead, in its zenith. If the altitude of the body were 80°, the observer would be 10° away from the body's GP. This value of zenith distance describes a circle upon which, at any point, observers will see the body at equal altitudes of 80°. Such circles of equal altitude may be thought of as circles of position, or better, circular lines of position. Its like having a cone whose point is at the sky-body's position and the open end of the cone on earth and we are on the circle described by the end of that cone.

While it is theoretically possible to plot such circles of position, their large size and considerations of chart scale and distortion usually make it impractical. Since the navigator is only interested in that part of the circle which passes through his position, there is another, more practical, method for plotting the line of position.

First, the altitude of the body is measured and corrected to give a value called *observed altitude* (Ho). Next, for the exact moment of sighting, the *theoretical altitude* of the body is calculated giving the computer altitude (Hc). For the computation of Hc, a position near the actual position is assumed.

Now, Hc and Ho define the radii of two circles of equal altitude, and the difference between them is called the altitude intercept (a), or the altitude difference. Following the computation of intercept, the direction from the assumed position to the body's GP is determined, and we now have the following:

1. the assumed position of the observer (AP)
2. the altitude intercept (a)
3. the *bearing* or azimuth of the GP of the body designated by the symbol Zn

The reduced sight can now be transferred to a plotting sheet. First, the assumed position (AP) is plotted. Next, using azimuth (Zn), a line is drawn from the AP toward the geographic position (GP) of the body. This line is extended from the AP for a distance equal to the intercept toward or away from the GP of the body. If it is away, the navigator extends the Zn line through the AP so that the actual angle is 180° *away* from the azimuth indicated. At that point a line of position is constructed perpendicular to the azimuth line. While this is actually a circular line of position, it is customarily approximated by a straight line except for very high altitude sights. It is good practice to label the line with the name of the body it represents and the time of the observation. The interpretation of the plot is facilitated by the equivalence of minutes of latitude and nautical miles.

It is useful to note the effect of the bearing of the body on the resulting line of position. A celestial body to the south yields a line running east and west, etc. When the number of available observations is limited, careful selection of the celestial bodies may provide the most useful navigational information, i.e., by providing lines of position which cross at 90° angles.

Solving the Navigation Problem with a Computer

Now let us consider how the Galaxy 1 Navigation Computer is used to reduce a celestial observation to a line of position. We will use a specific example.

In this example, the ship is navigating in the Pacific Ocean in the vicinity of latitude 30° N (north) and longitude 137° W (west). The log shows the date to be November 30, 1973. The navigator is using a sextant having no index correction and always makes his celestial observation from a place on the deck which is 12 feet above the water line.

At 02 hours, 36 minutes, 30 seconds GMT (Greenwich Mean Time), the navigator observes the star Markab at an altitude of 70 degrees, 35.5 minutes. To reduce this sighting using the Galaxy 1, he first pushes the button designated STAR and immediately the sextant altitude indicator SEX'T ALT lights up, as well as the degrees indicator DEG. Then the navigator enters 70 followed by a + (plus). After a number has been keyed into the computer, an ENTER key must be pushed before the computer will proceed to the next step. These ENTER keys are labeled as follows: The + (plus) key, performs the same function as the ENTER N/W key. Either of these keys are used to enter data which consists of positive numbers or signless numbers of direction in the northerly or westerly direction. The − (minus) key, performs the same function as the ENTER S/E key. Either of these keys are used to enter data which consists of negative numbers or signless numbers of direction in the southerly or easterly directions. The + key transfers the data into the computer. The SEX'T ALT indicator light remains on, the DEG light goes off, and the minute light, MIN, comes on. The navigator then enters 35.5 minutes followed by a +, whereupon the SEX'T ALT light goes out and the height of eye HT EYE light comes on. The navigator responds by keying 12 followed by a +. The computer then skips to sidereal hour angle S.H.A. and also lights the DEG indicator. The navigator responds by keying 14+. The Galaxy 1 then requests S.H.A. in MIN. The navigator responds by punching in 7.8+. These values are taken from the 1973 Nautical Almanac, page 232, (November 30, December 1,2). The Galaxy 1 next steps to TIME EXCESS in MIN at which time the navigator enters 36+ whereupon the computer steps to TIME EXCESS in SEC. The navigator enters 30+. The computer then skips to Greenwich hour angle of Aries abbreviated in the readout as G.H.A. and ARIES. The DEG also lights and the navigator, taking information from the Nautical Almanac, enters 99+. The G.H.A. and ARIES indicators remain on, requesting the time in MIN. The navigator enters 47.5+ and Galaxy 1 moves on to light *assumed* longitude (ASSUME LONG) in DEG. The navigator enters 137W and the instrument moves on to ASSUME LONG in MIN; the navigator enters 0.0 W (west). The Galaxy 1 moves on again, this time to declination, DEC, in DEG. The navigator enters 15 N (north). The unit moves on to ask for SEC in MIN; the navigator enters 4.1 N. Galaxy 1 moves on to assumed latitude (ASSUME LAT) in DEG. The navigator enters 30 N whereupon the computer asks for ASSUME LAT in MIN. The navigator keys in 0.0 N whereupon the Galaxy 1 will compute intercept. The Galaxy 1 will then display 11.6 minutes and INTERCEPT (or 11.6 nautical miles), also lighting up the toward (TOWARD) indicator. The navigator would then set his dividers to 11.6 nautical miles and key the ZN + key, at which time the Galaxy 1 will compute azimuth. In this particular case, ZN and 136.3° are displayed.

If you desire more information and a more detailed discussion, we suggest you obtain from Micro Instruments, 580 Opper St.

Escondido, California, 92025, their little booklet on the Galaxy 1 which goes into much detail on celestial navigation theory and practice.

Of course the previous discussion may seem like Greek to those who are uninitiated to celestial terms and what they represent. So, we recommend, for a brief discussion which explains circles of position more visually and simply, our book *Aviation Electronics Handbook* TAB No. 631, wherein on page 213 the use of celestial bodies or fixed satellites for navigation purposes is more completely explained.

THE U.S. NAVY NAGIVATION SATELLITE SYSTEM (NNSS)

The use of satellites makes it possible to determine position very accurately anywhere on the oceans of the world. It takes a radar type receiver to get the signals as the satellites pass overhead or somewhere in the viewing hemisphere and a computer to resolve the data that the satellite sends down to the ship.

As an introduction to the system, consider Fig. 9-37, which shows in an exaggerated manner the typical orbit of a satellite above the earth. From any point on earth, A or B in the figure, there will exist a unique set of distance lines between the point and the satellite, as the satellite moves from horizon to horizon. These distances are called the slant ranges; typical of these slant ranges are the lines S_A1, S_A2, and S_A3 (or S_B1, S_B2, and S_B3). It can be seen that the length of the slant range lines change as the satellite travels in its orbit; the shortest length occurs when the satellite is closest to point A or B. This normally happens when the satellite is directly overhead.

A radio transmission from the satellite, as received at either point A or B, will experience a doppler shift in frequency as the slant range changes because of the relative motion between the satellite and either point. Since the satellite orbits the earth, its position at any time, as well as the position of either points A or B, can be expressed in an earth centered coordinate system.

To use the satellite for fixing the position of the point, based on the Doppler (See *Modern Radar,* TAB No. 575, pages 67, 68, and 74) phenomenon, the following steps must be executed:

1. Determine the location of the satellite in an earth centered coordinate system, and its precise orbit. This is based on reception of data transmitted from the satellite. (Data defining the precise orbit of the satellite is periodically injected into the satellite by ground stations. The navigation message, transmitted by the satellite, contains the latest information on its orbit at the time of transmission.)
2. Determine the estimated position of the point on earth in the same coordinate system, based on dead reckoning from the last known position.
3. Calculate the predicted change in slant range that should occur over a very precise interval of time. Again, data for this calculation is derived from other data transmitted by the satellite, and the estimated position of the point in step 2. If the point is moving, consider its velocity, resolved into the same coordinate system, in the calculation.
4. Determine the actual change in slant range that occurs over the same precise interval of time by measuring the doppler shift of the received radio signal and converting this into a change in the slant range (steps 3 and 4).
5. Calculate the offset from the estimated position of step 2 by determining the difference between the predicted and actual change in slant range (steps 3 and 4).
6. Apply the offset from step 5 to the estimated position of the point (step 2); this is the corrected position of the point.

The computations are performed repeatedly following the termination of the satellite pass to yield a least-squares estimate of position offset from the system-estimated position at the end of the pass.

The navigation satellites have been in continuous operation since 1964, and have been available for commercial use since 1967. The U.S. Navy system consists of six satellites (more may be added) which are in circular, polar orbit around the earth. Every point on the earth passes under each satellite's orbit twice daily. These satellites are continuously tracked by monitoring stations which compute an accurate prediction of each satellite's orbit every time the satellite passes the station. The predicted orbit data is transmitted to each satellite approximately every 12 hours.

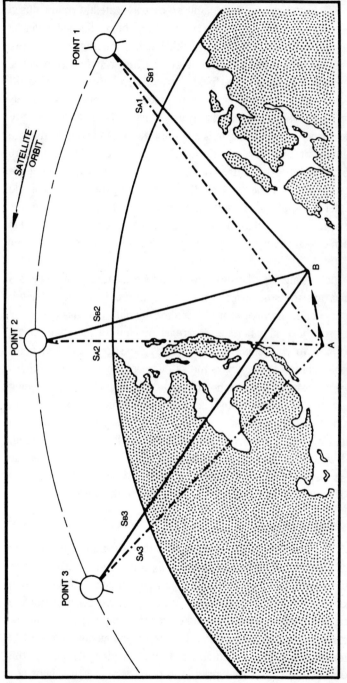

Fig. 9-37. Illustration of slant range between orbiting satellites and points A and B on earth.

The orbit data is retransmitted by each satellite continuously. The message lasts for exactly two minutes, beginning and ending at the instant of each *even* minute. Each 2 minute message contains two parts: one part is fixed and the other changes each time a navigation message is relayed. The fixed part of the message is called the Kepler parameter set. These parameters (numbers) define a perfectly smooth, precessing elliptical orbit around the earth. The variable portion of the message is a set of time-based variables that are the current corrections to the Kepler parameters. These data are the *ephemeral* (orbit) data. Together, the two sets of data define the actual position of the satellite; the ephemeral parameters, with the Kepler parameters, are sufficient for defining the satellite's position for eight 2 minute increments of time. A new correction is added to the message every 2 minutes, and the oldest correction is then deleted.

Each satellite, therefore, is an independent navigation beacon which transmits a navigation message that defines the satellite's position at each timing mark. Since the satellite will pass over your ship from horizon to horizon, and reach minimum slant range when it is closest to your ship, the transmitted message will experience a doppler shift in frequency as the satellite approaches, then recedes from your ship. The reception of the satellite signal over succeeding intervals while the satellite is in range will provide a measurement of the rate-of-change of slant range between the satellite and your own ship. This information combined with the satellite's known position, and your ships estimated position, permits the calculation of the offset between your ship's position derived from satellite data, and your ship's estimated position at the end of the pass.

The Satellite Receiver

The Raytheon satellite receiver detects the satellite message as phase modulation on a very precisely controlled 400 MHz carrier and recovers the doppler frequency by comparison with a precision internal oscillator. The receiver functions to decode the satellite message, derived from the doppler count, and format this data for transmission to the computer. The receiver functions completely automatically after an initial warm-up. Panel lights advise the operator when a satellite pass is in progress (as you cannot see them). A self test function is also provided on this receiver so you know it is working correctly.

DIRECTION FINDING AND AUTOMATIC DIRECTION FINDING

As the subtitle indicates, some of these units are so designed that you manipulate them to get bearings and fix information. Others are so designed that they supply this data automatically.

The direction finder is one of the most valuable pieces of equipment on board. These, when properly used, can give you data from which to plot your position. They can provide a direction to steer so that you have a course relative to a land based station, and they can also help by giving you some weather information in bad conditions as they give storm directions by bad reception on the storm bearing.

Some homing (direction finding) equipment operates in the 160 to 415 kHz band, which is long wave. Some use the 600 to 1650 kHz band, which is medium wave, and some use the 1600 to 4150 kHz band which is the marine radiotelephone band. General frequency coverage is available in most equipment for all these ranges of frequency.

The primary difference between this kind of receiver and others is that on some the antenna itself, like radar antenna, must move and be positioned physically so that it gives a null, or a minimum, reading on a meter or in the sound from a speaker. The direction giving antenna is a loop, not a vertical type. The types of loop antenna and sense antenna (which may be a straight rod) are shown in Fig. 9-38.

It is the manner in which the connections are made to the two perpendicular loops shown in the figure that determine whether the signal received is the loop signal or the sense signal.

It is to be noted that the loop antenna consists of two loops and a pedestal. The outputs from the ends of the transformers are fed to the *goniometer*, a transformer that has one coil which can be rotated with respect to the other. See our book *Modern Radar*, TAB No. 575, page 12.) The output from the center taps of the primary windings of the transformers are fed to the receiver through the azimuth indicator. The former are the loop-sensing signals and the

Fig. 9-38. Navimatic automatic direction finder. (Courtesy Raytheon Marine.)

latter is the sense antenna signal. The sense signal is a general signal required to determine the phase of the loop signal.

Operation of the Direction Finder

This information is courtesy of Raytheon Corporation. The azimuth indicator displays bearing information derived by the automatic direction finding (ADF) system. Two sensing signals from the fixed loop antenna (note that this kind of ADF does *not* require that the loops rotate) to the goniometer in the indicator are combined in its secondary winding, and the combined signal produces controlling power in the receiver to feed to the servomotor in the azimuth indicator.

A fiducial marker (reference) located at the top of the indicator face, corresponds to the FWD lubber line of a compass and represents the bow of the vessel. A manually rotatable azimuth ring permits the introduction of heading information into the indicator. The radio bearings may be taken directly in terms of magnetic or true reference. The center knob of the indicator rotates the goniometer manually, and manual direction finding is performed. On

ADF mode, the indicator knob is used to check the ADF bearing indicated. When the knob swings off the bearing, and is released, the indicator bearing will return quickly to the original bearing. If this action does not occur the bearing should not be trusted because the signal is too weak for an accurate bearing.

Before going further in this discussion, let us take a few moments to examine Fig. 9-39. This unit is the portable type and operates from self contained batteries. The loop antenna is built-in and the sense antenna can be clearly seen in the upper left hand corner of the receiver. This type unit is important to those boatmen who may have smaller vessels and would not want a permanent installation. It too, however, will give position fixing information as well as homing information, weather information, and distress and calling monitoring on channel 16. As shown, the unit may be used on the chart table.

Now, with these two units in mind we want to examine in some detail the installation and use of such receivers. We will be con-

Fig. 9-39. This Raytheon portable direction finder tunes to aviation and marine radio beacons and all standard broadcast stations. It also has crystals for immediate tuning to channel 16, the international calling and distress frequency, and the two continuous weather advisory channesl in the VHF/FM band. The set operates with ordinary flashlight batteries.

cerned, in the installation, with one ADF such as the Navimatic, which was shown in Fig. 9-38.

The location and installation is usually determined by the needs and desires of the operator. In general, the unit should be protected from adverse environmental conditions and installed in a manner providing the greatest utility. Consideration should be given to adequate air circulation and to the clearance required at the back of the unit for servicing.

It is desirable to orient the receiver so the operator may readily view the azimuth indicator while manipulating the controls.

Potential installation sites in the wheel house and in the immediate vicinity of engine instrument panels should be investigated for high interference level from ignition, lighting, and ammeter leads. As is the case of any equipment of equivalent sensitivity, a reduction in the ship's electrical system interference level may be necessary to insure optimum performance.

Azimuth Indicator Installation

The azimuth indicator unit may be installed in any position or altitude convenient to the operator. It is usually desirable to orient the indicator so that the fiducial marker is logically associated with the bow of the vessel as viewed from the operating position.

When so installed the indicated bearing may be readily associated with the respective quarters of the vessel. For greatest utility, it should be possible to read the azimuth indicator and the magnetic compass and operate the receiver from the same position.

Loop Antenna Installation

The loop antenna should be installed topside in an area as free as possible from rigging or railings forming large closed circuit metallic loops *in the vertical plane.* Maintain the maximum possible separation from existing transmitting and receiving antennas. Investigate potential installation sites for the proximity of cabin or running light wiring which conduct engine ignition or generator interference. Either the base plate or the stanchion method of mounting is recommended. The installation site should be high as practical with respect to its cable length, Fig. 9-40.

Fig. 9-40. The ADF antenna is at the right front corner of the flying bridge canopy.

The loop marked N and S must be carefully aligned with the fore and aft axis (keel line) of the vessel, N to fore, S to aft, or a constant displacement error will be introduced into the azimuth indicator.

In the event of an approximate 180 degree error, check the loop assembly for proper orientation of the N and S marking or the loop cable connection. Also, for 90 degree error, check the loop orientation or the loop cable connection.

When overall alignment is complete, the loop should be secured by fastening all screws.

Sense Antenna Check

Sense antenna sensitivity compared to the loop antenna sensitivity must be checked. This ratio, V/L, is very important for the ADF. When the loop antenna is installed at the highest site, from sea level, sensitivity of the sense antenna becomes better, and when the loop antenna is close by metallic materials grounded to the vessel or seawater, the sensitivity becomes lower. The V/L is checked as follows:

1. Receive a clear signal in the beacon band on MANUAL DF, and read the S meter reading while rotating the indicator by its knob to a maximum reading.
2. Change the mode switch to ADF and read the S meter. When the S meter indicates the same or slightly larger than in MANUAL DF, it is good.
3. When the indication is less than MANUAL DF, an antenna wire of a few feet must be connected to the sense loop antenna top.
4. Poor sense antenna sensitivity gives poor ADF and REC sensitivity.

Care should be taken to avoid the proximity of other antennas, electrical wiring, or areas where the loop antenna will be surrounded by a cage of grounded metallic rigging. There are things you must be very careful of when making an installation. The loop cable must be handled with extreme care during the installation to prevent damage to the inner conductor. It must be fastened so that damage in use doesn't occur.

Bearing Errors

On small vessels, for all practical purposes, the ADF performs without errors, but on large vessels it is seldom possible to select a loop antenna site that will assure complete freedom from bearing errors due to the metallic rigging, railings, superstructure, or electrical wiring. The magnitude and sign of such errors will vary widely with frequency, and with the relative bearing of signal arrival with respect to the particular vessel. In general, the errors tend to increase with frequency,   and the apparent absence thereof in the beacon band will constitute no guarantee of error free performance at any higher frequencies.

The presence and magnitude of bearing errors and other shipboard effects may be determined by conducting a radiocompass swing. Planning a course in relation to known landmarks and taking DF bearings and plotting positions from DF readings. Thus you will know what your errors are.

Radio Triangulation Position Finding

Triangulation is the basic principle of direction finding by radio. Figure 9-41 illustrates this principle. Assume that radio transmitting stations are located on a coast line at points A, B, and C and that the ADF system is on your boat. You will do the following:

1. Set the scale of the azimuth indicator to correspond with the magnetic heading of your ship.
2. Tune in station A. The azimuth indicator pointer will indicate the bearing of station A in magnetic terms.
3. Construct a line of position on your chart through the station extending seaward on the reciprocal of the radio bearing obtained. Notice that this reciprocal corresponds to the tail of the azimuth indicator pointer.
4. Tune in station B. Construct a second line of position through station B extending seaward on the reciprocal of the radio bearing obtained from station B. The intersection of the two lines thus obtained will give your position fix at the intersection.
5. To confirm your fix, tune in a third station (C) and repeat the procedure outlined in step 3.

Types of RDF Stations

The ADF equipment operates in the beacon, broadcast, and marine radio bands from 190 to 3500 kHz. Any radio station operating within its range can be used by the ADF provided the station

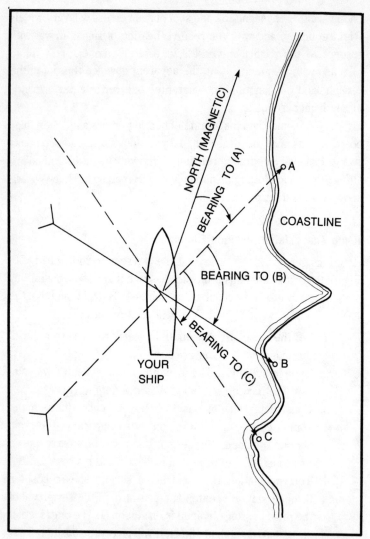

Fig. 9-41. Principle of an ADF fix.

meets certain requirements. The six most common radio stations used for direction finding are:

1. Marine radio beacons, mainlands, islands, and breakwaters.
2. Marine radio beacons on lightships.
3. Marker radio beacons on breakwater entrances or jetties.
4. Aeronautical range stations on mainlands or islands.

5. Broadcast stations.
6. Ships equipped with radio transmitters.

Each type of station is identified by a specific marker on the recent navigational charts.

Marine radio beacons. Most marine radio beacons are on the air twice each hour except during fog conditions when they are on the air continuously. The beacons are arranged in groups of two or three stations. Each station of the group uses an identical frequency, and alternates its transmissions periodically with one minute on and two minutes off. The interrupted signal permits other stations in the group to transmit during the off period. In some areas, one station of the group is on the air continuously. Some marine radio beacons transmit an interrupted carrier (keyed on and off), and an increasing number superimpose the identification signal on a continuous wave carrier. This latter type provides more dependable bearings as the azimuth indicator needle will hold steady during the full minute that the station is transmitting. On recent marine charts, the two transmission periods are shown adjacent to the location of the station. If a time period is not shown, the station is on the air continuously. The two types of marine radio beacons and their chart symbols are as follows:

1. Marine radio beacons on mainlands, islands, or breakwaters. See Table 9-5(a).
2. Marine radio beacons on light ships. See Table 9-5(b).

The notation for the chart symbol of station "a" above is read: RB_n designates the radio beacon and 287 designates the frequency of the station as 287 kHz. The code symbol $X = - \cdot \cdot —$ designates *identification code*. 10m-20m and 20m-50m indicates that the station is on the air from the 10th minute to the 20th minute, then from the 40th minute to the 50th minute of each hour.

Marker beacon (radio) on breakwater entrances or jetties. Marker radio beacons are low power, short range stations that are on the air only during fog or poor visibility conditions. The chart symbol for these appear in Table 9-5(c).

Aeronautical range stations on mainlands and islands. Aeronautical range stations are on the air continuously and usually provide very reliable radio bearings when located reasonably close

Table 9-5. Marine Chart Radio Beacon Symbols.

(a) MAINLANDS, ISLANDS, AND BREAKWATERS

ANACAPA ----

RBn 287

10m-20m and 40m-50m

(b) LIGHTSHIPS

RBn 314

20m-30m and 50m-60m

(c) BREAKWATER ENTRANCE AND JETTIES

RBn 300

(d) AERONAUTICAL RANGE STATIONS ON MAINLANDS AND ISLANDS

AERORANGE

(e) BROADCAST STATIONS

RTR

Station KBIG 740

to the coastline. They broadcast weather information each half hour at 15 and 45 minutes after the hour. A typical chart symbol appears in Table 9-5(d).

Use of broadcast stations. Standard broadcast stations are generally on the air continuously the greater portion of a 24 hour period. A number have continuous 24 hour schedules. If the stations are clear channel, employing non-directional antennas, and they are located near the coastline, they provide excellent and reliable bearings. The chart symbol for these appears in Table 9-5(e).

Ships equipped with radio transmitters. Relative or magnetic bearings may be taken on ships with radio transmitting equipment operating in the frequency range of the ADF (2.182 MHz, 2.638 MHz, 2.738 MHz, etc.). This feature permits the location of such vessels by homing or triangulation techniques. It is invaluable in effecting a rendezvous, locating distressed vessels, or directing other vessels to the scene of an incident.

398

Selecting Stations for Radio Direction Finding

Only certain stations which can be heard on your ADF meet the conditions required for accurate direction finding. Some stations which may provide clear reception cannot be used successfully. In most cases, natural phenomena determine which stations are satisfactory for a given geographical location.

At distances greater than 50 to 75 miles from the transmitter, depending upon frequency, the sky wave may be reflected from the ionosphere. This is that belt of highly ionized gases we had discussed previously. Signals, as you recall, reflected by the sky belt can vary constantly in apparent direction and strength. Figure 9-42 illustrates the problem. The reflected skywaves produce varying effects dependent upon the time of day and transmitter frequency.

The skywave effect is caused by *polarization* changes and by combining of the direct ground wave and the reflected skywave at the receiving point. As the skywave has traveled a greater distance, it arrives slightly later than the ground wave, and therefore is displaced in *phase*. Skywave effect is usually attended by sporadic garbling, fading, or varying signal strength.

The three bands covered by ADF usually exhibit little or no sky wave effect during daylight hours and can be used for accurate and reliable bearings.

Frequency and Usable Distance for DF

Usable distance for direction finding varies with frequency. The relations are depicted in Fig. 9-43. Longer distance is expected for propagating waves oversea; over land gives shorter distance. Stations intervened by mountain ranges from the direction finder have

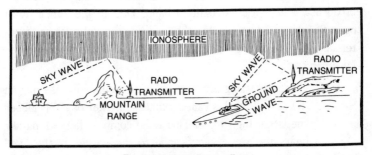

Fig. 9-42. Ionosphere effect.

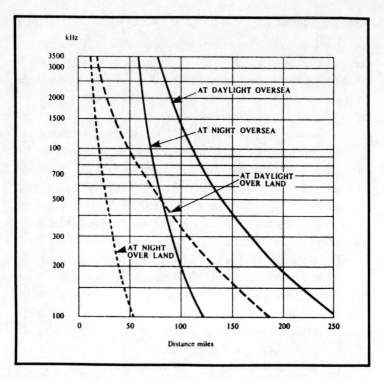

Fig. 9-43. Distance and usable frequency of DF.

shorter distance. Bearings taken during sunrise and sunset hours are subject to large errors and should not be relied upon for precise navigation.

Obtaining a Fix

In the receive mode the ADF functions exactly like a conventional tunable receiver capable of receiving signals in the beacon, broadcast, and marine telephone band. Due to the simplicity of operation designed into ADFs, the following *general* rules and pointers are provided rather than a detailed step-by-step procedure for DF tuning.

1. The fixed triangular mark adjacent to the compass ring on the azimuth dial is called a fiducial marker or FWD lubber line. (See Fig. 9-44.) This radio compass fiducial marker bears the same significance to the vessel as the fixed lubber line bears to a magnetic compass. During installa-

tion, the ADF antenna and azimuth indicator are aligned with respect to the fore and aft keel line. Thus when the 0° on the azimuth indicator compass ring is positioned adjacent to the fiducial marker, all bearings read from the dial will be relative to the boat. (See Fig. 9-45)

2. To read bearings directly in magnetic terms, set the compass ring on the azimuth indicator to correspond with the magnetic heading of the vessel. (See Fig. 9-46)

3. Always select the desired signal with the mode switch in the REC position. Observe the front panel signal strength meter and tune the receiver to obtain a peak reading. After tuning the receiver, set the mode switch to ADF.

4. Positively identify the signal source before utilizing the bearing obtained.

5. It is quite common for the actual transmitting sites of broadcast stations to be located at points remote from their respective studios. In many cases formerly used towers and antenna systems have been allowed to remain standing

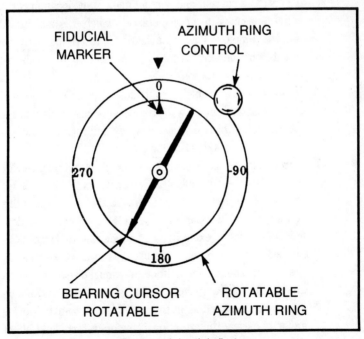

Fig. 9-44. Azimuth indicator.

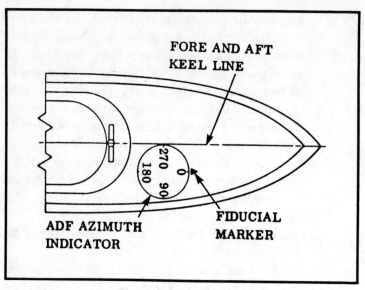

Fig. 9-45. Relative bearings.

and may still be listed in some radio navigation facility charts. The current and correct geographic location of the active antenna site of any station, which it is anticipated may be employed as a navigational reference, may be readily obtained by directing an inquiry to the technical operator of the station.

6. Jepson charts available through most local aircraft sales and service organizations will provide information permitting the utilization of many civil airways and military low frequency (200 to 420 kHz) facilities.

7. During sunrise and sunset hours, night effect may render certain bearings unreliable. Fortunately, the rate of response of the ADF will usually make the presence of this condition readily apparent. Night effect will cause random indicator-pointer excursions of moderate to large magnitudes. This phenomenon is usually more predominant at the higher frequencies. Although manual direction finders are equally subject to night effect, the condition may not be as vividly displayed as in the case of an automatic device and may escape the attention of the operator. Night effect seldom lasts very long and satisfactory bearings on a par-

ticular facility, subject to this phenomenon, may usually be obtained within one to two hours.

8. Occasionally severe bearing errors may be encountered due to a condition known as *coastal refraction*. (See Fig. 9-47.) Coastal refraction is the abrupt change in the direction of an electromagnetic wave as the characteristics of the medium, in which the wave is propagating, changes. The wave bending is most severe when the direction or propagation is nearly parallel to the interface of the mediums involved. In this case, the interface is the coast line, and the mediums are land and water. To avoid potential errors due to coastal refraction, select signal sources that do not result in bearings which intersect the coast line at angles of less than 45°.

9. Errors due to vessel rigging and existing antenna systems will vary with the complexity of these factors, the relative direction of signal arrival, and with frequency. It is important to understand that errors due to such causes are not peculiar to automatic direction finders alone, and may not be corrected by ADF receiver adjustment. Only techniques directed at the source of errors will prove satisfactory.

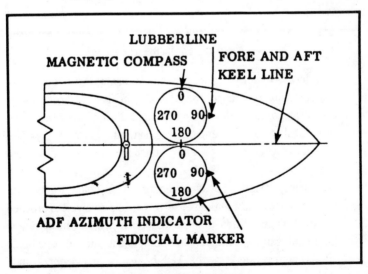

Fig. 9-46. Magnetic bearings.

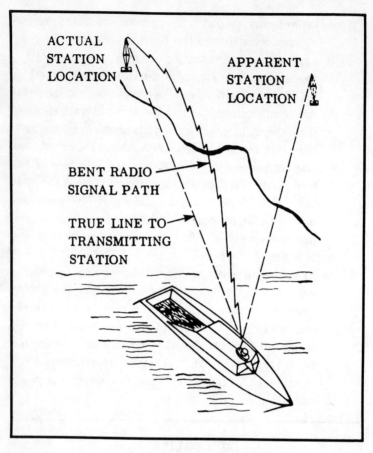

Fig. 9-47. Coastal refraction.

10. In the event of an emergency involving the need for immediate assistance, the ADF may be used to direct rescue craft to the scene by requesting that they steer the reciprocal of the magnetic bearing on their signals. This procedure is particularly useful when visibility is limited or when exact position is not known.

Warning: When providing requested or voluntary bearing information, always advise the vessel or vessels involved to proceed with caution since you assume no responsibility for the accuracy thereof or the safety of the vessel(s) employing such information.

It is recommended that the ADF be used at every opportunity to work practice navigational problems under conditions where the results may be visually verified. This will develop operator skill and confidence for when the instrument is really needed.

Operation in Crystal Positions

In crystal positions, there are provided 5 frequencies, including 2182 kHz, which aids the operator in rapidly obtaining or presetting a specific frequency reception from a transmitter which is not necessarily continuously on the air. The operator simply tunes to noise maximum, without signal, in either REC, ADF, or manual DF mode. The receiver is now precisely pretuned and is properly adjusted to receive the frequency of interest without additional searching by the operator.

For example, the Los Angeles, California, beacon station broadcasting at 302 kHz transmitts commencing the second minute after the hour for a one minute duration, and is off for five minutes— so the time is on one minute, off five minutes, etc. If you pretune the station, with crystal tuning, the station automatically becomes monitored during transmission times and you don't have to search for it during its off times. The equipment can be provided with four additional crystals in addition to the one on 2182, which is provided.

Homing

Specifically, homing involves steering a course derived from a radio signal originating at your destination. It is accomplished as follows:

1. Select a suitable radio station.
2. Swing your boat so the azimuth indicator pointer aligns with the fiducial marker.
3. Then, when constructing your lines of position, always construct a line of position on the chart so that it originates at the station employed and extends seaward on the reciprocal of the magnetic bearing indicated. This procedure will disclose the presence of any charted obstacles such as islands, lightships, jetties, etc.
4. Steer the boat to maintain the azimuth indicator pointer aligned with the fiducial marker. If it is noted that in doing so the magnetic compass heading continually changes, drift due to wind or tide is present, and your actual track will be a

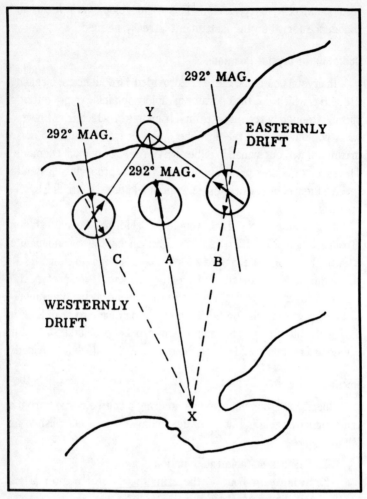

Fig. 9-48. Determination of drift.

curved line in lieu of a straight line to your destination. If this happens, then re-examine your course often on the chart to see if you are getting any obstacles in your way.

Indicator pointer deflections during homing operations show that you are getting drift due to wind or tide. As an example, assume that the magnetic course from point X to point Y at 292° is held constant as in Fig. 9-48. Also assume that your ADF is tuned to a station at point (Y) at the time of departure. Now the following can be expected:

- If the desired track, A, is being made good, the azimuth indicator pointer will remain on the fiducial marker, or FWD lubber line. Note the following, however. If a station at the point of departure is employed, the point *opposite* the fiducial marker is used as a reference point. The indicator deflection will be shown by the pointers drawn with dashed lines.
- Drift due to wind or tide, resulting in actual tracks approximating B or C, will produce indicator deflection as shown by the solid pointers of Fig. 9-48.

CROSS BEARING AND TRIANGULATION

Cross bearing and triangulation provide a means of obtaining a location, or a fix, by the use of two or three radio stations, respectively, or more, as we have previously discussed. For the greatest bearing accuracy remember that you want to select stations that have an angle of at least 30 degrees to 90 degrees between them, in relation to the assumed position of your vessel. Refer now to Fig. 9-49, and also back to the procedure on triangulation discussed previously.

Let's discuss the accuracy of this procedure. The actual location of your ship by triangulation will be somewhere close to the

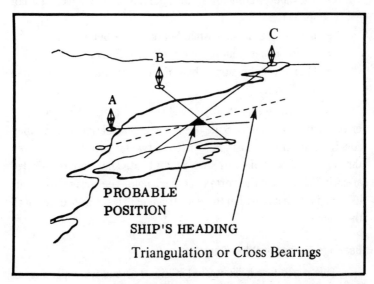

C

B

A

PROBABLE
POSITION
SHIP'S HEADING

Triangulation or Cross Bearings

Fig. 9-49. Triangulation of cross bearing.

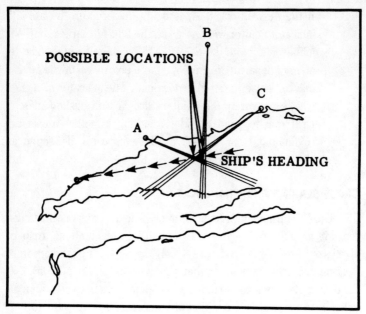

Fig. 9-50. Probable position.

assumed position of intersection of your three lines of position. The intersection will actually form a small triangle because:

- The inherent reading accuracy of the azimuth indicator is not perfect.
- The ship is moving while bearings are being taken.
- Radio signals bend during their propagation.
- There will be some bearing errors due to installation peculiarities.

By examining Fig. 9-50 you will see that assuming an average error of plus or minus 5 degrees for each bearing taken when constructing lines of position (construct two for each bearing) gives three areas of possible position for your boat. These are the shaded areas in Fig. 9-50 at the vertex of the triangle. You will find that your location is probably within the dark triangle. This is the center of all the lines of position.

Bearings Taken on Other Ships

This procedure is illustrated in Fig. 9-51 and we expand on an earlier mention of it. If you want to home in on another ship which might be in distress, you may instruct the operator of that ship to send a continuous signal and you home in on that. In general the location of another ship is determined as follows:

1. Tune in the radio of that ship.
2. Turn your vessel until you obtain an approximate off-the-beam relative bearing.
3. Set the azimuth indicator to agree with your magnetic heading and read the magnetic radio bearing.
4. Project a line extending from your known position on the magnetic radio bearing obtained.
5. Proceed on the magnetic heading employed in 3 till you reach a new known position. Then obtain a second magnetic radio bearing.
6. Project a line from your new position on the second magnetic radio bearing obtained.
7. The position of the other vessel will be indicated by the intersection of the lines on the chart.

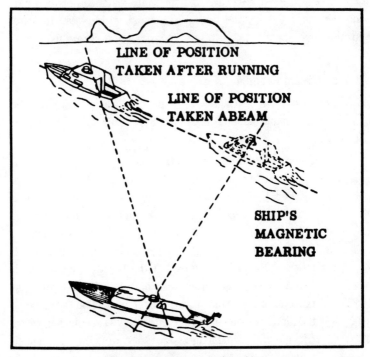

Fig. 9-51. Bearings on other ships.

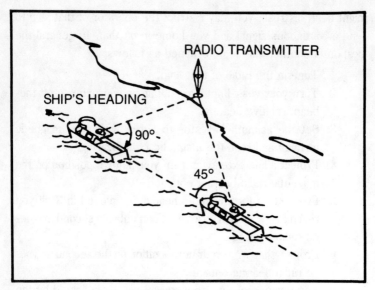

Fig. 9-52. Bow and beam bearings.

Of course you must be aware that the more distance between you and the other vessel, the farther you must go between the two positions mentioned above to get a reasonably accurate fix.

Bow and Beam Bearings

Bow and beam bearings with respect to a radio facility may be used to determine distance offshore. Refer to Fig. 9-52. Do the following:

1. Select a loud and clear radio station.
2. Position 0° on the azimuth indicator scale with the fiducial marker. Obtain a relative bearing on the station, between 0° and 45°. Proceed on course until the radio bearing is 45°, *relative.* Record the time at which this is noted.
3. Proceed on course until the radio bearing reading is 90° *relative.* Record the time that the 90° bearing is noted. Knowing your speed you can quickly calculate your distance offshore. Your distance offshore will be the same as the distance you have traveled since you are dealing with a triangle with equal length sides (of course the hypotenuse is longer).

Track Determination

Using the ADF to determine actual track brings us to an examination of Fig. 9-53. Again you select a radio station on shore as shown. Then you do the following:

1. Set the indicator scale to agree with your magnetic heading. Assume a heading of 272° magnetic as shown in our example figure.
2. Take a bearing on the radio station and note the time. Assume it to be 2:00 p.m.
3. Take additional bearing at some equal time intervals, assume in our example every fifteen minutes.
4. Construct lines of position on your chart though the radio facility on the reciprocal of the individual bearings.
5. Calculate the distance traveled during each fifteen minute period. If, for example, your speed was 12 knots, then you traveled 3 miles between each bearing taken. Mark off the 3 mile segments between the lines of position, and construct a line across the series of points. This line is your actual track. The distance offshore and course can be quickly obtained from the chart.

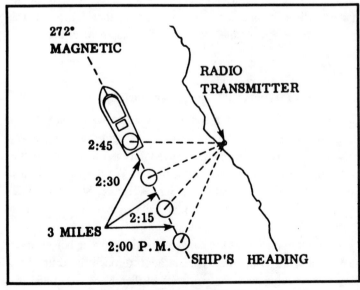

Fig. 9-53. Track determination.

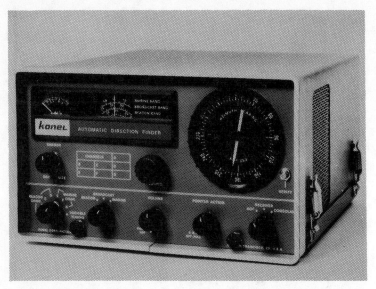

Fig. 9-54. Konel KDF-363 Automatic Direction Finder. (Courtesy Konel.)

We must point out that manual direction finding is very useful when the air is disturbed by statics which cause the pointer on the ADF mode to become erratic. The operators hearing, when he is skilled, will still give reliable information when you have to operate under such poor conditions. It is very wise, therefore, to get as much practice as possible using the DF equipment in the manual mode.

Constructing DF Equipment and Its Technical Operation

We have considered in some detail the navigation procedures using ADF equipment. We do not want to forget those of you who may be electronics buffs and who are as interested as we are in some technical details of this kind of equipment. We point out that it is possible to obtain kits (Heath Co., Benton Harbor, Michigan 49022) for ADF equipment and so you may build your own if this is your desire.

But for many it isn't the building, its just knowing how it works that is satisfying, and so we include next, through the courtesy of Konel, a description of the workings of ther Konel KDF-363 Automatic Direction Finder which is illustrated in Fig. 9-54.

412

The KDF-363 operates by comparing signals received by a loop antenna and by a sense antenna. The signal received by the loop antenna is always shifted in phase by 90° as compared to the signal being received by the sense antenna.

As the block diagram shows (Fig. 9-55), the incoming loop antenna signal is amplified by a loop amplifier and shifted in phase 90° by a phase shifter. It is important to note that the loop signal after being phase shifted is either in-phase or directly out of phase with the signal arriving from the sense antenna, depending on whether the loop is to the right or left of the incoming signal.

Output from the phase shifter is applied to a balanced modulator which is being switched at a 60 cycle rate. Output from the balanced modulator is an rf signal either in phase or 180 degrees out of phase with its input signal.

Output from the balanced modulator is combined at this point with the signal arriving from the sense antenna. The amplitude of the sense antenna signal is adjusted to be approximately equal to that of the balanced modulator output so that during one half of the 60 cycle switching frequency, the two rf signals cancel; during the other half cycle the two signals add. This adding and cancelling effect is shown in the mixing and phasing diagram. Fig. 9-56.

The combined signal is applied to a conventional superheterodyne receiver consisting of an rf amplifier, mixer, i-f amplifier and a detector. The detector demodulates the signal to a 60 Hz tone that may be either in phase or out of phase with the 60 Hz switching frequency, depending on whether the loop is to left or right of the incoming signal.

The 60 Hz detector output is applied to a 60 Hz amplifier and a highly selective 60 Hz filter which removes noise and any modulation from the incoming signal. Output from the filter is again amplified and applied to a servo amplifier.

The servo amplifier, Fig. 9-57 is essentially a phase comparing device that controls the rotation of the dc motor coupled to the loop. If the phase of the 60 Hz tone from the receiver detector is in phase with the 60 Hz switching frequency, the loop motor rotates in a given direction; if the two 60 Hz signals are out of phase, the loop motor rotates in the opposite direction. If no 60 Hz tone is being received from the receiver detector, no power is applied to the motor and no

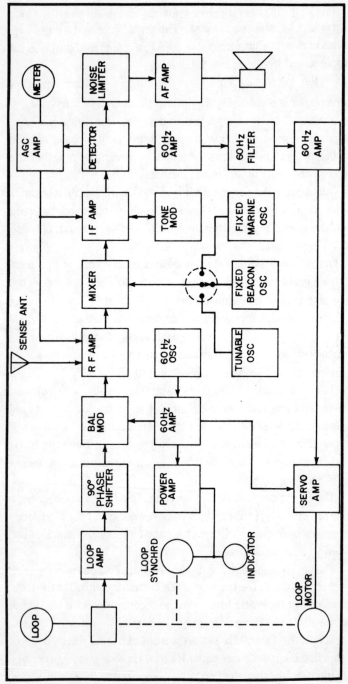

Fig. 9-55. Block diagram of the Konel KDF-363.

414

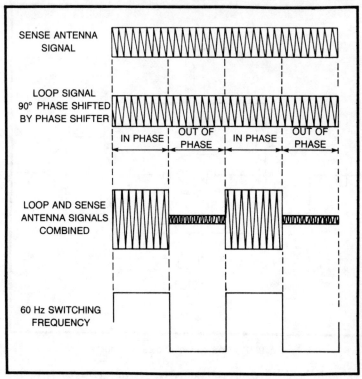

Fig. 9-56. Signal mixing and phasing.

rotation occurs. The KDF-363 system is adjusted so that the loop motor rotates the loop to *null* position at which time the motor stops.

Loop azimuth position is indicated by a transmitter synchro coupled to the loop and a receiving synchro controlling the needle on the front panel azimuth indicator. The ac power to operate the two synchros is obtained by amplifying the 60 Hz switching frequency to the necessary power level.

The KDF-363 also contains a conventional noise limiter and audio amplifier which operates a built-in speaker.

Errors Due to Installation

It is seldom possible to select a loop antenna site on the average vessel that will assure complete freedom from bearing errors due to metallic rigging, railings, superstructure, or electrical wiring. The magnitude and sign of such errors will vary widely with frequency

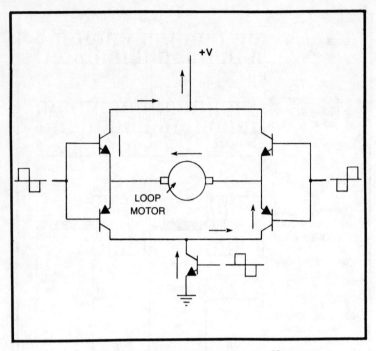

Fig. 9-57. Motor control and servo amplifier.

and with the relative direction of signal arrival with respect to the particular vessel. In general, the errors tend to increase with frequency; so, the apparent absence thereof in the 190 to 420 kHz band constitutes no guarantee of error free performance at higher frequencies.

The presence and the magnitude of bearing errors and other shipboard effects may be determined by conducting a radio compass swing. Any strong steady signal near the high frequency end of each band may be employed for this purpose provided that the source of the signal is known and visible. Coastal marine telephone stations are usually suitable for the high frequency band swing.

Radio compass swings should be conducted during the midday and well away from docks, bridges, power lines and other vessels to assure reliable results. If the ship's magnetic compass is to be used as a directional difference during the radio compass swing, its characteristics should be well known since any magnetic compass error will introduce an apparent radio bearing error. A suitable remote visual reference point and a sighting device provided with a calibrated azimuth scale may be employed to obtain more accurate results.

Radio compass swings should always begin with the source of the signal directly over the bow and aligned with the fore and aft axis of the vessel as indicated by the alignment of the indicator pointer and the heading marker. The indicator azimuth ring should be set to zero prior to starting the swing. Radio bearings should be recorded every 15° or relative ship's heading, as indicated by the directional reference employed, while making a tight circle. The resultant data may be plotted as an error curve for the particular frequency selected. See Fig. 9-58.

In the event that large errors are observed, it may be necessary to employ suitable insulators to break up any electrically continuous metallic loops, (whether ferrous or not) which may exist in the rigging, railings, or metal canopy supports. As previously mentioned such terminated antennas can introduce such errors, and this area should be investigated prior to more extensive corrective activity. It should be noted that errors due to the above or other related factors can not be eliminated by receiver adjustment.

CONCLUDING COMMENTS

Thus we conclude this important chapter on electronic navigation equipment. We remind you that the equipment is only as good as the operator, the care and maintenance, and the adjustments. All three must be above the level of adequacy. You must check and practice and know your equipment to have the best and most reliable performance from it.

It is a truism that electronic equipment—like a ship—is very much like a woman. Each one will have its own peculiarities. Even though you may have a similar or identical type to a thousand other units, yours will be unique in some manner. It takes a lot of affection, care, polishing, and caressing to learn just what its strengths and weaknesses are and how to use them to your own best advantage. Again, we say learn your equipment as a distinctly singular individual group of units. Learn each piece of it, each knob, each adjustment. Know what kind of touch each piece likes best and you'll find the rewards beyond your expectations.

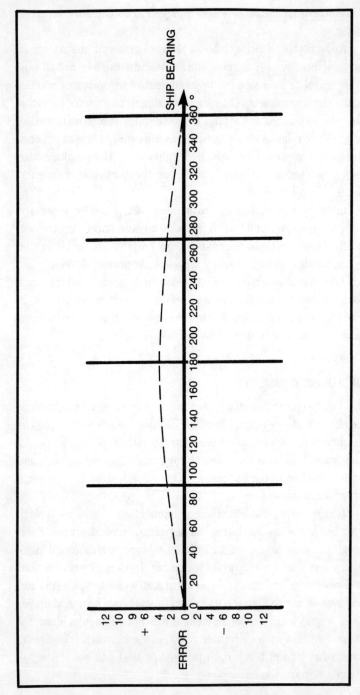

Fig. 9-58. Plot of error vs. bearing.

But when any doubts exists concerning your equipment, if it becomes the least bit erratic, or you even suspect that it might not be operating up to par, then call one of the countless fine servicemen who are trained and who have a reputation for knowledge, ability, fairness, and courtesy, and have them make whatever adjustments or repairs are required. Don't sacrifice good work and service for a few dollars in price or quickie-type fixes. Have it done and done right. Remember, as the saying goes, all this may save a life—and that life may be your own.

Now, how about an examination of some radar systems?

Chapter 10
Radar and Collision Avoidance Systems

For many pleasure boaters Fig. 10-1 is a familiar sight. To the left, silhouetted against the sky is a special TV antenna for boats; in the center rests an ADF antenna system like those discussed in the previous chapter; and on the right, one of the many radars that are available for use with pleasure craft. Not shown are the various communication antennas which, you may be assured, form an important part of this vessel's equipment.

RADAR FOR PLEASURE CRAFT AND SMALL COMMERCIAL VESSELS

In this chapter we want to discuss the use of radar on board craft of the small to commercial size: how to use the radar, how it works and how to select from the types available. It is to be noted that radar has two important functions. The first is for *collision avoidance,* and the second is for *navigation*. Within its range, radar can give the captain information on fixed landmarks from which he can plot his course.

Avoiding collisions at sea and finding objects that might cause damage, destruction and death, before they become a menace, is one of the primary duties of the person at the wheel. This has to be accomplished in all kinds of weather and under every possible circumstance. Radar can penetrate the night, fog, rain (to a limited degree), and turbulence to give the information required. But

Fig. 10-1. TV, ADF, and radar antennas on a pleasure craft.

operating radar requires some special knowledge—not anything beyond the most inexperienced landlubber's ability to learn, but only the desire to learn about. Use and practice using this kind of equipment until becoming quite expert in two aspects: First, the equipment must be known thoroughly, its capabilities and limitations, for each unit is unique. Second, the operator must be able to interpret its visual information with precision, and this requires practice.

Just having a radar on board is not enough. You must constantly use it by taking bearings on objects, monitoring other boats' progress in your waters, learning how buoys appear and how false echoes appear, and studying how to adjust the controls for the best and clearest picture information. It is not difficult, it just takes practice.

Now, what about licensing? Yes, radars, as all transmitting equipment, must be licensed. Even an emergency position indicating radio beacons (EPIRB) must be licensed. It is nice, however, that one license will cover all your transmitting equipment. Form 502 has this universal use.

When you put your radar on board be sure your station license has listed 9300 to 9500 MHz for radar and 121.5 MHz and 243 MHz for the EPIRBs. If you already have a license which does not list these, make a photocopy of it to post while you send the original and

Fig. 10-2. Radar antenna and Hatteras pleasure craft. (Courtesy Hatteras.)

a completely filled out form 505 to the FCC. It is suggested that you mark 156 to 158 MHz under item 13A for the addition of VHF frequencies, and under remarks, item 18, state "Request is made to modify my existing radio station license for inclusion of the new VHF frequencies." Send the application to the Federal Communications Commission, Gettysburg, PA 17325. No fee is required for this modification to your license.

Also, when filling out the 505 form under item 13A check the box "Other Frequencies" and write, "EPIRBs 121.5 and 243 MHz" next to this box. For your radar, check the box labeled 9300 to 9500 MHz under item 13B. If you do not have a 505 form you can get it from a dealer or you can send directly to the FCC, asking for one along with information on how to fill it out. Your transmitting equipment must be licensed to be legal.

Radar equipment on a boat can take many forms, but it can almost always be recognized by the rotating antenna which must be placed high and clear of surrounding structures. The indicating screen, or scope, may be located in the cabin or at any other

422

convenient location. Figure 10-2 shows one type radar on a Hatteras pleasure yacht, located above the flying bridge.

Before going deeper into this subject, let us consider for a moment an important passive device which will help you avoid trouble. This is the radar reflector as shown in Fig. 10-3. These are known as corner reflectors. They will cause the echo returning to a vessel to be large, bright, and clear. Often the masthead or sail alone will not provide a good return to a boat which may be using its radar to see if the way is clear. The radar reflectors tend to enhance the echo which is exactly what is desired.

Two such reflectors are shown. They are metal or have a metallic cover and will show two very distinct spots close together on a radar screen. Actually, at some distance the echoes will tend to blend together and show a fairly large object where this boat is located. Use them if you do not have radar or even if you do have radar. Use them to provide a good return to others who are searching for the position of other boats. They will see yours. Reflectors are cheap, consume no power, and last a long time. Talk to your dealers about them.

THE NAUTIC EYE RADAR

Now let's begin discussing radars. They come in a variety of sizes, shapes, and costs. One type for the small-boat owner is the

Fig. 10-3. Corner radar reflectors.

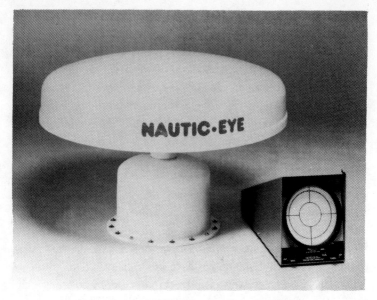

Fig. 10-4. Nautic Eye radar. (Courtesy Bonzer.)

Nautic Eye, shown in Fig. 10-4. This unit is said to be specifically designed for short range navigational needs for small boaters. It has ranges of 100, 250, 1,000 and 2,500 yards. It has a 5 inch scope and only two knobs for adjustment. It has only the two components shown.

Your own boat is always at the center of the scope display with this type gear. Targets in the form of bright spots will be on the scope around your position at the scope screen center—as the trace sweeps around the face of the scope like the second hand of a clock, but much faster. To make adjustments, set the gain control to obtain distinct targets but with very little of the snow caused by reflections from wave tops, etc. Set the range selector knob to the desired range and the outer ring will then have this range from the center position. You can estimate (or measure) the distance to objects inside the outer ring knowing the distance to the outer ring. Thus you can determine how far the objects are from your boat position.

It is always wise, with whatever radar you put on board, to begin using it by setting the controls and determining the range on the scope to a fixed land target. Then sail away from this target and observe how the pip changes position on the scope face. Make some maneuvers and check the changing position of the spot. Thus you learn how motion affects the echo spot, or trace, as it is sometimes called, whether your motion is caused by you, or the target, or from both causes.

Of course, even if you are moving, your position is always the center of the scope in this kind of system and display. Your individual radar instructions will tell you where your position is for other kinds of equipment. We would like to mention here that for a detailed discussion of how radars operate, including some types of radars not included in this work, obtain a copy of *Modern Radar*, TAB No. 575.

THE FURUNO RADAR SYSTEM

Now we begin an examination of some other kinds of equipment to learn how they operate and are installed and maintained. These are more complicated radars that do more things as you would suspect. Examine the Furuno system shown in Figs. 10-5 and 10-6.

The basics of a radar installation are shown in Fig. 10-7. Notice the use of a rotary converter to supply the needed high power from

Fig. 10-5. Furuno radar display unit. (Courtesy Konel.)

Fig. 10-6. Furuno radar antenna on a boat.

the 220 volt dc mains. Also note the 110/220 volt ac input to a rectifier that will furnish power without using the rotary converter if the ac power is available.

In any installation, the antenna must be positioned so that it points over the bow when the display scope strobe line is at zero degree heading. This is a mechanical adjustment which must be made during the system alignment. The adjustment requires two persons: one at the display and one at the antenna. The heading (flash marker) should appear on the scope just as the antenna front passes the ship's bow. This alignment is the last step of the radar installation. It is to be noted that you must operate the system during this alignment because the electromagnetic zero angle may differ from the geometric zero angle. You may have a squint angle. This means that the antenna may not physically be facing directly over the bow when you get the zero heading marker flash. For example, at the operating frequency of this radar, the squint angle is about 2.5 degrees advanced in the direction of the antenna turning direction. This means that when the antenna is physically pointing 2.5 degrees off the bow, *electrically* it is looking directly over the bow. This is nothing to worry about so long as proper alignment has been made.

OPERATING THE RADAR

Plese refer back to Fig. 10-5. You must preset the controls, as follows, before turning the radar on.

Control	Setting
Function	Off
Brilliance	Fully counterclockwise
Gain	Fully counterclockwise
STC	Fully counterclockwise
Others	May be in any position

1. Turn the rotary converter or rectifier unit on, if provided. Turn the FUNCTION switch from OFF to STBY. The cursor plate will be illuminated and the antenna starts rotating. In approximately 3 minutes, the tuning meter will light, indicating that the radar is ready for transmission.
2. Turn the FUNCTION switch to TX (Transmit).
3. Select range with the RANGE switch.
4. Turn the GAIN Control amost fully clockwise, with the BRIL (Brilliance) control set to the minimum position.
5. Turn the BRIL control clockwise to regulate the brightness of the picture scope.
6. Tune the receiver by turning the TUNING knob until the best each appears on the scope. The best tuning is obtained when the tuning meter on the top right of the front panel is showing maximum deflection.
7. Adjust the GAIN control again for best picture definition. Probably a slight reduction in gain will be required.
8. Flip the HEADING ALIGN switch upward, at the top left on the display panel. After a while, the heading flash will appear at zero azimuth scale position. If, however, the flash does not appear at zero but 2 degrees, momentarily depress the HEADING ALIGN switch downward. This switch is spring loaded and will flip back to the off position (center) when it is released. One depression will move the flash position 2 degrees anticlockwise and successive depressions will move the flash with a step of 2 degrees beyond the zero azimuth scale position. If it is required to place the heading flash at the optional position, then de-

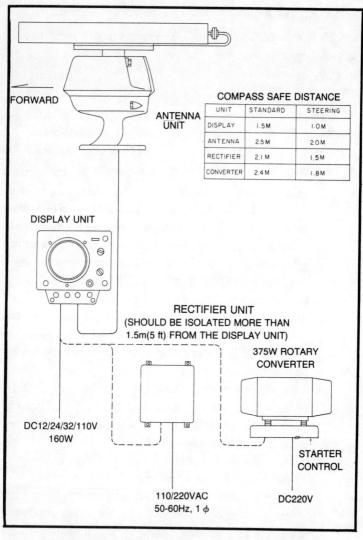

FORWARD

ANTENNA UNIT

DISPLAY UNIT

COMPASS SAFE DISTANCE

UNIT	STANDARD	STEERING
DISPLAY	1.5 M	1.0 M
ANTENNA	2.5 M	2.0 M
RECTIFIER	2.1 M	1.5 M
CONVERTER	2.4 M	1.8 M

RECTIFIER UNIT
(SHOULD BE ISOLATED MORE THAN
1.5m(5 ft) FROM THE DISPLAY UNIT)

375W ROTARY
CONVERTER

DC12/24/32/110V
160W

STARTER
CONTROL

110/220VAC
50-60Hz, 1 φ

DC220V

Fig. 10-7. Furuno system block diagram. (Courtesy Konel.)

press the switch downward the proper number of times. When finished adjusting, leave the switch at the off position.

9. Adjust the Hor. and Vert. (horizontal and vertical) CENTERING knobs so that the sweep starting point is positioned at the center of the display scope.

428

10. To measure the distance of a target, pull the BRIL RINGS knob out. Ring spacings are indicated in red around the range switch.

11. If the target close by cannot be discriminated among the sea return echoes, turn the STC control *slowly* clockwise. Do not use too high a setting; a small amount of sea return indicates the proper adjustment.

12. When the observation of the echo is difficult due to heavy rain or snow or when the identification of close-in targets is difficult, turn the FUNCTION switch to FTC. This helps to clear the echoes.

13. When a target has been obtained on the scope, the range is determined by using the range rings. The exact range is straight line distance from the center spot to the nearest edge of the target.

14. The bearing angle is the angle from the heading flash at 0 scale to the target. Turn the bearing CURSOR knob located at the lower left on the front panel so that the cursor cross line extension is on the center of the target and then read the bearing angle on the azimuth ring touched to the cursor line.

If you do not use the radar continuously, place it in STBY (Stand-by) operation by positioning the FUNCTION switch to this position. The antenna will still rotate. If you want to stop radar operation, turn the FUNCTION switch to OFF and set the controls to the initial position stated at the beginning of this discussion. Of course you will then turn off the main switch of the rotary converter or rectifier unit, whichever is provided.

It is important that you understand the limiting factors on the range of such a radar. They are the same for all radars. The maximum range is much affected by the propagating conditions of the radar pulse, such as the height of the radar antenna and the size and shape of the target. The reflecting characteristics of such targets also is important.

Under normal conditions the maximum range will be equal to the radar horizon or perhaps a little shorter. The radar horizon is longer than the optical horizon by about 6 percent because of the diffraction properties of the radar pulses. The maximum radar range is stated by the equation:

$$R_{max} = 2.2(\sqrt{h_1} + \sqrt{h_2})$$

Where: R_{max} is the radar range in miles.

$_1$ is the height of the radar antenna in meters.

$_2$ is the height of the target in meters.

For example, if the antenna height is 5 meters and that of the target is 10 meters, the maximum radar range is:

$$R_{max} = 2.2(\sqrt{5} + \sqrt{10}) = 11.9 \text{ miles}$$

Another factor that is most important is that of minimum radar range. There is a close range over which you cannot see a target, no matter how large it may be. This minimum range is governed by the radar pulse width and the height of the antenna. More on this in a moment. Right now we will state that for normal pulse widths used, the blind range is about zero to 30 meters from your radar.

Radar Resolution (Target Discrimination Ability)

The bearing resolution is an ability to discriminate two targets which are in two different points of the compass but at the same range. This bearing discriminating ability is proportional to antenna length and reciprocally proportional to wavelength. Usually the bearing resolution is from 1 to 3 degrees. If you want to pick out targets that are very close together, you need a long antenna, and a high frequency.

The range resolution is the ability to pick out targets which are on the same bearing, but at different ranges. This is determined by the pulse width only. With a wide pulse (in microseconds) you will find that your targets have to be separated more widely in range to be seen. Narrow pulses means they can be closer together and you can still see the separate echoes. Usual range resolution is from 20 to 30 meters with a 0.1 microsecond pulse.

ECHO STRENGTH

The strongest echoes are those which are directly swept, or head-on swept, by the antenna. When the antenna sends out a pulse and an echo returns from some angle to the antenna, this echo will necessarily be weaker than the head-on echo. Sometimes, of course, the target mass—such as sand on a beach or low hills with gentle slopes or some lighthouses—will send back echoes which are scattered. This means you get just a small amount of energy back from the amount you transmitted. Such echoes are therefore weak and dim. We say in this case that the incidence angle of the return is very small. The echo from a flat plate such as the broadside of a steel ship hull has a very large incidence angle (the angle is 90 degrees to the plane of the hull) and the echo is very large, giving a good bright picture. So be aware that the brightness of your echo can depend on the orientation of your target as well as its range.

FALSE IMAGES

When the target is wide and plane (for example the sideboard of a ship, a bridge, a building on a pier, or a breakwater), the radar waves are multireflected and will appear on the scope as if many targets existed there. In the case that the target is 200 yards away from the ship radar, the true image appears at the position of 200 yards, and the *false images* appear at positions of 400, 600, and 800 yards on the CRT screen as shown in Fig. 10-8(a).

When the radar waves are emitted from the antenna some of the energy actually goes astray from the main radar beam. This energy goes to the sides and is therefore called sidelobes. Because they pick up echoes at about 90 degrees from the main beam, images due to sidelobes will appear at right angles to the real echo on the scope face. This can be seen in Fig. 10-8(b). Sometimes these kinds of images can be eliminated or reduced by adjustment of the STC gain control. A real direct-image will remain even though you reduce the gain.

A relatively large target close to your radar set can appear as two images on your radar scope. One of these images is the real target and the other is what is called a reflected image. It is a false image. The cause of this kind of echo is the mirror effect of adjacent large objects. Its appearance is shown in Fig. 10-8(c) and it is called a compound image.

Sometimes, when the propagation of the radar waves is abnormal due to some kinds of atmospheric conditions, echoes will return to the radar much later than they are supposed to. When this happens you will have additional echoes which appear as very close

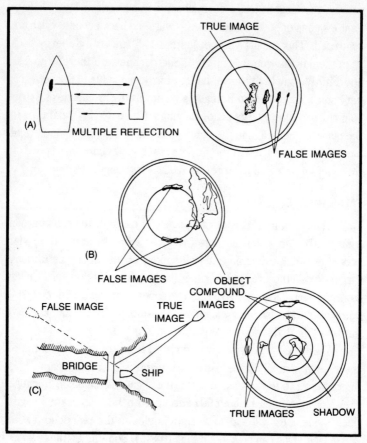

Fig. 10-8. Radar scope pictures false target.

targets, even though the echoes come from a target which is a long way off. What happens is that the echoes return during a second sweep of the scope trace. This does not happen often, but it can occur.

Any radar can have a *dead angle*. This can be caused because the radar is not high enough and funnels, masts, and derrick posts near the antenna actually cut off the transmission of radar energy in some direction. The angle shown in Fig. 10-9(a) is an example of a dead angle and in its zone you cannot see a target. Always keep your radar antenna high and clear for an unobstructed view.

You can have radar interference from other radars when they are close-by. In this case, bright dotted lines are presented on the

432

entire screen of the scope as indicated in Fig. 10-9(b). There isn't much you can do about this and the shapes of these lines will vary according to how close to your frequency the other radars may be and how much power they have, etc. Learn to recognize this kind of interference so that you can identify it and know its source.

We said earlier that a radar has a minimum range. This means that for very close ranges, the radar is blind to objects it bounces signals off. The shortest range which a radar can see is that at which the transmitting pulse if off—in time—and thus an echo can appear on the receiver scope which is blanked out during the transmitting time.

For example, if the pulse width is 1 microsecond, the radar is on for this period of time. The energy will travel out at 168 meters per microsecond, so it will go out half this distance and return half this distance in the one microsecond that the transmitter is on. Anything, then, in the range out to about 80 meters will not be seen as the receiver will be blanked out during this time.

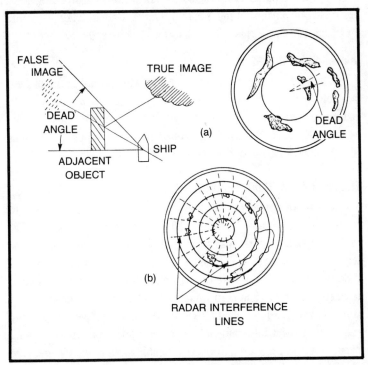

Fig. 10-9. Radar beam masking and interference.

Fig. 10-10. The antenna (center) should be mounted higher, clear of the crew and flying bridge.

Of course much shorter pulse times are used. For example 0.1 microsecond pulses cut the minimum range to about 20 to 30 meters in practical cases. This allows also for circuit recovery time.

Antenna Installation

Figure 10-10 shows a radar antenna which is not at the highest possible location. In fact, if persons stand on this flying bridge they may absorb some of the radar energy when the antenna points to the stern direction and may thus reduce its effectiveness. Antennas should always be far out in the clear and high up.

THE RAYTHEON 3100/3900 RADAR

For more details on the operation of a marine radar we turn to another example, the Raytheon 3100/3900 radar. This radar, as all of them, when properly maintained will give good reliable service on any boat. Maintenance must be periodic. The cleaning of the antenna radome (cover) or the antenna transparent cover must be done at least once a month. Salt spray builds up on this radome and can cause a deterioration of its ability to sent out and receive the energy required for accurate ranging and object detection. Also, moving parts must be greased and exposed cables and plugs cleaned and checked on a periodic basis. It's work, we agree, but don't put it off.

434

The display unit of the Raytheon 3100/3900 radar is shown in Fig. 10-11. The controls are few in number and the scope face is large and easy to read. The system block diagram is shown in Fig. 10-12.

Installation

Selection of an adequate location for the antenna T/R (transmit-receive) unit involves careful consideration. On many boats, the unit can be mounted directly on the top deck of the wheelhouse near the ship's center line. The unit should be mounted as high as possible to ensure best performance at the maximum range.

The antenna scanning beam should not be obstructed by nearby large objects. Locate the unit where large structures such as the superstructure or stacks are not in the same horizontal plane, particularly in a forward direction; otherwise, blind areas and false

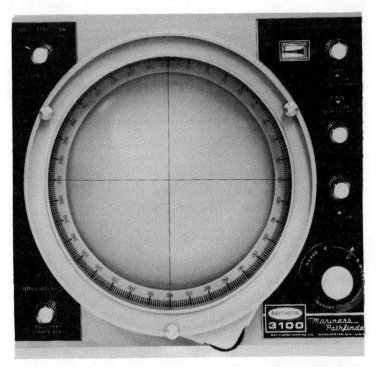

Fig. 10-11. Raytheon 3100 display unit. (Courtesy Raytheon Marine.)

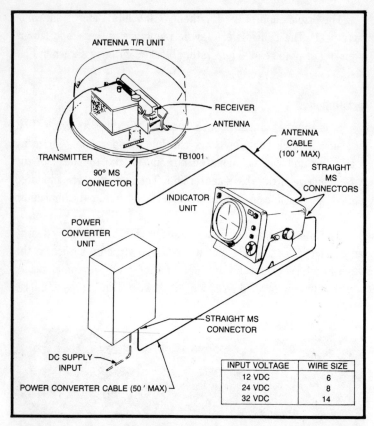

INPUT VOLTAGE	WIRE SIZE
12 VDC	6
24 VDC	8
32 VDC	14

Fig. 10-12. Raytheon 3100 Radar system block diagram. (Courtesy Raytheon Marine.)

echoes will appear on the display. Installation near the top of a stack must be avoided to minimize exposure to excessive heat and corrosive effects of stack gases.

Operating Controls and Procedures

Figure 10-13 shows the controls on the indicator front panel and briefly describes their functions. The figure also includes a sequential turn-on procedure keyed to the controls by circled key numbers.

Range. The range selector switch permits one of six scales in nautical miles (1/2, 2, 4, 8, 16, or 32) to be chosen for the range displayed. The number and range intervals of the marker rings are predetermined and automatically selected by the position of the

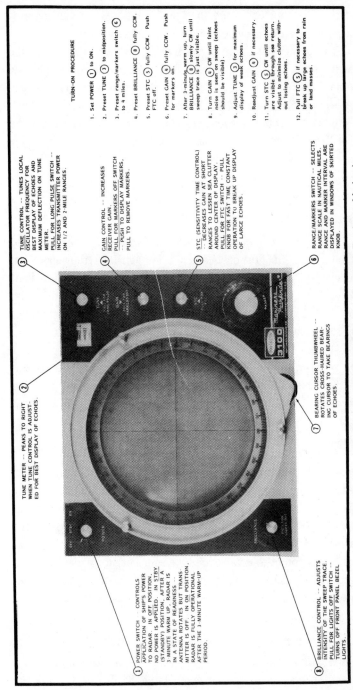

TUNE CONTROL -- TUNES LOCAL OSCILLATOR FREQUENCY FOR BEST DISPLAY OF ECHOES AND MAXIMUM DEFLECTION ON TUNE METER.

PULL FOR LONG PULSE SWITCH -- INCREASES TRANSMITTER POWER ON 1/2 AND 2-MILE RANGES.

TUNE METER -- PEAKS TO RIGHT WHEN TUNE CONTROL IS ADJUSTED FOR BEST DISPLAY OF ECHOES.

GAIN CONTROL -- INCREASES RECEIVER GAIN.
PULL FOR MARKERS OFF SWITCH -- PUSH TO DISPLAY MARKERS, PULL TO REMOVE MARKERS.

STC (SENSITIVITY TIME CONTROL) -- DECREASES GAIN AT SHORT RANGES TO LESSEN SEA CLUTTER AROUND CENTER OF DISPLAY.
PULL FOR FTC SWITCH -- PULL KNOB FOR FAST TIME CONSTANT OPERATION TO BREAK UP DISPLAY OF LARGE ECHOES.

RANGE/MARKERS SWITCH -- SELECTS RANGE SCALE IN NAUTICAL MILES. RANGE AND MARKER INTERVAL ARE DISPLAYED IN WINDOWS OF SKIRTED KNOB.

BEARING CURSOR THUMBWHEEL -- ROTATES CROSS-HAIRED BEARING CURSOR TO TAKE BEARINGS OF ECHOES.

① POWER SWITCH -- CONTROLS APPLICATION OF SHIP'S POWER TO RADAR. IN OFF POSITION, NO POWER IS APPLIED. IN STBY (STANDBY) POSITION, AFTER A 3-MINUTE WARM UP, RADAR IS IN A STATE OF READINESS -- ANTENNA ROTATES BUT TRANSMITTER IS OFF. IN ON POSITION, RADAR IS FULLY OPERATIONAL AFTER THE 3-MINUTE WARM-UP PERIOD.

⑧ BRILLIANCE CONTROL -- ADJUSTS INTENSITY OF THE SWEEP TRACE. PULL FOR LIGHTS OFF SWITCH -- TURNS OFF FRONT PANEL BEZEL LIGHTS.

TURN-ON PROCEDURE

1. Set POWER ① to ON.
2. Preset TUNE ③ to midposition.
3. Preset range/markers switch ⑥ to 4 miles.
4. Preset BRILLIANCE ⑧ fully CCW.
5. Preset STC ⑤ fully CCW. Push FTC off.
6. Preset GAIN ④ fully CCW. Push for markers on.
7. After 3-minute, warm up, turn BRILLIANCE ⑧ slowly CW until sweep trace is just visible.
8. Turn GAIN ④ CW until faint noise is seen on sweep (echoes should be visible).
9. Adjust TUNE ③ for maximum display of weak echoes.
10. Readjust GAIN ④ if necessary.
11. Turn STC ⑤ CW until echoes are visible through sea return. Adjust to minimize clutter without losing echoes.
12. Pull FTC ⑤ if necessary to break up large echoes from rain or land masses.

Fig. 10-13. Front panel controls of Raytheon 3100 Radar. (Courtesy Raytheon Marine.)

437

switch. The shortest range that covers the desired viewing area should be used to provide the greatest detail of display.

Brilliance. Rotation of the BRILLIANCE control varies the brightness of the CRT display. This control should be adjusted (turned clockwise or counterclockwise) so that with the STC and GAIN controls completely counterclockwise and the FTC knob pushed in, the rotating sweep trace is visible. At this setting of the BRILLIANCE control, a display of maximum contrast is provided without the possibility of overlooking small echoes.

> **CAUTION:** Too high a setting of the BRIL-LIANCE control will burn the center of the CRT and also reduce echo contrast.

Gain. Rotation of the GAIN control varies receiver gain, and thus the strength of the echoes (and noise signals) as they appear on the display. The normal setting for this control is for a light background speckle on the display. The equipment is in the most sensitive condition when this background speckle is just showing; objects will then be detected at the greatest possible range (see Fig. 10-14).

With too little gain, some weak echoes will be missed, and there is a decrease in the range at which objects can be detected. With excessive gain, additional echoes are not seen, but the contrast between echoes and the background noise signals is reduced, making observation more difficult.

A temporary setting at a lower or higher gain than normal may be useful to assist in detecting significant echoes. For example, with the GAIN control at its normal setting, clutter from rain or snow may obscure the echo from a nearby ship (or other object) within a squall or storm. Reducing the gain temporarily will usually permit the stronger and more distinct ship echo to override the clutter; however, detection of objects beyond the squall or storm may require a higher GAIN control setting than normal. At the longer range, clutter may attenuate, but not completely obscure, echoes from distant objects.

> **CAUTION:** Too high a setting of the GAIN control will burn center of CRT. Use STC to decrease gain at center when on 2 mile or longer range setting.

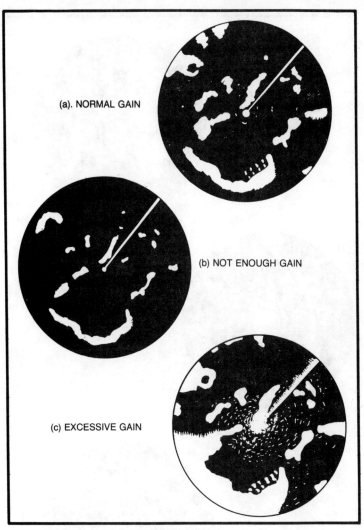

(a). NORMAL GAIN

(b) NOT ENOUGH GAIN

(c) EXCESSIVE GAIN

Fig. 10-14. Effect of the GAIN control setting on the display.

Tuning. Rotation of the TUNE control varies the fine tuning of the local oscillator to accommodate slight frequency changes in the transmitter or drift in the local oscillator. A readjustment on the TUNE control may be necessary after the radar warms up. The absence or decreased strength of echoes on the display is an indication that the equipment is off the tuning peak. Retune by selecting a weak echo and rotating the TUNE control clockwise and coun-

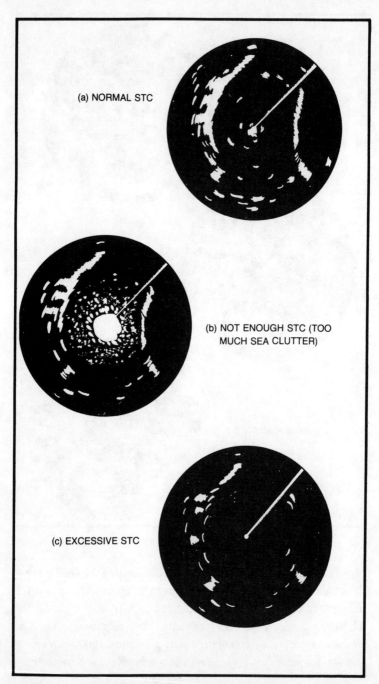

(a) NORMAL STC

(b) NOT ENOUGH STC (TOO MUCH SEA CLUTTER)

(c) EXCESSIVE STC

Fig. 10-15. Effect of the STC on the display.

terclockwise until maximum strength of the echo is observed. This adjustment can also be performed by observing the tuning meter. The pointer fluctuates when the antenna is rotating and picking up echoes, but when the average reading is highest (farthest right) the adjustment is correct. However, the finest adjustment is obtained by observing echoes on the display.

Pulling out the TUNE control provides long-pulse operation on 1/2 and 2 mile ranges where short-pulse operation is normally used. Long pulse operation provides stronger returns from weak targets but range resolution is poorer. Short pulse operation is usually preferable.

STC. The STC (sensitivity time control), sometimes known as swept gain control, is an auxiliary gain control. While the GAIN control affects echo strength uniformly throughout all ranges, the effect of STC is greatest on short-range echoes, becoming progressively less as range increases. Also, STC is effective only up to a maximum range of about 2 miles.

In particular, STC reduces the strength of the mass of random signals (echoes) received from nearby wave fronts. Just enough STC should be used to reduce the strength of the echoes so the clutter appears only as small dots but small objects can still be distinguished (see Fig. 10-15).

CAUTION: At short ranges the setting of the STC knob should never be advanced so far as to completely obliterate all clutter since this setting could result in the loss of echoes. At long ranges (8 miles and up) turning the knob fully clockwise will reduce bloom at the CRT center without any loss of useful information. This will help prevent burning of the center of the CRT.

The degree of STC effectiveness is fully variable, allowing an optimum presentation to be obtained under adverse weather conditions. Maximum reduction in the strength of nearby echoes occurs when the STC knob is turned fully clockwise; when it is turned fully counterclockwise, there is no reduction in echo strength.

The STC can be used to reduce clutter from storm and rain squall returns as well as sea returns from the immediate vicinity of your vessel. Clutter appears on the display as a very large number of small echoes. The position of these echoes varies from scan to scan, usually covering a considerable area. Sea clutter may appear out to a range of about 1.5 to 2 miles from the vessel when the sea is rough. The area of sea clutter is roughly oval in shape, not centered about the vessel, with the largest part lying to windward.

When the STC knob is adjusted for the best setting to minimize sea clutter, a crescent of clutter will probably remain in the windward direction. A common error is to apply too much STC so that a zone of darkness is around and beyond the maximum range to which the clutter extends. This may eliminate many significant echoes, particularly if the GAIN control is set so that the speckled background is not clearly visible at longer ranges. In any event, small readjustments of the GAIN control may be necessary after adjusting the STC knob.

FTC (Fast Time Constant). Pull out the FTC knob to make this feature effective. The function of this control is to diminish the displayed magnitude of large unwanted echoes that generally clutter up the display and which, by virtue of their size, may overlap and obscure smaller echoes in their immediate vicinity. This is particulary true of large echoes from precipitation, and sometimes true for large land-mass echoes. The FTC control appears to sharpen such echoes so that only the front edge of the echo is displayed, while smaller echoes are only slightly affected. FTC is generally used only on short ranges.

INTERPRETATION OF A MARINE RADAR DISPLAY

The radar display is a maplike representation of the area in which the radar is operating. Your boat is at the center of the display. The dead ahead bearing is indicated by the heading line flashing at the zero degrees bearing with every revolution of the sweep trace.

Contours of the coastline are depicted as solid echoes. Other surface vessels and channel buoys are displayed as small single echoes. Prominent landmarks (such as bridges, lighthouses, and dockside installations), which are readily seen from the boat, are large enough for the radar to detect and display. Greater detail is shown when using a short range scale, but the best technique is to start with a long range scale and switch to shorter ranges as you approach the coastline, harbor, or other vessels in the area.

Figure 10-16 illustrates an example of display interpretation. Figure 10-16(a) shows a nautical chart of Cuttyhunk Harbor (chart 263), and Figure 10-16(b) shows the Raytheon 3900 radar corresponding display. The radar is on the 0.5 nautical mile range scale; the inner bright circle represents the 0.25 mile range and the outer circle the 0.5 mile range. The ship's position is indicated by the small circle on the chart. The radar display is oriented to the ship, so the ship's heading is always toward the top of the display at 0° relative bearing. The radial lines on the rotatable bearing cursor are set to read a bearing on the docks to port. The relative bearing is 260. True bearing is equal to relative bearing plus or minus the ship's heading (add or subtract to get a positive number less than 360). In this case the ship's heading is 0°, so relative bearing and the true bearing are the same. A radar display can be thought of as a picture taken from above with the landscape (seascape) illuminated by a powerful revolving searchlight located at the radar antenna (center of the picture). Thus, a headland or building will be illuminated, but all areas behind it will be in its shadow. They will not be seen.

Note in the display that the ship is at the rear of an anchored fleet and that the boats off the bow are apparent. The land promontory and Coast Guard Station (now abandoned) are off the stern. Note that the beach areas are so low in elevation that they do not reflect (recall the incidence angle discussion earlier?). Thus these areas do not show on the scope.

EFFECT OF A BOAT'S MOVEMENT ON RADAR DISPLAY

The radar display changes shape and relative position according to the boat's speed and course. With no movement a steady display of fixed radar echoes is shown. If your boat is moving ahead on a straight course, echoes appearing at the top of the display move downward across the display. If your boat alters course to the right, the displayed echoes will be displaced by an equal amount in bearing in a counterclockwise direction, and vice versa. These changes in display patterns with the boat's movements are extremely important when plotting the ship's course and the course of nearby vessels.

Until the operator becomes thoroughly familiar with the interpretation of the radar display, every opportunity should be taken to compare charted coastal areas with their corresponding display

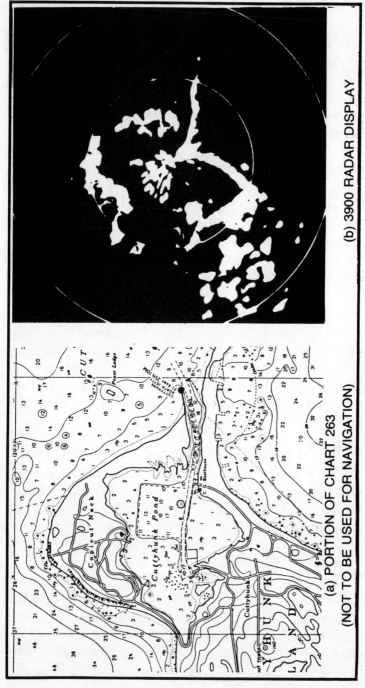

(a) PORTION OF CHART 263
(NOT TO BE USED FOR NAVIGATION)

(b) 3900 RADAR DISPLAY

Fig. 10-16. Display interpretation in harbor.

444

patterns. Harbor and coastal navigation should be practiced during daylight and clear weather conditions.

NAVIGATIONAL ECHOES

Echoes displayed on the indicator unit screen will be large or small, bright or faint, depending on the size and range of the object. The radar indication is similar to an observer's visual indication; a nearby object which is small may appear the same size as a distant large object. With experience, however, the approximate size of different objects can be determined by the relative size and brightness of their radar echoes. Of course corner reflectors, discussed earlier, produce a strong return even though they are small and may be a long way off.

Buoys and small boats are easily identified. Since they bob and toss about in the waves, they do not present a consistently uniform reflecting surface. Consequently their echoes have a tendency to fade and brighten and at times to disappear momentarily.

High coastlines and mountainous coastal regions can be picked up at the longest range of the equipment. However, the first sight of landfall on the radar display might be a mountain several miles inland from the coastline. The actual coastline may not appear until the distance is closed.

SEA RETURN DISPLAYS

Echoes may be displayed from irregularities on the surface of the water, particularly at close range, by breaking wavecrests in heavy seas. This type of clutter appears as dense background noise in the shape of an almost solid disc, as far as one mile in all directions from the display center. If the amount of sea return appearing on the display is not controlled, the desired echoes may be obscured. But with careful use of the STC control, the sea return can be diminished considerably to permit the desired echoes to be recognized. The use of long-pulse operation on the short range scales may aid in observing desired targets. However, land masses should be clearly visible even during heavy sea conditions.

STORM AND RAIN SQUALL RETURNS

Echoes from storm areas and rain squalls are readily identified by their returns, which generally present a large hazy area on the display scope, being made up of countless small echoes continually changing in intensity, size, and position. These returns may be very helpful for bad weather warnings. When storms or rain squall returns are not desired, either because they pose no threat or you want to see what else is in the area, pull out the FTC control knob to minimize them.

We had discussed false and ghost images earlier. Recall that they have the appearance of true echoes, but in general they are intermittent and poorly defined. A ghost image retains a fixed relationship to the true image and has a more arc-like appearance with a tendency to smear.

We had also mentioned interference from other radars which may appear as a line of dots from the center of the screen, many lines about the face of the tube, or as curved lines radiating out from the center. In this case you are simply picking up some other radar and there isn't a lot that can be done about it except to move away.

RANGE AND BEARING MEASUREMENT WITH THE RAYTHEON 3900

To measure the range of an echo proceed as follows:

1. Display the range marker rings by pushing in the MAR-KERS knob.
2. Note the range scale in use and the nautical mile intervals between the range marker rings.
3. Add the range represented by the number of rings between the center of the display and the echo to an estimate of the range between the inner edge of the echo and the nearest inner ring.

To measure the relative bearing of an echo proceed as follows:

1. Adjust your line of sight so the center spot is directly under the intersection of the cursor lines.
2. Rotate the bearing cursor until one of the radial lines engraved on the cursor passes through the center of the echo.
3. Read the bearing indicated at the intersection of that cursor line and the graduated scale. The reading so obtained will show the relative bearing to the object.

Relative bearing means the bearing in degrees from your boat's heading, or fore-aft axis. To obtain a true bearing (or magnetic bearing) add the relative bearing and the boat's true (or magnetic bearing) heading. If the result is more than 360, subtract 360 from the total to obtain the bearing.

NAVIGATING WITH RADAR

Radar is an accurate and reliable navigational aid for determining the boat's position. Figure 10-17 shows examples of alternative methods of using radar sightings from prominent navigational points which can be identified on a chart. A position fix based on two or more navigational points will furnish a more accurate fix, especially when the points approach 90° apart from your position. The following is how to obtain an accurate fix:

1. Finding your position by obtaining the ranges to three identifiable points and plotting them on the chart as shown in Fig. 10-17(a) results in a highly accurate position fix. Radar rangefinding is more accurate than visual rangefinding. The distances (ranges) are plotted by using dividers to measure the distance on the chart scale and transferring it to the chart. One end of the dividers is placed on the point, and the other end is used to trace the range arc.

2. Figure 10-17(b) illustrates the method used when only one point is available. The range is plotted as just described. The bearing is plotted from the point back to intersect the range arc using a plotter. The relative bearing must be converted to a true bearing before plotting.

3. Figure 10-17(c) illustrates how to find your position at the intersection of two plotted bearings. The two points selected should be as near 90 degrees apart as possible; greater accuracy is obtained if bearings to three objects each 60 degrees apart are plotted. Convert to true bearings before plotting. This method may be less accurate than plotting range arcs, since radar bearings, due to the beam width of the radar, are less exact than radar range.

AVOIDING COLLISION

As soon as an echo appears on the display, its range and relative bearing should be noted. This is best done on a plotting sheet or

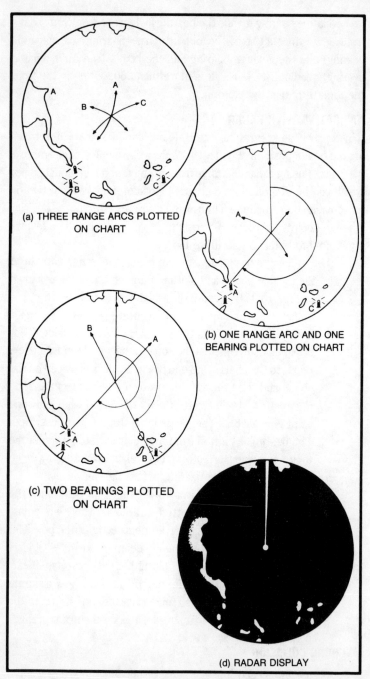

(a) THREE RANGE ARCS PLOTTED ON CHART

(b) ONE RANGE ARC AND ONE BEARING PLOTTED ON CHART

(c) TWO BEARINGS PLOTTED ON CHART

(d) RADAR DISPLAY

Fig. 10-17. Alternate methods of determining position fixes.

chart. As in visual observation, *a constant bearing indicates a collision course.* As soon as a series of plots indicates a closing range and no significant change is sucessive bearings, positive action should be considered mandatory. The Regulations for Preventing Collisions at Sea should always be observed. We will discuss just a little further on the Raytheon Collision Avoidance System which is most appropriate for larger and commercial vessls. It is worth study.

DETERMINING RADAR LINE OF SIGHT RANGE

When searching for distant echoes, the radar line of sight range to the echo can be a limiting factor. Radar waves behave like light waves but are refracted slightly more, increasing the distance to the radar horizon to slightly more than that to the optical horizon (the radar range displayed on the scale is, however, correct). As Fig. 10-18 shows, the radar line of sight range is a combination of what would be considered to be the radar horizon of the boat's radar antenna and the radar horizon of the reflected target echo. The nomograph provides a convenient method for determining any one of three factors involved when the other two are known.

THE SPERRY COLLISION AVOIDANCE RADAR SYSTEM

It is a logical development from the tracking radar to an integrated system that will present an evaluation of all possible dangers of nearby ships and of other radar reflective objects so larger ships may maneuver in time to prevent collisions.

This system, of course, requires the alert attention of the bridge, but under educated guidance, the system will help to avoid tragedies. In this section we want to learn what the system consists of and how it works. Its display unit and console, which will be found inside the bridge, are shown in Fig. 10-19. Here are the details we want to learn about. The Sperry integrated navigation and collision avoidance system is designed to present the bridge with:

- Reliable collision threat data in a unique indicator display that permits immediate maneuver decisions with minimum interpretation.
- Automatic on the hour or on demand output display at time and date, ship's estimated position, water and ground speed, set and drift, heading, and waypoint data.

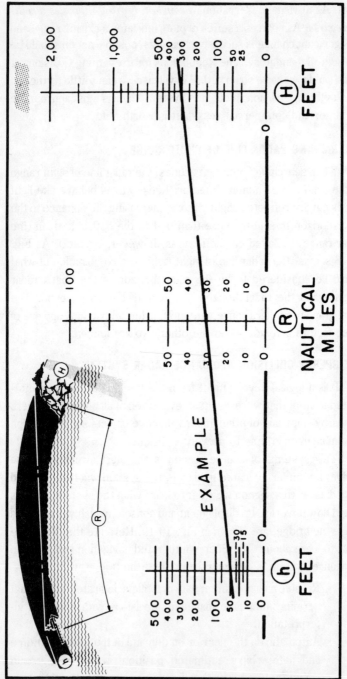

Fig. 10-18. Radar line of sight range nomograph.

450

The collision avoidance displays show real time, true situations with automated design features which reduce operator functions and permit early assessments of traffic, leaving more time for the important decision making process. Systems with expanded capabilities and optional features offer increased traffic assessments, automatic data readout on specific targets, automatic radar watch of approaching targets, radar interswitching, automated navigation with special

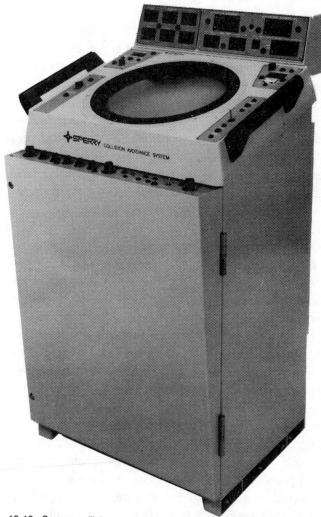

Fig. 10-19. Sperry collision avoidance system control indicator. (Courtesy Sperry Marine Systems.)

451

charting displays, and automatic position fixing from more than one source.

The basic system consists of a navigation computer/tracker electronics unit and the Control Indicator unit interfaced with a satellite receiver CRT data terminal, and shipboard radar, gyrocompass, and speed data generating equipment. System functions are controlled and coordinated by a general purpose, digital computer. The computer is programmed to periodically sample input information from interfaced shipboard equipment and, working with the tracker electronic circuits, to develop collision threat data on tracked targets. The computed results are used in the control indicator to generate a synthetic display of symbols which visually defines the degree of collision threat offered by the tracked targets. The synthetic collsion avoidance display is superimposed on a normal radar video presentation for rapid target recognition. Simultaneously, but independent of the collision avoidance function, the computer program calculates continuously the ship's dead reckoned (DR) position based on interfaced ship's gyrocompass and speed log input combined with manual or automatic values for set and drift. Automatic position fixing data from the satellite receiver using data from orbiting satellites is periodically available to correct the DR calculation. The waypoint subroutine provides heading-to-steer, distance-to-go and time-to-go to an operator-designated position. All navigation displays appear on the hour or on operator demand via the CRT data terminal. Update of navigation parameters is also accomplished via the data terminal.

For the system to compute collision data, radar video returns are received from interfaced radar equipment and processed in the tracker electronics for target data. Targets are manually selected by the operator with a joystick on the indicator which communicates the selection to the computer. The real time display situations shown on the indicator require that the system continually maintain track on the selected targets, generating new threat data and new displays as the situation changes. Computed threat assessments are based not only on video track information of targets, but also on speed and heading parameters sampled from your ship's heading, and velocity information is formulated from one of three speed sources: engine revolution rate, manual speed settings, or speed log equipment. The computer furnishes current numerical readouts on the indicator for your own ship's speed and heading, and instantaneous bearing cursor position. Programmed computer operations also provide for automatic monitoring of the displays for collision threat situations dangerous to your ship. When these conditions occur, the ship's bridge is automatically alerted with visual and audible alarms on the indicator. A magnetic tape reader is incorporated with the system to provide a means for reloading the computer program and to generate test functions and patterns for system realignment.

For the system to compute accurate navigation data, there must be continuous input of your ship's heading and speed. Given these inputs, initial set and drift, and an initial estimate of position, the system computes estimated ship's position every 3 seconds. The periodic input of position fix data from the satellite receiver serves two functions:

1. To correct the DR position
2. To update set and drift used in DR calculation.

If two speed axis data is available, ground speed is measured directly and set and drift and waterspeed are not computed. The waypoint data is updated every minute or so on demand, and the first display after waypoint entry is based on the operator entered value for groundspeed, allowing course predictions to be made before the data reverts to real time. Of course all navigation parameters may be operator updated at any time, but normal operation requires periodic updating only of the geometric correction factor, geoidal height.

The system collision avoidance operation is basically designed for operation in the collision avoidance mode with the capability to continuously track and display collision threat data on ships within the vicinity of your ship. This mode eliminates the need for manual plot and calculations of approaching ships to determine maneuver requirements, since the system automates all such functions and operations. The resulting indicator displays in this mode visually resolve all possible safe-travel areas surrounding your ship, leaving the operator free to make rapid and accurate maneuver decisions even in heavy traffic areas.

The basic orientation display for all computer generated synthetic patterns in this system is the familiar radar PPI (plan position indicator) presentation as in Fig. 10-20. Thus targets, land masses, and other reflecting objects can be quickly acknowledged. The 360 degree video sweep on the indicator is synchronized with the rotating antenna of the radar, generating images of surrounding objects on the screen. Your ship appears as a cross at the sweep origin. Six range rings permit accurate visual range measurements. A range scale switch setting on the control panel determines overall scaling of the display, the distance from screen center to outer edge of the screen. The direct readout of the scaling indicator gives the current range scale and range ring spacing in nautical miles so that you can make range measurements.

Your ship's heading is continually displayed as a dotted line (heading flasher) from your ship to the screen edge. A flasher off switch momentarily disables this function so that targets can be discerned under the heading flasher. The electronic cursor, consisting of a dotted and dashed (blanked) line, can be positioned through 360 degrees around your ship in 0.5 degree increments, using a bearing cursor rocker switch on the bearing panel. The electronic cursor permits automatic true bearing readout of any object on the display, and cursor degrees are read directly on the bearing cursor indicator. Both the heading flasher and bearing cursor lines are segmented to indicate distance traveled by your ship in 6 minute intervals. The dots on the bearing cursor are at 1 minute intervals.

Two different orientations of the compass stabilized indicator display are available with north up/course up switch selection. In north up position, a true course display is presented as in Fig. 10-20(a) with all video oriented and referenced to compass north, which is located at the top center, zero degree position on this indicator.

In this display, your ship is centered on the screen and approximate bearing degrees may be read at heading flasher intersection with the outer bearing ring which surrounds the screen. The ring is automatically illuminated for use in this mode. The accurate cursor true bearing can be read directly from the bearing cursor indicator.

In course up position, the display orients all video relative to your ship's entered course as in Fig. 10-20(b). Here it is now located at the top center, zero degrees position. To provide more forward collision assessment area, the entire display is offset, with your ship

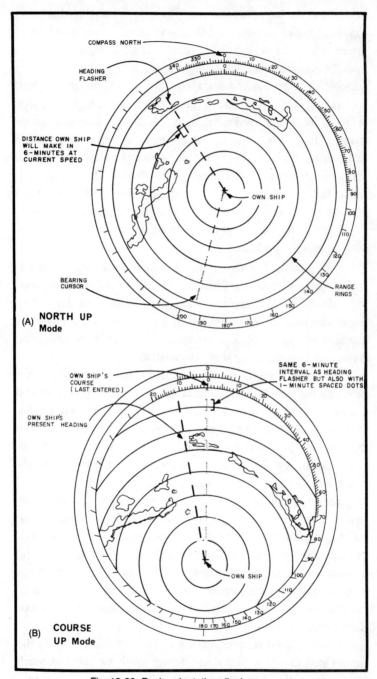

Fig. 10-20. Basic orientation displays.

located three-quarters of the way down the screen. In this offset condition, range ahead is 1 1/2 times the range scale and range astern is 1/2 the scaling. Approximate bearing degrees are read from the illuminated inner bearing ring, designed for offset reading and containing graduations from 0 to 180 degrees on either side of your ship's course. A feature of the course up mode is the retention of display information and orientation regardless of your ship's maneuvers. The effects of course changes are readily discerned because the heading flasher moves as your ship moves but the original situation data remains unchanged on the display. Once permanent course change is resolved (or at any desired time), the operator can depress a new course up switch to automatically realign the entire display so your ship's new course is in course up, zero degrees position on the indicator.

The system provides a true situation display of all danger imposed by intruding ships within a 24 nautical mile range of your ship (36 miles in offset display), as long as the ships are under system track. The unique, generated display patterns allow instantaneous assessment and visual determination of all possible maneuvering areas with minimum operator manipulation.

The system interface with shipboard radar equipment permits radar returns from selected ships in the vicinity to be processed and analyzed by the system to fix positions and determine movements. Radar returns are normally processed with every antenna scan so that situation progress and threat to your ship are recomputed. Computations are therefore always current and the resulting collision avoidance displays represent real time conditions.

These computations also require sensor data inputs for your ship's heading and velocity which are obtained from system interface with the ship's gyrocompass and selected speed sources. Based on these parameters and radar information, the true track, speed, and position of all selected vessels are predicted, as well as the intercept point of your ship with each, regardless of your ship's heading. Around these points are computed the possible danger areas to your ship offered by these intruders.

The computed information on each tracked ship is used by the control indicator to generate and display synthetic patterns which visually define this data for the operator. The patterns are superimposed on the standard PPI radar display and are visually associated with the respective ships so that the maneuver decision can be readily made with confidence.

The collision avoidance synthetic display is generated by computer data and superimposed on the basic radar screen return pattern to provide quick evaluation of the collision threat situations. The computed collision avoidance data generates a picture on the indicator showing the possible area of danger (PAD), if any, associated with each tracked ship as in Fig. 10-21.

These elliptical PADs on display represent all possible danger areas to your ship and the simplicity of a maneuver decision using this type of presentation immediately becomes apparent. Your ship merely has to maneuver in areas outside these PADs. This assumes the operator has used good judgment in selection of ships to be tracked. All approaching ships should have been placed under system track, beginning with those closest to your ship. If there are more ships than the system's capability, each should still be systematically evaluated long enough to determine its immediate threat to your ship and subsequently dropped or tracked on a priority basis.

Once your ship's maneuver is made and underway, display orientation remains stabilized so that maneuver progress and results are visually apparent to the operator, even though your ship's heading may change several times. After completion of the course change (or at any desired time), the operator can depress the new course up pushbutton on the bearing panel to reorient the display relative to the current gyrocompass heading.

Specific ships to be tracked are acquired by the operator manually, and the system has a capability to track and display data on as many as 20 acquired ships. The process of acquisition and track is as shown on Fig. 10-21. The operator manually moves the joystick control lever on the track panel to position a visual circle symbol over the selected ship. The acquire ship pushbutton is then depressed to inform the system of a ship track requirement. This results in generation of data by the computer/tracker electronics that establishes a tracking gate about the ship video on the next radar scan. The gate width and separation forms a tracking window with an initial area that is largely determined by the range scaling of the display.

On the next and subsequent scans, radar information from the ship received in the window is processed for tracking and collision threat assessment. When the first scan returns are processed to yield computed ship's position, computer lock on occurs and the track window is automatically reduced in size, more closely bracketing the ship return area in order to get increased accuracy.

If radar returns from the ship become insufficient for adequate processing on a later scan, the track window is widened to try to obtain sufficient return. Continued insufficient return data over 5 consecutive scans activates a flashing NO TGT RTN legend on the C/A WARNING indicator and an audible sound alarm. The threatened target is distinguished by its flashing collision avoidance symbols on the display. With 10 consecutive no returns scans, the system removes the track display and warning condition, dropping the ship from track and deleting all previously stored track data on that ship from the computer memory.

When the operator attempts to acquire a ship that yields insufficient return for lock on (or when the acquisition circle fails to properly encompass the designated ship video), track window size remains the same for the next three scans over the area (not reduced as in lock in), and is then dropped from display if the condition has persisted. Should the operator attempt to acquire a ship already under system track, the acquisition circle will flash for 2 1/2 seconds and the system will ignore the track request. To avoid confusion on the display, the operator can delete the acquisition circle display by depressing a reset pushbutton on the track panel.

After eight radar scans over the newly acquired ship, an initial assessment of the ship is made by the system. The result is a dashed velocity vector displayed at the ship video return as in Fig. 10-21(b). Vector origin is at computed ship position and display direction is set to the predicted ship's course. Each segmented combination of the vector (one dash line plus one space) is the distance the tracked ship will make in 1 minute at its current rate of speed, and total overall vector length is 6.5 minutes. The velocity vector enables quick visual evaluation of the ship's relative speed since 6 consecutive (1 minute) segments can be directly compared with one heading flasher segment.

If the 6 segment interval, for example, is twice as long as the flasher segment, that ship's speed is 2 times your ship speed read-out. The length and direction of the velocity vector are modified by the system as variations in acquired ship's speed or course are detected from processed radar returns. This initial assessment of ships is important to the operator in helping to assign tracking priorities at an early stage and is especially beneficial under crowded harbor and close trafficked conditions where attention must be quickly directed to the most threatening ships.

After 30 scans through the track window, sufficient data has been accumulated and refined by the system to accurately compute the point (or points) where your ship passes within the operator selected CPA of the acquired ship, for all possible own ship headings. Acquired-ship's speed and true course as well as your ship's speed is assumed not to change in these calculations. If the results indicate such points exist, and they lie within the PPI display area, a PAD is formed on the display. Simultaneously, a track line is drawn from inside the track window to the PAD center for identification and association. Superimposed on the track line is the velocity vector previously described as an aid in the target evaluation.

PAD size established the danger area about the intercept point which must be avoided. The minimum passing distance afforded your ship in the intercept area is set by the desired closet point of approach (CPA) with the tracked ship. The operation selects CPS (0, 1/8, 1/2, 1 or 2 nautical miles) using a CPA miles thumbwheel switch. As a margin of safety to account for radar variations, an additional 300 yards is added to the CPA. Although a PAD exists, there may not be a point of collision since it is possible to pass within the CPA set by the operator and not collide. If the point of collision is to be evaluated, set the thumbwheel switch to 0 CPA temporarily to show the area where the miss distance will be within 300 yards. If the miss distance will be greater than 300 yards, no PAD will be displayed.

The track line is drawn from the acquired ship's present position to the center of the PAD. Your ship's time to CPA with the tracked ship is estimated visually by comparing heading flasher 6 minute segments with your ship's remaining range to the PAD. More accurate comparison is made by rotating the bearing cursor

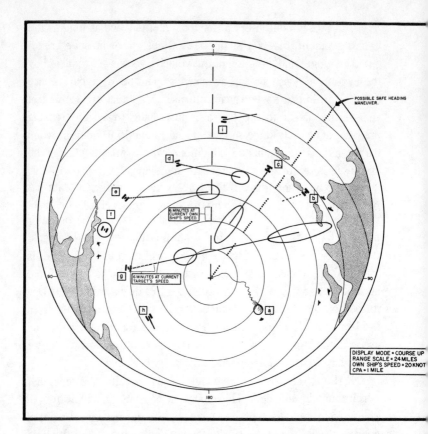

until it lines up with your ship's range track to the PAD, then using the 6 minute groups of 1 minute dots for measurement.

Since the time to interception is the same for both your ship and tracked ship, a visual comparison of range to go for each vessel yields a quick indication of tracked ship's relative speed. Tracked ships with greater range to intercept than your ship—long track lines as in Fig. 10-21(c)—are moving at relatively higher speeds, posing an immediate concern. Tracked ships with shorter range to intercept—short track lines as in Fig. 10-21(d)—are moving at a slower rate. For accurate estimates of relative speeds and distances, the velocity vector appears superimposed on the track line and originates at the video end of the track line. It allows direct 6 minute comparison to your ship's flasher segment for relative speed evaluation of targets as described for the initial 8 scan assessment. But in addition, it can be used to measure tracked ship's remaining

460

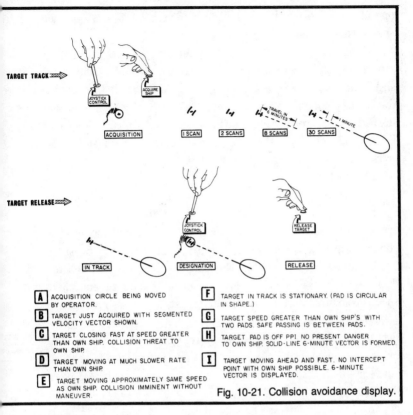

A — ACQUISITION CIRCLE BEING MOVED BY OPERATOR.

B — TARGET JUST ACQUIRED WITH SEGMENTED VELOCITY VECTOR SHOWN.

C — TARGET CLOSING FAST AT SPEED GREATER THAN OWN SHIP. COLLISION THREAT TO OWN SHIP.

D — TARGET MOVING AT MUCH SLOWER RATE THAN OWN SHIP.

E — TARGET MOVING APPROXIMATELY SAME SPEED AS OWN SHIP. COLLISION IMMINENT WITHOUT MANEUVER.

F — TARGET IN TRACK IS STATIONARY. (PAD IS CIRCULAR IN SHAPE.)

G — TARGET SPEED GREATER THAN OWN SHIP'S WITH TWO PADS. SAFE PASSING IS BETWEEN PADS.

H — TARGET PAD IS OFF PPI. NO PRESENT DANGER TO OWN SHIP. SOLID-LINE 6-MINUTE VECTOR IS FORMED.

I — TARGET MOVING AHEAD AND FAST. NO INTERCEPT POINT WITH OWN SHIP POSSIBLE. 6-MINUTE VECTOR IS DISPLAYED.

Fig. 10-21. Collision avoidance display.

range and time to any point on the display. One heading flasher segment is equivalent to 1/10th your ship speed readout, the value is both the speed (knots) and distance (nautical miles) your ship will make in 6 minutes.

If, for example, the readout is 10 knots, your ship is moving at 1 nautical mile every 6 minutes and the segment length equals 1 nautical mile. Assuming the 6 minute measure of a tracked ship's velocity, the vector is twice the length of a flasher segment, that ship is moving at 20 knots and will make 2 nautical miles in the 6 minutes. By estimating the number of these measures in the ship's range track to any point ont he display, the total range or time to go (for that ship) can be determined. Your ship's range and time to go to the same point can be quickly evaluated using the flasher (6 minute) segment measure in the same manner. The velocity vector remains displayed over the track line as long as the ship is under track. The

461

operator can easily observe changes in tracked ship course and speed using the vector.

Computations on ships moving at higher speeds than your ship actually result in two separate areas of interception with your ship—and two PADS as shown in Fig. 10-21(g). If the relative tracked ship speed is not much greater, the second PAD lies outside the PPI display area and only one is shown, Fig. 10-21(c). When two PADs can be displayed they are interconnected by extension of the track line. Safe passage is between the two PADs, or any area outside the PADs.

Ships tracked close to the edge of the display may compute PADs that also lie partially, or completely off the PPI. These ships are of no immediate concern but some threat potential may exist as conditions progress. No PAD is drawn; instead a solid 6 minute vector is displayed as in (h). The length is held to the predicted distance the tracked ship will move in 6 minutes at its current rate of speed. Ships that pose no immediate threat to your ship (no area of interception computed) will not generate PADs but will have a solid 6 minute velocity vector while under system track. This is shown at (i) for a ship holding the same course but ahead and moving faster than your ship. If the tracked ship alters its heading such that it becomes a threat to your ship, the PAD will automatically be generated and displayed by the system. The special illustrated case at (f) shows a ship or other object that has been acquired for tracking but is not moving. A circular PAD is formed about the video equal to the selected CPA plus 300 yards which distinguishes this stationary condition.

As radar information continues to be processed and updated on a tracked ship, track window parameters are varied as necessary around the video for most effective tracking. Parameters are re-computed from the data obtained on each scan and depend on such factors as tracked ship range, target size, and tracking conditions. In the latter case, operator positioning of the MODE switch is impor-tant to establish the tracking conditions. In harbor mode, gate size is reduced and only the leading edge of ships are tracked to give maximum distinction between ships that are close together. In sea mode, the entire ship is tracked for optimum track capability of more distant ships.

Ships being tracked on the same bearing from your ship are time shared by the computer which will cause some delay in displayed data. For two ships on the same bearing, the first assessment vectors appear after 16 scans (instead of 8) and threat symbols are established in 60 scans (instead of 30). A group of three ships will take three times as long as one ship to establish data display. With antenna scan rates of 3 to 4 seconds per revolution, the delay is not significant but will be noticed by the operator.

If the system attempts to interpret radar returns from ships passing too close to your ship, there is a possibility of losing track or generating inaccurate threat data because of your ship's effect on the radar return information. The system therefore automatically drops track on any ship whose track window moves to within 0.1 mile (200 yards) of your ship. It will also not accept track of any newly acquired ship under these minimum range conditions.

When full tracking capabilities are reached by the system (20 targets), it will accept no further acquisitions. The acquisition circle will flash if additional acquisitions are attempted. At any time the operator can release specific targets from track as shown in Fig. 10-21. This is done by again moving the joystick control to locate the acquisition circle over the computed ship position. The release target pushbutton is depressed which directs the system to drop track on the ship and all stored collision threat data. If the acquisition circle is incorrectly positioned so as not to encompass the computed ship position or is positioned over more than one tracked ship position, the circle flashes for 2-1/2 seconds and the system ignores the release request. It is important to note that computed ship position is at track line termination, normally where the ship video lies. There are cases (before target recomputations have taken place) when the video may separate from the track line end or computed ship position. It is good practice for the operator to *always* position the acquisition circle over the track line end, not the ship video, to avoid confusion when these conditions occur. The release function allows complete operator control over display tracking requirements, limiting track to those ships of immediate concern, deleting track on those which no longer pose a threat to your ship, and eliminating needless symbol cluttering on the display.

Computed data for displays such as the heading flasher 6 minute segments, and dotted cursor grounds and PADs are affected by your ship's speed. The system receives speed data from one of three sensor sources determined by the speed source switch position on the indicator speed panel. In rpm position, the system converts input voltages defining ship's engine revolution rate to your ship's speed. In log position the system counts incoming speed log pulses to obtain your ship's speed. A third, manual speed position of the switch permits using a fixed, operator selected speed value. In this mode, the speed input thumbwheel switch is adjusted to your ship's estimated speed and, when the enter pushbutton is depressed, the system computer stores the selected value. This mode, therefore, does not provide continuous monitoring of your ship's speed as do the other two speed courses. Accurate threat data computations in this mode require that your ship maintain its speed as entered or the operator promptly update the manual speed entry once a change is made.

The Sperry collision avoidance system incorporates a trial speed mode capability which allows the operator to visually observe the effects of your ship's speed changes on the collision threat situation without having to actually accomplish the speed change maneuver. In this mode, the operator selects the anticipated speed change on the speed input thumbwheel switch and depresses the trial speed pushbutton. The collision avoidance display is updated by the system to show the effects of the speed change, and all tracked ships appear with revised threat assessments. In basic systems, your ship's dynamics do not enter the trial speed computations made by the system; that is, the system assumes the speed change was made immediately. The operator should insure that the time required for the ship to assume the new speed is taken into account when the displayed situation is evaluated. During a trial speed mode, the system maintains continuous track on all acquired ships so that when normal operations are resumed with release of the trial speed pushbutton, the display reverts back to the real situation.

In conclusion, we are certain that you, as well as ourselves, realize the importance of collision avoidance systems as our world shrinks, day by day, and traffic on the high seas and in congested port areas becomes almost intolerable. There are many fine jobs available for those persons who would make the operation and maintenance of these systems a career.

This has been radar of the above water type. Now let us examine what might be called underwater radar—the sonar systems.

Chapter 11
Sonar, Depth Measurement, Fish Finders, Speed Log, and Doppler Docking Systems

A long title, but we have much to include in this chapter, and it all relates to the same basic physics phenomena—sound echoes and the Doppler effect. One might say it is the underwater mirror of radar systems.

OVERVIEW

We will discuss the principles, equipment, and operation of sonar which is the basis for all under water communication and measurements. Like radar, sonar systems depend on the transmission of impulses of energy and the return of some of this energy after it has impacted upon various reflective substances. With sonar it is ultrasonic sound waves that are being transmitted, and the echoes are received through the heavy medium of water—either fresh water or seawater.

Just as atmospheric conditions influence the transmission of radio and radar waves, the water presents conditions which affect the transmission of the lower frequencies which form the energy pulses used in sonar systems. Temperature is a very important consideration, and it varies with depth. The salinity of water affects the transmission as do bubbles, air pockets and other foreign matter. There are particles in the water which can reduce the range of transmission by the absorption of the sound energy, as well as causing spurious echoes on the sonar screens.

It is just possible that someone may ask why radar cannot be used underwater. The reason is that at high frequency the water particles absorb all this energy. It is really pretty difficult to even get radar energy out through the atmosphere, as water vapor and various other impurities decrease the energy content of the pulses very rapidly. We get it out by using lots of power for relatively short ranges. But it just won't go underwater. No way!

We will find in this chapter that radiation of other types of equipment such as the radiotelephones and radars may affect the equipment used for sonar detection. All the various equipment on a boat attempts to contribute interference to the electronic gear. These interference signals, or impulses, may appear in sensitive circuits to cause display interference. We must remember that just because it is sonar and operates at lower frequencies, this doesn't mean that it is not be be shielded and have its leads isolated and be kept away from electrical fields caused by electrical wiring. Sonar must have all these measures taken to insure proper performance. This equipment is also subject to vibration and corrosion problems just as is all the other electronics equipment.

Our range in this chapter is great. We start with a brief review of sonar, then the physics of sound as applied to sonar, courtesy of the U.S. Navy, and then progress through various kinds of fish finding and depth sounding equipment. We will examine the use of sonar Doppler effects to determine movement and speeds of ships. We will see how this phenomena is used to help dock the giant superliners and tankers, where movement is, at times, so slow that a human is incapable of knowing they are actually moving. Yet, with the ponderous masses of these big vessels, even with these incredibly slow motions the momentum is so great that one mistake in docking can wipe out the dock itself.

Finally we will examine some speed measuring devices and wind direction indicators which do not operate on sonar, but seem to fit well into this chapter as a kind of auxilliary equipment for boats. Perhaps these are most closely associated with sailing yachts which use more wind power than motor power.

In any event we have found this to be an interesting chapter to prepare for this work. We do recommend to you, that if you are familiar with the physics of sound, you may not want to study this

Fig. 11-1. Sonar display and recorder. (Courtesy Konel.)

section in detail. If not, then hurry over to the discussion of individual equipment. We caution you however, that all knowledge is most helpful to obtain the best possible performance from your equipment, such as a good understanding of the phenomena upon which it works, then its capabilities and limitations. So, really, to get the best and most from your systems and equipment—and the dollars you've spent on it—it might be worthwhile to take this chapter page by page and fill whatever gaps may exist in your memory or knowledge on this most important basic phenomena which is vital to boating.

SONAR

First, then, let us examine the equipment shown in Fig. 11-1 and then the block diagram of a sonar system shown in Fig. 11-2. With these in mind, we turn to a discussion of some types of sonar and some principles of transducers—a transducer is to the sonar what the radar antenna is to radar.

Searchlight Sonar

Early active sonars utilized the searchlight principle for transmitting sounds. Like a searchlight, the transducer had to be beamed to a particular bearing to transmit sound on that bearing. The sound beam was narrow in bearing width, about 5 degrees, consequently the echoes were received from only a small sector of the surrounding area. An arrangement of this type was necessary at this time because sufficient power for omnidirectional transmission could not be generated. The scanning sonars in widespread use today develop tremendous power—enough to be transmitted 360 degrees in azimuth simultaneously.

Later modifications to active sonars allow the selection of directionally transmitted sonic pulses, somewhat related in principle to the earlier searchlight sonars. This feature called rotating directional transmission is like that used in radar systems.

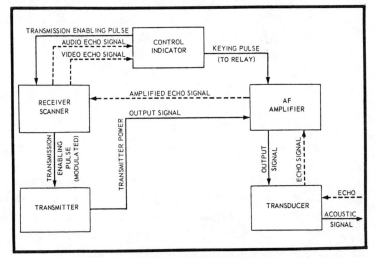

Fig. 11-2. Sonar system block diagram.

The main advantage of the searchlight type of sonar was getting more power in a given direction. The main disadvantage was the length of time required to scan the area around the ship. Search procedures called for the operator to transmit, listen for echoes, train in the transducer to a new bearing, transmit, listen, and so on, first on one side of the ship, then on the other. Thus it was possible for a submarine to slip by undetected on the port side, for example, while the operator was searching on the starboard side. Moreover, maintaining contact with a target that had a rapidly changing bearing required a high degree of proficiency on the part of the operator. Another disadvantage was that searchlight equipment had only an audio presentation, whereas today's scanning sonars provide both a video and an audio presentation.

Scanning Sonar

Modern submarines and antisubmarine warfare ships are equipped with scanning sonar, which transmits sound pulses of high energy in all directions simultaneously. One of the features of scanning sonar is a cathode ray tube display of all underwater objects detected in the area surrounding the ship. Targets' echoes appear as bright spots on the CRT, similar to the display of radar displays. Some of the data given to you by the sonar display is:

- The size of the target may be estimated from the size of the echo. Don't rely too heavily on this feature, though, because echo appearance depends on such factors as target speed, target aspect, range, and the performance of your own equipment.
- The distance of the echo from the center of the CRT represents range to the object from your ship, when the CRT is used in the ship center display (SCD) mode.
- True bearing of the object can be determined directly on the scope.
- Target movement can be determined from its scope presentation. Fixed objects such as reefs and sunken ships will move in a direction parallel to your ships movement and in the opposite direction. Moving objects may have motion in any direction with respect to your own ship.

- The wake of a submerged vessel or of a ship can often be seen. By examining the wake you may be able to establish the underwater craft's heading even before its movement can be determined by tracking. The shape of the echo may give you this information.
- Submarines that are too far away for detection by echo ranging may yet emit enough noise to be detected. Under these conditions, a small segment of the scope appears to be filled with a rippling pattern. The general direction of the noise source can be ascertained by taking a bearing to the center of the noise pattern.

Transducers

The piezoelectric transducer sends out the sound pulses and receives the echoes like the radar antenna. Various kinds of crystals have been employed in these units, but the most commonly used type is ammonium dihydrogen phosphate (ADP). The arrangement of the crystals on a diaphragm is as follows. One end of the crystal is attached to a bakelite-covered steel plate and the other end allowed to vibrate freely. The free ends of the crystal block constitute the transmitting and the receiving elements.

The entire arrangement of the crystals is to electrically give the effect of a single large crystal. The elements are housed in a chamber filled with castor oil, which has sound transmission qualities similar to seawater. The oil also protects the sensitive crystals from being damaged by exposure to water or moisture.

When an electric current of the desired frequency is passed through the crystals, they change shape as a unit causing a vibration. Vibrations are passed by the castor oil through a "window" in the sonar dome into the seawater. When outside energy is received in the form of an echo, it is a water pressure ripple which exerts mechanical pressure on the crystals, which in turn produce an electrical current that is amplified and converted into visual and audible signals.

Nearly all transducers now being built are of the ceramic type. Ceramic compounds have a high sensitivity, high stability with changing temperatures and pressures, relatively low cost, and can be constructed in almost any reasonable shape or size. The most commonly used ceramic compound is lead zirconate titanate. Such transducers are known as electrostrictive transducers, yet they behave just like the piezoelectric tranducers described previously. They are widely used in modern sonar systems. Although a ceramic material is essentially electrostrictive, it behaves like the piezoelectric crystals when it is permanently polarized. Polarization is accomplished by impressing an extremely high voltage on the heated material for a period of several minutes to align the molecules. Once the molecules are aligned properly, the cooled compound can then be treated just as though it were a piezoelectric crystal type material.

Magnetostriction is a process whereby changes occur in metals when they are subjected to a magnetic field. If a nickel tube is placed in a magnetic field, for example, its length is shortened as a result of the magnetostrictive effect. The effect is independent of the direction of the magnetic field.

In the searchlight type of sonar, several hundred nickel tubes are arranged in a circle and mounted on one side of a metal plate called a diaphragm. Each tube is wrapped with a coil of wire to prevent frequency doubling. When an alternating current is applied to the coil, the tubes shorten and lengthen at the rate of the alternating current (its frequency). Each tube is polarized by a constant magnetic field, usually supplied by a permanent magnet, so that during one half cycle of the applied signal, the ac voltage and the polarizing field add, and during the next half cycle they oppose one another. The permanent magnetic field is always in one direction, which permits this to happen.

As the tubes contract and expand, the diaphragm vibrates and produces an acoustic (sound) signal of the same frequency as the applied current. This signal is sent through the water and some of its energy is returned as an echo. One type of magnetostrictive transducer is shown in Fig. 11-3.

REFRESHER ON THE PHYSICS OF SOUND (COURTESY U.S. NAVY)

Regardless of what kind of equipment you use in sound ranging, bottom detection, fish finding, or for other uses, this review will help you to understand what you see and hear in the form of those all important echoes. We begin at the beginning, and ask your in-

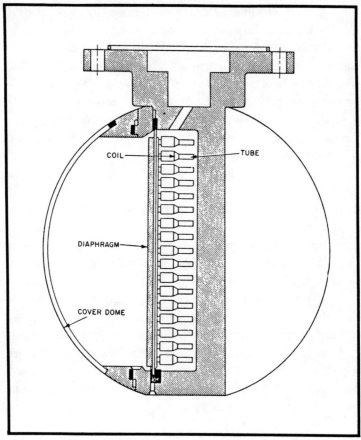

Fig. 11-3. Searchlight magnetostrictive transducer.

dulgence if you are already familiar with many aspects of this discussion.

Any object that moves rapidly back and forth, or vibrates, and thus disturbs the medium around it, may become a sound source. Bells, radios, and musical instruments are some familiar types of sound sources.

Sound waves are passed along by particles of the material through which they travel. The elasticity of the medium determines the ease, distance, and speed of sound transmission. The greater the elasticity, the greater the speed of sound. The speed of sound in water is about four times faster than in air, and in steel it is about 15 times faster than in air.

The limits of human hearing are determined by two interacting physical variables, frequency and intensity, and several other conditions that are dependent on the individual person, variables such as age, state of health, attention, and prior exposure to that sound type. The limits of hearing are normally between 20 and 20,000 Hz for young and healthy persons, provided the upper and lower frequencies are sufficiently intense. For a healthy middle aged person, the upper limit may lie between 12 to 16,000 Hz, although they may still hear the lower frequencies of 20 Hz.

It is common to refer to those sounds which can be heard as sonics, sounds below the 20 cycle range are called subsonics and those above the 15,000 Hz range are called ultrasonics or supersonics. The term ultrasonics merely refers to the acoustic phenomena above the level of human hearing. It is interesting that a 15,000 Hz vibration or sound might be called ultrasonic for a 60 year old person. They cannot hear it.

Early active-sonar equipment transmitted ultrasonic sounds through the water. Along with other sounds, they received echoes of these ultrasonic sounds and converted them into sounds which could be heard by the average ear. Modern active-sonars transmit sounds within the audible range, but because these sound transmissions are very high tones, the sonar equipment converts them into lower tones for ease of hearing.

Energy Waves

Waves may be classified by types as *tranverse* or *longitudinal*. A transverse wave is one wherein the particles of the medium through which the wave is traveling, move at right angles vertically to the wave's direction. The surf has an up and down motion while the wave moves toward shore. In the longitudinal wave the particles move back and forth along the wave's direction of travel, resulting in a compression and rarefaction of the wave as it moves.

Another example of a transverse wave is that created when you throw a stone into the water. A series of circular waves travel away from the disturbance. In Fig. 11-4 such waves are diagrammed as though seen in cross section. Observe that the waves are a series of crests and troughs. The wavelength (1 cycle) is the distance from the crest of one wave to the crest of the next wave.

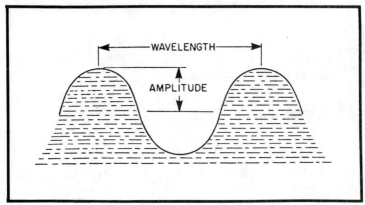

Fig. 11-4. Elements of a wave.

The amplitude of a transverse wave is half the distance, measured vertically from crest to trough, and serves to indicate the intensity of the wave motion. Half the distance is used because the trough is as far below the undisturbed water level, as the crest is above it.

Sound waves are longitudinal or compression waves set up by some vibrating object such as the sonar transducer. In its forward movement, the vibrating transducer pushed the water particles lying against its dome, producing an area of high pressure or compression. On the backward movement of the transducer dome (you can't see it move, but it does), the water particles return to the area from which they were displaced during compression and travel beyond, producing an area of low pressure or rarefaction. The vibrations of the transducer continue this process and produce the kind of waves shown in Fig. 11-5.

The dark rings are the compressions and the light areas the rarefactions. As the sound waves spread out, their energy simultaneously spreads through a larger and larger area. Thus, as you can see, the energy becomes weaker, the farther the waves travel.

Another way of representing the actions of the sound wave are shown in Fig. 11-6. Compressions are shown as hills, above the reference line, and rarefactions are shown as valleys below it. The wavelength is the distance from one point on a wave to the next point of similar compression. The change occuring between these points is called a cycle.

475

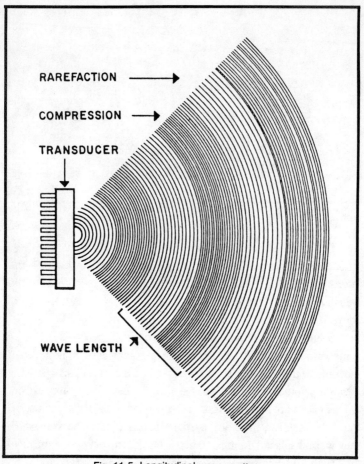

RAREFACTION →

COMPRESSION →

TRANSDUCER

WAVE LENGTH ↗

Fig. 11-5. Longitudinal waves pattern.

The frequency of a sound wave is governed by the number of vibrations per second produced by the sound source. A sonar transducer, for example, may transmit on a frequency of 5,000 Hz (5,000 vibrations per second). Motion is imparted to the sound waves in the back and forth movement of the water particles which, in effect, pass the wave along, even though the waves themselves may have very little actual movement. The *wave*, however, may travel great distances at a very high rate of speed. Not as great as the speed of radar waves, however.

Perhaps you've heard people speak of a heavy fog as being "thick as pea soup." This murky condition would be a dense fog caused by the atmosphere being filled with small particles of water called vapor condensation. A fog filled atmosphere is heavier (because of the weight of water particles in it) than a clear atmosphere. The measure for this thickness of a substance is called its density. This is defined as the weight per unit volume. In the study of general physics, density of any substance is a comparison of its weight to the weight of an equal amount (volume) of pure water. Because of the salt content (salinity) of seawater, it has a greater density than fresh water.

Density is also an indication of the sound transmission characteristics of a substance, or medium. When a sound wave passes through a medium, it is transmitted from particle to particle. If the particles are loosely packed (as they are in fresh water as compared to seawater), they have a greater distance to move to transmit the sound energy—one to another. In doing this time is consumed, and the overall result is a slower speed of sound than in a very dense medium.

Density and elasticity are the basic factors that determine the sound velocity. The formula for the speed of sound is:

$$C = \sqrt{\frac{E}{P}}$$

Where:

C = Velocity
E = Medium elasticity
P = Density

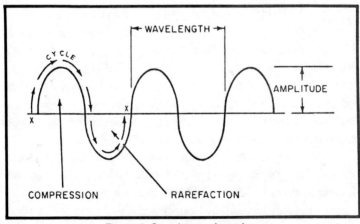

Fig. 11-6. Sound wave dynamics.

Variations in the basic velocity of sound in the sea are caused by changes in the water temperature, pressure, and density. In fresh water of 65°F the sound velocity is about 4790 feet per second (ft/s). In seawater, velocity, depending upon salinity, temperature, and pressure, is normally about 4800 ft/s at 39°F.

If a sonar transducer vibrates at the rate of 25,000 vibrations per second, and if the temperature is 39°F, the first wave will be 4800 feet away at the end of the first second. Between the transducer and the front of this wave there will be 25,000 compressions. Thus the wavelength, that is the distance between points of similar compression, must be

$$\text{Wavelength} = \frac{4800}{25,000} = 0.192 \text{ foot}$$

because there are the 25,000 compressions extending through the distance of 4800 feet. The formula for wavelength is the same as for radar except that the speed of propagation is less:

$$\text{Wavelength} = \frac{\text{Velocity}}{\text{Frequency}}$$

This formula can be algebraically manipulated to find any term if you know the other two.

Sound has three basic characteristics: pitch, intensity, and quality. Taken all together they make up the tone of the sound. Sometimes the result is pleasant, sometimes it is not. When the tone is low the frequency is low and the wavelength is long, and vice versa.

Intensity and loudness are often mistaken as having the same meaning. Although they are related, they actually are not the same. Intensity is a measure of the sound wave energy. Loudness is the effect of this intensity on the individual, in the same manner that pitch is the effect of frequency. Increasing the intensity causes an increase in loudness, but not in direct proportion. To double the loudness of a sound requires about a tenfold increase in the sound's intensity because of the way in which our ear works.

The quality of a sound depends on the complexity of its sound waves. Most sounds consist of a fundamental frequency, called the first harmonic, plus several other frequencies that are exact multiples of this fundamental. The fundamental is the lowest frequency of a sound wave. By combining different fundamentals in suitable proportions, a tone can be built up to a desired quality. Musical tones are produced by regular vibrations of the source. When the source vibrates irregularly the sound is called noise. If you cause the proper organ pipes to sound at the same time, you can imitate any vowel produced by the human vocal chords. On the other hand if you draw a fingernail across a blackboard you create what many call a noise of a distasteful kind.

Sound Power

The power output and reception sensitivity of sonar equipment are measured in decibels, which are used to express large power ratios. In the decibel system, the reference level is zero dB (0 dB) which is the threshold of hearing. The pressure level, or signal strength, of underwater sounds is compared to the 0 dB level, and is given either a positive or a negative value. Sonar receivers and similar equipment are capable of detecting sound levels far below this 0 dB level, down into what is called the minus dB range (−dB)

The reason for using the decibel system when expressing signal strength may be seen in Table 11-1. It is much easier to say a sound level has increased 50 dB, for example, than it is to say that the power output has increased 100,000 times. The amount of power increase or decrease from the reference level is the determining factor—not the reference level itself. Whether power output is

Table 11-1. Decibel Power Ratio Equivalents.

Source Level (dB)		Power Ratio
1	=	1.3
3	=	2.0
5	=	3.2
6	=	4.0
7	=	5.0
10	=	10
20	=	100
30	=	1000
40	=	10,000
50	=	100,000
60	=	$1,000,000 = 10^6$
70	=	$10,000,000 = 10^7$
100	=	10^{10}
110	=	10^{11}
140	=	10^{14}

increased from 1 watt to 100 watts, or from 1,000 watts to 100,000 watts, it is *still* A 20 dB increase.

Take particular note of the power ratios for course levels of 3 dB and 6 dB (also 7 and 10 dB). It can be seen that to increase a sonar's source level by 3 dB, it is necessary to double the output power. As an example, if the sonar source level drops from 140 dB to 137 dB the sonar has lost half its power. Any 3 dB loss, no matter what the source level, means a loss of half the former power. Decibels are used in all audio, radio, and radar descriptions.

Now let's see what is required to increase a sonar's range. To double the range of a sonar requires a source level increase of approximately 27 dB. This power increase is equivalent to about 500 times, which obviously is impractical. By another method, such as increasing receiver sensitivity, the range can be increased fairly easily, although it may not be doubled.

So far we have discussed the decibel mainly in relation to power output, but the decibel also is used to determine receiver sensitivity. Receiver sensitivity is measured in minus numbers, which represent the number of decibels below a reference level that a signal can be detected by the receiver. The larger the negative number, the better the sensitivity. Although the range would not be doubled, it is more practical, for instance, to increase a receiver's sensitivity from 112 dB to 115 dB than it is to double the output power of the sonar transmitter. Also it is not always necessary to increase the sensitivity of the receiver itself. An effective increase of several decibels may be achieved if local noise levels can be reduced in such sources as machinery, flow noise, crew noise, etc.

NOISE

The most complex sound wave is one in which the sound consists of numerous frequencies across a wide band. Such a form of sound is called noise because it has no tonal quality. The source of several types of noises may be identified easily, however, because of the standard sound patterns of the noises. Ship noise, for instance, consists of many different sounds mixed together. You may be unable to distinguish a particular sound, but, on the whole you could recognize the sound source as a ship. Some noise sources are shown in Fig. 11-7. The sources of many noises detected by sonar have not

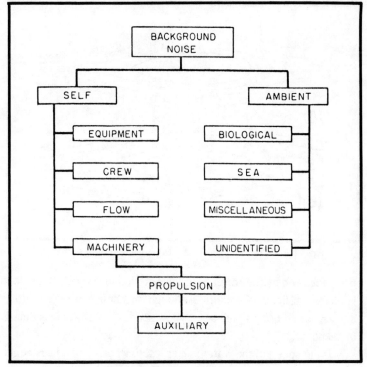

Fig. 11-7. Shipboard noise sources.

yet been identified. Explanations of some kinds of noises that have an adverse effect on a sonar operator follow.

Ambient noise is background noise in the sea that is due to natural causes. Different phenomena contribute to the ambient background noise. Many of the sources are known and their effects are predictable, but many still are unknown. From this unwanted background noise, the sonar operator must be able to separate weak or intermittent target noises. In general, the average operator requires a target signal strength of 4 dB above background noise.

Flow noise is the noise generated as an object moves through water. The relative flow between the object and the medium generates it. This flow is easiest to understand by assuming that the object is stationary and that the water is moving past the object. If the object is reasonably streamlined and its surface is smooth, and if it is moving very slowly, a flow pattern known as laminar flow is set up. Such a pattern is shown in Fig. 11-8(a) where the lines represent the

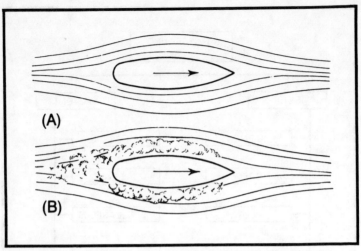

Fig. 11-8. Patterns of flow noise, (a) laminar and (b) turbulent.

paths followed by the water as it flows around the object. If the flow is laminar, all lines are smooth. Although laminar flow produces little, if any noise, it occurs only at very low speeds—perhaps less than 1 or 2 knots.

If the speed of the water is increased, whorls and eddies begin to appear in the flow pattern, as seen in (b), and the phenomenon is called turbulent flow. Within these eddies occur points where the pressure is widely different from the static pressure in the medium. Thus we have, in effect, a noise field. If a hydrophone is placed in such a region, voilent fluctuations of pressure will occur on its face, and what is called flow noise will be observed in the system.

As pressures fluctuate violently at any one point within the eddy, they also fluctuate violently from point to point inside the eddy. Moreover, at any given instant, the average pressure of the eddy as a whole differs but slightly from the static pressure. Thus, very little noise is radiated outside the area of turbulence. Hence, although a ship mounted hydrophone may be in an intense flow noise field, another hydrophone at some distance from the ship may be unable to detect the noise at all. Flow noise, then, is almost exclusively a self-noise problem.

Actually, not much information is known about flow noise, but these general statements may be made about its effect on a ship-borne hydrophone: (1) It is a function of speed with a sharp

482

threshold. At very low speeds there is no observable flow noise. A slight increase in speed changes the flow pattern from laminar to turbulent, and strong flow noise is observed immediately. Further increases in speed step up the intensity of the noise. (2) It is essentially a low-frequency noise. (3) It has very high levels within the area of turbulence, but low levels in the radiated field. In general, the noise field is strongest at the surface of the moving body, decreasing rapidly as you move away from the surface.

As the speed of the ship or object is increased still further, the local pressure drops low enough at some points to allow the formation of gas bubbles. This decrease in pressure represents the onset of cavitation. The noise associated with this phenomenon differs from flow noise.

Cavitation is produced whenever a solid object moves through the water at a speed great enough to create air bubbles. After a short life, most of the bubbles collapse. The sudden collapse of the bubbles causes the acoustic signal known as cavitation noise. Each bubble, as it collapses, produces a sharp noise signal.

Because the onset of cavitation is related to the speed of the object, it is logical that cavitation first appears at the tips of the propeller blades, inasmuch as the speed of the blade tips is considerably greater than the propeller hub. This phenomenon, known as blade tip cavitation is illustrated in Fig. 11-9. As the propeller speed

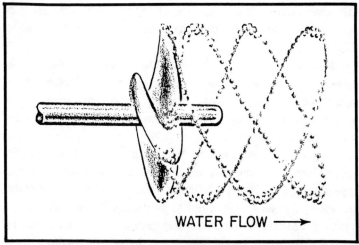

Fig. 11-9. Blade tip cavitation.

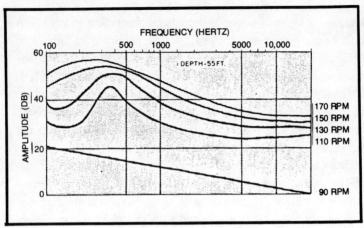

Fig. 11-10. Sheet cavitation.

increases, a greater portion of the propeller's surface is moving fast enough to cause cavitation, and the cavitation area begins to move down the edge of the blade. As the speed increases further, the entire back face of the blade commences cavitating, producing what is known as sheet cavitation.

The amplitude and frequency of cavitation noise are affected considerably by changing speeds. Cavitation noise versus speed at a constant depth is diagramed in Fig. 11-10. The curves shown are idealized.

Thermal noise is the absolute minimum noise in the ocean. As the name implies, it is a function of temperature. This noise is created by the motion of the molecules of the liquid itself and is difficult to measure.

Residual minimum is the lowest noise level that normally is measurable. Different unknown phenomena undoubtedly contribute to the minimum observable value. The point of interest, however, is that you are never likely to encounter ambient noise levels below the residual minimum.

Surface agitation can contribute much noise. For a sizable region above the residual minimum noise, the ambient noise levels appear to be related to the surface agitation. Usually, agitation of the surface of the sea is measured as sea state. Surface windspeed however, ordinarily is a more reliable measure of expected ambient noise than sea state. As the wind rises, the surface becomes more and more agitated, causing the ambient noise level to rise. Normally noise levels in this region are associated with what is called sea noise to distinguish them from other noises, which really are not caused by the sea itself. A heavy rain, for instance, will add greatly to the ambient noise.

Machinery noise is produced aboard ship by the main propulsion machinery and by any or all of a large number of auxiliary machines that may or may not be connected with the main propulsion system. Machinery noises are usually produced by rotating or reciprocating machines. Most noise of this type is generated by dynamic unbalance of the rotating portion of the machinery so that it causes a vibration within the machine. This vibration may then be transmitted through the machine mounts to the hull and from there it is radiated into the water as acoustic energy. In addition to the machinery, there are other shipboard noises which radiate into the water, such as fire and flushing pumps, air compressors, refrigeration machinery, air conditioning systems, diesel generators, gasoline pumps, blower motors and portable power tools. Any, or all, of this equipment may be operating at any one time, and this really adds to the noise radiated by the ship.

Another noise source is *circuit noise* and this comes from within the equipment itself. This noise may be in the form of a 60 Hz hum, static like noises may be present due to improper cable shielding, or leakage currents from other sources and wires which enter into the sonar receiver. Unlike ambient noise, however, this type of noise may be tracked down and controlled.

Fish Echoes and Sounds

Much equipment is devoted to fish spotting and depth sounding. We will have more on this in a moment. First consider some of the sounds of an audible nature and a supersonic nature which may be present in the sea. If you can listen to the sea sounds, you may try to identify the sources of whistles, shrieks, buzzes, pings, knocks, cracklings, and other weird noises not normally associated with the sea. Most of these noises probably come from different species of fish, but only a few have been identified positively.

Porpoises give out a whistling sound and sometimes a sound like a chuckle. Rudders of ships may give off a whistling sound.

Snapping shrimp are common around the world between latitudes 45° N and 45° S in waters less than 30 fathoms deep. As you approach a bed of snapping shrimp, you hear a buzzing sound. As you go closer, the sound resembles fat sizzling on a fire, them becomes similar to that given off by burning brush.

Whales, which are found in all oceans, give off a variety of sounds including knocks, groans, pings, and one resembling a rusty gate. The knocking sound of the sperm whale resembles the noise of hammering. Sperm whales and other large species seldom are heard in waters of less than 100 fathoms. Blackfish, which are similar to whales, emit a whistling sound like a porpoise, but clearer in tone.

There will be other sounds which you may learn to recognize and even possibly identify if your underwater sound system has a means for listening to the echos and creations from the depths.

SONAR TRANSMISSION LOSSES

To gain full benefit of echo ranging sonar systems you must be able to transmit an underwater sound pulse and recognize the returning echo from whatever target you are interested in. Detection of the echo depends upon its strength and relative quality compared to the other sounds which tend to mask it. It can be helpful to you to know:

- What can weaken sound as it travels through water.
- What conditions of the sea determine the path and speed of sound.
- What objects affect the strength and character of an echo.

This helps you to evaluate the information you get from your sonar instrument, whatever type it may be.

When a sound wave travels through water, it encounters elements that reduce its strength. Any signal strength lost in this manner is known as a *transmission loss*. As a sound pulse travels outward from its source, it becomes more and more weakened. Much of its energy is lost because of sea conditions and distance. There are three factors directly related to sound transmission which we need to examine. These are *divergence, absorption,* and *scattering*. The latter two of these is called the *attenuation* loss and these are dependent upon the frequency of transmission. Divergence loss is independent of the frequency of transmission.

It is interesting to know and realize that, like radar, water has *frequency windows*. Certain freqencies can travel much further with less loss than others. Two identical equipments, operating on different sounding frequencies may therefore have marked differences in ranging ability. It is always wise to check this feature.

When a sound wave is projected from a point source it assumes a spherical shape, spreading equally in all directions. The spreading is called divergence, and the further the wave travels, the more energy it looses. *The loss is inversely proportional to the square of the distance from the source, or 6 dB each time the range doubles.* In shallow water areas, the surface and bottom are boundaries that limit the vertical divergence of the sound wave. Consequently the expanding wavefront is cylindrical, rather than spherical in shape. *Cylinderical spreading loss is only half that of the sphere or about 3 dB each time the range is doubled.* Spreading loss at close range is very high, but beyond about 2000 yards the loss becomes less significant.

Some energy, of course, is lost in the form of heat. This happens when the diaphragm moves to compress the water. The energy lost due to this phenomenon is called *absorption* loss.

Besides losses caused by divergence and absorption, a sound wave loses energy due to the composition of the medium through which it passes. Composition of the sea naturally varies from place to place, and from time to time. In general, however, seawater contains large amounts of minute particles of foreign matter and many kinds of marine life of all sizes and shapes. Each time the sound waves meet one of these particles, a small amount of the sound is reflected away from its direction of movement and is lost. The reflection losses to the water are known as scattering losses. Some of the scattered energy is reflected back to the transducer and is then called *volume reverberation*.

When a sound wave strikes the boundary between two mediums of different densities, the wave will be reflected, just as light is reflected by a mirror. Some of the energy will be lost, but most of it will be reflected at an angle equal to the *angle of incidence*. The angle of incidence is the angle, with respect to the perpendicular to the direction of wave motion, at which the wave strikes the boundary. According to the physics law of regular reflection, which is reflection from a smooth surface, the above statement is true; the angle of reflection equals the angle of incidence. Reflection takes place whenever the sound hits the boundary between sea and air (sea surface) and between sea and bottom, and when it hits a solid object in the water. The amount of energy reflected depends upon the object's size, shape, and aspect.

Because the density of water is several hundred times that of air, practically all of a sound wave is reflected downward when it strikes the sea surface boundary. This effect is true, of course, only when the sea is smooth. When the sea is rough, scattering will take place.

The bottom of the sea also reflects sound waves. In deep water you are not concerned, but in waters of less than 100 fathoms the sound may unwantedly be reflected from the sea floor. It has been noted that losses are least over soft mud, and greatest over rough and rocky bottom where the sound is scattered and often gives strong bottom reverberations.

You have been in an empty room and heard your voice echo all around you as you talk. The sound often continues after you stop talking. It bounces around the room from wall to wall and ceiling to floor, if they are smooth and hard. This is the reverberation effect, sound waves bouncing around in a hard surfaced room.

The same effect can be observed in the ocean. Reverberation in the ocean is usually divided into three categories. They are:

1. Reverberation from the mass of water.
2. Reverberation from the surface.
3. Reverberation from the bottom.

It would seem that reflections are reverberations but this is not necessarily true. Reverberations *are* reflections but all reflections do not continue to bounce so as to cause strengthening of the sound and so all reflections do not become reverberations. That is a good morsel to think on for a while.

All processes contributing to reverberation are random in nature, with the result that reverberation amplitudes vary over wide limits as reinforcement and cancellation take place. Moreover, reverberation level is proportional to source level and pulse length.

Reverberation from the mass of water is called *volume reverberation* —recall that we mentioned this in the discussion on scattering. Suppose we have a transducer which sends out a short pulse. As the pulse of sound travels through the water it encounters various particles that reflect and scatter the sound. Because almost all of these particles are much smaller than a wavelength of sound, they do not reflect the sound as a flat mirror reflects light, instead they absorb energy from the sound wave and reradiate this energy in all directions. Some of this reradiated energy returns to the transducer at the source location and could be heard as a gradually fading tone at the same frequency as the source.

Some of the energy from the source strikes the surface, the point of impingement moving farther and farther from the source as the sound travels. If the surface were perfectly flat, this sound energy would be reflected as though from a mirror, and would bounce away from the source in accordance with the law of physics on reflection. But the surface of the sea is not perfectly smooth and each wavelet tends to reflect the sound in all directions. Some waves then return to the transducer, adding to the reverberation.

In general, reverberation effects from both the mass of water and the surface are small compared to bottom reverberation. The bottom of the sea is usually much rougher than the surface. Thus, more of the sound is reflected in other directions than those you would expect from a reflecting mirror. If the water is fairly deep, no bottom reverberation occurs for quite some time after the pulse because the sound wave must be given time to reach the bottom and be reflected. Normally, a sharp rise eventually occurs in the reverberation level after the source is cut off.

If there were no temperature differences in the sea, the sound wave would travel approximately in a straight line, because the speed of sound would be approximately the same at all depths. As indicated in Fig. 11-11, the sound would spread and become weakened by attenuation at a relatively constant rate.

Unfortunately, however, the speed of sound is not the same at all depths. The velocity of sound in seawater increases from 4700 feet per second to 5300 feet per second as the temperature increases from 30° to 85° F. Salinity and pressure also affect the sound speed, but their effects are small in relation to the large effects commonly produced by temperature changes. Because of the varying temperature differences in the sea, the sound does not travel in a

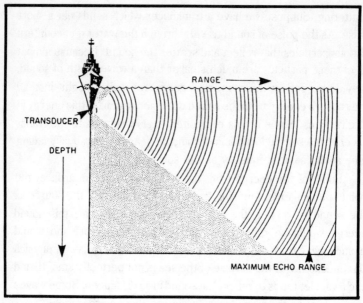

Fig. 11-11. Sound travel in water of constant temperature.

straight line. Instead it follows curved paths, resulting in bending, splitting and distortion of the sound beam.

When a beam of sound passes from one medium in which its speed is high, such as warm water, into one in which its speed is low, such as cool water, the beam is *refracted*, or bent. A sound beam bends *away* from levels of high temperature and high sound velocity, and bends *towards* levels of low temperature and low sound velocity. Figure 11-12 illustrates the refraction of a sound beam.

In strong winds and heavy seas, the roll and pitch of an echo ranging ship make it difficult to keep the sound directed on the target. Additionally, the turbulence produces air bubbles in the water, weakening the sound waves. Occasionally this envelope of air bubbles blankets the sound emitted by the transducer. Sonar operators can tell, by a dull thudding sound, when the sound beam is being sent out into air. This action is known as *quenching*.

THE ACOUSTIC SEA

We have discussed the various basic phenomena that cause power loss in transmitting sound; divergence, attenuation (absorption, and scattering), reflections, reverberations, refraction (bending), and quenching. Now, we must consider the structure of the sea as an *acoustic* medium, and learn the effects of this structure on the transmission of sound.

Of the many conditions affecting sound wave travel through the water, the following factors influence its speed; temperature, pressure and salinity. Figure 11-13 shows reasonably normal curves for temperature, salinity, and pressure as a function of depth in the Pacific Ocean and also the resulting velocity structure. It should be noted that the salinity variation plays a minor part in the form of the depth-velocity curve. This effect is almost entirely evident in the first 500 feet below the surface. The temperature curve also shows wide variations in the top 500 feet. From 2000 feet, downward, the temperature is nearly uniform as the water approaches the maximum density point at about 40°F. The pressure effect is represented by a straight line as the velocity increases linearly with depth.

On the composite curve, it easily can be seen that the velocity in the top 2000 feet is a somewhat skewed replica of the temperature

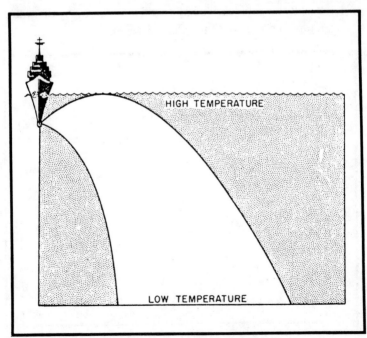

Fig. 11-12. A refracted sound beam.

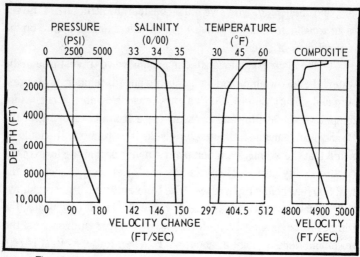

Fig. 11-13. Normal curves for pressure, salinity and temperature.

curve. Below 2000 feet it follows closely the straight line gradient of the pressure curve.

Except at the mouths of great rivers, where salinity may be a determinant, the path followed by sound in governed by the water temperature and the pressure effect of depth.

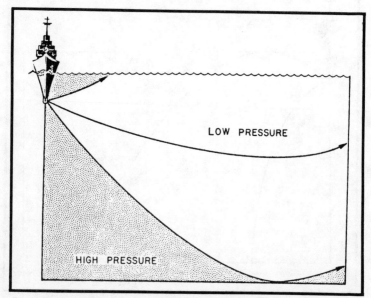

Fig. 11-14. Pressure tends to bend sound beam upward; the pressure effect.

The pressure effect is always present and always acts in the same manner, tending to bend the sound upward. Figure 11-14 illustrates the situation when the temperature does *not* change with depth. Even though the temperature does not change, the speed of sound increases with depth, due entirely to the effect of pressure, and the sound bends upward.

Figure 11-15 shows what happens when temperature increases steadily with depth. When the surface of the sea is cooler than layers beneath it, the water has a positive thermal gradient. Although this condition is unusual, it does happen, and causes the sound to be refracted sharply upward. In certain areas of the Red Sea, between Africa and Arabia, temperatures of well over 100°F have been recorded in depths exceeding 1 mile. Moreover, the salinity of the water in those areas approaches 30 percent, compared to between 3 and 4 percent in most ocean areas.

When the sea grows cooler as the depth increases, the water is said to have a negative thermal gradient. Here the effect of temperature greatly outweighs the effect of depth, and the sound is refracted downward. This common condition is illustrated in Fig. 11-16.

If the temperature is the same throughout the water, the temperature gradient is isothermal (uniform temperature). In Fig.

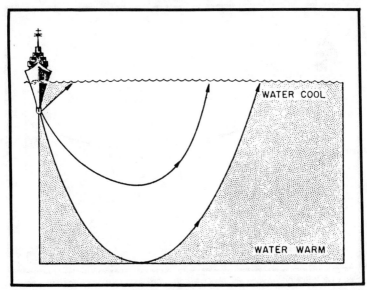

Fig. 11-15. Thermal effect.

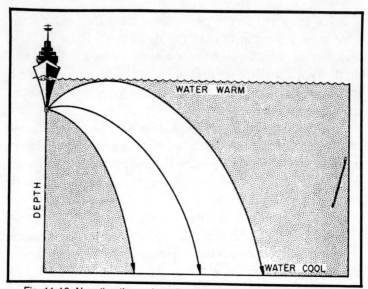

Fig. 11-16. Negative thermal gradient tends to bend sound downward.

11-17 the upper layer of water is isothermal; beneath this layer the temperature decreases with depth. This temperature change causes the transmitted sound to split and bend upward in the isothermal layer and downward below it.

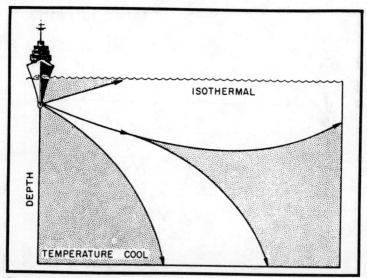

Fig. 11-17. Sound wave splits when temperature is uniform at surface and cool at bottom.

When no temperature difference exists, the sound beam bends upward. When the temperature changes with depth, the sound beam bends away from the warmer water.

Under ordinary conditions the sea has a temperature structure similar to that in Fig. 11-18. This temperature structure consists of three parts: a surface layer of varying thickness, with uniform temperature (isothermal) or a relatively slight temperature gradient; the thermocline, a region of relatively rapid decrease in temperature; and the rest of the ocean, with slowly decreasing temperature down to the bottom. If this structure changes, the path of a beam of sound through the water also changes.

Layer depth is the depth from the surface to the top of a sharp negative gradient. Under positive gradient conditions the layer depth is at the depth of maximum temperature. Above layer depth, the temperature may be uniform. If it is not uniform, a positive or weak gradient may be present.

SHALLOW WATER ECHOES

Echo ranging is difficult in shallow water because the sound is reflected from the bottom. When the ship is in shallow water, and the ocean floor is smooth, the sound bends down from the surface to the

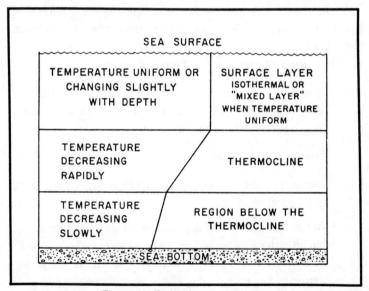

Fig. 11-18. Typical layers of the sea.

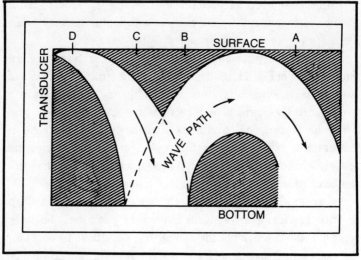

Fig. 11-19. Shallow water effect on transmitted waves.

bottom, then back up to the surface, and again down to the bottom, creating *shadow zones*. The *shaded* spaces in Fig. 11-19 are called shadow zones. Contact is regained when the target enters the wave path again. As shown in the illustration, contact is made at long range (point A), it is lost (point B), and regained at short range (point C). Note, however, that without the reflection, the maximum range would have been the short range at which the contact was regained (point C).

Here are some general conditions for hearing echoes.

- Usually poor near coasts (50 miles) as compared to sea conditions further out. Conditions for hearing are particularly poor at the mouths of rivers.

- Better in winter than in summer.

- Better at night than in the middle of the day, especially in spring and summer.

- Better in morning than in afternoon, in spring and summer, but little change if whitecaps are present. In many localities, however, conditions are better in the afternoon than in the morning, because of the effect of prevailing winds that freshen in the afternoon.

Deep Water Echoes

Now, let's examine some of the phenomena that take place in very deep water.

Theoretically, if the sound waves were not affected by velocity gradients, all the sound waves would be straight lines, and would travel in a direct path at whatever angle they left the source. In actual practice, however, the sound beam follows a path, or paths, as determined by the sea condition at the time.

Figure 11-20 illustrates a combination of two gradients of equal slope, one negative and one positive. Their function is a point of minimum velocity. If a sound source transmits at this depth of minimum velocity, all of the sound beams that start in an upward direction will be bent back down, and those that start downward will be bent back up. When such a condition occurs, we have what is called a *sound channel*. The depth of minimum velocity is called the axis of the channel. In this symmetrical situation, a beam that starts out downward will rise as high above the channel axis as it went below it and then will be bent downward again. Sound will remain in the channel as far as the channel exists, and will suffer very little loss as it progresses through the channel.

Sound channels are a rarity in shallow water (under 100 fathoms), but are always present in the deep water areas of the world. The depth of the axis of the channel is about 350 fathoms in the central Pacific and somewhat over 500 fathoms in the Atlantic. In the polar regions, where the surface water is materially colder, the axis of the channel lies nearer the surface.

Another effect that is closely related to the deep sound channel is called the *convergence zone effect.* The convergence zone effect is

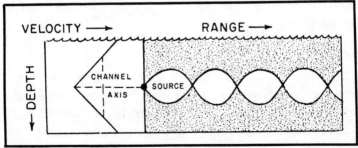

Fig. 11-20. A sound channel.

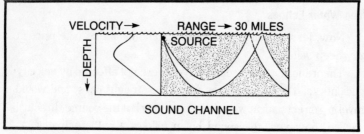

Fig. 11-21. Deep water sound channel from shallow source.

now applied to all long range active sonar. If the sound source is placed near the surface instead of near the axis of the sound channel, the path followed by the sound beam looks like that of Fig. 11-21. Sound energy from a shallow source travels downward in deep water. At a depth of several thousand feet, the signal is refracted due to pressure, and returns to the surface at a range of about 30 miles. The surface zone is from 3 to 5 miles wide.

The sound that reaches the surface in the *first convergence zone* is reflected or refracted at the surface, and again goes through the same pattern again. It produces another zone approximately 6 miles wide at 60 miles, and another 9 miles wide at 90 miles. Experienced personnel are familiar with this convergence zone effect and often they have picked up signals from targets that appear suddenly, show up for a few minutes and then quickly disappear.

A surface or near-convergence contact detected in the first convergence zone will have about the same signal strength as a target detected at 3 miles when no zone is present. Minimum depth required along the path of the sound beam is about 1000 fathoms. The usual requirement is 2000 fathoms for conducting convergence zone searches in naval applications. The minimum depth required is related to the surface velocity of the sound and increases as the velocity increases.

DOPPLER

Doppler is an important concept and phenomenon in both radar and sonar. We will discuss its application in the docking or large ships just a few pages further on. A good, modern physics book will have detailed information about this subject. We will review its concept briefly here.

You probably are familiar with the changing pitch of the sound from a train whistle as the train passes near you at high speed. Or, you may be familiar with the changing sound from an ambulance siren coming towards and going past you. This is due to the Doppler effect. As a train approaches, the whistle appears to acquire an increasing frequency. As the train goes by, the frequency seems to drop abruptly and becomes a long and drawn-out sound. This *apparent* change in the source frequency is due to the relative motion between the source and the receiver, and is known as the Doppler effect.

Each sound wave produced by the whistle in Fig. 11-22 is given an extra "push" by the motion of the train. So, as the train comes toward you, the resultant effect is an increase in pitch, caused by the compression of the sound waves. As the train moves farther away from you, the sound waves are spread farther apart resulting in a lower pitch. It is important to note that because the Doppler effect varies inversely with the velocity of sound, the effect is much less marked in the sea than it is in the air. But it is present in all sea ranging sound systems, where there is relative motion of an increasing or decreasing range direction between the sound source and a receiver.

DOPPLER AND ECHOES

Earlier we said that a sound wave pulse moves through the water and loses some of its energy to water particles. The particles then reradiate this energy in all directions. Part of the reradiated energy is returned to the receiver in the form of an echo, and the effect known as reverberation is heard. The water particles become

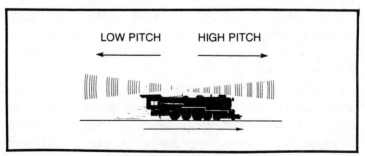

Fig. 11-22. Doppler effect with train.

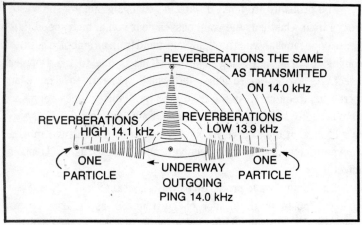

Fig. 11-23. Illustration of Doppler.

sound sources, and as your boat moves through the water, a Doppler effect can be noticed if you have proper sensing equipment. The Doppler effect of reverberations is illustrated in Fig. 11-23.

Aside from the manner used by U.S. Navy personnel, there are some types of docking and speed determining equipment, as we shall learn, which will automatically compare the frequency of the transmitted tone to that of various echoes to determine speed and/or position movement of big ships.

But consider the echo from a target that is neither going away from nor coming toward your ship, a target that is either stopped, or is crossing the sound beam at right angles to its direciton of travel, a target that may be following a constant radius circular course around your transducer. In this case there will be no Doppler echo. The returned echo will have exactly the same frequency as that of the emitted wave.

If you have sensing equipment which can detect the Doppler effect and you note that your echo frequency is higher in pitch than the emitted sound, then the target is either coming toward you or you are going toward it.

If the sound of the echo is lower in frequency than the emitted sound, then the object is either going away from you, or you are going away from it. This may be helpful in finding some types of objects which are underwater or in determining the relative movement of fish or underwater craft. You will find that even though the target does not move, a sunken ship for example, if it has a good strong echo, and you close on it, the Doppler effect will be present and will be a higher pitched note in the echo than the transmitted note. The reverse of this situation is also true. The sound will be lower in pitch if you are going away from this object.

SMALL CRAFT DEPTH SOUNDERS AND FISH FINDERS

We now examine some existing systems using the sonar principle. Let us first look at a simple, basic depth sounder, Fig. 11-24. This shows the kind of dial used to display depth information. With this kind of system we can determine how far the bottom is under us, and knowing the general contour of the bottom we can use readings from such a system as this to assist us in navigating the waterways. There are charts prepared which have depth information. Of vital importance would be cases where channels are used for water travel, and one must know his channel depth to avoid trouble.

Another type display unit is that shown in Fig. 11-25. We will gain some good general information about similar types of depth

Fig. 11-24. Raytheon fathometer. (Courtesy Raytheon Marine.)

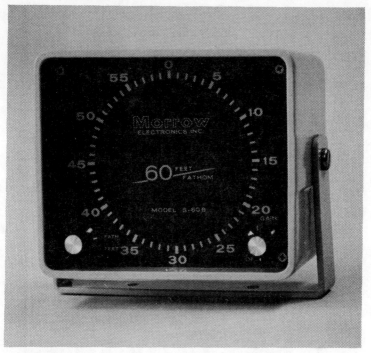

Fig. 11-25. Morrow S-60B depth sounder.

sounders from an examination of this one as to its installation and operation.

Refer now to figure 11-26. When the red light inside the dial flashes at zero position, a pulse (the main band) is generated and is transmitted into the water by the transducer. The pulse travels through the water to the bottom and is reflected back to the boat. The transducer picks up the echo pulse and sends it to the indicator where the light will flash a second time. The distance between the two flashes is calibrated in feet or fathoms so we can read the depth of the water from the dial scale.

When operating this sounder you select either feet or fathoms mode by the switch on the left side of the front panel. This selection may be made at any time whether the set is turned on or off. When in shallow water it is suggested that the operation be in feet because greater accuracy is then assured, due to the expansion of the feet scale. As you approach the 50 foot depth and deeper, the fathom mode is then recommended.

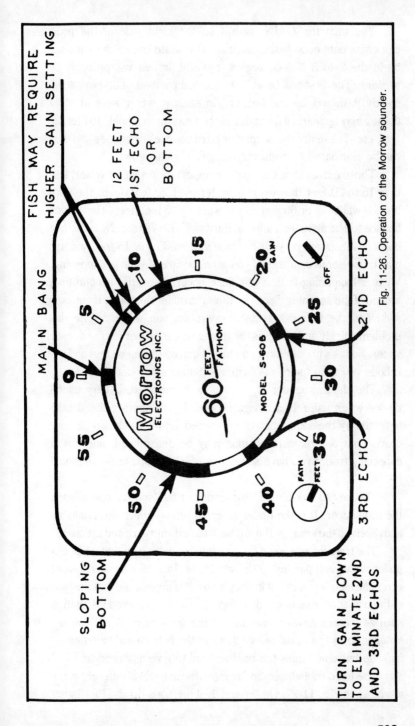

Fig. 11-26. Operation of the Morrow sounder.

You turn the GAIN control on the right side of the panel clockwise until echo flashes appear. The white line on the knob will be in the 2 to 3 o'clock region. Several flashes will probably be present. The first will be at the zero dial position. The next solid, steady flash will be the bottom. In shallow water several other flashes may appear, all multiples of the first, for example, 10 feet, 20 feet, etc. These are the second or third bounces or echoes and they can be eliminated by reducing the gain a small amount.

These extra echoes are not too important in shallow water, less than 15 to 20 feet; however, in water over 20 feet deep, the third bounce will be over 60 feet. If the water is 25 feet deep, the second bounce will be at 50 feet, and the third will be at 75 feet. Now this last bounce will appear on your dial face *as a reading at 15 feet*, and this may cause some confusion if you aren't aware of what is happening. What is happening is that this flash occurred on the second time around of the scanning disc. The timing is off for this flash. If you now switch to the fathoms mode of operation you will eliminate this problem quickly and easily as the timing now is proper for the deeper water. So, as a precaution if you have been operating on feet and get echoes you aren't sure of, switch to fathoms and double check.

The depth sounder is, as we have indicated, a very useful device when used as a navigation aid. By comparing the depths indicated by the sounder to the recorded depths as shown on your chart, your approximate position may be determined, and this is especially true if you have some idea of where you are—or should be.

The key to reliable depth sounder or fish spotter operation is the transducer. It is the underwater "antenna" which both radiates and receives the energy. It must be installed with care and precision.

The transducer should be mounted in such a way that its face is under water and parallel to the waterline. In shallow water a small error can be tolerated, but in deep water it is imperative that the face of the transducer be pointed straight down, if it is a fixed installation such as we are now considering. If the transducer is not pointed straight down the signal will go down to the bottom and be reflected back up but could miss the boat and fail to give any reading.

The fixed transducer can be mounted in several different ways as shown in Fig. 11-27. On through hull methods (a) and (b), flaring

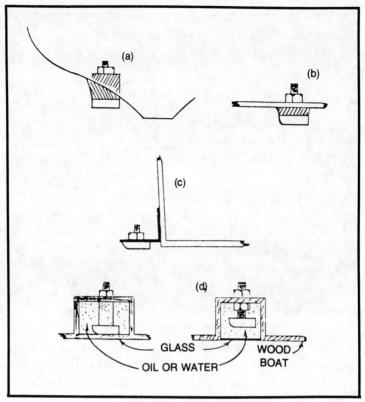

Fig. 11-27. Installing the transducer.

blocks are used to make the curved bottom of the boat fit the top of the transducer. Bedding compound should be used and the jam nut run up tight. The transducer wells (d) are very effective, and on glass hulls the loss of the echo going to the bottom is very small. The face of the transducer must still be pointed straight down. Water or oil must fill the space between the face of the transducer and the bottom skin of the boat. Be sure the well is over the skin of the boat, and not over a layer of flotation material which would deaden the echo energy. On some types of wood hulls, a glass patch can be installed for the transducer well. This keeps the transducer out of the water stream, and on some high speed boats this can be very important to the boat's performance. The transducer must be mounted in a place where the air bubble stream is at a minimum. In fact, when a boat is first put in the water, the sounder may not work

Fig. 11-28. Wesmar digital depth sounder. (Courtesy Wesmar.)

at all until the thin layer of air bubbles on the surface of the transducer, or bottom of the boat, has been dissipated. These bubbles
cannot be seen but until the bottom of the boat is wet, the sounder
cannot transmit a signal into the water.

The Wesmar digital depth sounder shown in Fig. 11-28 gives a
readout of the depth directly in feet or in fathoms. This unit has
several features which may be of importance. First it will sound an
alarm when the depth is less than a given setting. This alarm is
audible and draws your attention to the unit when it goes off. It also
has a provision which enables it to be used for fish locating, and this
equipment will give you another type alarm when there are echoes
which might indicate fish. This prevents you from having to constantly monitor the unit to see whats happening below you. Its
accuracy is said to be within 1/2 foot which is quite precise.

We have mentioned the use of a depth sounder for fish locator
use. One unit which does this is the Heathkit Fish Spotter which can
be built if you have the inclination to do this, following the excellent
instructions provided by this company. Figure 11-29 shows time
relationships when the electrical pulses from the Fish Spotter are
applied to the transducer.

506

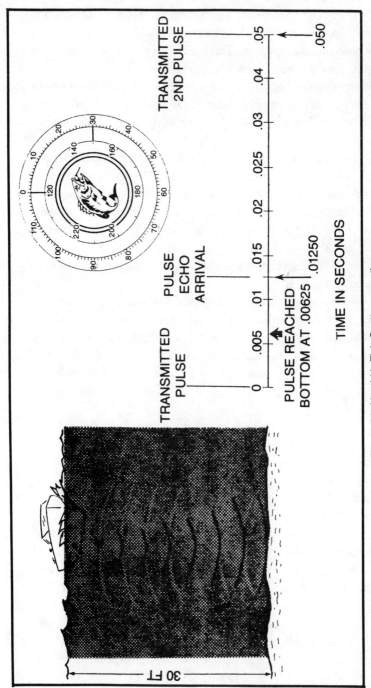

TRANSMITTED 2ND PULSE

.050

PULSE ECHO ARRIVAL

.01250

TRANSMITTED PULSE

PULSE REACHED BOTTOM AT .00625

TIME IN SECONDS

30 FT

Fig. 11-29. Heathkit Fish Spotter operation.

Inside the transducer, a piezoelectric ceramic element oscillates at approximately 200 kHz and vibrates in much the same way as the cone of a loudspeaker. This vibration introduces a motion, or signal, into the water which is directed toward the bottom in a relatively narrow beam. Because this signal is not audible, it may be considered as a silent sound traveling at an average rate of approximately 4800 feet per second in water, or, 0.0002083 seconds per foot.

As the signal leaves the transducer, it causes the neon lamp to flash at the zero depth mark on the scale. The time required for a signal to travel from the transducer to the bottom is the product of water depth (in feet) times the speed of sound in water (in seconds/foot). For example, let's assume that the depth of water under your boat is 30 feet. Then 30 feet times 0.0002083 seconds/foot = 0.00625 seconds of sound travel time from the transducer to the bottom.

As the signal strikes the bottom, it is bounced, or reflected, back up to the transducer at the same speed. Since the bottom seldom has a smooth flat surface, the reflected signal is widely scattered. Therefore, only a small amount of the reflected signal actually reaches the transducer. The return times for the reflected signal is another 0.00625 seconds which makes a total travel time of 0.01250 seconds.

Upon reaching the transducer, the reflected signal causes the ceramic element to vibrate at the same frequency that was originally generated. This vibration causes the element to generate a pulsed 200 kHz signal that is sent back to the Fish Spotter where it is amplified. The amplified signal is then applied to the neon lamp and causes it to flash.

The nylon disc spins at 1200 rpm. This speed represents a time of 0.05 second for each revolution. Therefore, the nylon disc would have rotated 1/4 of one revolution during the signal travel time of 0.01250 seconds. This causes the neon lamp to flash at the 30 foot mark on the scale.

Since the transmit-receive cycle is repeated 20 times per second, the overall effect is that of a continuous sounding. Therefore, even relatively small variations of the bottom contour can be observed while the boat is in motion.

The accuracy of the Fish Spotter is highly dependent upon the speed of the rotating nylon disc. Therefore the preset motor speed has been determined carefully by the speed of the sound waves in the water. Although water density has an effect on the speed of these sound waves, the overall accuracy of the system is well within the desirable limits.

This system has been engineered so that motor ignition noise and most other kinds of normal interference will not affect its operation. However, if random flashes do occur often enough to become a problem, an ignition interference kit should be installed on the boat engine. These kits can usually be obtained from the engine manufacturer.

Ignition pulses induced into the power cable and/or the transducer cable may cause random flashes to appear on the dial. This can only occur, however, if you have routed these cables too close to any other cable that carries ignition pulses, such as a tachometer cable or magneto ground wire. Therefore keep your Fish Spotter cables as far as possible from these sources of interference.

Keep in mind that interference does not have to originate from your own boat, but may occur and come from a bad electrical condition on a boat near you. In such cases the interference will cease when those engines are shut off, or when you move away so that there is sufficient distance between you and the interference source.

If you are running with an inboard engine, the usual actions taken to suppress automotive ignition interference will usually be effective with your Fish Spotter. These actions include: suppressors in the distributor cap, spark plug leads of resistance wire, suppressor spark plugs, bypassing with *coaxial* capacitors, bypassing of gauges with capacitors, bonding metal parts together, and using shielded wire. Figure 11-30 shows some of these actions which have been effective on electrical system on internal combustion engines, while Fig. 11-31 shows how a coaxial capacitor is mounted on a generator and an alternator.

If you are running with an outboard engine, use the engine manufacturers recommendations for noise suppression.

Ship to shore radiotelephone transmissions tend to radiate a large amount of rf energy. If these transmissions originate close to

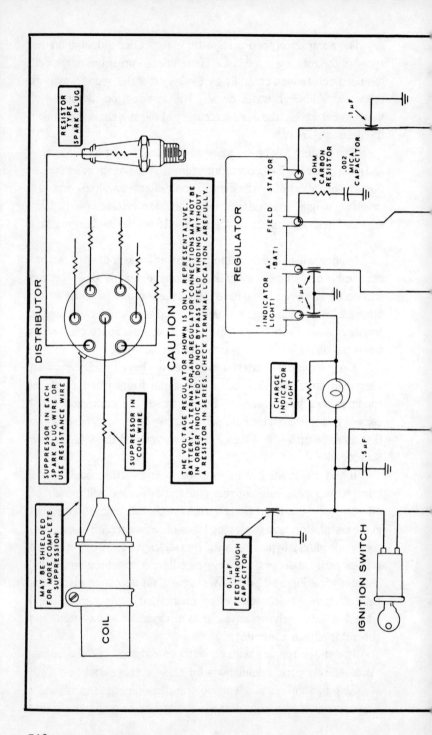

DISTRIBUTOR

RESISTOR TYPE SPARK PLUG

SUPPRESSOR IN EACH SPARK PLUG WIRE OR USE RESISTANCE WIRE

SUPPRESSOR IN COIL WIRE

MAY BE SHIELDED FOR MORE COMPLETE SUPPRESSION

COIL

0.1 μF FEEDTHROUGH CAPACITOR

IGNITION SWITCH

REGULATOR

INDICATOR A. (BAT) LIGHT

FIELD STATOR

4 OHM CARBON RESISTOR

.002 MICA CAPACITOR

.1 μF

.1 μF

CHARGE INDICATOR LIGHT

.5 μF

CAUTION

THE VOLTAGE REGULATOR SHOWN IS ONLY REPRESENTATIVE. BATTERY, ALTERNATOR, AND REGULATOR CONNECTIONS MAY NOT BE IN ORDER INDICATED. DO NOT BYPASS FIELD WINDING WITHOUT A RESISTOR IN SERIES. CHECK TERMINAL LOCATION CAREFULLY.

510

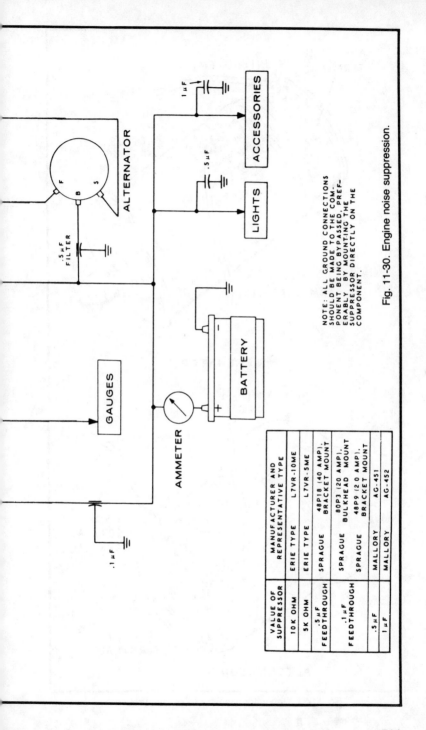

Fig. 11-30. Engine noise suppression.

NOTE: ALL GROUND CONNECTIONS SHOULD BE MADE TO THE COMPONENT BEING BYPASSED, PREFERABLY BY MOUNTING THE SUPPRESSOR DIRECTLY ON THE COMPONENT.

VALUE OF SUPPRESSOR	MANUFACTURER AND REPRESENTATIVE TYPE	
10K OHM	ERIE TYPE	L7VR-10ME
5K OHM	ERIE TYPE	L7VR-5ME
.5 µF FEEDTHROUGH	SPRAGUE	48P18 (40 AMP), BRACKET MOUNT
.1 µF FEEDTHROUGH	SPRAGUE	80P3 (20 AMP), BULKHEAD MOUNT
	SPRAGUE	48P9 (20 AMP), BRACKET MOUNT
.5 µF	MALLORY	AG-451
1 µF	MALLORY	AG-452

511

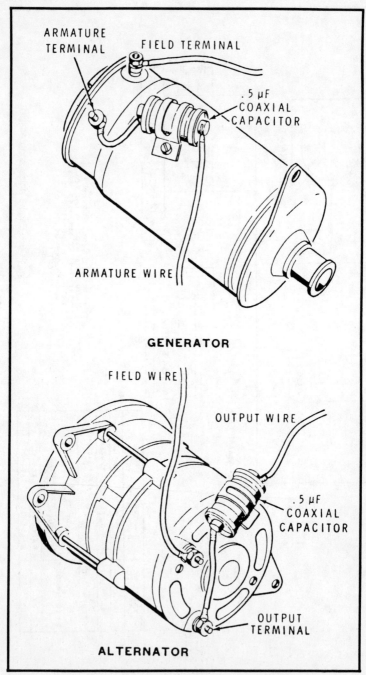

ARMATURE
TERMINAL

FIELD TERMINAL

.5 μF
COAXIAL
CAPACITOR

ARMATURE WIRE

GENERATOR

FIELD WIRE

OUTPUT WIRE

.5 μF
COAXIAL
CAPACITOR

OUTPUT
TERMINAL

ALTERNATOR

Fig. 11-31. Generator-altenator noise suppression.

your location they may show an interference on your Fish Spotter. However, these transmissions are usually of such short duration that, if encountered at all, they will cause only minor annoyance.

A TILTING TRANSDUCER SYSTEM

Now we want to examine another kind of system, one that has a transducer which can be tilted and turned to compensate for boat roll or pitch, and which can be lowered into the water and then retracted when going into drydock or when putting the boat back on a trailor mount. This unit is the Wesmar scanning sonar. The control and display appear in Fig. 11-32. The unit is depicting a school of fish on its scope screen, which gives you some idea of how these kinds of echoes appear. In Fig. 11-33 a channel on the ocean bottom is clearly shown. This represents another kind of echo. Figure 11-34 depicts a beam moving as it scans the ocean bottom. Figure 11-35 shows the type components which comprise this system.

Now let us refer back to Fig. 11-33 and take note of the dials and switches. We want to elaborate on them, what they are and what they do.

The SENSITIVITY control determines the ability of the transducer to sense (see) a target. The further the sensitivity control is

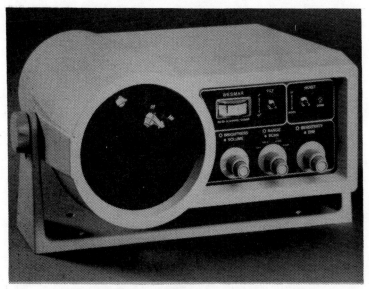

Fig. 11-32. Wesmar scanning sonar with fish indicated.

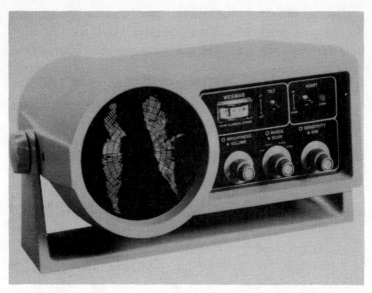

Fig. 11-33. Wesmar scanning sonar with bottom channel depicted.

rotated clockwise, the smaller the target it can see at any given range. Using too high a sensitivity level may cause the sonar to see too many targets, making it difficult, if not impossible to distinguish one target from another. Correct sensitivity level is critical for proper sonar operation. A very slight change in sensitivity will dramatically affect the operators ability to identify specific targets.

A VOLUME control regulates the loudness of the external speaker. At the same time a target is displayed on the CRT screen, a sound will be generated in the speaker of this system. Because of this, the speaker can be used as an audible alarm to tell the sonar operator when a target is encountered. Also, different targets make different sounds in the speaker. This fact makes the speaker useful for identifying different types of targets. That is, large targets will be heard as a thud while smaller targets will pop or crackle. These sounds from the speaker may free the sonar operator from constantly viewing the CRT screen. He may relax until a sound is heard then he can look and see what the sonar is looking at.

A RANGE control selects the distance which is to be displayed from its center to the edge of the sonar screen. The CRT screen is divided into 10 rings of range and 12 bearing marks. The boat is at the center of the screen and each ring out is 10 percent of the range selected with the range control. For instance, on the 100 foot range, each ring represents 10 feet from the transducer to the target. On the 500 foot range each ring represents 50 feet. The targets will appear in true range and relative bearing on the CRT.

Note the school of fish echos shown on the scope picture of Fig. 11-36. The bearing is about 60 degrees to 170 degrees, and the

Fig. 11-34. Scanning sonar in action. (Courtesy Wesmar.)

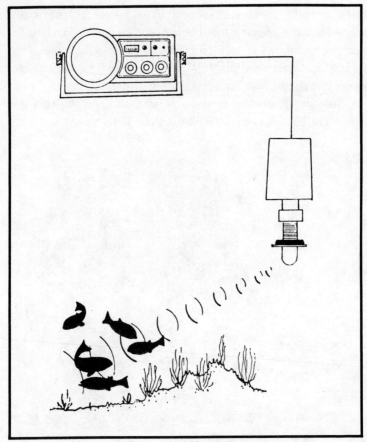

Fig. 11-35. Components of scanning sonar.

range, depending upon the scale range chosen by the RANGE control may be out to as far as 500 feet.

Let us assume for this example that you have set the range at 500 feet with the range control. Now examine the school of fish. This is a good size bunch of fish going from about 150 feet from your position to over 400 feet from your position. Each ring of the display scope will represent 50 feet.

THE SCANNING TRANSDUCER PROCESS

Now let us examine the scanning process of this system's scanning transducer. A scan control determines the direction in which the transducer rotates. When turned all the way to the left the

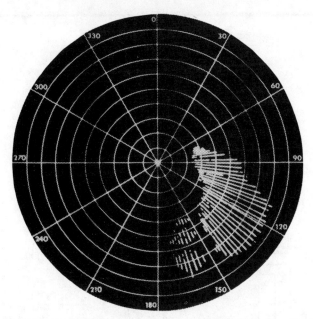

Fig. 11-36. Wesmar's CRT sonar locked onto a school of fish. (Courtesy Wesmar.)

transducer scans counterclockwise and the trace moves counterclockwise on the CRT screen. When the knob is in the far right position the movements are clockwise. With the knob in the middle

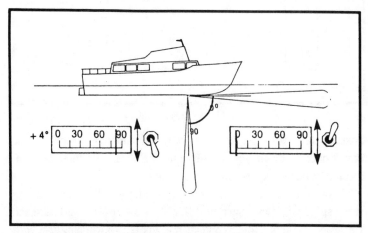

Fig. 11-37. Using the tilt control, the SS-80 transducer may be tilted from 4° above horizontal to 90° vertical. Any desired tilt angle between these postions may be selected on the console as shown above.

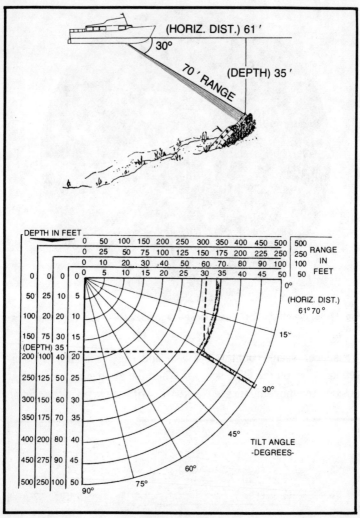

Fig. 11-38. Range chart use.

position the transducer beams in only one constant direction. The scan control allows you to reverse the scan direction and immediately take a second look at a sighting.

For example, if you are cruising and your Wesmar scanning sonar spots what you think may be a school of fish to starboard and you want to immediately confirm the sighting, switching the scan knob back to the area avoids having to wait for the transducer to make a full circle before sighting the object again.

A tilt control, Fig. 11-39, (left toggle switch) controls the angle at which the sound beam is projected out of the vessel. At 0° the sound beam will be horizontal just underneath the surface. At 90° the sound beam will be pointing straight down to the bottom like a depth sounder. To change the tilt angle hold the toggle switch up or down until you obtain the desired angle.

Of course, as always, the way to get maximum use of such a system as this is knowing how to use it properly. It takes practice. Here are some recommended ideas.

What the sonar sees in the water is presented on the CRT screen in the shape of dots, slashes, streaks, coloration from very intense to very weak, and also a variety of sound changes. The appearance of all these signals at any one time indicates that there are many different things under your boat. A similar situation would be when you look at a rich landscape and see many different shapes, sizes, colors and forms. Of course, you can recognize most of these instantly because your eyes have seen them before.

The best way to learn to recognize targets on your sonar is to take a known target and submerge it in the water, locate it with the sonar, see how it is displayed on the sonar scope, and hear how it

Fig. 11-39. Morrow chart sonar unit. (Courtesy Morrow.)

sounds on the speaker. A radar reflector usually makes a good sonar target when submerged. If not available, try other objects until a suitable echo is obtained.

The first step in practicing with your target is to find a very calm area without much boat traffic and preferably about 100 feet in depth. This is not always practical, but find the calmest, deepest place that is available in your area. Submerge the target with a weight attached about 10 to 15 feet below a buoy. The buoy, of course, will mark the location of the target, and the weight will keep the target under the buoy.

Set the sonar tilt to 90° and make sure that you have a good return off the bottom. Adjust the range switch so that the sonar is set at 50 feet. Launch your target close to either side of the vessel. Tilt the transducer until the target becomes visible on the CRT screen. This will probably occur at a 45° tilt when you are next to your marker buoy.

If you are drifting away from the marker buoy, keep track of the target by raising the tilt and by adjusting the range. If you are not drifting away from the marker buoy, move the boat away from the buoy and do the same thing. You will notice as you get farther away from your target you must decrease the tilt angle.

Reverse your scan direction and have the sonar scan in the same sector that your target is in. This is done by having your sonar scan clockwise, then counterclockwise. When reversing scan direction, there will be a slight shift in the location of the target due to drive mechanism tolerances. Switch your sonar into manual, and point the beam directly at the target. Adjust the tilt and notice how it affects the target display on the CRT screen. See how far you can go from your target and still track it. When you track at the maximum distance, come back towards your target and track it as you approach the marker buoy. You will notice that when you get close to the target you will have to tilt downward (increasing the tilt angle) as well as adjust your range, to maintain the image on the screen. Do this a few times with the target until you understand all the control functions of the sonar.

Now that you have tracked and followed the target with your sonar, replace the radar reflector or other strong target you have been using, with a fish or other small object, still keeping it under the buoy. Try tracking it. When you use a fish to track, you will notice that the CRT reading is not consistent. This is because a fish does not have the same reflective characteristics at every point. If the sonar intersects the fish head-first or tail-first, the fish will return a weak echo. If you hit the fish broadside, the fish will return a strong echo.

Practice using your sonar on buoys, breakwaters, shore lines, and shallow bottoms until you are familiar with the differences of the targets and how they are displayed. This will help you when you come into unfamiliar areas. The trick is to practice with your sonar often. The more familiar you become with your sonar the more fun and use you will get out of it.

Using a scanning sonar like this Wesmar SS-80, you can determine range to a submerged target using a chart-graph which converts the slant distance to depth and horizontal range figures. Examine Fig. 11-40(a) and (b).

Your CRT screen makes it easy for you to tell the distance from the transducer to a target. The chart enables you to compute the approximate distance to and depth of a target. For example: with the range setting on the console at 100, and the tilt angle at 30°, you pick up a target 70 feet away. Now you want to know how far away *horizontally* is the target and what its depth is.

To quickly find this out, read on top right of the graph, and on the 100 foot range scale find 70 feet. Now follow the curved line until it intersects with 30°. Now read straight over to the left axis to find the *vertical depth* (approximately 35 feet), and straight up to the top axis to find the *horizontal distance* (approximately 61 feet).

When using this graph, always read your figures on and for the correct range scale.

Finally we want to examine a chart type recording sonar and gain some information on how to read the information presented on such a chart. One such sonar is the Morrow unit shown in Fig. 11-39.

The operation of this unit requires attention to the sensitivity control to get a good graph. Units are designed for various depths. For example, 0 to 8 fathoms for the SR-80, and 0 to 320 fathoms for the SR-320.

One of the first things to be seen on the recorder is the multiple bottom echoes—these are like light flashes on the nonrecording

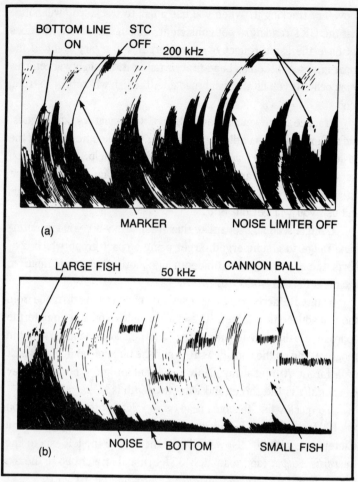

Fig. 11-40. Recording of fish.

equipment. With this kind of equipment in shallow water 6 to 10 echoes will be seen on the paper strip, and in deeper water, down to 50 fathoms, 2 to 3 echoes will appear.

The echo reflected by fish is much weaker than the echo reflected by the sea bottom and the gain control on the equipment must be advanced to where the second or third bottom echo appear before the equipment is sensitive enough to show the fish echos. The fish will be seen on the chart as shown in Fig. 11-40. But also note the crescent shape of the echo in this figure. This is due to a frequency of 50 kHz being used, and with the boat moving under power. Actually the boat gets closer to the fish and then farther away, and this makes the record look like a crescent because of the change in distance to the fish and other targets.

As we have said, you have to adjust the gain control to be able to record the fish on the tape, or chart. When you advance the gain or sensitivity control electrical noise generated on the boat usually appears. The noise looks like the streaks or small specks on the recording chart as in Fig. 11-40(b). In the figure, you can see the noise when the noise limiter is off, at the top of the crescent swing. But you can see the fish in this recording also. The fish shown (spots) are 8 to 10 inch trout. The sea bottom in this recording is from 10 to 30 fathoms.

Again, it takes practice to get used to the picture that you see portrayed on the chart. One nice thing is that you have a permanent record and this can be the subject of much interesting conversation in home port. It is always enjoyable to see how experienced sailors interpret the findings.

DOPPLER SPEED LOG AND DOCKING SYSTEMS

Sonar, including its Doppler effect, have many other uses besides sounding for depth or locating fish and other submerged objects. The Doppler phenomenon can be used to give a speed indication to the helmsman. This is very necessary in the cases of large ships, such as supertankers, where the speeds may be so slow that it is impossible to recognize that the ship is actually moving. We mean speeds down to near zero. With the mass of these giant ships, even at near zero speeds, the momentum can be so great that a slight mistake can wipe out a dock. Yes, this system of determining very slow (as well as normal speeds) can be very important.

One system which uses Doppler to determine speed is the Sperry SRD-301 Doppler sonar speed log. The basic installation of this system with its multiple transducers is shown in Fig. 11-41. Notice that there are five transducers used to obtain information required about the ships motion. Three of these transducers are transmitter units, and two are receiving units. The display unit is shown in Fig. 11-42.

There are other electronic packages required, and these, along with the display units are shown in Fig. 11-43. Now let use examine

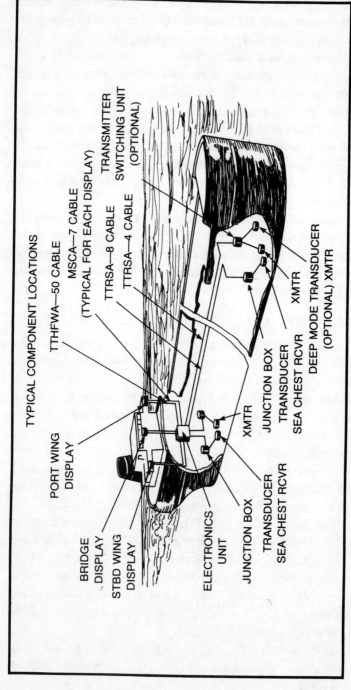

TYPICAL COMPONENT LOCATIONS

TTHFWA—50 CABLE

MSCA—7 CABLE
(TYPICAL FOR EACH DISPLAY)

TTRSA—8 CABLE

TTRSA—4 CABLE

TRANSMITTER
SWITCHING UNIT
(OPTIONAL)

PORT WING
DISPLAY

BRIDGE
DISPLAY

STBD WING
DISPLAY

ELECTRONICS
UNIT

JUNCTION BOX

TRANSDUCER
SEA CHEST RCVR

XMTR

JUNCTION BOX

TRANSDUCER
SEA CHEST RCVR

XMTR

DEEP MODE TRANSDUCER
(OPTIONAL) XMTR

Fig. 11-41. Sperry Doppler speed log installation.

the technical details. The Sperry system provides very accurate measurement of vessel speed and distance traveled through the water. The speed range is from zero to 35 knots, and the distance is measured to 9999.9 nautical miles.

The ship's speed is measured by transmitting *pulsed* sonic energy into the water and detecting the Doppler shifts of the reflected signals. The resultant signals are then processed and the speed displayed visually on the digital readout. The distance traveled is also computed and is displayed by a mechanical counter.

It is of interest to know that when you compare the out-going signal to the reflected signal you get what is known as *Doppler beats*. These may sound like a tone in the audible hearing range even though you cannot hear the original signal nor the echo because of its

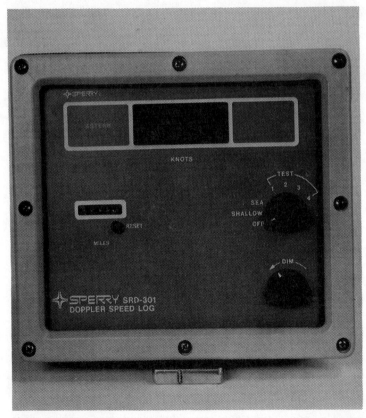

Fig. 11-42. Sperry SRD-301 Doppler speed log display. (Courtesy Sperry Marine Systems.)

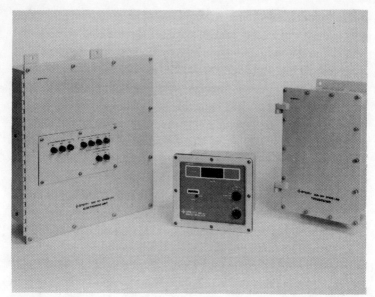

Fig. 11-43. Doppler speed log electronics units. (Courtesy Sperry Marine Systems.)

higher frequency. Now if you count the beats, and you know the wavelength represented by the beating tone, you can determine the distance moved per second. If you then sum up these beats, you will be able to determine the distance traveled. One beat equals one wavelength of travel.

Back to the installation. The transducer assembly sends the sonic energy into the water and gets back the Doppler shifted echoes. The unit consists of two active elements (piezoelectric crystals), a pair of impedance matching transformers, and a temperature sensitive thermistor. This thermistor is connected into a temperature compensating network that removes the greatest source of environmental errors from the system.

The two active elements in the transducer assembly are arranged so that one element directs its energy down and forward while the other element directs its energy down and astern. This arrangement eliminates Doppler shift errors due to vertical motion or heave, and minimizes the Doppler shift errors due to the ships pitch motion for pitching angles up to 10 degrees.

The speed log system alternately transmits and receives pulses of *2 megahertz* energy. Notice how much higher this frequency is than the other systems have had. The higher frequency means a shorter wavelength and more accuracy. Now, if there is motion through the water, the frequency of the transmitted energy will be different from the frequency of the received energy, and the difference will be directly proportional to the speed through the water, and will be inversely proportional to the water temperature.

If the ship is moving forward, the received frequency of the forward looking transducer element will be higher than the transmitter frequency, and the received frequency of the aft looking transducer element will be lower then the transmitted frequency.

The difference between the forward and aft channesl is measured and averaged over a large number of transmit-receive cycles. Timing circuits controlled by the mode switch provide a *water gate* (how about that name!) signal to accept Doppler return signals from water approximately 4 feet (shallow) or 10 feet (sea) below the transducer assembly.

The speed measurements are made by counting circuits in the electronics unit. At the end of the required number of transmit-receive cycles, the speed information is transmitted from the electronics unit to the master display unit, and any one of several optional remove display units. When a count equivalent to 0.1 mile of travel is accumulated in the distance counters, a pulse is transmitted from the electronics unit to the master display unit and optional display equipment to advance the miles counter 0.1 mile.

A Doppler Docking System

The use of Doppler to determine ship movement has another application which is important. This is for docking purposes. Just imagine trying to dock a super tanker the size of the Empire State Building and weighing about half a million tons. Again, this docking maneuver requires perceptions of speed so slow that we, with our human sensors, cannot feel the movement or see it. It is said that as much as 6 miles are required to bring such a vessel into dock, and that a fraction of a knot misjudgement is speed can mean the difference between a safe docking and badly damaged ship and docking facility. Of course either would mean the loss of millions of dollars.

What the Doppler docking system can give is zero speed concept and zero error at this imperceptible speed. The system can operate within one foot of the ocean bottom, so low draft is not a disadvantage. The Sperry docking system, using Doppler, can detect a movement of 0.01 foot per second in a ship one thousand feet long, and that should give sufficient information in docking and anchoring (where ship movement may be offset if this movement is known) so that complete and accurate handling of the vessel is accomplished.

This system, like the Doppler speed log previously described, uses transducers that monitor the Doppler effect on ultra high frequency sound waves in all four of the ship's possible directions of movement. The information is displayed on the bridge, using the readout display shown in Fig. 11-44. When the system is turned on, power is applied to all electronics. A solid-state power oscillator in each transmitter-transducer drives four crystals at a frequency of 400 kilohertz. The crystals are bonded to windows in the transmitter-transducer housing, and they are oriented to produce four beams of ultrasonic energy that are directed obliquely toward the bottom. One beam is directed forward, the second beam to aft, the third beam to port, and the fourth beam to starboard. The ultrasonic signals from each transmitter strike the bottom and are reflected. This reflected continuous wave energy is received by the receiver transducers which use crystals bonded to windows in the same mechanical configuration and orientation as the transmitter transducers. The signals are amplified by a four-channel preamplifier located in each receiver transducer. When there is relative motion between the vehicle and the bottom, each received signal will be shifted in frequency by an amount proportional to the speed vector in that direction. The received signals are applied to three processing channels in the electronics unit to produce the appropriate speed displays.

In forward motion the frequency received by the forward-looking receiver will be a higher frequency than the transmitter, and the aft-looking receiver will receive a signal lower in frequency than the transmitter. The frequency shift is measured and displayed as velocity in the selected units. The direction of motion is also detected and indicated as an arrow pointing in the direction of travel of the vessel over the ground.

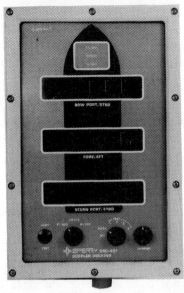

Fig. 11-44. A display unit for Sperry Doppler docking system. (Courtesy Sperry Marine Systems.)

Forward and aft data pulses generated by the Doppler pulse generator are applied to a true motion generator. This unit contains counters that scale the resultant count to produce 200 pulses per mile along the fore-aft axis. The output pulses are only produced for forward motion.

You will notice in Fig. 11-44 that the output can be in feet per second, knots, or meters per second, as desired, by simply positioning the selector switch on the display unit.

WIND VELOCITY AND DIRECTION INDICATORS

Although this next bit of equipment does not necessarily fall into the electrical-electronic category, there is some use of electronics to obtain the necessary data by which sailing craft and even power boats may obtain wind direction and the vessel's speed of movement and use this information to navigate. Thus we believe it is of value to include here and examine in some detail.

The Hornet is a combined log, speedometer, anemometer and wind direction indicator. One control box is used taking input signals from an underwater unit and a masthead unit. Outputs are taken from the control box to four indicators.

1. 360 degree wind direction indicator
2. A magnified wind direction indicatior
3. 0 to 60 knot wind speed indicator
4. 0 to 10 knot boat speed indicator.

The distance meter is mounted in the control box and is not resettable. The system operates at 12 V dc from the vessels main supply. There are no operating controls, the on/off switch being at the vessels main switchboard. The indicators may be either of the 4 inch type with square bezels, or of the 3 inch circular type. They have integral scale illumination operating form the 12 V dc via the indicator cable.

The control unit is fitted with two calibration controls inside the rear cover. They are: the speed log calibrator and the magnified direction misalignment corrector. The speed/log calibrator provides five increments of adjustment each giving a 3 percent change. Clockwise rotation of the control causes the log to run more slowly, and the speed indication to decrease. The magnified direction misalignment corrector is used to run more slowly, and the speed indication to decrease. The magnified direction misalignment corrector is used to remove any error from the magnified direction indication, after the masthead unit has been adjusted for alignment.

A valveless housing is used with the Hornet underwater unit for small craft. A valve type housing is available as an alternative for installation in vessels of larger draught. In both types, however, the underwater unit may be withdrawn into the boat for cleaning while afloat, or may be retracted into the housing for protection when not in use. The impeller fin is secured to the main body of the underwater unit by means of two screws. There are no electrical connections between the two parts, and the impeller fin is easily replaceable at sea should the need arise.

This impeller is also removable from the fin by unscrewing the rear bearing screw. The rotor is a molded nylon propeller with a stainless steel shaft running in bearings that do not require lubrication. A weed deflector in the form of a streamlined fin with a sloping leading edge is incorporated in the flange of the valveless housing. For the valve type model, it is provided as a separate unit and must be screwed to the hull a short distance ahead of the impeller. Both types conform to Lloyd's requirements for classified yachts.

The valveless housing is a simple tubular skin fitting in molded plastics, which is closed by means of a sealing cap after removal of the underwater unit. Alignment of the deflector fin with the direction of the water flow is achieved by rotating the housing within its outer sleeve, which is fixed to the hull, and locking it in place by means of its retaining ring nut. Alignment of the impeller fin with the deflector fin occurs automatically on lowering the underwater unit into its operating position. The plunger of the underwater unit contains two neoprene sealing rings and a bronze piston ring, the purpose of which is to scrape marine growth from the bore of the housing.

The valve type housing is of special design and incorporates a sliding gate valve enabling tubes to be closed when the underwater unit is in the retracted position so that the latter may subsequently be withdrawn without admitting water into the boat. Alignment is maintained by a dowel pin which must be inserted into a hole before the handle can be fully lowered. A locknut is provided to clamp the alignment device once the correct setting has been found. The underwater unit is held down against external pressure by means of a threaded retaining ring.

The transmission of signals from the impeller is effected by means of a magnet contained in it, the field from which induces very small pulses of electric current in a coil contained in the pickup unit. Recall the sonar scanning disc? These pulses are carried by cable to the control unit, where they are amplified and used to actuate the speed and distance indication circuits and dials.

In the interest of accuracy the underwater unit should be placed as far forward as possible consistent with maintaining immersion when pitching, or in the case of a power boat when it is planing and pitching. In a sailing yacht the best position is generally ahead of the ballast or fin-keel. It must not be installed further aft then 10 feet from the forward extremity of the waterline length. The installation of two underwater units, one on either side of the center line, together with a gravity operated selector switch (see Fig. 11-51), is recommended. This switch must be mounted on a transverse bulkhead. If only one underwater unit is fitted there may be a difference of up to 5 percent between the speed readings obtained on the two tacks when sailing to windward. Do not install the underwater unit within 6 feet of an alternator, dynamo, or electric motor.

Calibration

It is essential to calibrate the log before using it for dead reckoning, as the scaling is affected by the shape of the boat's hull and the position of the impeller. The log/speed calibrator, which is located at the rear of the control unit is set on the assumption that the flow rate of water beneath the hull is 6 percent less than the true speed. This is normally correct for a conventional displacement hull when the housings have been sited well forward as is recommended.

Having checked that the underwater unit is pushed down into the water completely, and is properly aligned, you will want to run the vessel up and down a standard measured distance under power at a constant speed which should be at least 10 times greater than the speed of the current. Choose a time when the tidal current is constant. Note the log readings at the start and finish of each run, and so obtain the total indicated distance sailed on the two runs. The difference between the total indicated distance and twice the standard measured distance is the log error and it should be expressed as a percentage of the standard measured distance. We will consider an example of this a few lines farther on.

First, be informed that the log calibrator control is a screwdriver operated rotary switch having six positions which provide five 3 percent increments of correction. Clockwise rotation causes the log to run more slowly. One tick movement in an anticlockwise direction would therefore reduce the 2 percent underreading error of the first example we shall consider in just a moment to a 1 percent error overreading. If it is found that there is insufficient clockwise movement of the calibrating shaft available to correct the error, an impeller of longer pitch, colored white, can be fitted in place of the standard black propeller. This will reduce the rate of the log by some 15 percent.

Examples

If the standard measured distance were 6,080 feet (one nautical mile) and the two distances indicated were 1.01 miles upstream and 0.95 miles downstream for a total distance of 1.96 miles, as against the actual 2.00 miles then the log error is 4 parts in 200 or 2 percent underreading.

It is to be noted that for ship-current ratios lower than 10 a correction factor must be applied to convert the standard measured distance to the distance actually sailed through the water. You multiply twice the listed distance by this factor before comparing it with the log reading. Here are the correction factors for ship speed to current speeds of 4 to 10.

Ship Speed Ratio: Current Speed	10	7	6	5	4.5	4
Correction Factor:	1.01	1.02	1.03	1.04	1.05	1.07

If you maintained a constant speed on the courses, the ship/current ratio is simply calculated as the sum of the two distances divided by their difference. Let's consider example two.

Let the measured distance be 6,080 ft (one nautical mile).

Now assume that your indicated distance upstream is 1.18 nautical miles and your indicated downstream distance is 0.93 nautical miles. The total indicated would then be 2.11 nautical miles.

If the ship's speed/current speed ratio is calculated:

$$\frac{\text{Ship speed}}{\text{Current Speed}} = \frac{1.18 + 0.93}{1.18 - 0.93} = \frac{2.11}{0.25} = 8.4$$

Then the correction factor from the table above is 1.015. You know that the distance sailed is 2.00 × 1.015 or 2.03 nautical miles, as against the 2.11 indicated, so the log error is 0.08 miles or 4 percent overreading of the log indicator. You would rotate the switch one click clockwise and this gives a 3 percent correction so in this position the error is 1 percent overreading. Be aware that the calibration of the log as just described will automatically calibrate the speed circuits.

Wind Direction

Here you must be careful. If the masthead bracket is not correctly aligned parallel to the fore and aft line of the boat, an error appears on both the 360 degree and magnified direction indicators and this is equal to the angle of the misalignment. To compensate for this, the bracket can be adjusted by up to 10 degrees either side by sliding it over the baseplate. A *fine* adjustment of the magnified section direction indicator *only* may then be carried out using the control at the rear of the control box. If the masthead unit misalignment is to port, the control is turned clockwise and vice versa. Each division of the control compensates for 1 degree of misalignment.

General Considerations of Sailing with these Units.

The four indicators are damped to an optimum degree to give average readings. When sailing to windward, tacking downwind, or running, the magnified direction indicator should be used, as its sensitivity is 2-1/2 times that of the 360 degree indicator.

By observing the magnified direction indicator, the speedometer and the anemometer, it is possible to calculate the speed that the boat is making good into the eye of the wind with considerable accuracy. If this resolved speed is maintained at its maximum value, the boat will take the least possible time to ready the windward mark when tacking.

When sailing downwind in light to moderate winds it frequently pays to steer an indirect course since the yacht's speed may increase considerably when the wind is brought from dead astern to the quarter. The leeward mark will be reached in the shortest time if, again, the resolved speed in the direction of the true wind is maintained at its maximum value, the yacht being gybed at the correct point to fetch the mark of the last leg of the zig-zag course. This rule holds good even if the wind is not blowing directly from, or toward the mark. To windward, it holds good wherever it is impossible to fetch the mark without tacking. To leeward it applies if, when the speed made good in the direction of the true wind is a maximum, the mark is on the leeward side of the boat. One then tacks downwind to reach it. If it is on the windward side it pays to alter course and head straight for it.

The main purpose of these type controls is to enable the speed made good to be determined, and having found the apparent wind angle corresponding to a maximum speed made good, to enable the helmsman to steer accurately to this angle. Other uses are to improve the accuracy of downwind steering, to obtain the best sail trim on a reach, and to predict the sail requirements and the gybe after rounding the next mark of the source.

Thus we conclude this book and hope that in it you have found some information of value and application to your own situation. The work may be set aside as a reference until such time as you do have occasion to examine its pages for the answers to some specific problem or to find an answer to some specific question.

We again thank you for your acceptance of our various books published by TAB, and trust you will accept this one and those which we undoubtedly will prepare in the future.

Index

Index